REMNANTS
the
R.E.M.
COLLECTOR'S HANDBOOK AND PRICE GUIDE

REMNANTS

the

R.E.M.

COLLECTOR'S HANDBOOK AND PRICE GUIDE

GARY NABORS

The publisher will not be held responsible for losses which may occur in the purchase, sale, or other transactions of items because of the information contained herein. Readers who feel that they have discovered omissions or errors are invited to write and inform us so that they may be corrected in subsequent editions. With the publication of this work it is not the intention of Eclipse Publishing to promote or encourage the production or sale of illegally manufactured "bootleg" records.

All items shown are from the collection of the author, with the exception of the following: p.10, Kurt Wood; p.52, Jefferson Holt; p.83 (right), Randy Fix; p.84 (bottom), p.204 (bottom left), p.209 (bottom), p.230 (bottom), Jimmy Cohrssen; p.136, Greg Nicoll; p.141, Jon Halper; p.156, Pete Jackson; p.212 (bottom), p.213, p.237, Todd Ploharski; p.230 (right), Peter Buck; p.229, p.238, Paul Butchart

All photographs by Jimmy Cohrssen, with the exception of the following: p.8, p.244, reprinted with permission from The Athens Observer; p.12, p.236, p.239, Terry Allen; p.14, Gary Nabors

Published by: Eclipse Publishing
P.O. Box 398
Bala Cynwyd, PA 19004

Manufactured in the United States of America

ISBN: 0-9636241-4-8

Library of Congress Card Catalog Number: 93-70503

10 9 8 7 6 5 4 3 2 1

TABLE OF CONTENTS

PART III: A COMPENDIUM OF ODDITIES COLLARED

ACKNOWLEDGEMENTS

I would like to offer my thanks to **Liz Carter**, former director of the R.E.M. fan club, who provided me with much assistance back in 1987 when I began doing the research for this book.

I am also very grateful to **Peter Buck**, who sat for a three hour interview and answered an endless barrage of questions about R.E.M. and their records. I would also like to thank Peter Buck for access to his R.E.M. collection and lending items to be photographed.

Also thanks to **Bertis Downs** and **Jefferson Holt** in the R.E.M. office.

Thanks also go to **Jimmy Cohrssen** for superb photography, as well as for helpful suggestions. Copy editing thanks go to **Cecily Nabors**, **Jon Halper**, and **Pete Jackson.** I am also grateful to **Steve Raskin** of Ion Design for preparing the cover.

This book would not be nearly as comprehensive if it weren't for the help of the following people who helped me track down elusive records, other pieces of information, or lent items for photography: **Todd Ploharski, Peter Jackson, Gary Harvey, Alfred Kohl, Frank Poppe, Gregory Nicoll, Kurt Wood, Paul Butchart, Randy Fix, Eric Flaum, Michael Jones, Kipp Teague, Don Nelson** and **Lee Hammock**. I am also grateful to Todd Ploharski for assisting in the interview with Peter Buck.

Finally, I would like to thank **Cecily Nabors** and **Susan Casey Nabors** for undying faith, support, and understanding, and in Susan's case, putting up with a house full of R.E.M. junk.

REMNANTS

the

R.E.M.

COLLECTOR'S HANDBOOK AND PRICE GUIDE

Part 1:

Begin the Begin

PREFACE

I'll admit it. R.E.M. is easily the most over-analyzed, most dissected, and most picked-over band in popular music today, and I am adding to the glut. Fortunately for you, however, it was not my intention with this book to commit myself to an exhaustive study of R.E.M. and their music and attempt to squeeze deep philosophical Meaning out of every album cover, lyrical phrase, song title, or any other aspect of the band and their music. If you want heavy analysis, go buy *It Crawled From The South*, or meditate while playing *Murmur* backwards.

I am guilty, however, of wanting to write a book that would serve the needs of R.E.M. fans and record collectors by providing them with the most complete and accurate record of every existing R.E.M.-related item and their values ever published. To do this, I called upon literally hundreds of different resources, but the most important was my experience in buying and selling R.E.M. records, CDs, and memorabilia for the past six years as the proprietor of Athens Records. Buying and selling R.E.M. records internationally allowed me regular contact with fans all over the world, and as a result, I could compile an inventory of everything that was released in the U.S. and elsewhere, and could also get a good idea of their values. Another unquestionably valuable experience I had which put me in a better position to write a book such as this was living in Athens, Georgia, for five years while I was a graduate student. I made a lot of friends there who knowingly or unknowingly contributed information for this book, and met a number of people who were more than willing to talk about their town's most famous residents.

• • •

The first R.E.M. record I bought was the 45 of "Radio Free Europe" on I.R.S., which cost me $1.49 plus tax at Record Bar in 1983 (times have certainly changed, as the same 45, now ten years old, might cost you $45). That same year, The Police released their radio-ready LP *Synchronicity* and followed it up with a tour. I went to The Police concert in Landover, Maryland, that summer, where R.E.M. opened before a crowd that could care less about them and practically booed them off the stage. I found them interesting and strangely appealing, and was still humming their tunes when I returned to college that fall.

By 1984 I was becoming a devoted fan, and found myself looking in the R.E.M. sections of the local record stores to admire the artwork on the sleeves of *Murmur*, *Reckoning*, and *Chronic Town*. I eventually broke down and bought all three records, despite the fact that I had them all on tape. I finally got a chance to see R.E.M. again in 1985 in Winston-Salem, North Carolina. After D. Boon and The Minutemen shocked the house and R.E.M. finished out their encores, I went home and began to look through my tour book that I bought at the show. The book contained a discography, with pictures, that listed tracks on B-sides of singles that I had never seen or known about, but wanted to hear.

I moved to Athens to begin graduate school at the University of Georgia, and it was around the winter of 1986 that I found I was becoming a collector. I started going to record shows in Atlanta to buy R.E.M. records, and eventually discovered *Goldmine* magazine, which ran a cover story on R.E.M. and their releases in July of 1987. I soon found that my collection included items that were not included in the published *Goldmine* discography, or in the back of the tour books. I began to assemble a discography of my own which included international releases, CD-only releases, and others. I also began to send out letters to British collectors whose ads I saw in *Record Collector*, and eventually established a solid trading relationship with a few fans overseas. When I put forth the idea to my record-collecting friends that I wanted to have a go at cataloging all of the R.E.M. stuff was was floating around and publish the information along with pictures, they thought it was a great idea, and began to help me search out rare and obscure items for me to include. It took seven years and lightened my wallet more than I care to think about, but it's finally complete, and I hope you find it entertaining and useful.

• • •

So why should you collect R.E.M. records and memorabilia? If you've bought a copy of this book, you're probably already a collector to some degree. Many collectors start out trying to locate some of the more elusive B-sides like "Tighten Up," "See No Evil," or some of the live tracks that have been released commercially. Most of my friends who are collectors then graduated from that phase to attempting to find all of the different picture sleeves for the singles. Like me, they then found themselves buying the overseas releases regardless of whether the sleeve differed from the U.S. issue.

There's no doubt that R.E.M. has emerged as one of the most collectible bands to have arisen in the eighties. In fact, the second edition of *Goldmine's Rock and Roll 45 RPM Record Price Guide* called R.E.M. "the most collectible group in the hobby [of record collecting]." This is due at least in part to the wealth of non-LP and live B-sides that have been released. Another factor that contributes to their appeal to collectors is the relative scarcity of the band's early singles, because despite the rave reviews that the band consistently received in the early and mid-eighties, their early singles were not big sellers. A deluge of promotional releases followed the band's signing with Warner Brothers in 1988, and further contributed to the number of rarities available for collectors to find. Thus, R.E.M. satisfy all of the requirements that make for a great collector's band: non-LP and live B-sides, rare singles, lots of promotional material, and a strong, devout fan base. It also doesn't hurt to be a phenomenal rock band.

R.E.M. HISTORY

Saint Mary's Episcopal Church, built in 1871, once stood at 394 Oconee Street, close to the University of Georgia. Razed in May of 1990 to make room for condominiums, the building was perhaps even more decrepit than it had been ten years earlier, when R.E.M. made its debut there. It was an eery and dismal place in which to walk around, even in the middle of the day, when the sun shone through the broken windows and the gaping hole in the roof.

At the end of 1979, Peter Buck was working at Wuxtry Records in Athens, where he met Michael Stipe, an art student at the University of Georgia who had similar musical tastes. They shared a fondness for current American punk bands like Patti Smith and Television, as well as for bands that were the roots of the Punk movement-- the Velvet Underground, the New York Dolls, and Big Star. Peter and Michael quickly became friends and decided to move into the converted church along with a crowd of friends, few of whom actually paid rent. Among the collection of church residents, loiterers, and squatters were Mike Mills and Bill Berry, who moved together to Athens from Macon, Georgia, to enroll at the University. The two were arch-enemies in high school, where Mills looked upon Berry as a rebellious thug, and Berry considered Mills a world-class nerd. Later, following a chance encounter when Mills substituted for the bass player in a band that included Berry, the two hit it off and put their prejudices behind them. Berry was working for Paragon booking agency as a "gofer," performing critically important tasks like chauffeuring Gregg Allman and Cher, and was employed when the company hired Ian Copeland. It was Copeland who introduced Berry and Mike Mills to late seventies New Wave and Punk, by playing for them discs by such groups as The Sex Pistols, The Damned, The Police, Gang of Four, and Chelsea. The excitement that the two felt for this new raw and energetic music would inspire Mills to buy back the bass he earlier sold to Copeland and influence the two to want to play the type of music that R.E.M. would later create. A year later, Mills and Berry enrolled at the University of Georgia in Athens. Ian

■ A youthful Peter Buck shows off some comic books at the Baxter street Wuxtry in April 1980, about a week after R.E.M. made their debut at the church party. Buck met Michael Stipe at the shop, and worked there fairly regularly until the band signed with I.R.S. in 1982.

Copeland's brother Miles went on to found I.R.S. Records in 1979, while his brother Ian founded Frontier Booking International in 1978.

Another one of the residents of the church was Kathleen O'Brien, Bill Berry's girlfriend at the time, who in February 1980, introduced Stipe and Buck to Bill Berry at a party, and later to Mike Mills at the now legendary nightclub Tyrone's O.C. (The O. C. stood for "Old Chameleon," a reference to the club's previous name). The four future rock superstars began rehearsing together in late February 1980 in the church, and after a few months of constant rehearsing and partying with no clear-cut musical goals, the quartet were finally convinced to play in public by O'Brien for her birthday party, on April 5, 1980. Mills and Berry were already accomplished musicians, and although at the time Mills was the better guitar player, they decided that Peter Buck would be the guitar man. Stipe, who had fronted some garage bands in the St. Louis area, was to be the singer.

Between three and five hundred people showed up for the party-- a testament to the active music scene in Athens at the time, and to how fast the word spreads around Athens when something big is going down on a given night. Two other bands played that night as well: The Turtle Bay Band (later known as Men in Trees) and The Side Effects. The Side Effects concluded their set and it was time for the members of the fledgling band to take the stage. They were still contemplating the possibility of backing out. But fortunately, they overcame their stage fright and ripped through a set of twelve originals and a few covers. After they played out their set list and struggled through requests shouted from the crowd, including "Honky Tonk Woman," "God Save the Queen," and "Roadrunner," they invited audience members to get up on stage and sing. Quoting Peter Buck, "We got drunk and fell off the stage, Michael burned himself with a cigarette real bad, we smashed up a bunch of equipment. Yeah, it was real fun." Stipe recalled in an interview with Timothy White, "We wrote fifteen songs in a month so we could play that thing. The party was wild. We expected about one hundred people and five hundred showed up. There weren't a lot of clubs to play in at that point and parties are real common in Athens, and it just kind of happened that we stayed together as a band and kept playing."

The band's next performance took place a few days later at the Koffee Klub in Athens on April 19, which was promptly raided by Athens police officers and prematurely halted. R.E.M. debuted without yet settling on a name that everyone could live with, and having played their second gig still nameless, the four decided to lock themselves in a room, and vowed not to emerge without an acceptable title. Such possibilities as The Ninth Wave, Slug Box, and a strong favorite, The Twisted Kites, were tossed around. Can of Piss was another suggestion, rejected simply because they needed a name that they "could tell our mothers." Many empty cans of beer later, they resorted to a random flip-and-point session with the dictionary, eventually agreeing on R.E.M., an abbreviation for "rapid eye movement," a phenomenon which occurs during the dream stage of sleep. Peter Buck summed up the reason for their choice in 1982, saying, "In the beginning, when we started together, we didn't know what kind of music we would be playing. We didn't want to limit ourselves by calling the band "Punk Rock" or something. R.E.M. was perfect-- real non-descriptive."

Strangely enough, the reason that the band needed to pursue their first paying job together was because the taps to the kegs from the church party were stolen, and they had promised Kathleen that they would somehow get back the $200 she lost in deposit money. So it was that R.E.M. launched their professional career as musicians, to pay for some stolen beer keg taps. Fortunately, Mike Hobbs, who booked Tyrone's, asked them to open for The Brains for a show on May 5th. The band was instantly popular. One week later they were headliners, making a whopping $343 for a night's work. The essence of the sudden popularity of R.E.M. was in their ability to bridge the gap between the more experimental forms of music being tried in Athens in the early 80's, and the more traditional, approachable styles. The mixture of their own original, exciting compositions with Rock and Roll favorites like "Hippy Hippy Shake" and "Rave On" allowed them to appeal to audiences with both conservative and relatively liberal tastes in Rock music. For the members of R.E.M., who all came to Athens originally to pursue degrees at the University of Georgia, school began to drift down their priority lists as the band took off, and all four eventually dropped out.

R.E.M. was among a family of bands in Athens that arose in the early eighties that followed the Art-Punk/Do-It-Yourself musical philosophy. The B-52's, who performed for the first time on Valentine's Day 1977, are credited with establishing the new musical movement in Athens; however, they played only a handful of paying dates before moving to New York. About the time the B-52's left, the Tone Tones played the first New Wave gig at Tyrone's, and a month later, Pylon debuted on March 9, 1979. Tyrone's, which burned to the ground on January 8, 1982, was the springboard for such bands as Pylon and Love Tractor and was the one club that was not afraid of booking new bands.

In the audience at the Koffee Klub the night of the band's second public performance was a young law student named Bertis Downs, who would help R.E.M. with what would prove to be critical legal matters in their early days. He convinced the band to create their own publishing company ("Murmur Music," later changed to "Night Garden Music"), and to register the name

R.E.M. as a trademark. He helped them form a corporation, despite the fact that their only asset was an old Dodge van with a carpeted ceiling. The support and continual assistance provided by Downs kept the band going through the trying times of playing pizza parlors, "new wave nights," gay discos, and biker bars that reeked of stale beer.

The band members decided at the end of 1980 that they should have some songs on tape that they could use to secure bookings. A portable four-track machine was brought into Tyrone's, and in a few hours they had laid down "Dangerous Times," "I Don't Want You Anymore," "A Different Girl," "Narrator," "Just a Touch," "Mystery to Me," "Baby I," and "Permanent Vacation." These tracks were in fact used to help them get gigs as planned, but by early 1981, their songwriting had improved drastically over the simple boy-meets-girl compositions of only a few months before. These new songs that were now typical of the band's sound were not represented on the four-track tape, and an effort to make new recordings commenced.

They played their current tape for Jefferson Holt, an old acquaintance and number one fan from Chapel Hill, North Carolina, then the manager of School Kids Records, and part time band booker. Holt, who would eventually move to Athens and become the band's manager, was initially captivated by R.E.M. when they filled in for Pylon and the Method Actors, who cancelled their shows at the Station in Chapel Hill in July 1980. Unhappy with the quality of the tape, and agreeing that new recordings should be made, he directed the band to Bombay Studios near Atlanta, Georgia, and producer Steve Perry. On February 8, 1981, the band recorded eight new songs on Perry's eight-track machine, "Sitting Still," "Gardening at Night," "Radio Free Europe," "Shaking Through," "Mystery to Me," "(Don't Go Back To) Rockville,"

"Narrator," and "White Tornado." It was again the band's intention to use these tracks to secure bookings, but they were deemed unacceptable for release as an independent single.

Jefferson Holt asked his friend Peter Holsapple of the dB's to suggest a producer that could help the fledgling band. Holsapple suggested the newly outfitted Drive-In Studio in Winston-Salem, North Carolina, owned and operated by Mitch Easter of Let's Active, out of his parent's basement. Taking Holsapple's advice, R.E.M. travelled up to Winston-Salem and on April 15, recorded "White Tornado," "Radio Free Europe" and "Sitting Still" in Easter's studio, the later two songs being released on Johnny Hibbert's Hib-Tone label in July of 1981. Around the time the Hib-Tone single was released, the band also sent out approximately 400 copies of a demo cassette ("Cassette Set") that contained the Hib-Tone cuts as well as "White Tornado," and on some copies, Mitch Easter's dubbed version of "Radio Free Europe."

R.E.M. proceeded to establish a strong local following by frequently playing Athens clubs such as the I & I Club, Mad Hatter, Tyrone's, and the 40 Watt Club. The 40 Watt Club, currently co-owned by Peter Buck's wife Barrie, is the only one of these that remains, although not in its original location. Originally Pylon's practice space, the club took its name from the single forty watt light bulb that at one time provided the only light for the room. The band's attitude towards the pursuit of a professional career in music was at the time still quite carefree. "We do this as a hobby," Peter Buck told *The Atlanta Journal* in February 1981. "We don't take it so seriously that we're going after a record contract. Our ambition is to be the best unrecorded band in the Southeast." In the same month, Mills put it differently, saying, "What we want to do is make one single or demo tape that's the most killer thing ever done, then we'll die in a car wreck or plane crash."

All of the band members still continued to pursue outside projects, most noticeably by appearing in the lineups of other Athens bands. Stipe at one time was in bands called Gangster (his first Athens band prior to R.E.M. in which he sang under the alias Michael Valentine), Boat Of, 1066 Gaggle O' Sound (a solo project) and the later Tanzplagen. Bill Berry was still an on-again/off-again member of Love Tractor, and this confusion led to a 1981 photograph in *New York Rocker* that included Berry in the Love Tractor lineup, identifying him as "Leroy," while on the same page Berry was shown as a member of R.E.M. However, it soon became clear that R.E.M. was the band to which the four wanted to devote their time and energy.

The frantic touring pace which followed the release of the Hib-Tone single included a June 1981 trip to the The Ritz in New York. This, and the ensuing critical acclaim, helped attract the attention of a number of moderately-sized record companies. However, the band's desire to avoid the trappings of a major label deal prompted R.E.M. to start thinking about releasing their next record on their own as well, with the help of David Healey, who had moved to Athens from New Jersey to work with the band. In October 1981, they found themselves back in Easter's studio in Winston-Salem, this time recording "Ages of You," "Gardening at Night," "1,000,000," "Stumble," "Carnival of Sorts," and later, "Wolves, Lower." The band's relationship with Healey fell apart when he failed to support them, and after toying with the idea of signing with RCA (R.E.M. recorded seven tracks for them in New York in February 1982), they decided to sign with California-based I.R.S. Records, then distributed by A&M, who signed the band on May 31, 1982. I.R.S., not overly pleased with the band's Drive-in Studio recordings, but not wanting to delay, decided to release five of the songs as the *Chronic Town* EP in August 1982. One of the principal reasons for choosing I.R.S., a company that had been founded only three years earlier, was that the label would let the band retain a great deal of artistic control over their future. This was something that R.E.M. surely would have sacrificed if they had signed with a major label.

Following the release of the *Chronic Town* EP, I.R.S. suggested R.E.M. record their next album with Human League producer Stephen Hague at the helm. In a studio in Atlanta, Hague pressured the band into using click tracks and synthesizers, neither of which interested the newly signed band. After about fifty tries at "Catapult," they gave up and told I.R.S. that they were going to return to Mitch Easter, this time to record in the larger Reflection Studio in Charlotte, North Carolina, with the help of Don Dixon. *Murmur* was recorded in January 1983, and was released in April of the same year. The album title was chosen, as Michael Stipe flippantly pointed out, "Because it's one of the seven easiest words to say in the English language." The impact of *Murmur* on the relatively stale state of popular music at the time was immense. The award-winning album, released at a time when British synth outfits dominated the pop charts in the U.S., initiated a movement among young American rock bands, who would strive to pursue their creativity while retaining their individuality. The songs from *Murmur* beckoned unestablished bands to make the kind of music that pleased them, regardless of whether it fit into a preconceived formula.

■ Backstage at the I & I Club in Athens, 1982.

The follow-up, 1984's *Reckoning*, was again recorded with Mitch Easter producing, with Don Dixon also twiddling the knobs at Reflection Studio in Charlotte. This album was also successful and lived up to most fans' and critics' expectations, perhaps suffering only from having to hold its own against R.E.M.'s stunning debut a year earlier. The next album, *Fables of the Reconstruction*, was recorded with folk producer Joe Boyd in England, rather than with Easter and Dixon. R.E.M.'s experience in London recording the tracks was stressful and unpleasant, which may have contributed to the mixed reviews that the record subsequently received. The high level of tension present in the studio that spring in 1985 was partly the result of severe homesickness and a run of bad weather. But more importantly, for the first time in their career the band members were decidedly short of material, and were forced to write entirely new compositions in the studio. Besides having less than two weeks to compose, record, and mix most of the tracks, R.E.M. was looking at a number of months on tour following the completion of the uncomfortable session. The idea of cancelling the tour and continuing only as a part-time band, or splitting up entirely, began to look increasingly more attractive. However, their close friend and manager Jefferson Holt persuaded them to carry on as a professional, full-time band by convincing them that greener pastures (and more time off the road) lay ahead.

The harder-edged *Lifes Rich Pageant* followed in 1986, and for the first time, the band that once played second bill to a hot legs contest had a gold record. *Document*, released in 1987, brought even a greater audience to R.E.M., going platinum not long after its release. The album also yielded the band's first top ten hit, "The One I Love."

With the release of *Document*, R.E.M. completed its five-record contract with I.R.S., and a decision had to be made. Should they leave I.R.S., the label that had nurtured them, or sign with one of the major labels that were courting them? The major labels could offer better distribution outside the U.S., particularly in Europe, and this perhaps was one of their biggest selling points. In the winter of 1988, R.E.M. was at the center of one of the most intense bidding wars in recent history. After carefully weighing their options, they finally settled on one of the biggest of the big in Warner Brothers on April 20, 1988, and had to endure the painful experience of saying goodbye to their old friends at I.R.S.

With the Warner Brothers debut, *Green*, R.E.M. now experienced the luxury of having hundreds of thousands of devoted fans waiting eagerly for the album's release, ready to lay down their money in good faith regardless of critics' reviews. Not surprisingly, *Green* brought the band to a still higher plateau, and the Green World Tour found the band playing arenas rather than theaters, something that they earlier vowed never to do. The album spawned the band's second top ten single, "Stand," which expanded the roster of R.E.M. devotees, and, perhaps to the chagrin of the band's older, long-time followers, brought a much younger audience as well. The *Green* tour was exhaustive, and included shows in Japan, Australia, Europe, Great Britain, and virtually every state in America.

A trademark R.E.M. sound became even more difficult to conceptualize, with the 1991 release of *Out of Time*, the band's seventh studio album, and second for Warner Brothers. The driving, politically tinged rock anthems of old were cast aside for this release, which was largely replaced by more gentle, personal compositions. No arena tour followed the release of this album, but as a testament to the band's popularity, Warner Brothers shipped 500,000 copies of the album the day of its release. The popular single "Losing My Religion," plus a brief

■ The first public performance of "Losing My Religion" took place on December 19, 1990 at the 40 Watt Club. Michael Stipe, Mike Mills, and Peter Buck debuted the song on a night that also featured performances by Robyn Hitchcock and members of Drivin' 'n' Cryin'.

but effective publicity tour in the spring of 1991, contributed to *Out of Time* reaching the #1 position in the U.S., U.K., and a number of other countries. The band again decided not to tour behind their next release, *Automatic For the People*. The record reached #2 in the U.S. and again contained a number of popular singles.

As R.E.M. grows and more and more followers are drawn to their captivating music, an ever increasing number of interested new fans want to know how R.E.M. reached the elusive upper tier of rock bands in the eighties and nineties. This book attempts to document the history of the band by cataloging their multitude of releases, and by reproducing promotional material and other collectibles that are difficult to find today for any price.

R.E.M. AND I.R.S. RECORDS

In April 1981, R.E.M. released their first single, and for the first time in their career they had a product to sell. Though Johnny Hibbert, founder of the Hib-Tone label, placed a few ads in local magazines and newspapers for the single, R.E.M. and manager Jefferson Holt were essentially handling their own promotion. They prepared posters for the single that doubled as gig posters, and sent hundreds of copies of the record to newspapers, magazines, independent reviewers, and clubs.

One year after the single and the infamous "Cassette Sets" were released, R.E.M. was a successful up-and-coming band with great press, no problem getting gigs, and a loyal following, but no record label. Disillusioned with the way that major labels handled "New Wave" acts at the time, they decided that they would finance all aspects of putting out their next record. They began recording and mixing the tracks at Drive-in Studio in North Carolina with limited financial help from David Healey, but the relationship between the band and Healey rapidly decayed. By May 1982, R.E.M. decided that signing to a successful label that understood and legitimately appreciated the Punk/New Wave aesthetic (and knew how to market it) might be wise. This would allow them to concentrate on their music and on touring rather than on the manufacturing and distribution of their records. I.R.S. Records had been courting the band for some time, and it was with I.R.S. that R.E.M. chose to sign.

I.R.S. was founded by Miles Copeland III in 1979, a time when record labels were popping up at the rate of about one every hour. These upstart labels signed every band with pointy shoes and skinny ties in the late 70's and early 80's, but Copeland, who had experience with the Punk movement from its inception, could tell the more legitimately talented bands from those that merely jumped on the crowded New Wave/Post-Punk bandwagon. The son of a career C.I.A. man who moved around a lot and eventually settled for a time in London, Copeland began his career in the music business in 1969 where he managed a number of groups including Renaissance, Wishbone Ash and Al Stewart. His management company grew to be a sizable organization, but fell apart in a few years. Copeland remained in London, and in 1977, became fascinated with Punk rock and couldn't resist getting involved. He soon represented a number of Punk bands including The Clash, Blondie, The Police, Squeeze, and the most notorious of all, The Sex Pistols. He eventually decided to found his own record labels in order to take a more active role in the careers of the bands he represented, and had soon signed Chelsea, Squeeze, and The Police, with whom his brother Stewart played drums. Soon he had developed three labels, Step Forward, Illegal, and Deptford Fun City, and had considerable influence at A&M Records who signed his two most successful groups, The Police and Squeeze. Ever the entrepreneur, he hit upon the idea of bringing to America new acts from England that couldn't get American distribution, but to do this he needed a new and bigger label. In 1979 he founded I.R.S. Records with one million dollars of his own money.

Copeland set up a manufacturing and distribution deal with A&M in the U.S. for I.R.S., but it was not a traditional parent company relationship, as A&M did not provide I.R.S. with advances or monthly budgets. Promotional duties were handled by A&M and Copeland's first employee, Jay Boberg, then only 20 years old, and now president of I.R.S. The relationship between Copeland's new label and A&M allowed I.R.S. to succeed mostly because the A&M team could get I.R.S. singles played on college radio, and therefore, I.R.S. had a sizeable advantage over many other small labels that were having trouble promoting their singles. The indie label soon established a cult following of its own, and some fans were going as far as to make bootleg T-shirts emblazoned with the I.R.S. logo.

R.E.M. entered into a contractual relationship with I.R.S. in May 1982, at a time when the label's most successful bands were The Go-Go's, The (English) Beat, and Wall of Voodoo. The question of who actually convinced R.E.M. to sign with I.R.S. is still disputed (at least among Copeland and Boberg), but there seems to be no doubt that Miles Copeland did not want to sign the band unless his brother Ian at Frontier Booking International agreed to book them. Ian Copeland was already in the process of setting up a booking relationship with the band, regardless of the fact that they lacked the support of a label. That being the case, Miles offered R.E.M. a five-album contract which gave them a modest advance, but with respectable royalties. The contract stipulated that the band re-record "Radio Free Europe" for release on their first LP, and granted I.R.S. the rights to the *Chronic Town* EP, which R.E.M. had previously recorded.

While negotiating their contract with I.R.S. and discussing the way that the band wished to be presented to the public, it became clear that R.E.M. was steadfastly opposed to making many of the concessions that major labels generally require of their new acts, namely opening for big name bands on the road, making accessible videos with proven formats, doing endless promotion, and using high-profile producers. Copeland agreed to give R.E.M. an unusual amount of artistic freedom for a young, unproven band, though he assured them that there was a price to pay for such independence. The drawback was that the band was not to expect hit singles, or the same level of success that many of their peers might achieve in the same amount of time. The compromise was agreed to, and R.E.M. was allowed complete musical freedom, along with the power to select producers, design their own record covers, and release records on their own schedule. The band members often relate that Copeland's best attribute was in his allowing them to achieve success at their own pace and on their own terms, despite the fact that the label might have made more money in the short run had they succumbed to the aforementioned music industry concessions. Copeland's concession paid off. By 1984, the label's three most popular groups had broken up, and R.E.M., "The Beatles of college radio," became the focus of their attention.

Through their 1986 release *Lifes Rich Pageant*, the relationship between I.R.S. and R.E.M. flourished, and the band sold increasingly more albums with each release. But later that year when I.R.S. saw the opportunity to profit from the release of an R.E.M. album consisting of B-sides and studio outtakes, the relationship hit a snag. The band wanted the songs that I.R.S. planned to release on the album to remain as B-sides, and not be marketed in an album format, but I.R.S. was steadfast and told the band they would release such an album with or without the band's consent. The band cooperated, because if an album of B-sides was going to be released, they wanted as much influence as possible in the project. The result was *Dead Letter Office*, the album that made available rare R.E.M. tracks that up until then were only in the hands of collectors. Despite the fact that I.R.S. had switched from A&M to MCA for distribution in 1985, *Dead Letter Office* was distributed by A&M rather than MCA because, as the press release put it, "The vast majority of the songs emanate from a time frame during which I.R.S. was distributed by A&M." Four months after the compilation was issued, *Document* was released, and R.E.M. was suddenly propelled into the popular culture with a top ten hit and a *Rolling Stone* cover declaring them "America's Best Rock and Roll Band." With *Document*, their I.R.S. contract had been fulfilled, and R.E.M. felt that it was time that they moved on to a bigger label that could more successfully market and distribute their albums overseas. Warner Brothers was their choice, but the decision was a difficult one to make, and I.R.S. felt they had been betrayed.

Less than three months before R.E.M. was to release their debut on Warner Brothers, I.R.S. announced plans to release an album of the band's more successful singles, plus a few other interesting tracks thrown in to interest those who already had all of the albums. Once again the band members were not particularly in favor of the compilation, but I.R.S. insisted, so the band cooperated and the result was *Eponymous*, released in October 1988.

The international success of *Out of Time*, a record that I.R.S. might have had the opportunity to handle had they been able to convince the band to ink a new contract with them, was no doubt difficult for the label to swallow. But, in true entrepreneurial spirit, they released *The Best of R.E.M.* in England and Germany to capitalize on the band's new international fame. The continual re-release of singles like "The One I Love" and "It's the End of the World As We Know It (and I Feel Fine)" and the way that they were aggressively marketed to compete with the *Out of Time* singles probably soured the band's once genial relationship with I.R.S. However, it's easy to understand why I.R.S. continues to capitalize on R.E.M.-- the label still owns the rights to some of the best and most fascinating rock songs ever written.

PETER BUCK ON R.E.M. HISTORY AND RECORD COLLECTING

Shortly after the marathon Green World Tour ended, I asked R.E.M. guitarist Peter Buck if we could get together and talk about R.E.M. facts and figures. I drove across town to Pete's house, a beautiful and impressively restored Victorian home that looks partly like the Aadams Family mansion and partly like a giant wedding cake. A knock on the etched glass door to Buck Manor brings its owner, and I show him some old R.E.M. singles he's missed along the way.

The living room is decorated in early Howard Finster, and the walls in the dining room are lined with shelves full of records from all eras-- a Nick Cave green flexidisc, Prince singles, a Dylan box set, X's "Adult Books" single, and number of other interesting rock artifacts. Tapes are lying everywhere as are magazines and piles of clothes, and I get the feeling that things still haven't gotten back to normal since the Bucks returned home from the tour. Pete takes a seat on the red velvet Victorian couch and we get down to business.

Let's talk a little about the history of the Hib-Tone single and how you hooked up with Johnny Hibbert. I've heard conflicting stories about that. He approached you first, right?
Yeah, I'd met him before and he was a nice guy. He suggested we do a single and we had just recorded the stuff already so we said sure. So we remixed it and put it out.

So there wasn't really anybody else that was involved.
No, we really didn't know what we were doing. I think we were just trying to make something so we could get live dates. I certainly wasn't a...we weren't really thinking of making a record at that point.

That was the first time he had ever done anything, right? He hadn't put out a record before.
Right, that was the first thing. And then he did, let's see...The Incredible Throbs, a single by a

guy... Harold Kelling... or Keller, I can't remember which. The Harold Kelling single is really good. And then he did another band. I think I've got all the Hib Tone records. I don't really remember what the other band was though. Something like The Downstairs?

Did you really smash a Hib-Tone single when it first came out?

Yeah. We all played it and went "Fuck it!" I smashed the single and taped it up on the wall. See-- it was mastered badly. Johnny was new enough in the business and he didn't know the difference and he couldn't afford it, and we really didn't know. I knew it was horrible but I didn't know why. The idea of how to master a record just didn't occur to me until years later. We were young then.

And nobody really knows how many of the Hib-Tone singles were made. Can we assume that he did a few more than R.E.M. knows about?

We never got an accounting one way or another. I think that we guessed. He told us it was 5,000. We think it was 7,000.

But the first pressing without the address was less than 1,000.

I think the very first pressing there was 1,000 and we sent 600 of them out to people.

And you were sending cassette sets out at the same time, right?

I think the cassette sets were before that. That's the original version of "Radio Free Europe" that's on the cassette. It was re-mastered for *Eponymous*. We didn't remix it or anything.

Do you have a cassette set?

I don't know if I have one of the real ones. I think my brother, or maybe my mom has one that's never been opened. We sent out a bunch of those things. We spent so much time doing that. It's funny, because we're real successful now, but God, we must have been real arrogant then, because we sent out all these demo tapes, with packaging that made no sense that had that thing, "Do not open!" on the outside, and most of them had no addresses on them. I can't imagine what people thought. I'm sure that it's in the bottom drawers of lots of places, which I like. At this late date, God, I can't believe we did that, but I'm really glad we did. It was totally unpretentious. I remember talking to Mitch Easter, and I said, "It's funny, we got like three letters from record companies last week," and he goes, "Oh really? Did you send tapes to them?" I said, "No." He goes, "You got *letters* from record companies?" At that point, Mitch has been in the music industry for like, fifteen years, and he said, "Man, I don't know anyone who's ever got anything but a form letter from a record company when they sent a demo tape. You got a letter *without* sending a tape in?" And I was like, "Well... yeah." He goes, "What did you do with them?" I said, "We laughed and threw them out the window." We had tapes all over the place. We had a weird experience with Greg Shaw, who ran Bomp records. This girl told him that he would like us, and he wrote me a letter saying, "Would you send a tape, or if you are out in Los Angeles, come visit me." My mom and dad lived out there, and Jefferson and I and my girlfriend at the time were going to drive out to L.A., so I wrote him back and said, "Coincidentally, we're going to be out to L.A. in about a month, so we can come visit you." We played him the "Sitting Still"/"Radio Free Europe"/"White Tornado" tape, and I thought it was kind of cool, and he goes, "You know, you shouldn't quit your day jobs. It's not all that good." And another guy goes, "I kind of like the instrumental." He goes, "Yeah, we put out this record by this band in Nebraska, and it sold 100 copies. No one's gonna buy this stuff. You put this out, no one will buy your record. You're just going to be a failure, so why bother?" I was like, "Well thanks, Greg." Mister underground, Greg Shaw.

Do you have a tape of the first show you played?
No, in fact that was about the farthest thing from anyone's mind to tape that thing. I know exactly what we did, though. We did twelve originals and we did six covers...or five covers.

Do you remember what they were, originals or covers?
Originals... it was all the stuff from the Tyrone's bootlegs.

So like "Wait" and stuff like that?
Maybe "Wait" was later. It was "All the Right Friends," "A Girl Like You"... You know, I can't remember what we were writing in those days.

Some of the stuff you see on the early Tyrone's boots?
Yeah. There's that one...let me see, how did that go? (picks up acoustic guitar and plays). I have no idea what that's called. That was one of the ones that we first came out with. I remember it was twelve of our own songs and we did...I think it was even five covers.

"One Nation Under a Groove"?
We never did that one in front of real people.

I heard that during the show there was like a 20 minute version of that song.
Well, we did the set, and then after we were done, everyone was like, "God that was great, and it's still real early, too. It's only one o'clock, why don't you play some more?" So we went back and just did a bunch of covers. I think we might have done that. I don't really remember. Everyone at the time was really drunk. You know, it was like a party. It was the first time we had ever played in public, and everyone was really excited and happy. I think we probably did "Stepping Stone" when we did the first set...and that Eddy Cochran song "Nervous Breakdown."

And like "Rave On" or anything like that?
No, we didn't do "Rave On" 'till later. I think maybe it was..."I Can Only Give You Everything?" Something like that. Maybe "Gloria" too. Mostly it was things that were easy to learn that I could play.

How long were you in Winston-Salem to record *Chronic Town*?
I think we did two days.

Wow, that was fast.
As far as I can remember, the two or three days before we were supposed to go up there, our van broke down or something like that. And we were like, "What are we gonna do?" Because we

couldn't fly, we didn't have any money, and we couldn't even *borrow* money. And I don't remember if we asked Kurt Wood of if he offered, but the idea was that we'd pay his way up there and buy him a couple of meals and he'd go to thrift stores while we recorded. We cut a bunch of songs, too. We cut "Shaking Through," and we did that "Jazz Lips" thing. But then that was without "Wolves." That one had "Ages of You" instead, and we went back and did "Wolves" to kind of give the record a different feel. Although, when it comes down to it, we should have put "Ages of You" on the record, probably.

What are your feelings on R.E.M. bootlegs, now that you've heard over thirty of them?
I still don't mind bootlegs, as long as they're well done, they have a good cover, and it's a good performance. So many of them are mediocre and that really pisses me off, and I'd like to meet those guys and tell them not to put out inferior work.

How about the "Finest Lunchbox" package?
I can't imagine the guy made any money off that thing.

Yeah, especially if the guy only made 100 of them like it says.
I've never seen numbers match up. Every number I see has been different. You know, I'm flattered. I think that's an amazing thing. It's when I hear a really bad one, like a bad performance on our part, or really bad mastering, or just bad sound quality that really pisses me off. The very first bootleg that ever came out about us ("L.I.V.E.") was horrible. It was that one from Italy with Stonehenge on the cover and it was recorded in...Rhode Island back when we were opening for The English Beat.

In Rochester?
Yeah, and it was obviously a hand-held mic in a tinny room. All you can hear is like a banjo-sounding thing, cymbals, and a bit of mumbling and bass bleeding. It was just horrible.

How about things like the interview discs and stuff like "Rapid Mouth Movement?" Do you have that one?
No. What's that, just an interview disc bootleg?

Yeah, I think it was an interview that Michael did in England because it is obviously a British guy interviewing, in '86. And it must have been for some pretty small outfit. They pressed it on green vinyl and it's got this elaborate packaging and everything. I don't know if you've seen that one... but how about the interview picture disc?
Oh yeah, I've got the picture disc. I can't imagine why anyone would want to listen to us talking. I buy bootlegs of the bands I like and I wouldn't consider buying bootlegs of talking. That's really foolish. If they want to do it, go ahead. I'd just as soon someone not bootleg it, because at any given time anything you say could be lies anyway.

Some of the covers on R.E.M. bootlegs are really incredible. Like *Rolling Stone*. The color on that is really amazing. It looks really professional.

Unfortunately on those I don't think the sound quality is as good as the covers are. Then again, a lot of people like me will buy them and play like one or two things. Do you know if there's a bootleg that has the "Theme From Two Steps Onward" on it?

Yeah, on a cassette bootleg. It's like a packaged cassette with some cutesy name on it.
I just heard a demo tape with about four songs on it and that's on there. I forgot we had done that. We actually did a studio version of it with horns. It was really a good version. Michael's vocal wasn't finished exactly, but I mean, it was full vocals.

Do you think you are ever going to put it out?
We lost the tape! I don't know where it is. We were going to put it out as a B-side but we *could not* find it.

Well, you can always do it again though, right?
Naah. Now I don't remember how it goes.

Tell me about your experience with David Healey.
He was this guy that we knew who offered to pay for our records, and then absolutely had a total flip-out. Like when we were doing *Chronic Town*, he was supposed to be paying for it and we'd call up and go, "Our van broke down and we're stranded," and he'd go, "Fuck you, I'm not going to pay the bill!" And hung up on us.

Well, you were thinking of putting it out on your own label, right?
Yeah, and it was going to be his label. He was like, a talker, you know? Like he *almost* got Keith Richards to give him five thousand dollars. He was a good friend, but it was totally crazy. He'd have these breakdowns. We'd be depending on him and all of a sudden he'd not give us the money that we were supposed to get. So he got his name on the EP.

"Ex. producer."
"Ex. producer," which used to be "executive producer, " and then since we fired him we just put "ex. producer." He was just insane, but in a fun way, but he got weirder. He was always *going* to do everything. He was *going* to get money, and he was *going* to have a deal. It just got really weird. He had all these grandiose plans, then basically what it came down to was he wanted to be cut in forever for a big part of everything we wanted to do. And it was like, "Well, we don't do that kind of shit." It was like, "If you back us for this, we'll give you some money, and you'll get a percentage of the record." I mean, he wanted to sign ourselves to him for the rest of our lives. Then he would own us. And he would say, "All I want to do is help you out." And then he handed us this thing that said basically, "You will be my slaves for life if you sign this." And we just looked at him and went, "We can't do this. This is insane." And he says, "I just want my fair share!" And his fair share was like ten percent of us until the end of the century. It was pretty much insanity.

What about the video of the band that was shot at Wuxtry in Atlanta, was that right after the show at the church?

It was after we did the first show at the church, and it was after we did the show at the Koffee Klub. I can't even remember why we played there. That was the first time we played outside the church, was that place. I can't remember if it was a benefit, or if it was just a show, but we played at the Koffee Club, which had a little PA, and the police came and closed it down after like forty minutes. Someone complained, and the police shut us down, and took everyone's name and photos. It was kind of funny. There's a police report you can look up. Bert has it. It says, "An unidentified band was making a racket, people were dancing, and we think they were selling drinks." But then the thing at the Wuxtry, of course I worked there, and they had a video camera and I'd never seen a video camera before, and they suggested we should film some stuff to send out. I think it was the first time we played in Atlanta when we did that thing with Red Beans and Sprouts down at The Warehouse down on Spring Street. I think it was that day. I think we did the Brains shows before we went to Atlanta. I think we had done about five live shows.

What did you think of your performances back then?

There was a lot of energy, we were learning how to do it. There was kind of an innocence to it. We weren't certainly a great band, but we were interesting. I think there was a kind of chemistry between us that we could catch on stage. Sometimes we were really sloppy and fucked up, but it was pretty neat. I certainly would not want to have any of it captured on tape.

Although it has been.

But most of the boots come from a time when we were actually starting to play well together. Hell, half the time I couldn't keep my guitar on. I was just learning how to play.

What about the shows where you opened for Bow Wow Wow?

Yeah, they were really mean to us. I hated those guys. We played with them once in New Jersey and they had all this catering with tons of food, and one of us asked, "Do you have any food for us?" and they went, "No catering for the opening band, it's too expensive!" So we sat down in the catering room drinking our own beer, and these bodyguards came over to us and said, "You've got to get out of here. They don't want anyone around while they eat." In our dressing room we had, like...*shit* in it, and it was like *really* bad. And we said, "We don't have anywhere to go!" So we had to go sit out in the van and drink beer while they ate. Then we opened for them in Atlanta and it was just all a big hassle. They had bodyguards pushing us around and yelling. I got in this arguing match with one of them after the show.

Of course, where are they now?

I don't really wish anyone ill, but I don't mind hearing bad things about them. Most of the musicians that I've met have been really nice but the real pompous ones that think they are great are a problem.

It seemed to be the case for a lot of Athens bands that started playing, particularly in the early eighties, that they started playing really before they were good musicians. Like The Side Effects were always bad, but everyone loved them anyway.

Oh yeah, they were really fun, but if you were to judge them by their musicianship, they were horrible. They just went beyond it because they were so much fun. Those were the days. People would go out to see something that was different, and no one really expected a professional show. We were all kids. It was just a happening little town. You would go see bands and you'd have no idea what you would see. Some nights you'd see a guy with a banjo, some nights you would go see a real punk band, some nights you'd see Pylon.

How did you hook up with Bert?
He saw us at our second-ever show at the Koffee Klub and he used to come in the record shop that I worked at. He was still a law student, and he loved us. The day after he saw us play at the Koffee Klub he said, "Man, you're now my favorite band. You guys are going to be so big some day, and I'm going to be a lawyer in six months and I'll work for you for free."

And Jefferson was kind of the same way.
Jefferson booked us to play in North Carolina. We went to his town and then he moved here and started working for us. Pretty much everyone that's working for us has been working for us since the beginning.

So he was managing a record store and booking and he just happened to book you guys and went to see what you were like?
Well, he was trying to bring bands into Chapel Hill because nothing was going on there, and he just really liked us. When he moved to Athens to work in this record store called Foreign Legion and manage it, he started working with us, and then the store went under. It was only open for two months and it had three different names.

How long did you work at Wuxtry?
Full time, I guess it'd be 1978 to spring of 1980. Then I started taking time off, and I worked in 1981 and 1982, but sometimes it wasn't literally more than three weeks out of the year, because we were on the road *all the time*, and I kept the job, and finally they said, "You're never here *at all*. What good is it to have a manager that's in Iowa?"

How did you get the job?
I used to go in and buy records from the owner, Mark, in their Atlanta store. Most of the guys who would go to the store were real record queers who would bother him and push him around. I would just say, "Do you have this?" and he'd go, "Yeah" and I'd buy it, and I wouldn't argue about price. Then he needed someone to work at the store, and literally he said, "You know, you know music a lot and you're really not too much of an asshole. Do you want a job?" And I said, "I'm thinking I might move to Athens." And he said, "Oh, that's great. One of our guys quit a week ago and we don't have anyone working there right now, and if you're travelling and you want to go work in Athens, go ahead." At that point I had *just* quit my job. That was like December 21st or something, and I moved up here January 2nd of 1978.

What was your old job?

Working at another record store. I got in a big argument and I just quit and walked out. It's true, though. Mark at Wuxtry wanted someone to run the business that wasn't going to be a jerk about it. Because a lot of guys who are really into records are kind of weird, and a lot of them tend to be jerks. He told me it was okay to be rude to the customers, but do your job. We worked together in Atlanta for two days, and I came up to Athens and managed the store. I wasn't making much-- like $3.25 an hour. I met Michael in 1979. I guess I was there about a year and a couple months before I bumped into him. Then we started hanging out. I was doing other stuff-- I had friends. Then it looked like we were going to form a band, and all of a sudden we did. Then I started disappearing from work, and I'd go, "Man, I've got to take *all* of August off." I mean, 1981 was pretty bad. I worked through 1982, but in all of '82 I only did like two weeks' work, because we were on the road the *entire* time. I got back in '82 and went to work at night, and then he came over to my house and said, "Listen, I hate to fire you, but you're *never* here, and we just can't have a guy who manages the store who *isn't* in the store. I'm hiring all these temporary people, and they don't know what they are doing." So I said, "You're not firing me because you think I'm a thief or anything," and he said, "Oh, no, no, no."

You couldn't have been because you weren't there!

I said, "You're not thinking that I've been taking money out, or anything." And he said, "No, no...you're *never* there. We can't have somebody do that." which was fine. Perfectly acceptable.

When did it really hit you that the band could be something really huge?

I never really thought that. I knew it was going to be something a little bit out of the ordinary when we signed the record contract. I realized that very few people actually sign contracts with a major label. I guess I didn't even start thinking that people were even paying attention to what we were doing until...it might not even have been *Document*. I remember during *Document*, Scott saying, "Everyone's telling me that this next record is going to make you as big as U2." We were like, "What?" With *Green*, we knew that people would listen to it and buy it, but we never really felt that automatically we would have these results.

I went to the L.E.A.F. benefit concert in Atlanta and saw that you actually got to stand in front of a microphone and sing for a little while. That must have been a new experience for you!

I sing on two songs if I feel like it. I have trouble staying in pitch to tell you the truth, when I'm on stage. It has to be crystal clear for me to sing in pitch. So I really don't care, but then "Wild Thing," anyone can sing that. It was like, "What the hell, I'll sing." C is my key. I can sing in C. It's easy to sing. And "Get Up," Mike was tutoring me on how it goes. It was kind of fun.

That was a great show. Whose idea was it to do the songs from *Murmur* and *Green* in the order that they appeared on the albums?

Well, I think what happened was we were seeing The Who do *Tommy* and I just said, "God, who would want to do one of your old records? Can you imagine us doing *Murmur* in 2005?" And someone said, "Hey, what a great Idea! Let's do *Murmur* at The Fox!"

I noticed Michael had a music stand out there with him for the *Murmur* songs.

You know, "Catapult" we hadn't played since '84. "Laughing" we hadn't played...we played it twice in '85.

So that was pretty challenging for you guys.

We all *kind* of remembered them. It's just weird to start playing a song and get half way through and go, "Uh, guys--we're doing the wrong key and I can't do the bridge in this key." You know, if you have a weird tuning or something.

That must have been fun playing the *Green* songs at The Fox that you hadn't played live.

Yeah. We had actually *never* played "The Wrong Child" together, ever. I put down the acoustic guitar, Bill put down the mandolin, Mike put down the Mellotron, Michael did the vocals...there wasn't any time when two of us were in the studio at the same time.

When the next record comes out, will Warner Brothers put pressure on you to tour?

See, they don't really care at all where we tour, as long as we tour. If we didn't tour, they'd probably be disappointed.

To kind of get your name in the press.

Right. The thing is that it's not so much the people that come see you as it's just the idea that you'd be in the paper all over the country for a month. You talk to radio people and stuff like that. Especially if we make a different, kind of weird record for us, we might just play a smaller space. I want to tour-- I love touring, but I don't really want to do this again. I mean the big places.

That must have been a lot of work.

Nine months. And the thing is, we held up great. Nobody was really ill.

After the next R.E.M. album comes out, do you think there will be any 45s?

The people at Warner said probably not, but if we tell them we want them, they probably will let us. Because nobody seems to buy those CD 45s. We sold 300,000 of the American seven-inch of "Stand." I like seven-inchers.

The CD singles seem to sell really big in England, but not here.

Well, I don't think they've ever come up with a format that everyone uses. Everything's different...the five-inch, the three-inch with adaptors, and the seven-inch vinyl.

Do Mike Mills or any of the other guys collect the R.E.M. stuff like you do?

No, nobody cares. Jefferson collects some stuff, and Bertis sometimes tries. It's not like I play them. I don't have them in play rotation or anything like that. I've got them in a closet. Just because I like to have this shit. Eventually I'll probably have kids. I've got books and clippings and photos...I think it's kind of cool. I know it's stupid for me to buy R.E.M. stuff, but I do want to have it. I read those stories about John Lennon sending people to auctions to buy Beatles dolls for $4,000. The rare R.E.M. thing, of which there's only one, and I think Mike has it, is the ten-inch acetate of "Driver 8" with alternate mixes of "Can't Get There From Here." We don't make many acetates.

What kind of input do you guys have on what's going to be a single from an album and how it's going to be done?

We give them suggestions, but it's their job to pick it. Michael will design like five singles covers, and it's obvious that some songs will never be singles. So he'll design covers for some of the ones that are going to be singles, and they pick and choose and then we try to come up with alternate backing tracks. Sometimes it's hard. We finished *Green* and we had six extra songs, and they weren't finished. So that's why we just had "Memphis Train Blues" on there. It's kind of cute, but it's certainly not like "Ghost Riders" or something like that. "Ghost Riders" and...what else did we record at the same time... "See No Evil" and "Dark Globe," and acoustic "Pop Song."

Whose choice was it to do "Dark Globe?

Michael started singing it one day and we started doing it. I didn't know he knew anything about Syd Barrett.

How did "Dark Globe" end up as a flexidisc?

The people at *Sassy* wanted something and we didn't really have anything in the can that was finished that we could give them. They wanted something that was pretty much unavailable in America. That was like the only one that didn't officially come out in America. It was like an English B-side. So they wanted that and we said, sure, what the hell. We've known the editor for years, Jane Pratt. I'd seen it because I knew her. It's a teen magazine that actually talks about things you'd care about.

Michael quit doing autographs a while ago, right?

He does them on charity things.

Of course there are guys that follow musicians around airports and hotels and get them to do autographs and then sell them for fifty dollars or more. Is that why he quit doing them?

Yeah, plus he just got tired of them. Essentially it's a meaningless thing. I'm ambivalent about it. It used to be when people asked us for autographs, they'd go, "Why don't we just talk instead of having an autograph?" But I'd get asked to do autographs eighty times a day, and I just don't have that much time to have a private conversation with every person who wants an autograph. Especially if it's a twelve-year-old girl with braces on her teeth who's so awe struck with fear that she just looks at you and shivers. It's like, "Sure, I'll sign your T-shirt." I don't mind it. Michael just got a little tired of it, and that's fine. I do see those guys who... and they're at every show...there's like this eighty-year-old guy, and I go, "That guy's not a fan of us."

Tell me how the Bill Berry "13111" twelve-inch single came about.

He just writes all kinds of weird little songs by himself and he just decided to do it. I have no idea why. I think it's pretty cool.

Yeah, it is pretty funny. I noticed his name isn't on it anywhere.

No, he didn't want to make it The New Bill Berry Solo Record. He just wanted to do something interesting.

What did people think about you in Japan on the *Green* tour? Did they know you pretty well?

We did okay. A couple thousand people a show. We only did two dates I think. I'm not sure if they get it exactly, but some of the kids are really fanatical and they followed us around and gave us gifts. Everyone gives saki and also socks, because they have these really nice hand-done socks. I have tons of these Japanese socks that are really good.

You get to travel in different circles now, and I'm sure you wanted to meet famous people when you were younger. Who have you gotten to meet that you always wanted to? I just saw a picture of you with Jerry Lee Lewis.

I did meet Jerry Lee Lewis. You know, I didn't really have any interest in meeting these people at all. I always liked the records and I go see the bands, but I just never considered that it would be interesting to go see a guy in a band and talk to him. By and large, the people that I've met that I respected their work have been nice people. I've accidently met some people who were humongous jerks.

Have you ever gotten any feedback from the bands whose stuff you covered, like Lou Reed or Wire?

Yeah, I met Lou Reed. Actually, he called up the office when *Dead Letter Office* came out. A friend of his said, "You got to listen to this! Don't listen to the rest of it, it's outtakes and B-sides." And he played it, and called up Jefferson and said, "I just want you to know I think this is great. It's kind of the original feeling of the Velvet Underground." Then I met him this summer and he goes, "You guys do my stuff really good. I really appreciate the kind of looseness factor, that you did it direct to cassette." And I said, "Thank you very much."

So he didn't know about it when the "Radio Free Europe" single came out.

No, I don't think so. It was a B-side. He's a fan of ours, and of course I'm a fan of his. Fred Smith from Television, he saw us do "See No Evil." We got real drunk afterwards. He's in the Fleshtones, and we said "Let's do it 'cause Fred's here." He was like, "Man, that was great!" Mission of Burma doesn't know we do "Academy Fight Song" yet.

How about Wire? They must know.

Oh, I'm sure, it made them 25 or 30 thousand dollars. They thought it was pretty cool, I guess. A friend of ours had them sign one of our records, and one of them wrote, "You Hooligans! You ruined it!" I have no idea what they think of it. I'm sure that they appreciate the checks, because it was on a record that did well, and they made a lot of money off of it.

Is there stuff in your contract that says that by a certain amount of time you have to produce a certain amount of material?

Yes and no. If we just don't turn in a record they can yell at us and sue us or something, but Warner Brothers just let you do whatever you want to.

With you, yeah.

Well, maybe not with everyone, but a lot of people *need* someone to tell them what to do. They don't tell Prince what to do, they don't tell Randy Newman, they don't tell Neil Young, but I'm sure they tell a lot of the other acts, "You need to cut a record now." But everyone that's worked with us knows we're always prepared. We always write tons of songs, we're always ready to go in the studio before they think we're ready. I mean, *Green*, they were going, "Oh yeah, it will be out in March of '89. They won't even start recording until like around Christmas time." And we were like, "Hell no!" We signed the contract and Jefferson said, "Surprise, surprise, they're going in the studio in three weeks, and they've written all the songs, they've done demos for them, picked a producer, booked studio time, and we want the record to come out November eighth." And they were like, "Holy shit!" They had heard that we were going to take some time off; they thought it was going to be an eight month thing, or something.

How many guitars do you own?

A lot. Probably over forty.

Do you get people that send them to you and say, "Please play this on stage"?

Not really. Sometimes they'll go, "Do you want one?" but I usually don't take things unless it's something I really want, and usually I pay for them, because I don't want to feel like I have to endorse some guy's product. If I don't like it I'll just put it in a closet or sell it or something. Like those Les Pauls I used, I bought them. I paid cost, but that's about half-price. All my Rickenbackers, I paid cost. Occasionally someone will go, "I just want you to have this guitar," but usually I try to turn it down.

Speaking of endorsements, I saw Bill's doing one now for drums. Do you think that's good or bad?

I don't really mind if a musician does an instrument one. I don't do it. I don't really want to. He never gets his pictures in magazines. Like in that big Musician article, he wasn't even in there. He just kind of went, "Fuck 'em, so they're not going to put me in the article, that's fine. I'll have a full page in everything else." I'm ambivalent about that kind of thing, but he didn't get paid for it, so it's okay.

Tell me about the Nigel and the Crosses material. I know you've had one track on the Byrds tribute album.

At the end of that, when it starts fading out, it was a medley. We did "Oh Yeah" by Roxy Music. It was an *amazingly* good version of that. I mean a really good version, with all the 12-string guitar. We cut like an album's worth of stuff in one day, and we also cut for the Byrds thing "Tambourine Man," like this letter-perfect version. And we did "Wild Mountain Thyme," and then Robyn started playing this song and I just followed him into it, and I said, "What's that?" And he goes, "It's that Roxy Music song, 'Oh Yeah.' " I'd never listened to it and we just rehearsed it once and did it. It was like nine minutes long, and it's really good. Robyn plays it great. I thought it was one of his songs. There's a ton of that stuff. We could put out a two-record set of all the stuff me and Robyn have done.

How many times did the Hindu Love Gods play live?

Twice, I think. Twice, and that one time with Warren Zevon.

So you only played once with Warren Zevon.

Yeah, and then we did twice...once at the 40 Watt and once at that place...The Georgia Hotel or whatever that was. And then we did the Warren Zevon thing. It was after Love Tractor.

Do you get a lot of letters from small bands asking you to produce?

Yeah. Kids in junior high school. I really have to see a band or really just like them for me to want to do it. It takes a lot of time for me to do, I mean, ten or twelve days doesn't seem like a lot, but it is, and I never really ask for money because these people are all broke. So, I'm working for a week and paying for stuff.

What was it like going in the studio with the first band you produced, Dreams So Real?

I didn't really produce that. I was going to, and what happened was, they didn't have the material, and they were all fighting, so I was there when they cut like seven songs.

It was in someone's living room, wasn't it?

Yeah, it was in someone's house. It was a good studio--the guy was good. But it was kind of like, Bob would come in and go, "Man, this song sucks. I'm not going to play on it." Then they'd do one take of the song, and it would be horrible, and they'd go, "Oh, that's good enough." And then I said, "I thought you guys had enough songs for me." And they said, "Oh, well, we thought we did, but we don't." I co-produced about half the basic tracks for about half of that record. I played on that, and I was supposed to produce it, but it didn't work out that way.

What was it like helping to put together Kevn Kinney's solo record?

Well, we talked about it, and everyone knows that Drivin' n' Cryin' needs to have kind of a rockin' record to be a success, and they don't mind Kevn getting the acoustic stuff out of his system, and getting loosened up a bit. I think this was the first time he was really comfortable in the studio. They'll make a rockin' record that's really great, and maybe it will do something.

I think your first real performance on TV was the David Letterman show in 1983. What was that like?

They were really nice people, but it's no fun playing on TV. Actually, Dave came back stage and said hello. He was really nice. He isn't a good interviewer, but he did like us. I know that he liked us 'cause he said so, and when he met Warren Zevon he said, "You worked with R.E.M.? I love those guys. I listen to their tapes all the time when I'm jogging." But it's not fun to play when it's not one of your shows.

Do you think there's going to be another B-sides collection like *Dead Letter Office* coming out, or was that just like a one-time thing?

I don't know. I would prefer probably not to. I think probably Jefferson and Bert think we will, but I just don't really see it. We recorded enough stuff that we could put out...like if we died in a car wreck tomorrow, or if the band broke up, there's tons of stuff sitting around that I could put out. Maybe a couple records of it. But there's no real reason to have it out, and the B-sides should probably just stay B-sides. The reason we did *Dead Letter Office* mainly, was because we knew I.R.S. wanted to, and if we didn't get involved, they'd probably want to anyway, and it would come out eventually, and we'd rather be involved and have it look like one of our records, and have liner notes, and have it sound like one of our records. The way we did it, we ended up doing *Eponymous* the same way. I wouldn't have picked those to come out, but they wanted them out, and we'd rather be involved and have it come out representing us well, rather than have it come out and *not* be us.

What about the song selection on it, though. Were you happy with that?
That was us. That was our song selection. They really wanted "Superman" to be on there, and we were like, "Nope, that's not really representative of us."

So it ended up on the I.R.S. tenth anniversary CD.
The only review that I've read of that CD just said, "This is kind of weird, because it's totally unrepresentative of them, and it's not a song they wrote." But I.R.S. still kind of believed that it should have been a hit single. I don't really agree with that. They keep thinking that someday it will be.

What happened to Michael's rumored *Field Recordings* record?
Well, what happened was, he was doing some stuff that he was recording. Some of it, he just took a DAT out in the field and recorded things, some of it was instrumental things with other people. It wasn't anything like a solo record. It was just recordings, and he probably would have put it out under some name, but Dutch East Indiea heard about it and started saying Michael Stipe's solo album is coming out on this day, and it was like, wait a minute. Michael was like, "I don't want anyone to buy it thinking this is like me singing songs with the band." As far as I know, his voice isn't even on it. I haven't even heard the stuff. I heard little bits and pieces of things, but you know, he kind of just canned it because he didn't want people to be thinking, "Well, here's the new solo record," and buy it and go, "What?" It will be an arty little project whenever it does come out, if and when it does. It 'll be something that people don't pay much attention to.

What's the story behind the Vibrating Egg LP?
That's Jefferson's horribly deformed baby. It's just something he's always wanted to do, which was massacre some of his favorite songs. I didn't play on it, but I know a bunch of people that did. It was supposed to be some dumb, fun thing. As far as I know, Jefferson never really put it out for sale. For the longest time, the only way to get it was if you wrote to him and asked for a copy. And it was listed on the Dog Gone sheets, and I said, "Did you sell any of these?" and he said, "Yeah, I've sold about six." It never really got in stores. It's kind of cool. He said, "I want to put it out, and if people write to me and ask for it, we'll mail it to them." Now that his record company is doing the shake up thing, I don't know if you can get it. We all got promo copies, and thought it was kind of a hoot. You know, his label signs some good bands that he's working with, but mainly he does fun little things. If I ever made a solo single I'd do it for him, too, but I don't really have much interest in it right now.

You know that pretty soon most record stores aren't going to be selling vinyl albums anymore. I know people who are real audiophiles that try to track down first pressings of analog recorded records because they don't like things in digital sound. Are you kind of like that, or do you not care about CDs anymore?

Originally when CDs came out and everyone was switching to them, I, being someone who's around music all the time, I didn't think that they had reached, technologically, a place where they were sounding good. To me, the high end was kind of crisp and crunchy. It was an unpleasant sound. Maybe it's because people are recording things differently now. I think it's probably just the technology, but I think they're sounding real good. If records disappear I'm going to be real nostalgic for them. I still buy records. I like records. But for record companies, it's more profitable to make CDs. They charge more for them, and pay us less for them.

I understand it costs the same to make a CD as it does a record.

They charge more and you get less royalties on them. It's not like a ton of money less, but it's less royalty rates than LPs, even though they are making a bigger profit. I've heard some of our records on CD and they sound good, but they're not the way I heard them when we mixed them, and it's not the way they sound on the record. There are a lot of things on *Murmur* that don't come out or that aren't supposed to come out, but I can hear them on the CD.

That must be kind of annoying.

Well, it's not like it's anything horrible, but things that are supposed to be buried in there are kind of popping up. People tell me all the time, "I just listened to *Murmur* and it's a new record!" I heard *Blood on the Tracks* on CD and that ruined the record for me. It's so horrible-sounding on CD. I'm ambivalent about CDs. Records will be gone.

One thing you notice in reading *Goldmine* or *Record Collector* is that record collecting, especially of new releases, seems to be much bigger in the U.K. than in the U.S. Things are packaged in the U.K. clearly for collectors, like the "Stand" maple leaf CD. What do you think the difference is between the people in this country and that country, and why do you think it's like that?

I don't know. I think there are collectors in both countries. It's more of a marketing thing over there. They've always got an extra track on the CD, or a poster with the single, and that's just a marketing thing that they know works. But as far as the amount of people that collect the stuff, it's probably about the same per capita from country to country.

I've noticed in the ads in *NME* and other music magazines that they always have, in huge letters, "Previously unreleased B-side." You never really see that kind of thing over here.

No, it's not something that is a marketing tool over here very much, but people do buy that stuff. In England, I just assume that since it's just such a small populace buying the stuff that you need to appeal to those people to actually get a record on the charts.

I'm very fond of all of the promotional trinkets that I.R.S. and Warner Brothers have done. Whose idea was the "Stand" promo compass?

I guess the record company. We have to okay everything, but they'll come to us with ideas, and ask us if it's a good idea.

I also liked the "Inside-Out" T-shirt that was actually inside-out.

That was Michael's. We do the real merchandising. The stuff we sell, we design it. Michael does, essentially. We okay or veto it. But this record company stuff, we might say, "Gee, wouldn't it be nice to have a trash can," or something. Or a yo-yo, or whatever. They'll say either yes or no. Usually they'll go, "God that's a cool idea!"

How about the "Meadow in a Can?"

Yeah, I think that was Michael's idea. I don't know. Maybe it was the record company's. Michael just wanted it to be called "Meadow in a Can." He liked the name. All this stuff is kind of floating around. Actually, it's kind of interesting. I don't even drink coffee, but one of my favorite things is those R.E.M. coffee mugs. Bill Graham, the same guy that made the *Green* Tour water bottles, made these things. Every time you play at a Bill Graham place-- he's really good about treating people well. The dressing room door has a wooden sign with your name branded on it, "R.E.M." When you play his place you always get some little cool thing that was made especially for the show that commemorates the event. The mugs were really cool. I copped as many of them as I could.

I understand that every year you put together a collection of all of the band's TV appearances onto a video archive. Do you have any of those?

I don't have them all. I've got some of them. We've got hundreds of hours of that shit. We've got some really rare stuff. We retain the ownership to everything we do. When we do TV shows, it's in the contract that they can use it so many times, then it reverts to us. We've got acres and acres of TV footage of us, and all of the studio stuff we do, and the radio broadcasts. We've got a vault in Atlanta that's just filled with this shit.

What did you think of "Spam" by Weird Al Yankovick, the take-off of "Stand?"

We all talked about letting him do that, and we thought it was definitely kind of funny, but it's definitely not what I want to be known for in my career. I thought it was kind of cool. I mean, what the hell, he did Michael Jackson and he did us. It would have been nice if it was on a record that had actually sold a bunch, so we could make some money off it, but what the hell. Weird Al's lawyer called us up, and asked if they could do that, and we talked about it, and said, "Well, what do we say? If we say yes, people will go, God, this is some bullshit showbiz thing. If we say no, we look like humorless boobs." And I said, "What the fuck. Why not. Let him do it." It wasn't as funny as "Bad," because "Bad" *was* really funny, where he did the "Fat" thing. But it was okay.

MTV has really changed since its inception. Do you ever watch it?

I watch 120 Minutes, and I watch some of the special shows. I don't watch it every week. What I don't like is how they ghetto-ize everything. Like there's the heavy metal hour, and there's the rap hour. I'd rather have it all together, so you'll see Guns and Roses, and then, you know...

Big Daddy Kane.

Yeah, and then us, and then Whitney Houston, rather than, "Okay, now we'll have all white people, and now we'll have all black people, and now we'll have all white people with spandex pants and big guitars..."

A lot of people try to make comparisons between R.E.M. fans and Grateful Dead fans, especially when it comes to bootlegs, and tape trading. Do you think there's a comparison to be made, or do you think that's kind of silly?

Well, with The Grateful Dead, when you're one of their fans you buy a lifestyle. You wear certain clothes, and you do certain things, and I don't think that's quite so much us. Although what is similar is that they're real fanatical. We do have people follow us around, and they do trade tapes and all that. But that's good. Most bands that I really like have those kind of fans. The Smiths have those kind of fans, Dylan has those kind of fans and Whitney Houston doesn't. That's a different situation.

So what makes a band have those kind of fans or not have them?

It must reach them on some personal level rather than just be a good beat that you can dance to.

Do you have a new "desert island list" for records?

I don't know. It would change all the time. I'd probably cheat and take all those box sets. I'd take the Muddy Waters thirteen-record set, the Hank Williams fourteen-record set, and maybe the Stones one. I don't know if I had just a few records to take, what I'd do. Because the ones that I really love, I've probably played to death. I don't know when the last time I've played a Big Star record was.

How did the ritual of putting the plastic dinosaurs on your amps get started?

We just did it. The very first day of *Murmur*, the very first day I bought those, they've been on the amp for every single session we've ever done. The same ones. I get a lot of them from different people, but those were the very same ones we've used from the word go.

Is it like your good luck charm?

Well...yeah. I'm not very superstitious, but after you've done it this long you might as well keep doing it. When we did *Green* our plane was delayed and I accidently left them in a bar in Atlanta. We called up and we mailed the lady who ran the bar fifty dollars to Federal Express our dinosaurs. So we only missed half a day.

What's your relationship like now with the I.R.S. folks? Is it still friendly?

Yeah, I have a lot of personal friends there. It's kind of sad and kind of strange because we left, but we changed as a band while we were there, and the label changed a lot. Their emphasis on acts changed quite a bit between the time we signed and the time we left. It was time for a change. I know we hurt their feelings, and it was real tough for us, and real hard for us to do it. We felt it was the thing to do.

So you flew Jay Boberg out from I.R.S. to tell him in person?

We wanted to tell Jay because in a lot of ways, he discovered us and signed us. He had been a real important part of what we had done, and we wanted to tell him to his face. I think that if you are going to make the decision you should have the nerve to look someone in the eye and say it. It was hard. It really upset us all, and upset him, and I'm sure it still bothers him. I still think about it myself, but I think we made the right move.

How had I.R.S. changed?

When we started with them, they had The Cramps, The Buzzcocks, The Go-Go's, Howard Devoto... some fairly weird stuff. And as we got to the end of the run, there was us, and there wasn't a whole lot else. They had Black Sabbath, and some other things. And they changed the way that they did business a lot. Things just changed in the way that 1982 was a lot different than 1988, when we signed the Warner Brothers contract. It seemed like the right thing to do for us.

It seems like Warner Brothers allows you to be equally as creative.

We just give them the records and say, "This is our new record, and put it out if you want." That's what we do.

Here's a question you're probably tired of answering. Do you think a live R.E.M. album will ever come out?

We've got tons of shows recorded on 24 track. It's all labelled in the vault, and I'm sure if we break up we'll put something like that out just to have it. I don't really see us doing something like that now, or even in the next few years. It will be like, "Well, that's the end and here's the live record."

Are you contractually allowed to break up?

We can do whatever we want to. No one can force you to make a record. We'd still be under contract, as long as we wanted to. In a lot of ways it's like the I.R.S. contract. We can do what we want to, they can ask us to make records, but certainly if we don't want to work together they can't force us. Nobody can force you to do that. If we broke up, we all are signed individually, and could perform with other bands, but we don't have any...we're not going to break up. We're at the point now that if I decided that I'd rather not work with these guys for a year, we could just *not* work together. Warner Brothers is more than willing to let us slide on that kind of stuff, but we have no interest in breaking up anyway.

What exactly is R.E.M./Athens, Limited?

That is...it's like Public Image Limited. Like they said they were going to be, except we really are like that. It's the four of us and Jefferson. It's a corporation that provides records, songwriting, public performances, videos...and this corporation, which is also a band, makes all those, markets them, and then someone contracts that corporation to get our work. R.E.M., when it comes right down to it...when we signed with Warner Brothers, in the contract it doesn't say that the four of us are actually the people that are going to write the songs, or play on the records, or sing. It's the five of us, and we will provide music to Warner Brothers. Essentially, if we said, "R.E.M. is *these* people doing *this*," legally we could do that. We could have whoever make a record, and give it to them. They wouldn't be happy with that. Warner Brothers wants some kind of small assurance that most of the guys in the band will actually play on the records, and will tour sometime, and it's going to be you people, and it's not going to be three fat guys you found in Duluth and had them do the stuff. It's just a corporation that provides entertainment services. When it comes down to it, there's no description in our contract that says who plays what, who's gonna sing what, and who's gonna write what. The five of us can decide that whatever we decide is a record by R.E.M. *is* a record by R.E.M., and deliver it to them. Of course, no matter what it says in the contract, if we did pick some shit people and make a shit record under our name, I'm sure we'd get sued or something. But basically, we just provide them with records over a certain amount of time, and they say, "Thank you."

Are there any magazines that have persistently given you bad reviews?

A lot of fanzines, sure. At least in the last five years. But, you know, that's kind of funny. In *Forced Exposure*, for like a year I was the anti-Christ. I read that magazine, and I like it. It turned me on to a lot of stuff that I didn't know about. What am I going to say? It doesn't really bother me that much. I just think, "Okay, so they hate us, they hate me particularly and say slanderous libelous stuff." It doesn't bother me. Byron Coley, the editor of *Forced Exposure*, who was after me with an axe for years, saying all this really, really nasty shit about me...this girl that I was dating in 1986, she was looking at me and saying, "You and Byron Coley, all this shit he writes about you, the really weird thing is I knew him when *Murmur* came out, and we were talking and he goes, 'Man, this band R.E.M. are really great. You really have got to check them out. They're really wonderful.' " And then once we were real successful it was like we're some rotten horrible thing, and I'm personally this horrible person. But who cares. There's a lot of people that I don't respect, and if I'm not too respected by people, it really doesn't bother me.

I've noticed that your success, and the dropping off of some of your older fans, and having the older fans say that you've "sold out" is a very touchy subject among you guys. It seems that you want to make your point that you haven't changed, and a lot of people just don't like things that are big.

It's not too touchy. If someone comes up to me and says, "Gee, I think you've sold out," I just say, "In what way?" I do exactly what I want to do, I have no interference from anyone, and selling out...I think that's garbage. Of course, if someone said, "I really don't like you since you got successful," I understand it completely. I don't really go see many bands in arenas. I see Prince. That's the only band I see at the Omni since 1980. I've seen him three times. People who are like me that really like to discover new bands, and are excited about it--that's great. They go on to find someone else who's really cool, and they're willing to push them for a while, and then go on to someone else. Those are the people that keep Rock and Roll going. If everyone only went out to see bands that sold a million records, it would just wither on the vine. It's just when people say that we did all of this for the money...it's bullshit. We never did a thing for the money. We've turned down millions of dollars for things like endorsements. Literally millions of dollars. More money than I have, we've been offered that we've turned down. I won't name the company, but they offered us $800,000 just to *use* "It's the End of the World As

We Know It" in a commercial, and we turned it down, because I didn't want to. $800,000 dollars is a lot of money. If I was going to sell out, that's probably the time I would have done it. I mean, selling out? Fine. If you want to say that that's fine. To me it's just kind of bogus.

A lot of people probably equate the phrase "selling out" with being successful, regardless of how you became successful.

We're successful because we're good, and we're kind of unique. I'm not saying that we're a great band, but there aren't a lot of other bands like us. If you don't want to be in a big crowd, that's fine. I go see bands in front of 200 people all the time. I went to see NRBQ, and that was the biggest crowd I'd been in in a long time, and there were 300 people.

I always thought that you were doing the right thing from the beginning, when the songwriting credits were shared for every single song. Then that can't get in the way.

Even all the instrumentals, the four or five of them that we're recorded on B-sides, they are instrumentals without vocals or words, and Michael's still involved, because that's the way we want to do it. We share the money, we share the credit...we share the bad stuff, too. If someone says, "That song sucks," that's fine. That was my decision when we started out. When we were publishing stuff we started talking about it, and I said, "I think we should publish all together, because most bands break up because of money and ego. This way we'll have the same amount of money and everyone will be involved equally. There are songs I didn't have anything to do with. There are *years* when members of the band didn't contribute much in the way of songwriting. It gets shifted around. At one point or another, just about all of us have been really weak, and someone else has been strong. I'm not going to say which albums are ones that I contributed heavily to, but there are records where I wrote almost all the songs chord-wise. There are records where Bill and Mike did almost all the work. Guess which ones they are and I think you'd be surprised. We're not going to sit down and break up who wrote the chords to one song. Of course Michael writes the words and the melodies, although the melodies a lot of times are Mike's bass line parts, but I think people would be really surprised at seeing me as the Rock and Roll dude, how many of the things are not Rock and Roll that I wrote. I write *a lot* of the slow stuff, for some reason, and I can't tell you why.

What are the songs that the band has written over the years that you feel most attached to?

Right now, not thinking about when I wrote them--the way I feel about them now...definitely from the first record, "Perfect Circle. " I like the way "Gravitys Pull" turned out as a recording. There are a lot of songs on there that I could see would be really personal. And essentially, the songs really turned out the way they were supposed to turn out. "Catapult" used to be one of my favorite songs, but I just hated it by the time we recorded it. I like the chords to "Fall On Me," I don't know if I like the song or not. It's not like I listen to them or anything. "Worksong" is one of my favorite songs that I ever wrote, because it's like two chords.

Did you like the remixed version?

Yeah, but that wouldn't have been on the album, I thought it was a neat remix. I think that you might as well use the technology and the ideas that you get from different disciplines of music.

We all sat there and did it. "So. Central Rain" I always thought was a real good song. That's like a song that you could just sit around on guitar and do.

It seems that one of Michael's favorites is "World Leader Pretend."

I like it too, a lot. And you know, the funny thing was, we *almost* didn't show it to Michael. We had written it, and we'd all said, "Okay, let's not do anything that sounds like R.E.M." I came up with the chords, and I said, "I think this is too R.E.M., but what the fuck? Let's do it anyway, and we'll show it to him." I thought he'd go, "Fuck this," because we had decided that we were not going to sound like ourselves. I could write a lot of R.E.M. songs in my sleep-- all that A minor/E minor stuff. And it was like, "What the hell, we'll show it to him, and he'll probably hate it," and he came up with these *great* lyrics! He goes, "Man, I heard the song, and it all came out in like one minute." It was just one of those things. That happens with us about every record. There's two songs where he just hears the music and goes, "I've got words." Then like an hour later we've got a complete song.

It sounds like he really approached that song as one of the most personal things he's ever written.

Yeah, I think it was. He's written real personal stuff, just more disguised. That's why they printed the words on the record, because that was like a real opening to the record, to show you that in a lot of ways we're trying to tear down the walls that we've created between ourselves and our audience, you know, from obscurity or whatever. It really moved me when I first heard it. I was shocked.

Are there any songs that you've wanted to cover that you haven't covered yet?

Most covers are thing we just do. It's not like someone says, "God this is my favorite song, we've got to cover it!" It's usually kind of like, "Oh, yeah, let's do that one. What the hell, it's fun." We've never done a cover of like a rhythm and blues song or a soul song that really we made our own. Whereas the kind of covers by white bands we've done, we really changed them around. When we do covers by black bands we kind of tend to be a little bit too respectful, or something. So I'd love to do a really cool song by someone that I really respect. I don't know, like maybe a Marvin Gaye song or something by Funkadelic, and do a really interesting version of one of those. Then again, I think those records are so great, I'd feel like a real honky trying to cover them.

You probably felt the same way about the Wire tune, right?

Bill and Mike, I don't think, heard the song until months after the record was out. Bryan Cook actually taught it to us. We played it with him and Michael singing, and we said, "Well, let's do it for a while."

So the *last* thing you do when you think you are going to do a cover is to go out and buy the album and hear what the original sounded like.

Just about everything we've learned we learned like old hillbillies in the mountains, by the oral tradition. Like, "See No Evil," Holsapple taught that to me. I know the Television records, and I love them, but I never actually sat down and listened to the song to figure it out right. You get the riff, and then you hear the record and you realize you played it twice as fast, changed the words, dropped a verse, and cut the solo in half. I don't think we've ever sat down with a record and actually *learned* the song, except for maybe one or two. "Superman" was one of the ones that we just kind of *did*.

Who was it that found that record and wanted to do a cover of it?
I found it years ago. I just had a pile of singles at Wuxtry and there were like two or three of those, and I played it and thought, "God, that's really good!" So I gave one to Mike and we talked about doing in in '81 or '82 and never got around to it. Mike and Bill's side band ended up covering it.

The Corn Cob Webs?
Yeah. They just ended up playing it one night, and I went to see them and went, "God, that was cool that you do that." Then we just started practicing it, and we were playing it with them singing it and Michael walked in and goes, "Oh, that's good. Let's record this." Then we recorded it in the studio and it sounded good with our stuff, and we said, "Well, let's put it on the record then."

I always like the good 70's AM radio songs for covers, like BTO.
We do "Taking Care of Business." "We've done that Fleetwood Mac song "Rhiannon." We used to do that. It's a good song. We did that Abba song... You know just doing covers, sometimes we just do it for five minutes especially if we've been on tour for a long time, you kind of tend to throw some in. Something we haven't played. No one has really rushed to cover our songs. There are some good ones. It has always kind of surprised me that people don't cover them.

I think that it would surprise a lot of people that you go in and do stuff that half the band doesn't know, and that they haven't heard the original.
That's fine. That's the way it is. Blues guys did that. You put your stamp on something if you really don't know it. We don't worship the originals. We may really like the song, but we're a different band. You just go in, and what the hell. That's the way we do it.

Have you heard from Tom Verlaine from Television?
Actually, he saw us one of the nights we played "See No Evil," and I said, "How did you like the song?" And he said, "What song?" So I said, "Your song!" He says, "My song? What song is that?" I said, "We did 'See No Evil' !" He goes, "You did 'See No Evil' ?" I said, "Yeah, we did it like the last song of the second encore." He said "Really?" I said, "Yeah, you didn't notice?" and he goes, "No."

How about Vega and the guys from Suicide?
I don't know those guys. I'd love to hear from them. Obviously I love their records.

Is there anybody that you have heard in the past that you want to play with but never really got together with?

Neil Young, we almost worked with him. I could be a great rhythm guitar player for Neil Young, and Bill and Mike would be great. We met several times, and when we met David Geffen, Bert and Jefferson met him, and he was talking about how Geffen's such a great label for artists and Jefferson said, "Yeah, but if Geffen is such a great place for artists, why did you *sue* Neil Young for making non-commercial records?" Geffen of course, about fell on the floor, and Neil heard about it. We had already met Neil and we'd been friends, and he likes our records and stuff, and he went around telling everyone we know that (in a Neil Young voice) "Yeah...I heard those "Reem" boys, they wouldn't sign with David Geffen, 'cause they treat ol' Neil Young *so* bad." I really like Neil's new record. I've always wanted to work with him.

Anybody else?

Well, you know, there's a lot of people I'd like to work with but Neil is one person that I think I could actually do justice to accompanying. Whereas, as much as I love Al Green, there's a million guitar players that are better than me.

Do you get bugged in Athens a lot?

I never get bugged here. Every once in a while, but not much. Every once in a while I bump into some little kid who's really shocked, or something, but by and large, this is my town. I live here. No one really gives much of a shit.

How much influence do you think Michael has on the music?

Usually what happens is, when we're going to rehearse, me and Mike and Bill will get together two weeks before Michael comes in and we'll just sit and jam, because listening to us coming up with ideas is just so fucking boring that it drives everyone insane. We just sit there and make noise and show each other ideas, and then after we've got eight or nine things that are kind of half done, but may not have a bridge, Michael will come in and go, "God, I love this," or, "I've got words for this already," or "I hate this, I'll never do it." Or he'll go, "Why don't you do this part *five* times," and then we start working together like that. And then maybe we'll do another week by ourselves and come up with another five or six. So that's like maybe three weeks of rehearsal by ourselves, and then it will end up with Michael there with him editing, and us editing.

Does he have a lot of lyrics that he keeps back?

He's got books *this thick* of lyrics. If we give him something that hits him he'll go, "I've got lyrics to that right now." "Worksong," he did in one take, the first time. "Swan" was the same way. He said, "I've got all these Civil War lyrics," and I said, "Well you know, that's funny, in my notebook I've got some Civil War lyrics, too." I gave him three lines that ended up in the song. I gave him really twenty lines, but he ended up using two or three. I said, "This is the kind of song I thought we'd do," and he went, "Oh, I can do that." I just played it all the way through, and he sang it *straight through*.

Which lines were yours?

"The whiskey is water, the water is wine." I don't remember what the rest of them were. Actually, that line was going to be, "The whiskey is water, the water is wine/I hear feet marching in time" or something. As usual, whenever we give him lyrics we'll give him all these batches of lyrics that make sense, and he'll take out a couple of lines, and add some of his stuff, which is fine. Another thing that Michael will do is say, "Man, I've got these words, and there really political words," and he showed me and he goes, "I need a song for this. I need a carnival song." So then we'll try and write a carnival song. He gave me some *great* fucking lyrics, called "Graveyards of the Air," and I've written three different songs for it, and I can't come up with the right thing exactly, but man, they're great lyrics.

Is the Michael Stipe of 1980 still the same now? Especially now that he's got the money to really be himself, has he really gone any farther out now than day one?

As a matter of fact, I've always thought that he was real normal, because to me, someone who decides what they want to do with their life, does it no matter what anyone thinks and is successful at it, they're not crazy, they're right on the money. With Michael, I understand exactly what it's like to be normal more now than I did in the period of 1983 and 1984. It's really great. It's like being in this marriage that's working out really great. You know, we finished the *Green* tour and we were on the road for *nine months* in each other's pockets the whole fucking time, and that usually would want to make us break up, like we always do at the end of every tour, but we finished the tour and it was like, "God, we've got all these great songs, let's start rehearsing!" We're really excited. I have this feeling that we're either diluting ourselves or we're coming into a really strong period for us. God, I'm writing songs *every* day. I sit around and play guitar, and I've got just a *pile* of shit now. That's what I do. I sit around, and I have the TV on real quiet, and do that. We've got tons of stuff. I'm really excited. I feel real lucky.

Do you think it's harder now for a band to start out, kind of like your band started out, or do you think it's easier?

I hate to say both, but it's both. The live scene is totally dead and fucked up almost everywhere you go, so it's really hard to build a reputation as a live band because there just aren't that many ways, what with the drinking age going up and all that kind of stuff. On the other hand, there are a lot of small labels that are willing to cater to bands. You can start on a small label and work, and reach a level that allows you to go to a major label, whether it's someone like Galaxy 500 making two really good records and maybe the third or fourth will be on a really big label, like Fetchin' Bones being on Capital. There's a way to grow in music, and there wasn't when we started. On the other hand, there's this kind of jaded awareness of what is going on in music. That's a drag. People have heard everything *too much*. When we went to New York, people were really excited about us. I don't think any band goes to New York now that people are excited about, unless they're God's gift to the world, and I know we weren't at the time.

One thing that I've wondered about in the movie *Athens, GA-Inside/Out* is when Jim Herbert is talking about Athens and he says that people aren't thinking about "taking it to New York." When you look at the bands like the B-52's, they left for New York immediately.

See, all the kind of arty bands skipped out on our learning experience, which for us was playing little small places around the South and learning what we were doing, and admittedly, the B-52's were a much better band when they started than we were, regardless of playing capabilities. They had really great songs, they had a great concept, a great look, a great stage show...they needed to go to New York. That was good for them. They weren't a three-sets-a-night bar band. We learned how to do that, and we had to throw that away and become something else. For us, on the other hand, we weren't ready. We were naive and young and as much as we thought we were men of the world and smart and all that kind of stuff... I thought I knew everything, I mean, God damn. We went to New York, and I was totally befuddled. For us, it was good not to go there for a year and a half or two years, or whatever it was. But if Jim meant by "going to New York" turning professional, nobody in Athens ever did turn professional. We're all still kind of amateurs, and I think that's one of the nice things about it. Jeez, professionals... professional shirt salesman, car salesman, but professional rock and roller?

What do you think could be done today to reverse some of the trends that make it hard for a young band trying to get off the ground and get heard, like the horrible state of FM radio?
Kill everyone in the music business including everyone who's *ever* played in public, everyone who's ever worked at a record company, everyone who's ever worked at, or owned, or dealt with a radio station, and then start over. And then again, you'd still have the bullshit.

How do you think you could get your foot in the door, and maybe get some radio stations to take a chance on playing more alternative acts and less Paula Abdul-- some of the bands that are kind of between underground and mainstream?
Right now? I don't know. The reason that we're successful is that we were good, and we persevered, and we really didn't give much of a fuck about radio or selling records. I *always* wanted to sell a million records. I wanted to from the first day I made my first single, but I didn't want to have to *do* anything about it. I wanted to make records, and someone would buy a million copies of it. We just did it. And, you know, you've got to be good. I know a lot of bands who persevere and aren't good, and didn't do anything, and I know a lot of bands who are *great* and persevered and didn't do anything. I wouldn't know how to say what to do and how to do it. I have no idea why we sell records, I don't understand our appeal. I know we're a good band, and I know we're unique, and that's it. There are a lot of good bands who were unique and didn't sell anything.

It seems like today it's so hard for an American band without a gimmick to be added to an FM radio play list. It's like a virtual impossibility.
Man, it's easier now. You should have been there when Mike and I would go around and do interviews at stations, and they would just look me in the eye and say, "Well, we can't put you in rotation because you just don't sound right." I would go, "Well, what are you playing?" and they'd go, "As far as New Wave, we're playing Berlin, The Cars, Missing Persons...that's *real* New Wave." And "Mickey," that song by that little rat-faced girl, Tony Basil. That was like the biggest stuff in the world, and none of those people are still around. We've persevered against all the prevailing music trends.

Why do you think in Europe, when the first two records were released and you got the most favorable press that anybody had ever gotten among American bands, the records still didn't sell very well?

They sold okay. It's just like it was in America. You've got to pay your dues, first off. We're just not a band that you can hear once on the radio, and go, "God, I really like this." You might like it, but I think a good thing about us is that over the space of time hearing us and hearing what we do and seeing us makes the records that much more meaningful, rather than just, "Oh man, that's a great single, I'm gonna buy it." Given the fact that we couldn't get played on the radio in England and that we weren't played on any radio station all over Europe, we were doing a word of mouth thing. People weren't hearing us, and it built up. This last tour was really pretty massive.

I understand that the BBC wouldn't play you because they thought you were a hippie band.
Well, that was John Peel. And John Peel *is* a fucking hippie, that's the thing that really blows my mind. He didn't like us, and that's his opinion, and that's fine, but we really weren't on BBC at all, and then all of a sudden we had a hit single.

This might be too heavy a question, but have you guys made *any* mistakes? Your success all seems so natural even from an outside point of view.
The weird thing is about the whole thing about making mistakes is that you only make mistakes if you regret the past, and I never felt that we did. When we were talking with Miles Copeland after our first record came out, he said, "Man, if you did *this* and *this* and *this* and *this*, you could be the biggest band in the world." And we went, "Well, we don't want to do that." And he goes, "Okay, well, don't blame me. There will be a time in your life when your peer group will have yachts, and big houses and millions of dollars, and you won't, and you're going to come to me and say, 'Why didn't we do that?' and I'll say, 'Because you didn't do the stuff that you were supposed to do.' If you can accept that, I can accept that." Which was one of the cool things about Miles. As much as we had our differences with him sometimes, he just said, "You choose where you want to be." We just said, "Well, we've decided we want to do it *this* way, and we don't really need the yachts," and that was perfectly all right. So we didn't do all the stuff that everyone else does. We didn't do the glitzy videos and big tours. Not to pat ourselves on the back, because, shit, we just didn't feel like doing it. But it's kind of like, you can't have regrets if... even if we weren't successful we would have ended up in the right place. We made the records we wanted to make. If every record sold 100,000 copies and if we had gone and been on DB records for the fourth record, that's fine. We could have done that and handled it and lived with it. As far as mistakes go, we make the little teeny mistakes. Very few. I've always said I think opening for the Police was *stupid*, but it wasn't a career decision mistake. I just thought it was a boring time, and didn't do us any good. There are certain things we should have done technically as far as production when we toured, like having a sound guy and a light guy, that we probably should have done earlier, and there are records where I could say, "Gee, I wish we'd finished some of these songs a little bit better." Every record just about, I think about that, except the last couple. We always just walked into everything with confidence and said, "We'll do our way and it will probably work out." And it will work out if you figure that any way that you are able to keep doing what you want to do is success. If we had been judging ourselves by the amount of records sold, really very few bands get to make four records without selling... we only sold 300,000 records by the third record, and we played to a lot of people, but if we were on a major label, that's not success. Even though we would be making the company money, that's

kind of considered failure. But we always thought, "God, we're selling a hell of a lot of records!" We were selling 100 times more than a lot of our peer group who were making equally good records and were playing to a lot of people, and were doing really well, but not making a lot of money at that point, but we were making those records. I remember feeling like I'm the luckiest guy in America because I was in this great band doing this great stuff and the idea of selling a million records or competing with U2, or whatever just never even occurred to us.

ABOUT THE PRICES IN THIS BOOK

The values in this book reflect the range of asking prices for R.E.M. items from dealers in the U.S. and overseas listed below. Asking prices were also obtained from ads placed by individuals in *Goldmine*, *Discoveries*, and *Record Collector* magazines in 1992 and 1993. In most cases, the highest and lowest asking prices were discarded and a range was created with the remaining values. The greatest difficulty in valuing R.E.M. collectibles is that the asking prices for most items are significantly higher in England than anywhere else in the world, including, interestingly enough, for items made in England. For example, one often sees advertised in England early singles like the U.K. promotional copy of "So. Central Rain" for £25, whereas in the U.S., the same single may generally trade for $25, or about half as much. In addition to the problem of regional variation in asking prices, many of the more scarce items are rarely if ever seen for sale, and in these cases, a number of dealers were consulted as to what their asking price might be if they had the item to offer. On a final note, all photocopied items such as lyric books and fanzines are not priced because they can easily be reproduced.

U.S. dealers
Athens Records, Pennsylvania
B & B Music Express, Washington
Chad and Jeremy Music, Washington
The Disc Junkie, Connecticut
Ellis Audiotics, New York
Fantastic Plastic, Pennsylvania
International Record Collector, Maryland
Metro Music, Maryland
Music Machine, Maryland
New England CD, Massachusetts
The Old Hippie, Kansas
Princeton Record Exchange, New Jersey
Rich Richards Posters, California
Vinyl Ink, Maryland
Vinyl Vendors, California
Jack Wolack Rare Necessities, New York
Wuxtry Records, Georgia
Yesterday and Today Records, Maryland
Yodelin' Pig CD and Collectibles, Maryland

non-U.S. dealers
Adrians, England
Bob Clayton, England
Esprit, England
Fantastic Plastic, Ireland
Minus Zero Records, England
Swordfish, England
Greg Vandyke, England
Vinyl Addiction, England
Vinyl Experience, England

Part 2:

What you want and what you need

ACETATES and TEST PRESSINGS

In addition to the vinyl albums, seven-inch singles, and twelve-inch singles described in this book, test pressings and acetates of each record also exist and are highly prized. An acetate, also known as a reference disc or master, is made of cellulose acetate-coated aluminum, and is cut in the studio directly from the master tape. These acetates are used for two purposes. First, the acetate, which can be played like a regular record on a turntable, gives the producer and the band the opportunity to hear what the song or songs will sound like on the record. Second, and more importantly, acetates are used in the process of making the actual records. One acetate that meets with the approval of all those concerned in the studio is chosen to be used for the production of the records, and is called the "master lacquer." The master lacquer is coated with nickel at the pressing plant, where the nickel coating is later peeled off, creating a negative image of the grooves in the original acetate. This metal "mother" is then used to press records. However, before the mother is used to press records that will be sold in retail outlets, test pressings are first produced to check the sound quality of the product. If the quality of the sound is satisfactory, promotional copies of the record are pressed, and then finally, the commercial copies.

Acetates are very expensive to make, and as Peter Buck said in the interview herein, "We don't make many acetates." Acetates generally have simple typewritten, or less often, handwritten labels. In England, while R.E.M. was with I.R.S. Records, acetates were made at Tape 1 Studios, and have the Tape 1 logo on the labels. English test pressings of R.E.M. records bear a large black "A" and "B" on their white labels, and often doubled as promotional records. Test pressings of R.E.M. singles originating from England seem to be much more plentiful than their American counterparts, but both U.S. and U.K. test pressings for the same titles generally sell for the same price.

I suppose one of the ultimate R.E.M. collectibles must be the metal mother that was used to press the Hib-Tone single. Ever wonder who has it? It hangs on Jefferson Holt's wall in his office in Athens. For Holt's thirtieth birthday, Bert Downs removed a label from a Hib-Tone first pressing, glued it to the mother, and framed it along with a sleeve, jokingly making it look like a platinum record award.

Test pressings of the early singles like "Radio Free Europe" and "So. Central Rain" go for about $50 and up, while those for later releases start at around $30. In addition to the band's singles on I.R.S. and Warner Brothers, test pressings of all the fan club singes are circulating. These have either plain, white labels or printed, "test pressing" labels, and sell for around $125. Some of the fan club singles were also pressed on marbled vinyl, and have sold for as much as $250. The marbled vinyl singles use the labels that are found on the stock copies and are generally accompanied with picture sleeves, indicating that they were presentation copies rather than true test pressings.

ALBUMS AND EPs

Since the virtual demise of the vinyl LP, original pressings of R.E.M. albums on vinyl with their original inserts have become increasingly more popular among collectors. Of particular interest are the promotional issues that bear a gold embossed promotional stamp on the back. In the United States, gold-stamped promotional copies of all of the band's LPs on I.R.S. have been released, and are otherwise identical to the stock copies. During the period when I.R.S. releases were being distributed by A&M (from *Chronic Town* through *Reckoning*, plus *Dead Letter Office*), the stamp reads, "For promotion only, ownership reserved, sale is unlawful." After I.R.S. switched to distribution by MCA, the stamp changed to read "For promotion only, ownership reserved by MCA Records, Inc., sale is unlawful," or simply, "For promotion only, ownership reserved, sale is unlawful." In England, early promotional R.E.M. albums from I.R.S. bore a stamp on the reverse that read "Property of A&M, demonstration only, not for sale."

In the U.S. and Holland, the early original LPs contained printed inner sleeves, which were replaced in the mid-eighties with clear plastic sleeves, making editions with their original inner sleeves collectible. Record club editions of many of the band's albums have also been pressed, which have a different label design, and are usually issued in thinner glossy jackets. Record club editions will also differ by having the abbreviation for the club appear on the jacket and label. For example, the letters "CRC" will appear on Columbia Record Club issues. In Japan, many records and CDs by U.S. artists are issued with a paper band called an "obi" (Japanese for "sash") wrapped around the jacket, containing information about the album and the artist, written in Japanese. R.E.M. albums that have this band intact are worth somewhat more than those without it.

In 1990, the band's back catalog was reissued in the CBS "Nice Price" series in Japan and Europe on LP, CD, and cassette. The Japanese CDs all contain fold-out inserts detailing the history of R.E.M. and I.R.S. Records, written in Japanese. The European reissue LPs were manufactured in Holland, and the CDs were made in Austria, with their paper inserts being printed in Holland. The country of origin of these issues on CD is listed as Holland in the catalog in this book. The priced items listed under each album in this section are the more collectible issues. The catalog numbers for releases from other countries in other formats are listed in the catalog.

Chronic Town

1,000,000 / Stumble / Wolves, Lower / Gardening at Night / Carnival of Sorts (Boxcars)

Release date: August 24, 1982
Producer: Mitch Easter, Drive-In Studio, Winston-Salem, North Carolina.

■ 10,000 copies of the EP were issued with the gargoyle label.

Canada	LP	I.R.S.	SP 70502		**$10-15**
Greece	LP	Illegal	ILP 26097		**10-20**
Holland	LP	I.R.S.	ILP 26097		**8-12**
Holland	LP	I.R.S.	ILP 26097	(Sade mispressing)	**50-75**
Japan	LP	CBS/Sony	20AP 2958	(with obi)	**40-60**
U.S.	LP	I.R.S.	SP 70502	(with promotional stamp)	**8-12**
U.S.	LP	I.R.S.	SP 70502	(original gargoyle label)	**25-40**
U.S.	cassette	I.R.S.	CS 70502	(advance promotional edition)	**30-40**

The first release from I.R.S. Records by R.E.M. was this five-song EP, which remained unreleased outside the U.S. until 1984. The record was an instant college radio favorite, remaining in the top five for three months after its release, and finished top 50 on The College Music Journal's 1982 year-end top 100 chart. *The Village Voice* penned the EP in at #1 on their EP chart for the same year.

Back in Mitch Easter's studio where they recorded their first single, the band threw in every studio effect they could come up with for this record, including recording a chorus of crickets for the end of "Wolves, Lower" and using kitchen utensils to get just the right sound. A few weeks after the release of the EP, the band described the mood and sound that they were trying to capture on the EP as "spooky gospel." The band's first major label debut was a moderate success in terms of sales figures, but more importantly it prompted critics to praise R.E.M. as the first band to fuse a folk feel with post-punk energy. Michael Stipe summed up his feelings about the EP in a recent radio interview, saying, "*Chronic Town* pretty much, like all our records, fit exactly where we were at that moment and we rushed right through it, and that's exactly what we were doing at the time. We were so terrified to be on stage that we would just kind of catapult our way through every single song. We would finish an hour and a half set in forty minutes, say. Things kind of moved at a fast clip back then. I mean, I even sang one song with a garbage can on my head to get the right echo."

The first 10,000-12,000 copies of the EP that were released in the U.S. featured a custom label, a miniaturization of the sleeve design, a gargoyle from the Cathedral of Notre Dame in Paris. These labels were fairly expensive to make, and since at the time R.E.M. was not a particularly strong money maker, the labels were discontinued. Close scrutiny of the label that appears on the first pressing reveals that the tracks were published by "Murmur Music," instead of the later adopted "Night Garden Music." First pressings of the EP can be distinguished from subsequent pressings owing to the addition of the UPC bar code on the back of the sleeve. Also the sleeves for first pressings were printed using a deeper shade of blue.

For the completist, the actual first-ever release by the band on I.R.S. is the *Chronic Town* advance cassette, which states "This copy precedes a test." These were shipped as promos, without an insert, to radio stations. Also for the devoted collector, an unknown number of copies of the Dutch issue of the EP were mis-pressed with tracks by easy listening radio favorite Sade on side 2.

A number of the tracks from the EP have cropped up elsewhere. An alternate take of "Gardening at Night," which features a stronger vocal rather than the falsetto that made it on the album, was later released on *Eponymous*. "Gardening at Night" also appears on a U.K. fanzine record, entitled *Jamming! A New Optimism*. In addition, the song "1,000,000" can be heard briefly in the movie *Strange Invaders*. "Wolves" was chosen to be a B-side for "Rockville" seven and twelve-inch singles outside the U.S., and a live take of "Gardening At Night" as well as the studio track of "Wolves" are found on both the U.K. and Dutch "Rockville" twelve-inch. The American new music magazine *Trouser Press* also issued a flexidisc of "Wolves" to subscribers only in December of 1982. All five tracks on the EP were released on CD format in 1986, tacked onto the *Dead Letter Office* disc.

Murmur

Radio Free Europe / Pilgrimage / Laughing / Talk About the Passion / Moral Kiosk / Perfect Circle / Catapult / Sitting Still / 9-9 / Shaking Through / We Walk / West of the Fields

Release date: April 13, 1983 (U.K.: August 1983)
Producers: Mitch Easter and Don Dixon, Reflection Studio, Charlotte, North Carolina.

Australia	LP	I.R.S./Epic	ELPS 4380		**$10-20**
Australia	LP	I.R.S.	ELPS 4380	(promotional edition)	**35-45**
Japan	LP	CBS/Sony	25 AP 2659		**15-20**
Japan	LP	CBS/Sony	25 AP 2659	(promotional edition with obi)	**35-60**
Japan	CD	I.R.S./EMI	TOCP-7266	(promotional edition with obi)	**30-50**
U.K.	LP	I.R.S.	SP70604	(with promotional stamp)	**15-20**
U.S.	LP	I.R.S.	SP70604	(with promotional stamp)	**7-12**
U.S.	cassette	I.R.S.	CS70604	("There She Goes Again" on insert)	**35-55**
other non-U.S. LPs					**10-20**
other non-U.S. CDs					**15-25**
other non-U.S. cassettes					**8-12**

R.E.M.'s first full-length LP is thought by many fans and critics to be among their best, and it must truly be recognized as an underground classic. Cut in just sixteen days for a mere $25,000, the album was recorded in January 1983 at Reflection Studios (the same studio in which Tammy Bakker once recorded), this time with the help of both Mitch Easter and Don Dixon.

Upon its release, the critics hailed R.E.M. as the leaders of a generation of new Southern rock bands. The record, which spent 30 weeks on the charts, sent reviewers flipping studiously through their thesauruses, attempting to find new superlatives to describe this intriguing work. *Rolling Stone*'s 1983 critics' poll was littered with R.E.M. praises, with *Murmur* standing tall as best new album, R.E.M. as best new artist, and as #3 for band of the year. The *Village Voice* placed the album at #2 for the year, and *Record* magazine listed *Murmur* as #1 top debut album, and #3 best album for 1983. For the members of R.E.M., the rave reviews were both a blessing and a curse, due to an old cliche in pop music circles: fantastic reviews for a debut album condemn a band's follow-up release to an all-out critical assault by reviewers.

From the eery mounds of kudzu on the cover to the background rumblings and haunting echoes on the tracks, the album has quite a dark and mysterious aura about it, which helped to create somewhat of a mystique around the band members as well. Strange sound effects and intense layering pervade the album. "We Walk" features the electronically altered sound of Bill Berry shooting pool in the basement of the studio, "Radio Free Europe" is prefaced by the amplified hum of the studio through Mike Mills' bass, and "Perfect Circle" features backwards guitar, and a piano solo that was played both on an antique out-of-tune upright and a correctly tuned new piano. Years later, band members confessed that they were out to make a "mystery record." The mystique of *Murmur* was further advanced by the band's refusal to include a lyric sheet for an album that contained, in many cases, largely unintelligible lyrics.

The album was originally released on April 12, 1983, in the U.S. with the catalog number SP70604, but releases after September 1 of that year carry the catalog number SP 70014. In fact, copies of the album exist with the new catalog number pasted over the old number on the spine. The album was originally to include the band's rendition of the Velvet Underground's "There She Goes Again," however, the track was pulled just prior to the release date. However, some copies of the *Murmur* cassette insert were printed and released with "There She Goes Again" listed among the song titles. *Murmur* has been released internationally, and the Japanese and Australian promotional copies of the album are particularly valuable. In August 1992, I.R.S. released a version of *Murmur* on CD in Holland and Japan that contained the bonus tracks "There She Goes Again," "9-9" (live), "Gardening at Night" (live) and "Catapult" (live), all taken from B-sides of commercially issued records. The live versions of "9-9" and "Gardening at Night," taken from the B-side of the import "Rockville" twelve-inch single, originally faded out prematurely, but on the *Murmur* reissue CD the tracks are heard in their entirety.

Reckoning

Harborcoat / 7 Chinese Brothers / So. Central Rain / Pretty Persuasion / Time After Time (Ann Elise) / Second Guessing / Letter Never Sent / Camera / (Don't Go Back To) Rockville / Little America

Release date: April 14, 1984
Producer: Mitch Easter and Don Dixon, Reflection Studios, Charlotte, North Carolina.

Australia	LP	I.R.S./Epic	ELPS 4439		**$10-20**
Australia	LP	I.R.S./Epic	ELPS 4439	(promotional edition)	**35-45**
Japan	LP	CBS/Sony	28 AP 2847		**15-20**
Japan	LP	CBS/Sony	28 AP 2847	(promotional edition with obi)	**30-50**
Japan	CD	I.R.S./EMI	TOCP-7267	(promotional edition with obi)	**30-50**
New Zealand	LP	Illegal	ELPS 4439	(promotional stamp on label)	**20-30**
U.K.	LP	I.R.S.	IRSA 7045	(with promotional stamp)	**15-20**

U.S.	LP	I.R.S.	SP 70044	(with promotional stamp)	**7-12**
U.S.	LP	I.R.S.	SP 70044	(promotional sticker and stamp)	**10-15**
U.S.	LP	I.R.S.	SP 70044	(purple vinyl)	**18-25**
U.S.	LP	I.R.S.	SP 70044	(brown vinyl)	**18-25**
other non-U.S. LPs					**10-20**
other non-U.S. CDs					**15-25**
other non-U.S. cassettes					**8-12**

■ The Japanese issue of the LP with the "obi" intact

The band's second LP, *Reckoning*, was so titled in anticipation of the inevitable scrutiny that the album would receive after the unexpected critical success of *Murmur*. Described by Peter Buck as "less of a mood record, more of a song record," the album contained far fewer overdubs than *Murmur*, and was more straightforward in its content. With *Reckoning*, R.E.M. wanted to make a record that captured the energy of the band's live sound. The tracks were laid down at a breakneck speed, with half of the album being recorded in two days, giving the band somewhat of a reputation as studio speed demons. The entire album, which was made for about $30,000, was completed in eleven days, prompting the band to cancel two weeks of studio time and head home.

The follow-up to *Murmur* was again greeted with praise by the American and European press, with one critic, Francis Dordor of the French rock magazine *Best*, going as far as to say that "The guitars seem to be carried away in perpetual arpeggios filtered by the ferns and sounding like the Celtic harps of fairyland. R.E.M.'s music is ageless. It was born before rock." The *Rolling Stone* review was favorable but somewhat lukewarm. Critic Chris Connelly, however, did correctly predict that "With skill and daring like theirs, the tiniest commercial concessions-- some accessible lyrics by Stipe and a major league drum sound, could win this band a massive audience."

The record was definitely not an initial success in terms of its sales in the U.K. despite the favorable reviews, partly because the BBC refused to play a "hippie record." R.E.M. had no hit single and made few major television appearances in Europe, two critical requirements for an American band to sell albums overseas.

The intriguing artwork on the cover of the album was designed by Georgia folk artist/preacher Howard Finster along with Michael Stipe. Finster is pictured in the lower right corner of the inner sleeve of the album, and the other two photos are somewhat historic pictures of Jefferson Holt and Bert Downs. Stipe recalled the undertaking of the *Reckoning* project, saying, "I came up with the idea, and I took it to him with this initial drawing of the two-headed snake. I told him what I wanted, then I went back to him about a month later and I asked him to paint the snake for me. We talked about it and agreed that we represent the elements. Parts of it is rocks, part of it a thunderstorm, part of it the sun, and part of it the sky. Trying to discuss long distance what I want, I'm not good at. There was a communication breakdown-- there was a lot more detail in the painting and it just didn't come out." The album artwork was selected simultaneously in *Musician* magazine as both best and worst album jacket of 1984.

Finster recollected in Tom Patterson's biography of the artist, "One of the things that really boosted me up these last years is doing these record covers for Rock 'n' Roll groups. And what started that was the R.E.M.'s (sic). They're from Athens and they knowed about me from my shows I had there with Andy Nasisse at the University of Georgia. They first started coming here about seven years ago and taking pictures of the garden and talking to me about buying a little of my art. And they done a video film of my garden that they run on TV with one of their hit records. And I done several record covers for 'em, and I done a T-shirt for 'em. And the singer, Michael, worked with me on one of them album covers. He's an artist too, and he done part of it, and I done part of it. And when I done them R.E.M. albums, I really fixed myself up with a lotta publicity and a lotta albums." Fans who make the pilgrimage to Finster's "Paradise Garden" in Summerville, Georgia, won't want to miss seeing the album and British "So. Central Rain" seven-inch sleeve hanging in his studio, or the cement sculpture "Seppents of the Wilderness," which appeared on the promotional poster for *Reckoning*.

First pressings of the album were pressed in colored virgin vinyl. Both purple vinyl and brown vinyl copies exist, and the coloration is so dark that in order for it to be seen, the album must be held up to a light. Some, but not all promotional copies of the album were issued with a sticker on the front, citing some of the awards that *Murmur* received. The Japanese pressing of the album is of particular interest to collectors, and was initially issued with a booklet written in Japanese entitled "The Impactive Rock Scene of I.R.S.," describing the band's background, as well as that of Let's Active, The Go-Go's and other I.R.S. bands. The Japanese issue also contains a larger insert describing the band's history in more detail. The British version of the LP differs from the U.S. edition in that the word "Reckoning" appears above the letters "R.E.M." on the cover. In Europe and Japan the album was reissued on CD in 1992, this time containing the bonus tracks "Windout" (with Jefferson Holt and Bertis Downs on vocals), "Pretty Persuasion" (live in the studio), "White Tornado" (live in the studio), "Tighten Up," and "Moon River."

Fables of the Reconstruction

Feeling Gravitys Pull / Maps and Legends / Driver 8 / Life and How To Live It / Old Man Kensey / Can't Get There From Here
Green Grow the Rushes / Kahoetek / Auctioneer (Another Engine) / Good Advices / Wendell Gee

Release date: June 10, 1985
Producer: Joe Boyd, Livingstone Studio, London.

Australia	LP	I.R.S./Epic	ELPS 4495		**$10-20**
Australia	LP	I.R.S./Epic	ELPS 4495	(promotional edition)	**30-45**
Brazil	LP	Epic	144.847	(with insert)	**15-25**
Japan	LP	I.R.S.	28AP 3058		**15-20**
Japan	LP	I.R.S.	28AP 3058	(promotional edition)	**25-45**
Japan	CD	I.R.S./EMI	TOCP-7268	(promotional edition with obi)	**30-50**
U.S.	LP	I.R.S.	5592	(with promotional stamp)	**8-12**
U.S.	cassette	I.R.S.	5592	(advance promotional edition)	**30-40**

other non-U.S. LPs	**10-20**
other non-U.S. CDs	**15-25**
other non-U.S. cassettes	**8-10**

For the band's third full-length record, R.E.M. took a change in direction, opting to record with producer Joe Boyd, whose previous credits included producing early Pink Floyd, The Incredible String Band, Fairport Convention, and Richard Thompson. After agreeing that a change in producers would add new life and diversity to the band's sound, Peter Buck suggested Boyd, being familiar with his earlier work. R.E.M. emerged from Boyd's studio in London with a record that maintained elements of the band's earlier sound, but with a distinct difference. This would be the last R.E.M. album to have an abundance of largely indecipherable lyrics, and the last to convey the dark and somewhat veiled atmosphere of the band's early recordings.

The band members describe the period when this album was recorded as a critical time for them, mostly because they were in the midst of feeling the pressure to decide whether or not they wanted to continue to perform as a band. Their stay in London was also marked by a stretch of horrible weather, which surely made everyone feel all the more distressed. Peter Buck recalled, "We fought a lot, and we were all in miserable physical and mental states when we made [*Fables*]. Because of the chaotic situation, a little more weird soul showed through." Joe Boyd, in an interview with *Record Collector*, said of making the record, "We couldn't agree with the spatial relationships between instruments. I had problems with the vocals-- Michael Stipe wanted them quieter than I did. It was a strange experience-- everyone wanted themselves turned down! I was very relieved when most reviewers really liked the album, but I don't think the group was that happy with it."

Actually, not all reviewers were as kind to R.E.M. about this album as they had been in the past. The album was panned by some critics, who saw R.E.M. losing their youthful brilliance and naive appeal in exchange for instrumental experimentation (strings, tuba and banjo), and tracks like "Kahoetek" were even described as "filler." Even Bill Berry went as far as to say in a 1988 *Rolling Stone* interview that "*Fables* sucked." Even so, the album sold 300,000 copies in a mere three weeks. I.R.S. seemed to put a bit more emphasis on the promotion of this record, perhaps due to the company's changing distributors from A&M to MCA. Nevertheless, the album managed to make *Record* magazine's #2 album of the year, second to Talking Head's *Little Creatures*. R.E.M. also took *Record*'s "Band of the Year" honors as well.

Collectors should look for the U.S. *Fables* advance cassette, which features totally different graphics than stock copies. In England, *Fables* cassettes were released with two different styles of cover graphics, and different catalog numbers. Also of interest is the Japanese promotional LP, which has a sticker on the cover and a slightly different label. The Brazilian and Portuguese issues differ from the U.S. or U.K. issues by having orange and pink inner sleeves, respectively, and the cover of the Brazilian LP has a thin green band around the top and left side on which is written "New Rock Collection." First editions of the U.K. *Fables of the Reconstruction* CD (DMIRF 1003) mis-titled the track "Green Grow the Rushes" as "Green Grow the Rushed." In August 1992, *Fables of the Reconstruction* was reissued on CD in Holland and Japan, and these reissue CDs contain the bonus tracks, "Crazy," "Driver 8" (live), "Burning Hell," "Bandwagon," and "Maps and Legends" (live), all taken from B-sides of previously released singles.

Lifes Rich Pageant

Begin the Begin / These Days / Fall On Me / Cuyahoga / Hyena / Underneath the Bunker / The Flowers of Guatemala / I Believe / What If We Give It Away? / Just a Touch / Swan Swan H / Superman

Release date: July 28, 1986
Producer: Don Gehman, Belmont Mall, Belmont, Indiana.
Certified Gold: January 23, 1987

Argentina	LP			(promotional edition)	**$20-30**
Brazil	LP	Epic	144.905	(with insert)	**12-20**
Japan	LP	I.R.S.	28 AP 3240		**18-25**
Japan	LP	I.R.S.	28 AP 3240	(promotional edition)	**25-45**
U.S.	LP	I.R.S.	5783	(with promotional stamp)	**8-12**
other non-U.S. LPs					**10-20**
other non-U.S. CDs					**15-25**
other non-U.S. cassettes					**8-10**

The follow-up to the moderately received *Fables of The Reconstruction* LP was an album with a harder edge, featuring the sounds the band sought from John Cougar Mellencamp's producer Don Gehman, thundering drums and heavy guitars. The monumental difference between this album and the band's previous work, however, would be Stipe's intentionally discernable lyrics; he was now clearly confident to call out to his audience with a message. Peter Buck often went as far as to refer to the album as "our Bryan Adams record."

The album takes its name from the movie *A Shot in the Dark*, in which Peter Sellers pronounces, after driving his car into a lake, "It's all part of life's rich pageant." The band adopted the phrase (dropping the apostrophe) and applied it to the never-ending string of minor catastrophes that they experienced while touring, where amps periodically blew up and PA systems failed. The album received rave reviews, and was certified gold in January of 1987 under the strength of the popular first single, "Fall On Me." That this album reached gold status was truly an achievement, in that the band's previous three albums collectively had sold only 600,000-700,000 copies. For many R.E.M. fans and critics, it was this record that marked the end of R.E.M.'s status as an underground, or cult band.

The album was the first to contain a cover song, The Clique's "Superman," and also contained the band's first instrumental release on LP, the flamenco "Underneath the Bunker," originally entitled, "Samba." The inclusion of these two tracks, which close either side of the LP, was meant to temper the nature of this otherwise very serious sounding record. The critics faulted them for including the tracks, perhaps not yet realizing that a band as serious sounding as R.E.M. can be can still have a sense of humor.

In February 1993 the album was reissued on CD in Holland containing the bonus tracks, "Tired of Singing Trouble" from the *Lifes Rich Pageant* sessions, a live in the studio recording of "Just a Touch" from the *Reckoning* sessions, "Rotary 10," the live acoustic versions of "(All I Have To Do Is) Dream" and "Swan Swan H" from the *Athens, GA - Inside/Out* soundtrack, and "Toys in the Attic." Some of these tracks were readily available as B-sides and on *Dead Letter Office*, but others were exclusive to this reissue.

Dead Letter Office

Crazy / There She Goes Again / Burning Down / Voice of Harold / Burning Hell / White Tornado / Toys in the Attic / Windout / Ages of You / Pale Blue Eyes / Rotary Ten / Bandwagon / Femme Fatale / Walter's Theme - King of the Road

Release date: April 27, 1987
Producer: various producers

Brazil	LP	Epic	235.502	(with insert)	**$12-20**
Japan	CD	CBS/Sony	32DP 799	(with obi)	**25-35**
Japan	LP	I.R.S.			**18-25**
U.K.	cassette	I.R.S.	70054	(advance promotional edition)	**15-20**
U.S.	LP	I.R.S.	70054	(1st cover, promotional stamp)	**8-12**
U.S.	LP	I.R.S.	70054	(1st cover, promo sticker & stamp)	**10-15**
U.S.	cassette	I.R.S.	70054	(advance promotional edition)	**15-20**
other non-U.S. LPs					**10-20**
other non-U.S. CDs					**15-25**
other non-U.S. cassettes					**8-10**

Much to the chagrin of many R.E.M. collectors who took pride in having laboriously assembled all of the band's B-sides, I.R.S. released this collection of B-sides and outtakes spanning from 1981 to 1986. The release of this compilation was an attempt to appease the legion of R.E.M. devotees who wanted to hear these long out of print and hard to find tracks. First pressings of the record (about 75,000) were released with a patterned light green sleeve, rather then the plain dark green sleeves of subsequent printings. Promotional copies of the album were issued with a special sticker on the front stating that the record was "a special collection for album radio." Sales of the album were healthy considering virtually all of the songs had been previously released, with I.R.S. shipping initially about 250,000 copies.

The inner sleeve contains liner notes by Peter Buck, written in his typical loose, self-deprecating style. Only one single was issued in support of the release, a promotional twelve inch of "Ages of You," an outtake from *Fables of the Reconstruction*. R.E.M. fans with CD players lucked out, as all five of the *Chronic Town* tracks, which had not yet been released on CD format, were included on the *Dead Letter Office* disc. Six years after its original release, *Dead Letter Office* was reissued in Europe, again containing *Chronic Town*, but adding two bonus tracks. These extra tracks were a live to two-track version of "All the Right Friends," and an acoustic version of "Gardening at Night." This particular recording of "All the Right Friends" had previously only been available on the bootleg *Pretty Pictures*, and the acoustic recording of "Gardening at Night" from the *Reckoning* sessions is exclusive to this CD reissue.

Document

Finest Worksong / Welcome to the Occupation / Exhuming McCarthy / Disturbance at the Heron House / Strange / It's the End of the World As We Know It (and I Feel Fine) / The One I Love / Fireplace / Lightnin' Hopkins / King of Birds / Oddfellows Local 151

Release date: August 31, 1987
Producer: Scott Litt and R.E.M., Sound Emporium, Nashville, Tennessee.
Certified gold: November 2, 1987; Certified platinum: January 25, 1988

Canada	LP	I.R.S.	42059	(with "11 New Songs" sticker)	**$8-15**
Japan	LP	I.R.S.	28 AP 3382		**18-25**
Japan	LP	I.R.S.	28 AP 3382	(promotional edition)	**20-35**
U.S.	LP	I.R.S.	42059	(with promotional stamp)	**6-10**
U.S.	LP	I.R.S.	42059	(with promotional sticker)	**7-10**
other non-U.S. LPs					**8-15**
other non-U.S. CDs					**15-25**
other non-U.S. cassettes					**8-10**

R.E.M.'s fifth offering was their angriest and most provocative album to date. Where *Fables of the Reconstruction* and *Lifes Rich Pageant* subtly confronted the political and social injustices in the world ("Green Grow the Rushes," "Cuyahoga"), *Document* rose one step higher and emerged as the band's starkest and most negatively-tinged work. Despite the nature of the album's content, which the band described as "chaotic" and "weird," the record went top ten, on the heels of the number nine single "The One I Love."

The tracks were recorded at Nashville's Sound Emporium, under the direction of producer Scott Litt, who was best known for his work with Katrina and the Waves and for producing The dB's second album, *Repercussion*. The band first hooked up with Litt in an Atlanta studio, where they recorded "Romance," the track that appeared on the *Made in Heaven* soundtrack. Litt later produced The Indigo Girls' 1989 breakthrough LP as well, which features guest appearances by all four R.E.M. members. In keeping with the scheme of *Lifes Rich Pageant*, *Document* included a cover song, this time a forceful rendition of Wire's "Strange," which originally appeared on their *Pink Flag* LP (Harvest/EMI SH SP4076). The album also includes an appearance by Los Lobos saxophonist Steve Berlin, who can be heard on "Exhuming McCarthy" and "Fireplace."

Collectors should keep an eye out for promotional copies of the album, some of which feature a sticker promoting the "Finest Worksong" single. Another interesting issue is the Japanese edition of the LP, which contains an insert with a biography of the band written in Japanese, and partial lyrics to all of the tracks in Japanese and English.

In 1993, I.R.S. remastered the album and re-released *Document* in Holland on CD. These CD reissues contain the "Other Mix" and "Lengthy Club Mix" of "Finest Worksong," "Last Date," the live versions of "The One I Love" and "Disturbance at the Heron House" from the McCabe's Guitar Shop performance in 1987, and the "Time After Time, Etc." live medley, which includes "So. Central Rain" and Peter Gabriel's "Red Rain."

Eponymous

Radio Free Europe (Hib-Tone version) / Gardening at Night (alternate vocal) / Talk About the Passion / So. Central Rain / (Don't Go Back To) Rockville / Can't Get There From Here / Driver 8 / Romance / Fall On Me / The One I Love / Finest Worksong (drum/horn mix) / It's the End of the World As We Know It (and I Feel Fine)

Release date: October 3, 1988
Producer: various producers

Japan	LP	I.R.S.	UDP 1426		**$15-20**
U.S.	LP	I.R.S.	6262	(with promotional stamp)	**6-10**
U.S.	cassette	I.R.S.	6262	(advance promotional edition)	**20-25**
other non-U.S. LPs					**8-15**
other non-U.S. CDs					**15-25**
other non-U.S. cassettes					**8-10**

After I.R.S. lost the heated bidding war for R.E.M. in the fall of 1988 to Warner Brothers, their thoughts turned to the band's rich back catalog, and they quickly put out this compilation. The album, which billed R.E.M. as "The band you grew up with," was designed to capture Christmas record buyers in 1988, and I.R.S. maintained that the release was not intended to compete with R.E.M.'s Warner Brothers debut, which was released only a month later.

If the members of R.E.M. and their associates had their way, they would have preferred that this collection never be released. However, since I.R.S. had been so good to them in the past, the band agreed to the label's plans, requesting only that they have a hand in the project. Ron Scarselli was asked to design the cover art, and the band was involved in the final selection of the tracks. Despite the fact that the album had only a month to sell before the release of *Green*, sales were still fairly strong.

Eponymous was not advertised as a "greatest hits" record, perhaps justly so, because the band had experienced only two top forty singles in their career. The major selling point of the album was the inclusion of the original Hib-Tone version of "Radio Free Europe" (though this time it was the brighter Mitch Easter mix of the track that was released, and not Hibbert's mix), and an alternate version of "Gardening at Night," which used stronger vocals than the track that appeared on *Chronic Town*. Also included was the alternate mix of "Finest Worksong" with the Uptown Horns.

Green

Pop Song '89 / Get Up / You Are the Everything / Stand / World Leader Pretend / The Wrong Child / Orange Crush / Turn You Inside-Out / Hairshirt / I Remember California / untitled

Release date: November 8, 1988
Producer: Scott Litt and R.E.M., Ardent Studios, Memphis, Tennessee.
Certified gold: January 10, 1989; Certified platinum: February 14, 1989

■ The U.S. promotional CD of Green.

Argentina	LP	WEA	80127	(promotional edition)	**$15-25**
Australia	LP	WEA	25795.1	(with tour sticker)	**10-20**
Brazil	LP	WB	670.8035	(with insert)	**12-20**
Japan	LP	WB	25P2-2389		**10-20**
Japan	CD	WB	25P2-2389	(promotional edition)	**40-50**
U.S.	CD	WB	PRO-CD-3292	(promotional edition)	**30-45**
Yugoslavia	LP	Jugoton	30727777		**10-15**
other non-U.S. LPs					**8-15**
other non-U.S. CDs					**15-25**
other non-U.S. cassettes					**8-10**

Seven months after signing a reported eight-figure deal with Warner Brothers, R.E.M. released *Green*, an album that easily went platinum and swelled the growing legion of R.E.M. fans to such a degree that the band found themselves having to play arenas during the *Green* tour. Upon signing with Warner Brothers, Pete Buck told the University of Georgia's *The Red and Black*, "It was a difficult decision to make, but we are all confident that Warner Brothers is the company most willing to help us musically and professionally." Michael Stipe put it differently, commenting that, "With significant energy and unprecedented outcome, we have pummeled and joined critical mass. The present is at hand-- we are now a fossil fuel."

One might have expected that for their major label debut, R.E.M. would have compiled a collection of tracks that were musically safe, sounding somewhat like their previous releases, and that would result in minimal nail biting by Warner's executives. As the band maintained, this was not at all such a record, but one that was quite experimental. They did, however, invest considerable time and energy to ensure that they gave it their all, spending a whopping eleven weeks in the studio to record the tracks, an eternity for R.E.M.

Original plans for the record, then tentatively titled *Think Tank Decoy*, called for an all-acoustic side and an electric side, but the final product contained only three acoustic numbers interspersed among the rest of the tracks. The reviews for *Green* were overall quite positive, and the British music magazine *Melody Maker* even went as far as to call the LP the best record in ten years. *Green*, released on November 8 to coincide with election day, bore a multitude of singles in various formats, which depending on a collector's point of view, is either wonderful or an awful pain. In the U.S., collectors quickly bought up the popular promotion-only edition of *Green*, which featured a cloth-bound book style cover, and a picture disc made to look like a miniature record. Another very interesting collectible that arose from this album was a test printing of the jacket that was rejected, many copies of which seem somehow to have escaped Warner Brothers' incinerators. These test printings differ somewhat from the original cover that was used in that the sleeve is yellow instead of orange, and that the "R" in *Green* is replaced entirely by a 4, both on the cover and on the spine. The "4" can be seen on the regular issue under both the "R" in *Green* and in R.E.M., and rumor has it that when Michael Stipe was playing around with possible titles for the LP on his manual typewriter, he typed a 4 over the "R" in *Green*, and thought the result looked interesting enough to make it onto the cover.

Out of Time

Radio Song / Losing My Religion / Low / Near Wild Heaven / Endgame / Shiny Happy People / Belong / Half a World Away Texarkana / Country Feedback / Me in Honey

Release date: March 12, 1991
Producer: Scott Litt and R.E.M., Bearsville Studios, Bearsville, New York, and John Keane Studios, Athens, Georgia.
Certified gold and platinum: May, 1991

Czechoslovakia	LP	Popron	50 139-2		**$12-20**
Germany	LP	WB	7599-26496-1	(limited edition w/7-inch single)	**35-60**
Japan	CD	WB	WPCP 4195	(promotional edition)	**35-45**
Spain	LP	WB		(alternate sleeve)	**75-125**
U.S.	CD	WB	9 26496-2	(limited edition in portfolio)	**20-30**
U.S.	CD	WB	9 26496-2	(as above, with promotional sticker)	**22-35**
U.S.	CD	WB	PRO-CD-4695	(Bullet Boys mispressing)	**30-50**
other non-U.S. LPs					**8-15**
other non-U.S. CDs					**15-25**
other non-U.S. cassettes					**8-10**

With *Out of Time*, R.E.M. had largely freed themselves from confronting political or environmental issues with their music, and instead gave us songs about love and relationships, topics they had steadfastly avoided in the past. Michael Stipe, in fact, sings on the track "Low," "I skipped the part about love. It seemed so silly." On *Out of Time*, R.E.M. offered the listening public eleven pop songs largely about the most common of themes in popular music, but still managed to make them sound noticeably different from the standard radio fodder. The album's title is a reference to the fact that the band literally ran "out of time"

■ The *Out of Time* collector's edition in "portfolio" packaging. Some copies had a slightly different sticker on the back and were sent out for promotion.

when attempting to arrive at an acceptable title. R.E.M. continued to expand their musical boundaries on *Out of Time* by infusing such varied instrumentation as harpsichord, flugelhorn, and pedal steel guitar into the tracks, which in addition featured guest performers Peter Holsapple, formerly of the dB's, Kate Pierson of the B-52's, rapper KRS-One and saxophonist Kidd Jordan.

Out of Time, which has sold more than twelve million copies worldwide, was the band's first number one album on the *Billboard* charts, reaching the position eight weeks after its release. The record collected more than its share of awards, the most significant of which being a Grammy for "Best Alternative Rock Album." *Out of Time* was also nominated for a Grammy as "Album of the Year." The album picked up a slew of other awards, including "Best Album" in the *Rolling Stone* readers' and critics' polls, the College Music Journal's "Album of the Year," *Billboard* magazine's "Top World Album," and "Best Album" by readers of the U.K. magazine *Q*.

Coinciding with the release of the album was a special limited edition CD in an elegant "portfolio" package, containing ten postcards, and a wood grain-patterned picture disc. The outer sticker on promotional issues lacks the UPC bar code and indicates that the disc was issued for promotion only, but otherwise is identical to the commercial release. Some limited edition copies of the album in Germany were issued with a free single, featuring live takes of "World Leader Pretend" and "Turn You Inside-Out" from *Tourfilm*. In America, the entire album was mistakenly pressed onto a promotional CD for the Bullet Boys single "THC Groove" (Warner Brothers PRO-CD-4695), which appeared some two weeks before the official release date for *Out of Time*. Another curious issue of the album comes from Spain, where a promotional contest was held in which students were invited to submit designs for the album's jacket. The winning entry was used on the cover of a small number of Spanish *Out of Time* LPs.

The Best of R.E.M.

Carnival of Sorts (Boxcars) / Radio Free Europe / Perfect Circle / Talk About the Passion / So. Central Rain / (Don't Go Back To) Rockville / Pretty Persuasion / Green Grow the Rushes / Can't Get There From Here / Driver 8 / Fall On Me / I Believe / Cuyahoga / The One I Love / Finest Worksong / It's the End of the World As We Know It (and I Feel Fine)

Release date: September 30, 1991
Producer: various producers

Holland or U.K. LP					**$15-18**
Holland or U.K. CD					**16-20**
Holland or U.K. cassette					**15-18**
Japan	CD	I.R.S./EMI	TOCP-7265	(promotional edition with obi)	**30-50**

Released strategically during the wave of popularity that R.E.M. enjoyed internationally with *Out of Time*, this "best of" compilation included most of the band's singles from their days at I.R.S., as well as a few additional album tracks. It might have been a bit misleading for I.R.S. to call this a "best of" compilation considering the album lacked the band's most successful singles ("Stand" and "Losing My Religion" from the band's Warner Brothers LPs both outperformed "The One I Love" on the charts). The album climbed past *Out of Time* on the U.K. charts, eventually reaching #7 in October 1991, but had little staying power. The compilation soon dropped off the charts while *Out of Time* remained.

Automatic For the People

Drive / Try Not to Breathe / The Sidewinder Sleeps Tonite / New Orleans Instrumental No. 1 / Sweetness Follows / Monty Got a Raw Deal / Ignoreland / Star Me Kitten / Man on the Moon / Nightswimming / Find the River

Release date: October 6, 1992
Producer: Scott Litt and R.E.M., Bearsville Studio, Bearsville, New York; Criteria Recording Studios, Miami, Florida; John Keane Studios, Athens, Georgia; Kingsway Studio, New Orleans, Louisiana; Bosstown Recording Studios, Atlanta, Georgia.

Japan	CD	WB	WPCP-4970	(promotional edition with obi)	**$30-50**
U.S.	CD	WB	9 45122-2	(collector's edition in wooden box)	**28-35**
other non-U.S. LPs					**8-15**
other non-U.S. CDs					**15-25**
other non-U.S. cassettes					**8-10**

Automatic For the People did not quite reach the level of worldwide chart success that its predecessor *Out of Time* achieved, though the critically praised, multi-platinum record did reach the number 2 slot on the *Billboard* chart in the U.S., and enjoyed very strong sales worldwide. The record suitably impressed *Rolling Stone* magazine's critics, who voted *Automatic For the People* "Best Album" for 1992, nine years after *Murmur* took the same award.

In addition to the four formats on which the album was released in the U.S., (LP, cassette, CD, and the yet unproven minidisc), Warner Brothers also released the CD in a special collector's edition in a wooden box, which contained sixteen vellum cards on which were printed the album credits, and photographs of the band members in Florida where a portion of the record was recorded. The inserts also remind you that " 'Automatic For the People' is the service mark of Weaver D's delicious fine food in Clarke County, Georgia."

BOXED SETS OF ALBUMS

Collection
Release date: August 1990
Holland I.R.S. 465885 **$60-80**

This limited edition 5CD boxed set of the band's albums included *Fables of the Reconstruction*, *Lifes Rich Pageant*, *Dead Letter Office*, *Document* and *Eponymous*. First editions of this package included the CDs that were issued when the individual albums were originally released, but subsequent editions included discs pressed for the "nice price" mid-line series, which used different catalog numbers, and had a "nice price" sticker on their jewel boxes.

R.E.M.
Release date: November 1992
Germany I.R.S. 131762 **in print**

This boxed set of three discs contains the three remastered and reissued CDs of *Murmur*, *Reckoning* and *Fables of the Reconstruction* that were issued in August 1992.

SEVEN-INCH SINGLES AND FLEXIDISCS

Of all the formats in which music has been sold, many collectors hold a special place in their hearts for the vinyl seven-inch single, known to people not obsessed with records as the "45." Particularly prized are singles sent out by record companies for promotion, which often have different labels or picture sleeves than the standard commercial issues. In the U.S., the first three promotional R.E.M. singles on I.R.S. were "Radio Free Europe," "So. Central Rain," and "(Don't Go Back To) Rockville," which have "promotion copy, not for sale" written on their labels, and were not issued with picture sleeves. Later, when I.R.S. records were manufactured and distributed by MCA, white label singles were used for promotion. These white label singles generally come in two varieties which have noticeably different label designs. The first variety can be distinguished easily from the second by the presence of a large black star on the right side of the label, whereas the second variety has the star on the left side of the label. The second variety also has the phrase "promotion only- not for sale" written over the song title, rather than on the left side of the label. These different labels are probably the result of the records being produced at different plants. All U.S. white label promotional 45s are stereo/stereo double A-sided issues with the exception of some promotional copies of "Superman" and "The One I Love," which retain their B-sides, "White Tornado" and the live version of "Maps and Legends."

Of the promotional singles released in the U.K., the first four singles on I.R.S. ("Radio Free Europe," "So. Central Rain," "Talk About the Passion" and "(Don't Go Back To) Rockville") are the ones that many collectors seek out. They have a large "A" in the center of one or both sides of the labels, and like U.S. promos, are all stereo/stereo double A-sided singles. Later promotional singles released in the U.K. were stickered with a generic label on the front of the sleeve showing the release date, and sometimes another sticker on the back indicating that the single was a promotional copy. Promotional copies of singles released in Germany are stickered on the reverse with a label that reads "PR-Copy," and are generally accompanied by a small press release, as are the later U.K. promotional singles. In addition, some copies of most of the I.R.S. singles pressed in Holland were used in France for promotion, and these bear an embossed silver promotional stamp on the reverse of the sleeve that reads, "vente interdite, enchantillon gratuit," indicating that they were promotional copies and not for sale.

R.E.M. promotional singles generally sell for more than their commercial counterparts. However, in cases where a commercial single did not sell well, promotional copies of the single may be more plentiful, and are not as valuable as the commercial issues. Of the R.E.M. singles, this is the case for the U.K. "Radio Free Europe," Spanish "Rockville" and the Australian "Radio Free Europe" and "So. Central Rain" singles.

Radio Free Europe/Sitting Still

Release date: July 1981

■ The photograph on the front of the sleeve was about as discernable as the lyrics to the song.

■ The back of the sleeve featured a photo of the band by Carol Levy.

U.S.	Hib-Tone	HT-0001	(first pressing without address on label)	**$135-175**
U.S.	Hib-Tone	HT-0001	(second pressing with address on label)	**90-125**

This now legendary single is probably the most popular R.E.M. collectible, commanding extremely high prices both in the U.S. and overseas. Johnny Hibbert, Atlanta lawyer and the owner of the record company responsible for pressing the single, did not keep a record of the number of singles pressed, and therefore it will never be known exactly how many of these actually exist. Estimates run from 5,000-10,000 copies, though first pressings of the single, which lack the record company's address on the record label but use the same picture sleeve as second pressings, number less than 1,000. The majority of the first pressings were sent out for promotion in the U.S., with an additional fifty copies being sent to Europe. The remainder were sold in retail record stores in the Atlanta and Athens area.

Hibbert originally approached the band in 1980 about recording the first single for his fledgling label, and at the time, R.E.M. had in mind totally avoiding outside help and were thinking only of putting a record out on their own label. Nevertheless, Hibbert won them over, and they made the trip to Winston-Salem to lay down the tracks at Mitch Easter's Drive-In Studio. The tracks, recorded on April 15, 1981, had a style somewhat typical of Mitch Easter's own recordings, upbeat and full of ringing Rickenbacker arpeggios. Tension between Hibbert and R.E.M. was created when the band preferred Mitch Easter's mix of the song to his, and since Hibbert was fronting the money for the venture, it was his mix that eventually made it to vinyl, despite the band's disapproval. Additional technical problems arose during the transfer to vinyl, and the songs somehow lost their brightness and emerged sounding like they were recorded underwater. Despite its muddy sound, the single made its way to the desk of New York Times critic Robert Palmer, who penciled it in on his 1981 top ten singles list.

"Radio Free Europe" quickly made its way into heavy rotation on college radio stations. Before long, it received outstanding reviews from other critics and attracted the attention of major record companies. One such critic, Tom Carson of the *Village Voice*, described the single in his January 13, 1982 review as "A celebration of possibilities still limitless that's so large-spirited, it makes the voice of experience sound all wet." The single went on to top the *Village Voice*'s year-end poll as "Best independent single," and suddenly, R.E.M. had popularized the independent single in the post-punk era.

The band, however, did not completely share the excitement that critics did about the single. In fact, Peter Buck, unhappy about how the record was mixed, ceremonially smashed a copy at a party and taped it up on his wall. Michael Stipe was unsatisfied with the reproduction of his photograph that appeared on the cover. Nonetheless, the record still embodies quite a bit of charm in its simplicity and naivete, and as a collectible, will no doubt stand the test of time.

The interesting but thoroughly confusing photograph on the cover is a somewhat blurry rendition of a room in Michael Stipe's old house on Barber Street in Athens, and the photograph on the back of the sleeve also appeared on early promotional posters for the single. Both A and B-sides of the single appear on an Italian bootleg from 1984 entitled *Really Exciting Music*, and the Mitch Easter mix of the Hib-Tone version of "Radio Free Europe" was included on the album *Eponymous* in 1988. The re-recorded versions of both the A and B-sides appear on the band's first full-length album, *Murmur*. In addition, both tracks, along with "White Tornado," appeared on the band's "Cassette Sets," early demo cassettes sent out by the band.

Little sense could be made from Stipe's garbled lyrics on "Radio Free Europe," which thoroughly perplexed listeners who tried to interpret the song. Later, when the re-recorded version of the single was released on I.R.S., and when lyrics to the song were published in *Song Hits* magazine in October 1983, and in *New Sounds* magazine in January 1984, the meaning of the anthemic single still remained unclear. Perhaps only Mitch Easter, who possesses the original lyrics to the song typed by Michael Stipe and left behind in the studio, truly knows what Stipe sings on the single. Peter Buck would offer some assistance a few years later, telling *Creem* magazine, "Michael and I were talking about weird commercials and we remembered the spot they used to run for "Radio Free Europe" where they had that Czech disc jockey talking and then he introduced 'de Drivters...On Broadvay'. When I was a kid I thought that stuff was perfectly natural, but as I got older I thought, 'Isn't that strange? America is spreading cultural imperialism through pop music?' We should send money so that they can listen to the Drifters. Now, I'd rather have them listen to the Drifters than have cruise missiles, but we thought that was really strange. So the song was related to that; to uncomprehending outsiders listening to Rock n' Roll and not having a clue as to anything about it. I can't imagine someone behind the

Iron Curtain figuring out what 'On Broadway' means. So it's an evocation of that without referring to the commercial."

At least two printing errors of the sleeve exist, one where the red color that fills the letters "r.e.m." is offset by at least half an inch, and the other where the sleeve opens to the front rather than the back. On a final note, if you're concerned that Hibbert will reissue the single and make your copy worthless, don't be. R.E.M. bought back the rights to the tracks from Hibbert for $2,000 in 1982.

Wolves, Lower

Release date: December 1982

U.S.	Trouser Press	flexi 12		**$35-50**
U.S.	Trouser Press	flexi 12	(with Trouser Press magazine)	**40-60**

The rarest of the R.E.M. flexidiscs was issued to subscribers of the now defunct *Trouser Press* magazine, in issue #80. The flip side of the flexi features a song off of the 1982 debut by Lords Of The New Church, another band signed by I.R.S. in the early eighties, who were more well known than R.E.M. at the time. When the choice between using either an unreleased version of "Gardening at Night," or a track from *Chronic Town*, *Trouser Press* chose to use "Wolves" rather than the unreleased material. The version of "Gardening at Night" that *Trouser Press* turned down, which features a heavier vocal track than that which appeared on *Chronic Town*, subsequently appeared on *Eponymous*.

A video was filmed for the song, at Club Lingerie in Los Angeles in 1982. The band was not pleased with the one-camera take, complete with Michael Stipe lip-synching the vocals, and that is most likely the reason why the video was never selected to be on any video compilations.

Radio Free Europe (edit)/There She Goes Again

Release date: April 13, 1983 (U.K.: August 1983)

Australia	Illegal	ES 875	(no PS)	**$70-95**
Australia	Illegal	ES 875	(white label, promotion only, no PS)	**70-95**
Holland	Illegal	A3567		**125-150**
U.K.	I.R.S.	PFP 1017		**50-80**
U.K.	I.R.S.	PFP 1017	(promotional label)	**45-65**

U.S.	I.R.S.	IR9916	(A-side is an edited version)	**40-60**
U.S.	I.R.S.	IR9916	(A-side is the album version, some w/o PS)	**55-70**
U.S.	I.R.S.	IR9916	(double A-sided, promotion only, no PS)	**20-35**
U.S.	I.R.S.	IR9916	(Spandau Ballet mispressing)	**30-45**

■ Sleeve design used for both U.S. and U.K. issues

■ Holland (Illegal A3567)

One of the agreements that R.E.M. made with I.R.S. Records when negotiating their contract was that they would re-record "Radio Free Europe" and "Sitting Still," both previously released on the Hib-Tone label, for an I.R.S. release. Capitalizing on the success of the Hib-Tone single, the first I.R.S. single by R.E.M. was chosen to be the revamped version of "Radio Free Europe," backed by a cover of the Velvet Underground's "There She Goes Again," one of many Velvet Underground songs the band have recorded. As the liner notes read on *Eponymous*, Mike Mills and Jefferson Holt thought that the Hib-Tone version of the single "squashes the other one like a grape." The B-side was recorded live to two-track with Mitch Easter on acoustic guitar.

Since the "Radio Free Europe" track on *Murmur* was 4:03 minutes long, perhaps a bit long for radio, it was decided that a special edited version of the song would be released as the single, at 3:07 minutes. However, some copies of the U.S. single exist that play the album length version of the song, backed with the same B-side. The single that runs 4:03 minutes is exceedingly rare; however, the distinction is only made among a few dealers and collectors.

British copies of the single are quite popular collectibles in the U.S., and stock copies of the U.K. and Australian singles seem to be somewhat harder to find than the promotional issues. Although there were no great differences in the sleeve designs between the American and British releases, the Dutch sleeve is entirely different, and is also quite rare. Also extremely hard to find is the U.S. seven-inch single of the sappy ballad "True" by Spandau Ballet (Chrysalis VS4 42720) which plays both the A- and B-sides of the I.R.S. "Radio Free Europe" single. These mis-pressed singles were issued in the picture sleeve for the Spandau Ballet seven-inch, and have Spandau Ballet labels. Since the error appeared on the A-side as well as the B-side for this single, no doubt most were returned, making this mispressing quite scarce.

Of the U.S. "Radio Free Europe" picture sleeve, Peter Buck told *Contrast* magazine, "The back of the 'Radio Free Europe' single is one of my favorite single sleeves. It's the one with the llamas on the back. Michael got an old 30's picture from Spain and it said 'do not copy.' The guy who took it is dead as a doornail so we stole it and put it on the back. Michael said, 'Look at this,' and I said, 'Why don't you put our names over the top?' and he did. It was really funny to me anyway. Everybody thinks we're so serious, but four llamas with our names over them--we're like, 'Yeah, that's us.' "

The video for the song was filmed on the grounds of preacher/folk artist Howard Finster's "Paradise Garden" in Summerville, Georgia by Arthur Pierson. After its completion however, I.R.S. decided that additional footage of the band playing live, interspersed with scenes of the band members in Finster's garden would be more palatable for MTV viewers. Therefore, two versions of the video exist, one with, and one without the live footage added. The version that was chosen for *R.E.M. Succumbs* does not include the live footage.

Talk About the Passion/Talk About the Passion

Release date: November 1983

U.K.	I.R.S.	PFP 1026	(promotion only, no PS)	**$30-45**

This single, issued without a picture sleeve, was released for promotion only in the U.K. The single was intended to support sales of the *Murmur* LP and the four-track "Talk About the Passion" twelve-inch single, which included "Shaking Through" from *Murmur*, as well as two songs from the then unreleased *Chronic Town* EP, "Carnival of Sorts (Boxcars)" and "1,000,000." In the U.S., "Talk About the Passion" was only released as a promotional twelve-inch single without a commercial counterpart. A video for "Talk About the Passion," directed by independent film maker Jem Cohen, was released in 1988 to support sales of *Eponymous*, and was included on *Pop Screen*.

So. Central Rain/King of the Road

Release Date: April 14, 1984 (U.K.: March 1984)

■ Sleeve design used for all issues with picture sleeves

Australia	Illegal	ES 971	(no PS)	**$50-60**
Australia	Illegal	ES 971	(white label, promotion only, no PS)	**35-50**
Canada	I.R.S.	IR9927	(no PS)	**30-40**
Holland	I.R.S.	A4255		**15-25**
U.K.	I.R.S.	105		**18-25**
U.K.	I.R.S.	105	(promotional label)	**20-35**
U.S.	I.R.S.	IR9927		**15-25**
U.S.	I.R.S.	IR9927	(double A-sided, promotion only, no PS)	**12-20**

"So. Central Rain" was chosen to be the lead single off of the *Reckoning* LP, and was the only single from the album to chart, climbing only as high as #85. That's Bill Berry on the cover of the sleeve, with the reverse showing a slightly altered section of Howard Finster's *Reckoning* cover. The B-side of the single, an odd combination of an experiment for a commercial for Walter's Barbecue in Athens and a drunken venture into Roger Miller's country classic "King of the Road," appears in a slightly edited version on the *Dead Letter Office* LP. Of R.E.M.'s version of "King of the Road," which features Mike Mills calling out chord changes, and Michael Stipe struggling with the lyrics and losing, Peter Buck has said, "If there was any justice in the world, Roger Miller should be able to sue for what we did to this song." A portion of the lyrics to the Walter's commercial originate from the Pere Ubu song, "Lonesome Cowboy Dave," which was released as the B-side to the single "Not Happy," issued on Rough Trade in February 1981 (RT 066).

(Don't Go Back to) Rockville/Catapult (live)

Release Date: August 1984 (U.K.: June 1984)

■ The U.S. picture sleeve

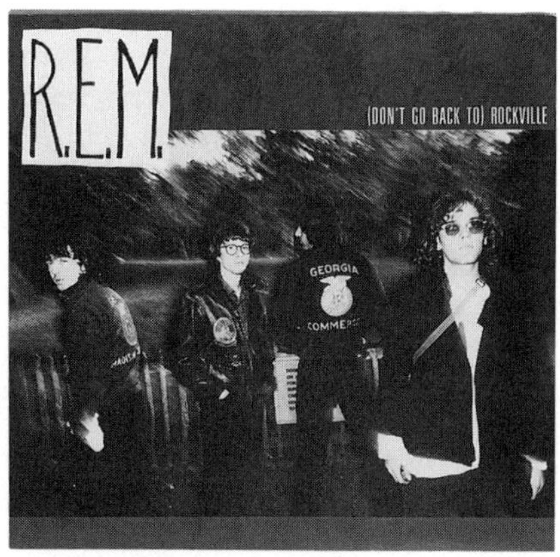

■ Sleeve design used for all non-U.S. issues

Holland	I.R.S.	A 4734	(b/w "Wolves")	**$18-30**
Holland	I.R.S.	A 4734	(b/w "Wolves," with French promotional stamp)	**20-30**
Spain	Illegal	ILSA 4734	(b/w "Wolves")	**35-50**
Spain	Illegal	ILSA 4734	(white label, promotion only, one-sided)	**35-50**
U.K.	I.R.S.	107	(b/w "Wolves")	**25-35**
U.K.	I.R.S.	107(DJ)	(edit/LP versions, promotion only)	**30-40**
U.S.	I.R.S.	IR 9931		**20-40**
U.S.	I.R.S.	IR 9931	(double A-sided, promotion only, no PS)	**18-25**

An early staple for the band, "Rockville" was being performed regularly by the middle of 1981. Written mostly by Mike Mills for a girl named Ingrid Schorr, the song was originally played about twice as fast as it was recorded for *Reckoning*, and was a straight ahead Rock and Roll song, rather than a country flavored tune. "Rockville" had long been a favorite of Bert Downs, R.E.M.'s lawyer, and the band decided to record a special version just for him, adding the country twang as a joke. Finding that they genuinely liked the country version, they added piano and tremolo guitar, and re-recorded the song for possible release on *Reckoning*, or as a B-side. Although the band agreed that the song wasn't particularly representative of their style, "Rockville" was chosen to be included on *Reckoning*, and was the album's second single. The country feel of the record prompted the single to make appearances on a number of country charts, but it was steady air play on college radio stations that popularized the single.

In the U.S., the single was released both for commercial and promotional purposes as a special 3:51 minute edit of the original 4:30 minute album track. Promotional editions of the single were issued in the U.S. and U.K., both using the same record number as the stock copies, but with different labels. The U.S. promos play the edited version of the song on both sides, while U.K. promos have promotional labels, and play the edited and LP versions of the single. A few promotional copies in the U.S. were shipped with the picture sleeve, but most were sent with the generic I.R.S. label sleeve. Of special interest to the collector are the Spanish stock and promo singles, which have the lyrics to the song on the back of the sleeve. The inclusion of the lyrics was not authorized by the band.

The B-side of the single was recorded on June 27, 1984 by The Source in Seattle's Music Hall for FM broadcast. The live take of "Catapult" also appeared on the promotional U.S. twelve-inch single of "Rockville."

Tighten Up

Release date: March 1985

U.K.	B.O.B./Lyntone	5/LYN 15742	(flexidisc)	**$25-35**
U.K.	B.O.B./Lyntone	5/LYN 15742	(flexidisc with magazine)	**30-45**
U.K.	B.O.B./Lyntone	5/LYN 15742	(hard vinyl test pressing)	**55-75**

After about a year and a half of trying to get I.R.S. to let them do a flexidisc for a fanzine, R.E.M. finally got their way and gave a track to the British fanzine *Bucketfull of Brains*. Fans of the new music magazine received a real treat with issue number 11, which included one of the better articles written about the band, and the "Tighten Up" flexidisc. Given the choice of either waiting until R.E.M. was back in the studio or taking "Tighten Up," the magazine chose to use the song, having already prepared the cover story on the band.

The song was recorded live at Mitch Easter's Drive-in Studio in Winston-Salem (Mitch adds vibes on the song) and was performed live by the band as early as February 1981. According to Peter Buck, Michael Stipe had never heard the original Archie Bell and the Drells version of the song when R.E.M. recorded it, and was merely briefed on the song's lyrics prior to its recording. In 1988, a number of copies of the flexidisc, and to a lesser extent, the magazine, surfaced, and it is suspected that additional copies were printed for collectors.

Can't Get There From Here (edit)/ Bandwagon

Release Date: June 10, 1985 (U.K.: July 1985)

Australia	Epic	ES 1082	(b/w "Driver 8," promotion only, no PS)	**$30-45**
Canada	I.R.S.	52642		**12-20**
Canada	I.R.S.	52642	(promotional label)	**30-45**
Holland	I.R.S.	A 6384		**12-15**
Spain	Illegal	ILSA 6384		**15-25**
Spain	Epic	M20618	(one-sided, promotion only)	**35-55**
U.K.	I.R.S.	IRM 102		**10-15**
U.S.	I.R.S.	52642		**6-10**
U.S.	I.R.S.	52642	(double A-sided, promotion only, variety 1)	**10-15**
U.S.	I.R.S.	52642	(double A-sided, promotion only, variety 2)	**10-15**

This lead single from the 1985 *Fables of the Reconstruction* LP, and first departure from the production skills of Mitch Easter and Don Dixon, was somewhat of a non-traditional sounding

■ Sleeve design used in the U.S., Canada, Holland, and U.K.

■ The Spanish commercial picture sleeve

■ Picture sleeve from the Spanish promotional issue

song for the band, and according to Peter Buck, was a bit of a self-parody. Featured on the track were horns and strings, instruments that R.E.M. fans probably didn't expect to hear following the guitar-oriented sound of the band's earlier releases. Upbeat and funky, in a tongue-in-cheek sort of way, the song was written with allusions to a small town outside of Athens called Philomath. "Can't Get There From Here," which originated from riffs used during sound checks while the band was on tour in 1984, did fairly well for R.E.M., who at the time were still definitely not a singles-oriented band. The music and lyrics to the song were published in *Guitar* magazine in the February 1986 issue.

The B-side of the single, described by Buck as "The Clever Ditty" and "The Fruity Song" due to its bizarre chord changes "as if The Lovin' Spoonful had discovered minor sevenths and ninths" was also released on the British and Dutch twelve-inch singles, along with a third track, "Burning Hell." "Bandwagon" was the band's reaction to the meaningless flag-waving nationalistic rock songs in rotation at the time.

Three different edits of the song were released as singles. The LP version was used for the Australian and Spanish promo singles, while in the U.S. and Canada, record buyers were offered a 3:40 minute edit of the track. In the U.K., Spain, and Holland, an even shorter 3:10

minute version was issued. Collectors should try to locate the "Can't Get There From Here" singles from Spain on Illegal Records, both commercial and promotional. The Spanish commercial sleeve has a black and white inset picture of the band, and the promotional sleeve for the one-sided Spanish single is unique.

Driver 8/Crazy

Release date: September 3, 1985.

U.S.	I.R.S.	52678		**$10-15**
U.S.	I.R.S.	52678	(double A-sided, promotion only)	**12-20**

"Driver 8," the follow-up to "Can't Get There From Here," was released commercially only in the United States, and was backed by a cover of "Crazy," a song originally recorded by another Athens band, Pylon. White label promotional copies of the single exist, and seem to be more scarce than those for their other I.R.S. singles. Band manager Jefferson Holt lends his skills as a backing vocalist on the B-side. Of Pylon's original recording of "Crazy," Peter Buck told *Contrast* magazine, "When that record came out I was so depressed because it was so much better than ours." Bill Berry even went as far as to tell *Rolling Stone* that R.E.M. was not "America's Best Rock and Roll Band," but that Pylon was. Pylon's recording of "Crazy" was originally released on Atlanta's DB Records in 1981 as a seven and twelve-inch single (both issued as DB 61), and on the LP *Chomp* (DB 65).

Michael Lachowski, bassist for Pylon, recently recalled the details of R.E.M.'s experience with "Crazy" for *The Bob*, saying, "I think they did the whole thing from memory. They did it while they were in England and they didn't have a copy of the record. They called their office and asked them to ask Vanessa (vocals) to write down the lyrics and then their office was gonna fax them to the band or something, or read them over the phone. All this got done, but not in time, so there was an effort there to try to make it a little more complete, but as it got recorded, I think they winged it." Pylon drummer Curtis Crowe also added, "I think it's great to hear somebody else do your thing. It's like that saying, 'imitation is the sincerest form of flattery.' "

Wendell Gee/Crazy

Release date: September 30, 1985

Canada	I.R.S.	IRSP 857	(Three track 7" with two songs by Beat Rodeo, no PS)	**$100-150**
Holland	I.R.S.	A 6587		**12-20**
Holland	I.R.S.	A 6587	(with French promotional stamp)	**15-25**
U.K.	I.R.S.	IRM 105		**20-35**
U.K.	I.R.S.	IRMD 105	(double single w/"Ages of You" /"Burning Down")	**20-25**

While "Driver 8" was chosen to be the second single from *Fables of the Reconstruction* in the U.S., the choice for England and Holland was the delicate, melodic "Wendell Gee." Peter Buck actually despised the song in its original form, but after the banjo track that closes the song was added, he became much more fond of the track, and didn't object too vehemently about having the song included on the album. Between Gainesville and Jefferson, Georgia, you'll find Wendell Gee's Used Cars, the source of the inspiration for the song.

A gatefold double single with "Bandwagon" and "Ages of You" was released as a limited edition in the U.K. only, and features artwork by Ron Scarselli. The standard U.K. single (IRM

105) is much more difficult to find than the double single, probably because record buyers preferred the double pack which contained the two previously unreleased extra tracks. A seven-inch single of "Wendell Gee" was also released in Holland with a slightly different picture sleeve and label than the U.K. issue. Easily the hardest of the "Wendell Gee" singles to find is the Canadian promotional "Official I.R.S. 3 Track Pack," which also plays two tracks by Beat Rodeo, "Just Friends" and "Without You."

■ Sleeve design for the U.K. and Dutch "Wendell Gee"

■ In Canada, "Wendell Gee" appeared on a three-track sampler along with two tracks by Beat Rodeo.

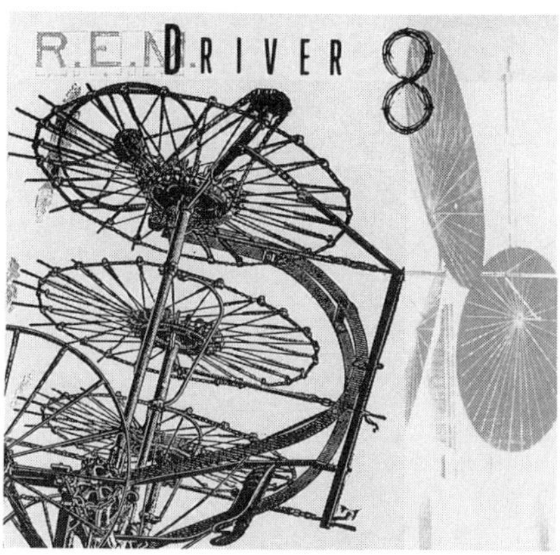

■ "Driver 8" was issued as a single only in the U.S.

■ The sleeve for "Femme Fatale" was issued to subscribers only

Femme Fatale
Release date: June 1986

U.S.	The Bob	REAL 005	(black flexidisc)	**$10-18**
U.S.	The Bob	REAL 005	(red flexidisc)	**15-25**
picture sleeve (numbered)				**12-20**
picture sleeve (not numbered)				**12-20**

When asked by the magazine *The Bob* to donate a track for issue as a flexidisc, R.E.M. gave them "Femme Fatale," a reworked cover of the Velvet Underground classic from their 1967 debut LP. The flexidisc, red or black, was stapled to the front of the magazine, which featured a nice cover shot and perhaps one of the most insightful articles on the band. The article was written by Fred Mills and Todd Goss, who followed R.E.M. for a number of dates on the Reconstruction Tour through the Southeast in late 1985. The authors recounted juicy tidbits about backstage conversations after the gigs, Stipe's lengthy song intros, and faithfully reproduced long and informative interviews with Peter Buck.

Picture sleeves featuring a cover photo by Sandra Lee Phipps of Michael Stipe "getting in trouble" were sent to subscribers only. The first 1,000 copies of the sleeve were hand numbered on the back with a green marker. The same marker was used to write the letter "e" on the end of the word "fatale" on the cover. On later copies of the sleeve, which weren't numbered, the "e" is written in red. The flexi was pressed on red and black vinyl, and the red copies are somewhat more scarce.

Fall On Me/Rotary 10

Release date: August 18, 1986 (U.K.: July 1986)

■ Sleeve design used in the U.S., Canada and Holland

■ The U.K. picture sleeve

Australia	I.R.S.	ES 1170	(no PS)	**$15-25**
Canada	I.R.S.	52883		**10-15**
Holland	I.R.S.	A 7302		**8-12**
Holland	I.R.S.	A 7302	(with French promotional stamp)	**12-15**
U.K.	I.R.S.	IRM 121	(gold label)	**10-15**
U.K.	I.R.S.	IRM 121	(silver label)	**10-15**
U.K.	I.R.S.	IRM 121	(blue label)	**15-20**
U.S.	I.R.S.	52883		**7-10**
U.S.	I.R.S.	52883	(double A-sided, promotion only, variety 1)	**10-15**
U.S.	I.R.S.	52883	(double A-sided, promotion only, variety 2)	**10-15**

"Fall On Me" was, according to Michael Stipe, inspired by a historic physics experiment that took place at the Leaning Tower of Pisa where an equal amount of feathers and lead weight were dropped in order to see which one would be first to hit the ground. Stipe has also described the track as "a song about oppression," and the song is most widely interpreted to have something to do with acid rain. The strong first single from *Lifes Rich Pageant* received more air play than any previous R.E.M. single, and as a result, helped the band increase the size of its ever-expanding audience. The B-side, "Rotary 10," was described by Peter Buck as, "The movie theme without a movie" and actually has been played live a handful of times.

British copies of the single feature a different sleeve than U.S. editions, and copies of the single were released with blue, gold, and silver labels. The Canadian issue uses the same picture sleeve as the U.S. editions, but with a bronze label. Australian copies of the single were issued without a picture sleeve.

Superman/White Tornado
Release date: November 3, 1986

■ Sleeve design used for all issues except at right

■ The rare Japanese promotional issue.

Australia	I.R.S.	6502257	(no PS)	**$15-20**
Canada	I.R.S.	52971		**10-15**
Canada	I.R.S.	52971	(promotional label)	**25-35**
Holland	I.R.S.	6502257		**8-12**
Holland	I.R.S.	6502257	(with French promotional stamp)	**10-15**
Japan	I.R.S.	XDSP 93083	(B-side by Timbuk 3, promotion only)	**190-235**
U.K.	I.R.S.	IRM 128	(gold label)	**10-15**
U.K.	I.R.S.	IRM 128	(silver label)	**10-15**
U.S.	I.R.S.	52971		**6-10**
U.S.	I.R.S.	52971	(double A-sided, promotion only, variety 1)	**8-15**
U.S.	I.R.S.	52971	(double A-sided, promotion only, variety 2)	**8-15**
U.S.	I.R.S.	52971	(white label promo issue with A and B sides)	**20-30**

Original plans for *Lifes Rich Pageant* did not involve the inclusion of the cover of The Clique's 60's pop tune "Superman," and in fact, the track is not listed on the album jacket. Ironically, "Superman" turned out to be one of the more popular tracks from the album. The original version of the song as recorded by The Clique was released on White Whale Records as the B-side of the single "Sugar On Sunday" (WW 323) and is also found on the LP *Sugar On Sunday* (WW 7126). Gary Zekley, who wrote "Superman," and who was surprised and excited to hear that R.E.M. was covering his song, joined the band on stage in Dekalb, Illinois on December 21, 1986 to sing harmony and play tambourine.

"White Tornado" was one of the band's earliest recordings, originally laid down in 1981 at the same time as the Hib-Tone tracks. The song was chosen to be one of three to be released on the band's early demo cassettes, along with "Radio Free Europe" and "Sitting Still." The original recording appeared on the 1983 bootleg *Smoking in the Boys Room*, and later on *Dead Letter Office*. A more recent recording of the song, recorded in January 1984 during the *Reckoning* sessions, is heard here as the B-side of the "Superman" single.

British copies of the single feature both gold and silver label varieties, while the Dutch issue uses a different layout and type style on the sleeve than U.S. copies. Three varieties of U.S. white label promotional singles exist, the one with the B-side being worth more than double A-sided promos.

The One I Love/Maps and Legends (live)

Release date: August 24, 1987 (U.K.: November 1987, reissued October 1988 and November 1991)

■ Sleeve design used for all original issues

■ Picture sleeve for the one-sided Japanese single

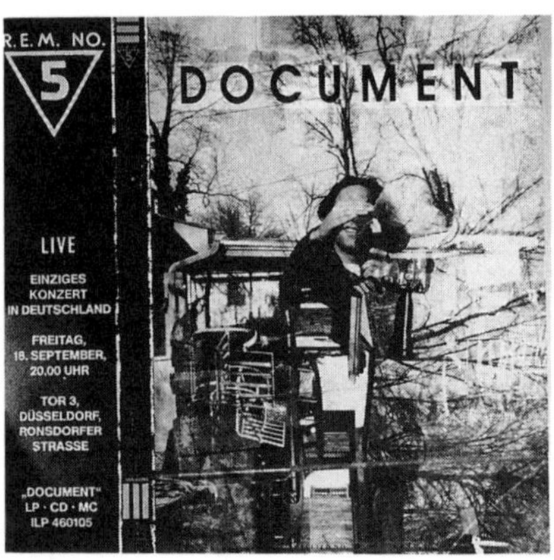

■ The German promotional sleeve uses the *Document* cover.

Australia	I.R.S.	6511137		**$8-12**
Canada	I.R.S.	53171		**7-10**
Canada	I.R.S.	53171	(double A-sided, promotion only)	**20-30**
Germany	I.R.S.	1C 006 2045377	(released November 1991)	**5-7**

Holland	I.R.S.	6511137		**7-10**
Holland	I.R.S.	6511137	(with French promotional stamp)	**10-15**
Holland	I.R.S.	6511137	(in German promotional sleeve)	**100-150**
Japan	I.R.S.	04SP 1072	(one-sided)	**15-20**
S. Africa	CBS	SSC 6067	(no PS)	**20-30**
U.K.	I.R.S.	IRM 146	(b/w "Last Date")	**6-10**
U.K.	I.R.S.	IRM 173	(October 1988 reissue, b/w "Fall On Me")	**5-8**
U.K.	I.R.S.	IRM 178	(September 1991 reissue, b/w "Crazy," gold label)	**5-7**
U.K.	I.R.S.	IRM 178	(b/w "Crazy," jukebox issue with black label)	**6-8**
U.K.	I.R.S.	IRM 178	(b/w "Crazy," with silver label)	**5-7**
U.K.	I.R.S.	IRM 178	(as above, Gloria Estefan mispressing)	**30-50**
U.K.	I.R.S.	WIRM 178A	(b/w "This One Goes Out" (live)/"Driver 8" (live), promotion only)	**40-50**
U.S.	I.R.S.	53171		**5-8**
U.S.	I.R.S.	53171	(double A-sided, promotion only)	**7-12**
U.S.	I.R.S.	53171	(promotional issue with A and B sides)	**7-12**

The powerful first single from R.E.M.'s 1987 *Document* LP became the biggest hit to date for the band, and eventually became their first *Billboard* top ten single. This, according to Peter Buck, was "one of the five warning signs of the end of civilization as we know it." "The One I Love" spent ten weeks in the top forty, making its first chart appearance on October 17. The single was passively assumed to be a love song by many, and was famous for containing Stipe's most misinterpreted lyrics, as they refer to the object of the song as, "A simple prop to occupy my time."

The photographs that were used on the sleeves that accompany the singles for "The One I Love" and for U.K. editions of "It's the End of the World" were taken in the Florida Keys, and in Athens by local photographer Karekin Goekjian, whose work Stipe first saw at the Aguar Video Productions offices in Athens. Stipe, an avid photographer himself, asked Goekjian for some of his photos. "I draw my inspiration from nature," said Goekjian about the photographs that adorn the sleeve for the single. "I get fascinated by seeing nature take over our possessions. Nature reclaiming things fascinates me. Michael liked a few of my photos and he thought that they all fit the theme of the album, and that's how it worked out."

The live take of "Maps and Legends" that was used as the B-side of the single was recorded in May 1987, during an in-store appearance at the legendary McCabe's Guitar Shop in Santa Monica, California. The guitar work was courtesy of Jeff Gans, a friend of the band, "who plays the song better than I do" according to Peter Buck. A live recording of "The One I Love" from the same show was used as the B-side of U.S. and U.K. commercial twelve-inch singles, and the entire show from which the B-side track was taken has been released on bootlegs.

In England, "It's the End of the World" was chosen to be the first single from *Document*, but fell flat, prompting the release of "The One I Love," which was doing very well in America. The B-side of the first U.K. issue was a cover of Floyd Cramer's "Last Date," and was recorded in John Keane's busy studio in Athens, where R.E.M. does their demo material. The U.K. single was released with both bronze and silver labels. Both double A-sided white label promos and promos with the B-side were released in America. The Dutch, Canadian, and English sleeves are all virtually identical to the American issue. In Germany, some of the Dutch singles were sent out for promotion in a special promotion-only gatefold sleeve featuring the *Document* LP artwork on the cover, and a brief year-by-year bio on the reverse. The Australian sleeve features an inset photo of the *Document* cover on the back, and the sleeve for the Japanese one-sided issue includes a brief biography of the band on the back, written in Japanese.

With the release of the album *Eponymous* in October 1988, I.R.S. again released "The One I Love" in the U.K., reaching back a few years into the R.E.M. catalog for the B-side, "Fall On Me." The sleeve design was re-worked and the reissue was released along with a twelve-inch and CD single that also included "So. Central Rain." In October 1991, the single was once again issued, this time in the U.K. and Germany in conjunction with the LP *The Best of R.E.M.* Both the U.K. and German singles used the same sleeve design as the 1988 issue from *Eponymous.* While the choice for the B-side on the 1991 German issue was the live cut of "Maps and Legends," in England, I.R.S. chose to use the band's cover of Pylon's "Crazy." Some advance promotional copies of these U.K. singles (IRM 178) play a Gloria Estefan track on the B-side, and are quite rare. Collectors may also want to try to locate a copy of the German pressing that was sold in Spain and stickered with a label indicating that it was a single from the album *The Best of R.E.M.* Advance white label promotional copies of the 1991 U.K. issue were backed with live versions of "This One Goes Out" ("The One I Love") and "Driver 8." In addition, some stock copies of IRM 178 were used for promotion, and carry an MCA promotional sticker.

It's the End of the World As We Know It (and I Feel Fine) (edit)/Last Date
Release date: January 1988 (U.K.: September 1987, reissued December 2, 1991)

■ Sleeve design used in the U.S. and Canada

■ Sleeve design used for all U.K. issues

Australia	I.R.S.	6513487	(no PS)	**$8-12**
Canada	I.R.S.	53220		**7-10**
Canada	I.R.S.	53220	(promotional label, no PS)	**18-25**
Spain	Illegal	ARI 2066	(one sided, promotion only)	**25-40**
Spain	I.R.S.	4024097	(double A-sided, promotion only, released 12/91)	**18-25**
U.K.	I.R.S.	IRM 145	(b/w "This One Goes Out" (live), gold label)	**6-8**
U.K.	I.R.S.	IRM 145	(b/w "This One Goes Out" (live), metallic blue label)	**6-8**
U.K.	I.R.S.	IRM 180	(12/2/91 reissue, b/w "Radio Free Europe," gold label)	**5-7**
U.K.	I.R.S.	IRM 180	(as above, with silver label)	**5-7**
U.S.	I.R.S.	53220		**5-8**
U.S.	I.R.S.	53220	(double A-sided, promotion only, variety 1)	**8-10**
U.S.	I.R.S.	53220	(double A-sided, promotion only, variety 2)	**8-10**

The edited version of this cut from *Document* was released as the follow-up to "The One I Love" in the U.S., but was chosen as the lead single from the album in the U.K. The track runs 4:07 minutes on the LP, and a number of different edits of the song were released. The American edit, which appears on the stock and promotional singles runs 3:29, and the U.K. single clocks in even shorter at 2:59. The labels on some copies of the U.S. promo single show the track running 3:27 minutes, while others indicate that the single runs 3:29 minutes.

The B-side of the single was initially intended to be an original composition entitled "Theme From Two Steps Onward," but the tape that included the track was lost en route from London to the U.S. The album version of "It's the End of the World" was reissued in the U.K. in December 1991 as a single from *The Best of R.E.M.*, this time backed with "Radio Free Europe," and issued with both gold and silver labels. Coinciding with the album's release was a special promotional issue of the single from Spain, which uses cover art from the album on its sleeve. Some copies of this later issue (IRM 180) were shipped for promotion, and were stickered with a label that reads "MCA radio promotion."

In August of 1989, Greenpeace released *Rainbow Warriors*, on LP, CD and cassette in the U.S., Russia, and Japan that included the track. The track also made an appearance on the soundtrack to Timothy Hutton's 1987 film *Dream a Little Dream*, solidifying R.E.M. as the band that has surely donated the most great songs to soundtracks from bad movies. Curtis Crowe of Pylon once told *The Bob* magazine, "There are people who write songs where you just go 'God, I wish I had written that. What an incredible song!' I mean, I listen to R.E.M.'s "End of the World" and I just go, 'You know, if I had written that song I'd just quit.' "

Finest Worksong/Time After Time, Etc. (live)

Release Date: April 18, 1988

The U.K. picture sleeve

Holland	I.R.S.	ILS 651320 7		**$8-12**
Holland	I.R.S.	ILS 651320 7	(with French promotional stamp)	**10-15**
U.K.	I.R.S.	IRM 161		**7-10**
U.K.	I.R.S.	IRM 161	(with promotional sticker on back of sleeve)	**25-40**

"Finest Worksong" was the third single from *Document*, and was released in England and Holland as a seven-inch single. The song made for a great album opener on *Document* and was first on the set list of most of the band's 1987 performances. One of the band's favorites to play live, the song embodied the themes of the album and tour as expressed by the band, "strength and work." "Time After Time, Etc.," a medley which uses lyrics from "South Central Rain" and

Peter Gabriel's "Red Rain," was recorded in Utrecht, Holland's Muziekcentrum, and was originally broadcast over FM radio.

Both the English and Dutch singles contain the LP version of the song, unlike the twelve-inch singles, which are remixes. The sleeves feature photo stills from the video for the song, which was directed and produced by Michael Stipe. Most copies of the English single were released with a yellow sleeve sticker indicating that it contained the live track. About 100-200 of the U.K. singles were issued as promos, with a release date sticker on the front and a promo sheet with a brief discography and biography glued on the back, containing one of the silliest sentences ever written about R.E.M., "R.E.M. is not a band-- but a concept, all embracing, all entity...R.E.M."

Parade of the Wooden Soldiers/See No Evil
Release date: December 1988

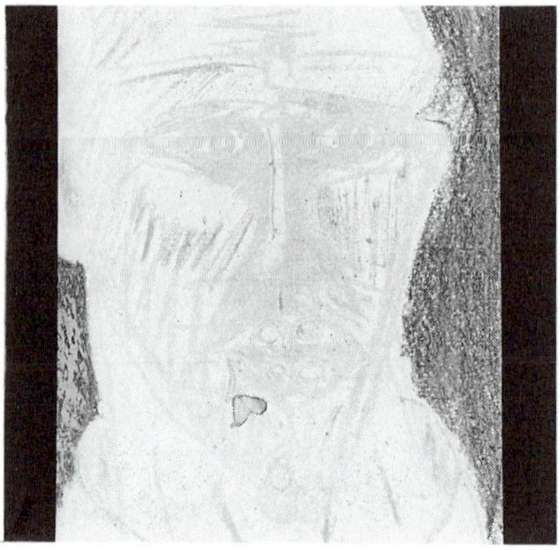

■ The band's first fan club single is highly coveted.

U.S. U-23518M (fan club only) **$125-175**

If you were a member of the R.E.M. fan club in 1988 you made out well, because for the first time a record was given out in the annual Christmas mailer to members. The A-side of the green vinyl single was performed by everyone at Ardent Studios who happened to be present during the band's recording session, with some participants picking up drum sticks and banging on whatever was close by. The actual title of the song performed on the A-side is "The March of the Wooden Soldiers" from *The Nutcracker Suite*, composed by Tchaikovsky, not Mussorgsky, as is indicated on the sleeve. The band's cover of Television's immortal "See No Evil" from their 1977 *Marquee Moon* LP is superb, and is a tune that R.E.M. has included in their live shows for years. Either track has yet to appear elsewhere, except on bootlegs. A segment of "Parade" can be heard on Warner Brothers' "Should We Talk About the Weather" interview LP, and "See No Evil" was broadcast nationally over FM radio during a "Rockline" interview.

The single was selling for upwards of fifty dollars immediately after its release, due to its limited pressing of 3,000, and to the fact that the record was not available commercially. At the time of the record's release, there were about 2,500 members in the fan club, leaving about 500 extra copies for the band members and office crew to dole out to family and friends. Letters arriving at the R.E.M. office complaining about records broken in the mail and asking for a replacement copy were answered simply by asking their authors to send in the broken records for new ones. To no one's surprise in the office, despite many claims of broken records, only one single was ever mailed back. Many letters also arrived in January written by latecomers asking if they could join the fan club and still receive the much sought-after single. These poor souls, who had no doubt previously thought joining a fan club was beneath them, were denied. The value of this record may eventually eclipse that of the Beatles' Christmas flexidiscs, especially if R.E.M. continues to expand its audience at its current rate. Rare to the point of absolute unavailability, is an alternate pressing of the single with a different B-side, the instrumental remix of the untitled song from *Green*, of which only two copies exist, both being in the hands of R.E.M. personnel.

Stand/Memphis Train Blues
Release date: February 1989 (U.K.: January 23, 1989, reissued August 1989)

■ Sleeve design used for all original issues of the single

■ Picture sleeve from the August 1989 U.K. reissue

■ The U.K. reissue in the "stencil pack"

■ The Spanish promotional sleeve

Australia	WB	7-27577		**$8-12**
Canada	WB	76887	(no PS)	**8-12**
Canada	WB	PRO 76887	(double A-sided, promotion only, no PS)	**20-35**
Ecuador	WEA	45-80156	(no PS)	**15-20**
Germany	WEA	927577-7		**9-12**

Germany	WEA	927577-7	(promotional tour date sticker on sleeve)	**10-15**
Philippines	WB	WB-77-661	(double A-sided, promotion only)	**25-30**
Spain	WEA	1033	(double A-sided, promotion only)	**15-20**
U.K.	WEA	W7577		**6-8**
U.K.	WEA	W7577X	(recycled paper sleeve)	**6-8**
U.K.	WEA	W2833	(8/89 reissue, b/w "Pop Song '89" (acoustic))	**7-10**
U.K.	WEA	W2833W	(as above in limited "stencil pack" with PS)	**8-12**
U.K.	WEA	W2833W	(as above in limited "stencil pack" without PS)	**8-10**
U.S.	WB	7-27688		**4-6**
U.S.	WB	7-27688	(double A-sided, promotion only, no PS)	**6-9**
U.S.	WB	7-21864	(b/w "Pop Song '89," Back to Back Hits issue, no PS)	**3-5**

The first offering from *Green* was the bubbly, somewhat tongue-in-cheek "Stand," a single that would outdo all previous R.E.M. singles by climbing all the way to number six on the *Billboard* Hot 100. The song was the closest that the band had come to a single with even a remote AM radio feel. It even included a wah-wah guitar solo, an effect that Peter Buck described as "one of the most despicable and overused effects possible." The single was backed by "Memphis Train Blues," which was, according to Buck, "a mandolin blues jam, if you can imagine anything that horrible." "Stand" received steady radio airplay for months in the U.S., and garnered additional attention when R.E.M. allowed FOX Television to use the track as the theme song to the now cancelled comedy "Get a Life" in September 1990. The band later allowed *Guitar School* magazine to publish the music and lyrics to the single in their March 1993 issue.

The cover of the U.S. sleeve uses a frame from the video for the song, and on the reverse, an old picture of Buck taken long before he knew what a Rickenbacker guitar was. The U.S. sleeve was a relatively limited release, with Warners issuing later copies of the single without the sleeve. Double A-sided U.S. promotional copies also exist, and were also shipped without the picture sleeve. In England, Warner Brothers released the track in an exhaustive variety of formats, in standard packaging, and in collector issues. The first issue of the seven-inch uses virtually the same sleeve as the U.S. release, though some copies of the U.K. single were issued in sleeves made from recycled paper, and the words "recycled paper" are printed on the reverse. Promotional copies of the German single feature a sticker on the cover proclaiming the song "Top 10 in U.S." and listing German tour dates.

After the single didn't fare too well on the U.K. charts, WEA next pushed "Orange Crush," which went over much better. Having a lot of faith in "Stand," based perhaps upon the outstanding success of the single in the U.S., WEA re-released "Stand" in the U.K., this time backed by the acoustic take of "Pop Song '89," and issued in a different sleeve. Recycled paper editions of the sleeve were again issued, and a special "stencil pack" was released which included the single. When the picture sleeves ran out, WEA issued subsequent stencil packs with no picture sleeve inside.

Orange Crush/Ghost Riders

Release date: May 1989

Australia	WB	7-27652	(b/w "Memphis Train Blues")	**$8-12**
Germany	WEA	7-927652	(b/w "Memphis Train Blues")	**6-10**
Germany	WEA	PRO-523	(double A-sided, promotion only)	**125-175**
Spain	WB	1008	(double A-sided, promotion only)	**18-25**
U.K.	WEA	W2960		**6-8**
U.K.	WEA	W2960X	(recycled paper sleeve)	**6-8**
U.K.	WEA	W2960B	(as above in boxed set with poster)	**10-15**

With the release of *Green* in the U.S., Warner Brothers bombarded radio stations and record stores with promotional releases in support of the song, including the orange vinyl twelve-inch

■ The U.K. picture sleeve

■ The rare German promotional sleeve

■ The Spanish promotional sleeve

single and picture disc CD single. Strangely though, "Orange Crush" was never released as an individual commercial single in this country. In England however, the single was quite popular, and was backed by a cover of Suicide's "Ghost Riders." It was issued in a standard sleeve, recycled paper sleeve, and recycled paper sleeve in a limited edition boxed set, which included a two-sided "Green World Tour/Ecology" poster ("The Green Package"). The standard U.K. issue single was later included in the U.S. boxed singles set, *Singleactiongreen*.

The Australian edition makes a nice collector's item, in that the B-side, "Memphis Train Blues" is mis-labelled as "Memphis Train Blues, The Eleventh Untitled Song," which leads one to assume that at one time the instrumental mix of the eleventh song from *Green* was considered as a B-side for this single. The Spanish and German promotional issues are also popular collectibles, owing to their unique sleeves. The original version of "Ghost Riders" (actually entitled "Ghost Rider") was released by Suicide in 1977 on their self-titled debut LP on the Red Star label in the U.S. (RS1), and on EMI/Bronze in the U.K. (BRON 508). The song is currently available on the Restless CD *Suicide* (7 72519-2) and the Reachout International cassette *Ghost Riders* (A-145).

Of the song's content, Peter Buck told *Billboard* magazine, "It's about Vietnam, but it could just as well be about Nicaragua or anyplace else they're going to send 18-year-old kids in the next year, and they're going to." Mike Mills told Timothy White in a radio interview, "It's largely about [Agent Orange]. It's also about the bad side of being drafted and having to go fight a war that you certainly may not believe in and don't want to go fight for. Once you turn eighteen it's something you live with. I missed the draft fortunately, but it's something that's very scary if you're very close to that age at all."

Pop Song '89/Pop Song '89 (acoustic)

Release date: May 1989

Australia	WB		(no PS)	**$20-30**
Canada	WB	76407	(no PS)	**6-10**
Canada	WB	PRO 76407	(double A-sided, promotion only, no PS)	**20-30**
Germany	WB	PRO 541	(b/w "Orange Crush," promotion only)	**160-200**
U.S.	WB	7-27640	(no PS)	**4-7**
U.S.	WB	7-27640	(with PS, from Singleactiongreen box)	**7-12**
U.S.	WB	7-27640	(double A-sided, promotion only, no PS)	**6-10**

This single dates back to about the middle of 1987, and was often played live as the more pretentiously titled "Pop Hit '89" during the *Document* tour, using quite different lyrics. The acoustic B-side was "recorded and mixed in four minutes" in John Keane's Athens studio. Much to the disappointment of American fans, the single was initially issued without a picture sleeve. However, when the single was released in the U.S. singles box set *Singleactiongreen* in November 1989, it was issued with a picture sleeve, which ended up being a rendition of the sleeve that was used for the cassette single. The standout of the "Pop Song" singles is definitely the German promotional issue, backed by "Orange Crush," complete with a stunning live shot of Michael Stipe on the sleeve, along with favorable review quotes from the British press.

Turn You Inside-Out

Release Date: 1989

Spain	WEA	1078	(promotion only)	**$18-25**

This single from the *Green* LP was never released commercially, and was only issued as a promotional single in Spain. The song did, however, make a brief appearance on *Billboard*'s "Album Tracks" chart. "Turn You Inside-Out" features a guest appearance by Sugar Hill Records session drummer Keith LeBlanc, who adds percussion.

Get Up/Funtime

Release date: September 1989

Canada	WB	27917	(no PS)	**$8-10**
Ecuador	WEA	45-80155	(no PS)	**15-20**
U.S.	WB	7-22791		**5-9**
U.S.	WB	7-22791	(double A-sided, promotion only)	**12-15**

"Get Up" was the last of the singles to be released off of *Green*, and not long after its release, it was issued in the U.S. boxed set of singles. "Funtime" was originally recorded by Iggy Pop, and the track appeared on his *The Idiot* LP, released in 1977. Promotional copies of "Get Up" were issued, using the same sleeve and record number. The Canadian release was issued without a picture sleeve.

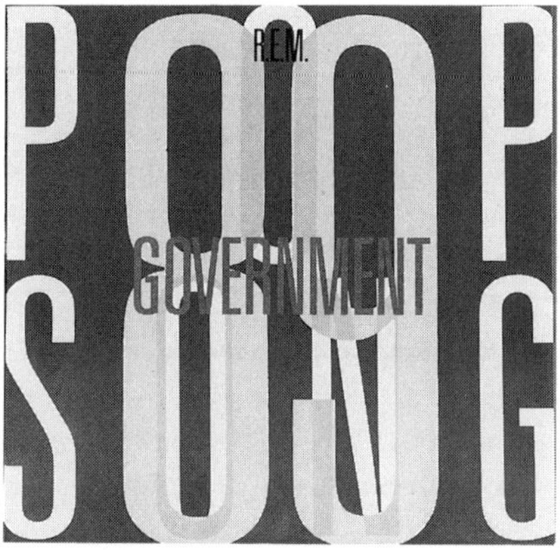

■ The U.S. "Pop Song" sleeve from Singleactiongreen

■ The Spanish promo issue of "Turn You Inside-Out"

■ The German promotional sleeve of "Pop Song" (front)

■ The reverse of the sleeve shown at left

■ The picture sleeve from "Get Up"

■ The "Dark Globe" flexidisc from *Sassy* magazine

Dark Globe
Release date: November 1989

U.S.	Evatone	105900-15	(five-inch flexidisc with magazine)	**$8-15**

The relatively new girls' magazine *Sassy* approached R.E.M. about releasing a flexidisc and they agreed, giving them the track "Dark Globe," which had still not been released in the U.S. A special Christmas message from Michael Stipe was dubbed onto the end of the track as it plays on the flexidisc. The relationship between R.E.M. and the magazine actually preceded the release of the flexi, as Michael Stipe and *Sassy* editor Jane Pratt were friends long before her magazine ever hit the shelves. The December 1988 issue of the magazine featured a nice original R.E.M. poster. The original version of "Dark Globe" appeared on ex-Pink Floyd member Syd Barrett's *The Madcap Laughs* LP, released in 1970, and is currently available on the LP *Opel* (EMI C1-91206) and the double LP *Barrett* (EMI SABB 11314) as "Wouldn't You Miss Me (Dark Globe)."

Good King Wenceslas/Academy Fight Song
Release date: December 11, 1989

U.S.	122589	(fan club only)	**$90-120**

The single that R.E.M. fan club members received for Christmas 1989 was a mostly *a capella* rendition of the old Christmas caroller's classic, backed with a studio version of an R.E.M. favorite, Mission of Burma's "Academy Fight Song." The single, mailed out to fan club members only, was issued in a special poster sleeve which unfolds into a photo of the band from a 1981 performance at the University of Georgia. The original version of "Academy Fight Song" can be heard on the Rykodisc CD compilation *Mission Of Burma* (RALP 0072) and was originally issued as a single in 1980 on Ace Of Hearts records (AHS 104), and in an eight-pack of singles on Ace Of Hearts in 1985 (AHS 100). Since the number of members in the fan club had increased since the Christmas 1988 mailout, 4,500 singles were pressed for 1989 rather than the previous year's 3,000.

■ The poster sleeve from the 1989 fan club single

■ The sleeve from "Ghost Reindeer in the Sky"

Ghost Reindeer in the Sky/Summertime
Release date: December 1990

U.S.	122590	(fan club only)	**$80-95**

For a 1990 Christmas present, the R.E.M. fan club mailed to members this single. Originally popularized by Vaughn Monroe when it was released as a single on RCA Victor in 1949, the song "Ghost Riders in the Sky" has since been recorded by an untold number of bands, and became well known upon the release of an instrumental version of the song recorded by the Ramrods in 1961. The B-side was co-written by George Gershwin, and can be found on the soundtrack from the film *Porgy and Bess*, released in 1959. Six thousand copies of the 1990 Christmas single were made. In 1992, the track was included on a compilation CD entitled *Rarities on Compact Disc volume 12*.

Losing My Religion/Rotary Eleven
Release date: February 19, 1991 (U.K.: February 25, 1991)

■ Sleeve design used for all original commercial issues

■ The German "Song of the year" reissue

Australia	WB	5439-19392-7		**$8-12**
Ecuador	WEA	45-80163	(b/w "Texarkana," no PS)	**15-25**
France	WB	5439-19392-7		**6-8**
Germany	WB	5439-19392-7		**5-7**
Germany	WB	5439-18963-7	(b/w "Losing My Religion" live acoustic, 3/92)	**5-7**
Italy	WB	Promo 412	(B-side by Escape Club, juke box edition, no PS)	**20-35**
Spain	WEA	WEA 1425	(acoustic version, double A-sided, promotional)	**18-25**
U.K.	WB	W0015		**5-7**
U.S.	WB	7-19392	(no PS)	**2-3**

The debut single from *Out of Time* was "Losing My Religion," a Southern exclamation meaning, according to Michael Stipe, "At the end of your rope, or on your last mile." Stipe also liked to refer to the single as a "classic obsession song." The lyrics to the single were published with permission in the April 1991 edition of *Sassy* magazine, and the music and lyrics to the song were later published by *Guitar School* magazine in September 1991. The video for the single, which was banned in Ireland because of its supposed sacrilegious imagery, took six of the nine MTV video awards for which it was nominated in 1991, including Video of the Year. The song also was awarded "Best Single" in the 1991 *Rolling Stone* readers' and critics' polls, and "Single of the Year" by the *College Music Journal*. In March 1992, "Losing My Religion" was awarded a

Grammy for "Best Pop Performance by a Duo or Group," and the video for the song won the "Music Video, Short Form" award. The song had been nominated for a total of four Grammy awards.

Collectors should try to locate the rare Italian jukebox issue of the single, backed with "Call it Poison" by Escape Club. As for the other issues, there is little difference between the picture sleeves of the Australian, French, German and U.K. editions. U.K. copies of the single exist that have both small and large center holes, as some copies were intended for use in jukeboxes. In March 1992, following the nomination of the song for a Grammy in the U.S., the single was reissued in Germany as a "Song of the Year" edition.

World Leader Pretend (live, edit)/Turn You Inside-Out (live)
Release date: March 12, 1991

Germany	WB	PRO 610	(promotion only, issued with limited edition LP, no PS)	**$20-30**

German fans might have found tucked inside their copy of the newly released *Out of Time* LP this "strictly limited edition" single, which features two live tracks from the *Tourfilm* video. The A-side is a 4:05 edit of the song which originally ran 4:25 on the video. Copies of the album that contained this single had a yellow sticker on the shrink wrap which indicated that it contained the limited edition single.

Shiny Happy People/Forty Second Song
Release date: September 1991 (U.K.: May 1991)

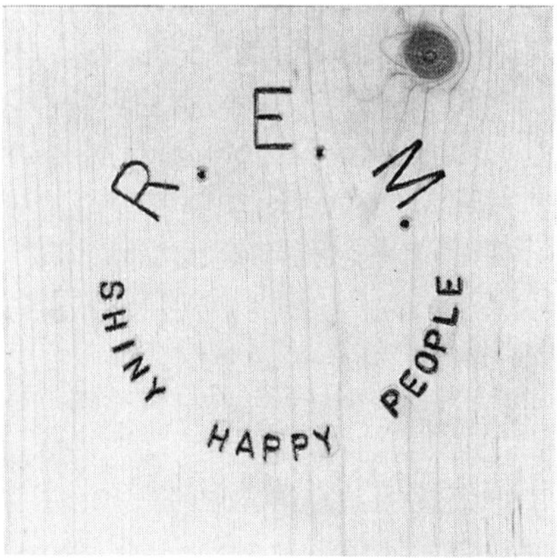

■ Sleeve design used for all issues except at right

■ The Spanish promo issue of "Shiny Happy People"

Ecuador	WEA	45-80165	(no PS)	**$15-20**
France	WB	5439-19307-7		**6-8**
Germany	WB	5439-19307-7		**6-8**
Spain	WB	1378	(promotion only)	**18-25**
U.K.	WB	W0027		**5-7**
U.S.	WB	7-19242	(no PS)	**2-3**

This was the second single released in England from *Out of Time*, which features Kate Pierson of the B-52's on backing vocals. The B-side, "Forty Second Song," (actually 1:20), is a bit of a throwaway, a harpsichord-tinged ditty that the band evidently could not fit lyrics to. Sleeves for the single were sold in the U.K. with both matte and glossy finishes. Some months after its release overseas, the single was released in the U.S. without a picture sleeve. The lyrics to the song were printed in English and Spanish on the reverse of the Spanish promotional sleeve, which uses the *Out of Time* jacket cover artwork on the front.

Near Wild Heaven/Pop Song '89 (live acoustic)
Release date: August 5, 1991

France	WB	5439-19179-7		**$6-8**
Germany	WB	5439-19179-7		**6-8**
Germany	WB	PRO 610	(b/w "Rotary Eleven," promotion only)	**35-50**
U.K.	WB	W0055		**5-7**

The infectious "Near Wild Heaven," which features Mike Mills on lead vocals, and Beach Boys *Pet Sounds*-era backing vocals by Michael Stipe and Bill Berry, was the third offering from *Out of Time* in England. The B-side to the single was recorded live at the Borderline in London, March 15, 1991, when R.E.M. was billed as "Bingo Hand Job." In Germany, the track was released as an extremely rare promotional seven-inch single, the sleeve of which is nearly identical to the one issued for "Losing My Religion."

Radio Song/Love is All Around
Release date: November 4, 1991

Germany	WB	5439-19246-7		**$6-8**
U.K.	WB	W0072		**5-7**
U.S.	WB	7-19246	(no PS)	**2-3**

Released a full eight months after the album on which it appeared, "Radio Song" did not outdo the singles that had previously been released from *Out of Time* in terms of sales or chart success, but nonetheless received steady air play. "Radio Song" was nominated for a Grammy for "Best Rock Performance by a Duo or Group." The single was backed with a live version of the Troggs' "Love is All Around," recorded in Los Angeles on Rockline in April 1991. The Troggs' version of "Love is All Around" was originally released in the U.K. in 1967 as a seven-inch single on Page One, and in the U.S. on their LP *Love is All Around*, released on Fontana in 1968.

■ The U.K. issue of "Near Wild Heaven"

■ The U.K. "Radio Song" sleeve

Baby Baby/Christmas Griping
Release date: December 1991

U.S.	122591	(fan club only)	**$75-90**

For Christmas 1991, R.E.M. fan club members received this single, a cover of the Vibrators' "Baby Baby," featuring Mike Mills on lead vocals, backed with "Christmas Griping." The B-side consists of the band members complaining about various annoying aspects of the Christmas season, over a constantly shifting backing track in which "Rudolf the Red Nosed Reindeer," "Frosty the Snowman," and "Jingle Bell Rock," among other Christmas melodies, are heard. The singles came packaged in Independent Projects Press sleeves which were individually numbered to 4,000, two thousand less than the number of singles pressed the previous year. The original version of "Baby Baby" appeared on the Vibrators' debut LP *Pure Mania*, and was released as a seven-inch single in the U.S. and U.K.

Academy Fight Song (live)/Watching Bluegrass Burn (The Coal Porters)
Release date: March 1992

U.K.	B.O.B./Lyntone	B.O.B.32		**$7-12**
U.K.	B.O.B./Lyntone	B.O.B.32	(white label test pressing)	**35-45**

The English fanzine *Bucketfull of Brains* released this live version of "Academy Fight Song" with double issue 39/40. The track was recorded by Westwood 1 during the Green World Tour for their "Superstars in Concert" radio show, and is widely available on bootlegs.

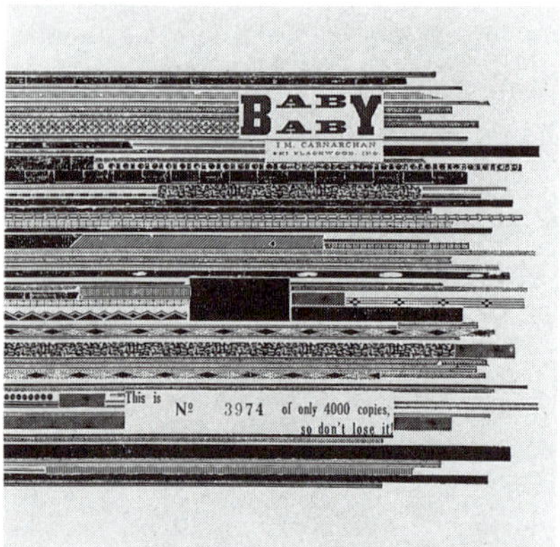

■ The 1991 fan club single was a cover of the Vibrators' punk classic "Baby, Baby."

■ The "Drive" picture sleeve

Drive/Winged Mammal Theme
Release date: October 1992 (U.K.: September 1992)

France	WB	5439-18708-7	(b/w "World Leader Pretend")	**$6-8**
Germany	WB	5439-18708-7	(b/w "World Leader Pretend")	**5-7**
U.K.	WB	W0136	(b/w "World Leader Pretend")	**5-7**
U.K.	WB	W0136	(as above, black label jukebox issue)	**5-7**
U.S.	WB	7-18729	(no PS)	**2-3**

The dirge-like first single from *Automatic For the People* was released in the U.S. backed with the non-LP track "Winged Mammal Theme," which sounded suspiciously like the theme from "Batman." In fact, the band submitted the track to the producers of the film *Batman Returns* for possible inclusion on the soundtrack, but it was not deemed suitable. Outside the U.S., Warner Brothers chose to use "World Leader Pretend" for the B-side of the single, probably with the intention of introducing new fans to their first R.E.M. album, *Green*. The picture sleeves for all of the non-U.S. editions of the single, with cover photograph by Michael Stipe, are virtually identical.

■ The picture sleeve from "Man on the Moon"

■ The fan club issued "Where's Captain Kirk" as the single for 1992.

Man on the Moon (edit)/New Orleans Instrumental #2
Release date: February 1993 (U.K.: November 1992)

Germany	WB	5439-18656-7	(b/w "Turn You Inside-Out')	$5-7
U.K.	WB	W0143	(b/w "Turn You Inside-Out')	5-7
U.S.	WB	7-18642	(no PS)	2-3

Outside the U.S., Warner Brothers again chose to use an album track from *Green* as the B-side of a single from *Automatic For the People*, this time selecting "Turn You Inside-Out" to back "Man on the Moon." In the U.S., "New Orleans Instrumental #2" was used. The non-LP track also appears on the U.S. cassette and CD single of "Man on the Moon."

Where's Captain Kirk? / Toyland
Release date: December 1992

U.S.	fan club	REM 92	(fan club only)	$70-80

The fan club's "Mystic & Merry 1992 Single" was a cover of "Where's Captain Kirk?," a song originally performed by Spizzenergi and released on the Rough Trade label in 1979. The studio version of the original single can also be heard on the Rough Trade album *Spizz History*, and a live version of the track appears on the A&M compilation *URGH! A Music War*. Six thousand copies of the individually numbered 1992 singles were pressed. Both grey and white sleeves were used for the singles, and of the grey sleeves, three different printing varieties exist.

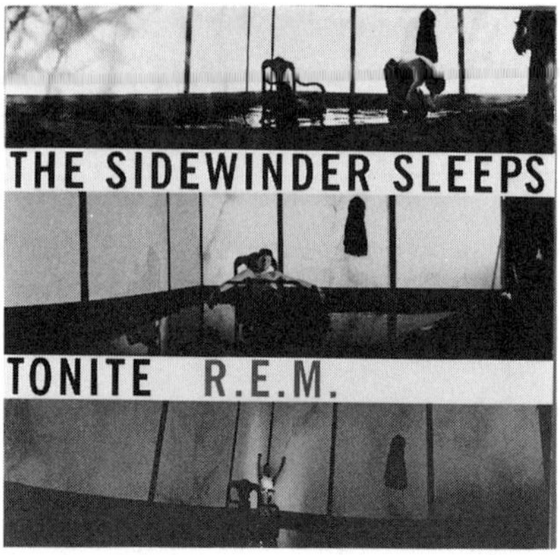

■ "The Sidewinder Sleeps Tonite"

■ "Everybody Hurts" was backed with "Pop Song '89."

The Sidewinder Sleeps Tonite/The Lion Sleeps Tonight
Release date: April 1993 (U.K.: February 1993)

Germany	WB	5439-18597-7	(b/w "Get Up")	**$5-7**
U.K.	WB	W0152	(b/w "Get Up")	**5-7**
U.S.	WB	7-18523	(no PS)	**2-3**

For the third single from *Automatic For the People*, Warner Brothers again chose to use a standard LP track as the B-side for European issues. U.S. record buyers, however, were offered the non-LP track "The Lion Sleeps Tonight." While recording *Automatic For the People*, the band made the decision to contact the owner of the rights to the song "The Lion Sleeps Tonight" and pay them for its use, because of the similarity of the two song titles. Peter Buck said of the decision, "We didn't want some guy down the road going, 'You owe me two million dollars!' So we called them up and said, 'We're calling it 'The Sidewinder Sleeps Tonite' and the singer kind of paraphrases the line.' In any court of law we couldn't have been nailed, because the song doesn't have anything to do with it. But you don't want someone to feel you're stealing from them."

"The Lion Sleeps Tonight," which has been recorded by a number of groups including The Weavers, The Tokens, Miriam Makeba, Karl Denver and The Tight Fit among others, is one that R.E.M. have dabbled with since the beginning of their career. They first recorded the track in November 1983 during a trial studio session in San Francisco with Elliot Mazer, a candidate producer for *Reckoning*. They later brought the song out a few times during the Reconstruction tour.

Everybody Hurts (edit)/Pop Song '89
Release date: March 1993

Germany	WB	5439-18513-7	**$5-7**
U.K.	WB	W0169	**5-7**

"Everybody Hurts" was the surprise fourth single from *Automatic For the People* in England, climbing all the way to #7 on the U.K. chart, and propelling *Automatic* back into the #1 slot on the album chart. The success of the single was due in part to strong crossover airplay.

BOXED SETS OF SEVEN-INCH SINGLES

Singleactiongreen
U.S. WB 7-22780 **$25-40**

This boxed set of singles was released strategically in November to entice Christmas buyers, and included the U.S. seven-inch singles of "Stand," "Get Up," "Pop Song '89" and the English "Orange Crush" single. The set also contained a poster for "Get Up," and another selling point was the inclusion of a picture sleeve for "Pop Song '89," which had previously been issued only in a generic Warner Brothers sleeve. Soon after the box set was issued, many were returned because they mistakenly included the German issue of "Orange Crush" with the acoustic take of "Pop Song '89" as the B-side, rather than the British issue, which was backed with "Ghost Riders."

TWELVE-INCH SINGLES

U.S. ISSUES

Talk About the Passion/Catapult/Sitting Still
Release date: 1983

I.R.S.	SP 70968	(promotion only, no PS)	**$25-35**

The first R.E.M. twelve-inch single to be released in the U.S. was this promotional disc, issued without a picture sleeve. "Talk About the Passion" was issued along with two other tracks from *Murmur* to promote the album.

Pretty Persuasion/(Don't Go Back To) Rockville (edit)
Release date: 1984

I.R.S.	SP 70979	(promotion only, no PS)	**$20-30**
I.R.S.	SP 70979	(as above, with error label)	**30-40**

"Pretty Persuasion" was an early favorite to be a single from *Reckoning*, but was never released commercially. Some copies of this single contained a labelling error, where the label for "Pretty Persuasion" was pasted onto both sides of the record, thus leaving no evidence that "Rockville" appeared on the B-side.

(Don't Go Back To) Rockville (edit)/Catapult (live)
Release date: August 1984

I.R.S.	SP 70982	(promotion only)	**$40-50**

This is probably the most popular U.S. twelve-inch single among collectors, chiefly due to its unique promotion-only picture sleeve, the first promotional twelve-inch to be released with a picture sleeve in the U.S. The B-side was recorded by The Source at the band's June 27, 1984 performance in Seattle.

■ The rare "bicycle" sleeve from the U.S. promo of "Rockville"

■ The U.S. promotional twelve-inch of "Can't Get There From Here"

Can't Get There From Here (edit)/Driver 8/Life and How To Live It
Release date: June 10, 1985
I.R.S. L33-17004 (promotion only) **$15-25**

The lead track on this promotional single is a special radio edit of "Can't Get There From Here," which clocks in at 3:09, about a minute shorter than the LP version. The picture sleeve for the single is unique.

Driver 8/Driver 8 (live)
Release date: August 8, 1985
I.R.S. L33-17034 (promotion only) **$20-30**

This single, with promotion-only picture sleeve, features a live cut, recorded in Seattle by The Source in 1984.

■ The promotional twelve-inch single of "Driver 8"

■ The "Life and How To Live It" single is one of the more difficult ones for collectors to locate.

Life and How To Live It/Bandwagon/Crazy
Release date: October 21, 1985
I.R.S. L33-17060 (promotion only) **$20-30**

As a collector's item, this promotion-only record released in support of *Fables of the Reconstruction* is quite popular, due to its unique promotion-only sleeve. The B-side tracks from this single were released on the LP *Dead Letter Office* in 1987.

Fall On Me/Fall On Me
Release date: July 21, 1986
I.R.S. L33-17159 (promotion only) **$10-18**

Issued with a promotion-only picture sleeve. The photos on the sleeve were taken from the band's 1986 *Athens, GA-Inside/Out* appearance.

Superman/Superman
Release date: October 20, 1986
I.R.S. L33-17200 (promotion only) **$10-15**

Issued in a promotion-only picture sleeve, which strongly resembles the commercial sleeves for the single.

I Believe/Toys in the Attic
Release date: January 5, 1987
I.R.S. L33-17199 (promotion only) **$12-18**

This single, issued in a promotion-only picture sleeve, was never released commercially as a single in any format. The B-side appeared on the U.K. twelve-inch of "Fall On Me," and on *Dead Letter Office*.

■ U.S. promotional singles of "Fall On Me" and "I Believe" from *Lifes Rich Pageant* were both issued in unique promotional picture sleeves.

Ages of You/Ages of You
Release date: April 7, 1987
I.R.S. SP 70146 (promotion only, no PS) **$10-15**

One of the band's earliest compositions, "Ages of You" was originally recorded in 1981, and was released as a single from *Dead Letter Office* some six years later. The track was initially recorded during sessions for *Chronic Town*, was recorded again during the *Murmur* sessions, and was recorded a final time during the sessions for *Reckoning*. The version that appears on this single and on *Dead Letter Office* is a 1985 remix by Steve Fjelstad of the *Murmur*-era recording. This single was released without a picture sleeve, and all copies bear a sticker on the jacket stating that the single is an "Early delivery from the Dead Letter Office."

The One I Love/The One I Love
Release date: September 1987
I.R.S. L33-17384 (promotion only) **$12-18**

Issued in a promotion-only picture sleeve in support of *Document*.

The One I Love/The One I Love (live)/Maps and Legends (live)
Release date: September 7, 1987
I.R.S. 23792 **$7-12**
I.R.S. 23792 (with promotional stamp) **10-15**

Some copies of this commercial single were issued for promotion, and bear a gold embossed promotional stamp. The B-side tracks were taken from the McCabe's Guitar Shop appearance in Santa Monica, California.

It's the End of the World As We Know It (and I Feel Fine)/ Disturbance at the Heron House (live)
Release date: 1987
I.R.S. L33-17430 (promotion only) **$10-20**

This single, issued in a promotion-only sleeve, contains the LP version of "It's the End of the World," and a nice acoustic take of "Disturbance at the Heron House" recorded at McCabe's Guitar Shop in Santa Monica.

■ The U.S. promotional issue of "Finest Worksong" (L33-17510) was issued in this unique sleeve.

■ An unknown number of copies of the single shown at left carry the "Finest Workshop" error label.

Finest Worksong (LP Version)/Finest Worksong (Media Version)
Release date: 1988

I.R.S.	L33-17510	(promotion only)	**$15-18**
I.R.S.	L33-17510	(as above, with "Finest Workshop" error label)	**35-50**

Some initial pressings of this promotional single have the B-side mistakenly titled "Finest Workshop," and were released in error. The "Media Version" is identical to the "Other Mix" found on the commercial twelve-inch single. The single was issued in a light blue promotion-only picture sleeve.

Finest Worksong (Lengthy Club Mix)/Finest Worksong (Other Mix)/Time After Time, Etc. (live)
Release date: March 1988

I.R.S.	23850		**$7-12**
I.R.S.	23850	(with promotional stamp)	**10-15**

Two different versions of "Finest Worksong" were released on this commercial single, which was also issued in Canada. The "Lengthy Club Mix" features the Uptown Horns and clocks in at 5:52, while the "Other Mix," which runs 3:48, is otherwise identical to the track as it appears on *Document*, but has the horns added. Original plans called for the release of the "Other Mix" on *Document*, rather than the mix without horns. Some copies of the U.S. single were shipped as promos, and were embossed with a promotional stamp.

Orange Crush/Orange Crush
Release date: November 1988

WB	PRO-A-3306	(promotion only)	**$22-30**

This beautiful orange vinyl single announced that Warner Brothers was not going to fool around with promoting their newly signed band. Though the track was promoted with a CD and twelve-inch single, "Orange Crush" was never released as a commercial single in the U.S. The sleeve for this release resembles the one shown for the "Orange Crush" seven-inch single.

■ The "Tower of Luv Bug" mix of "Radio Song" (PRO-A-5623) was issued in this title sleeve.

■ The U.S. promotional issue of "Drive" (PRO-A-5942) includes two exclusive mixes of the song.

Shiny Happy People (Dance to the Music Mix)/Shiny Happy People (Pop Mix)/Shiny Happy People (Hip Mix)
Release date: September 1991

WB	PRO-5060	(promotion only, no PS)	**$18-25**

This promotion-only piece features three non-LP versions of "Shiny Happy People," remixed by Michael Stipe and Scott Litt. The "Dance to the Music" mix samples the Sly and the Family Stone classic of the same name. All three tracks were also released as a promotion-only CD (PRO-CD-5060), which is far more common than the vinyl issue. Curiously, nowhere on the label of the vinyl single does it indicate that the record was issued by Warner Brothers.

Radio Song (Tower of Luv Bug Mix)/Love is All Around/Belong (live)
Release date: November 26, 1991

WB	9 40229-0		**$5-8**
WB	9 40229-0	(with promotional stamp)	**6-10**

The "Tower of Luv Bug" mix of "Radio Song," was released as a commercial five-inch CD single containing the identical B-sides as this twelve-inch vinyl issue. The live version of "Belong" was recorded in Greensboro, North Carolina, in 1989, and "Love is All Around" was recorded live in the "Rockline" studios in Los Angeles in April 1991. Some copies of the twelve-inch were embossed with a gold promotional stamp.

Radio Song (Tower of Luv Bug Mix)/(Monster Mix)
Release date: February 1992

WB	PRO-A-5263	(promotion only)	**$20-35**

This promotion-only single with unique title sleeve was quite difficult for collectors to find, even when it initially appeared. The "Hurby Luv Bug Mix" of "Radio Song" was available commercially in the U.S. and elsewhere, but the "Monster Mix" was only available on this twelve-inch.

Drive (Primary Remix)/(Secondary Remix)
Release date: December 1992
WB PRO-A-5942 (promotion only) **$20-35**

This twelve-inch promotional single contains two remixes of "Drive" by Scott Stuckey that are found exclusively on this single.

NON-U.S. ISSUES

Talk About the Passion/Shaking Through/Carnival of Sorts (Boxcars)/ 1,000,000
Release date: November 11, 1983.

U.K. I.R.S. PFSX 1021 **$35-55**

This rarest of the U.K. twelve-inch singles includes two *Murmur* cuts, backed by two from the *Chronic Town* EP. At the time of the single's release, *Chronic Town* had still not been released outside the U.S. Curiously, "Talk About the Passion" was not released as a seven-inch single in the U.K., though a promotional seven-inch was made available.

So. Central Rain/Voice of Harold/Pale Blue Eyes
Release date: March 26, 1984

Holland	I.R.S.	A12-4255	**$18-25**
U.K.	I.R.S.	IRSX 105	**18-25**

Released two weeks before the 1984 European tour, this twelve-inch single is now very popular among collectors due to its interesting B-sides and relative rarity. As in the case of many of the older R.E.M. singles, the 1986 release of *Dead Letter Office* made these once scarce B-sides available to all, and probably lowered the demand somewhat for the earlier singles. Nevertheless, this single, and many others like it which have had their B-sides re-released, are still fetching respectable prices.

"Voice of Harold" is not merely Stipe babbling stream-of-consciousness lyrics to the "Seven Chinese Brothers" backing track as a few critics supposed. In actual fact, the "lyrics" to the song were lifted from the liner notes from the album *The Joy of Knowing Jesus* by The Revelaires. "Pale Blue Eyes" originally appeared on the Velvet Underground's eponymous LP in 1969, and like all of the Velvet Underground songs that R.E.M. has covered, their version differs considerably from the original. The Dutch copy of the single, like all of the Dutch singles, differs from the U.K. single in that the sleeve is made of hard paperboard rather than flexible paper, and different type styles are used.

(Don't Go Back To) Rockville/Wolves/9-9 (live)/Gardening at Night (live)

Release date: June 18, 1984

Holland	I.R.S.	A12-4734	(LP version, issued in red sleeve)	**$35-45**
Holland	I.R.S.	A12-4734	(edited version, issued in blue sleeve)	**50-65**
Spain	I.R.S.	ILSA 12.4734		**60-80**
U.K.	I.R.S.	IRSX 105		**25-35**

This single is very popular among collectors, and would probably be even more so had it not been for the 1992 reissue of the two live tracks on the remastered *Murmur* CD. The live tracks were recorded in mono at the band's April 20, 1984 performance at the El Dorado in Paris. For some undisclosed reason, although the band had approved the two live tracks in their entirety for use as B-sides, when the single hit the shelves, the live tracks were found to fade out towards the end of each song, rather than during the applause that followed.

Of the Paris show from which the B-sides were recorded, Godfrey Cheshire wrote, "There are more [converts] to be found that night at the Theater El Dorado. Quite a few more, in fact. Clearly enjoying themselves, R.E.M. offers a lengthy energetic set to the exuberant fans that have packed the large nineteenth century theater. As Michael prefaces their first encore with a "merci beaucoup" to the French opening act, tour manager Geoff Trump notes the reaction of the show's promoter: 'The guy was astonished. He had no idea there would be this kind of turn-out. He thought he would have to keep the balconies closed and he's had to use both of them.' Indeed both balconies are filled with dancing, cheering fans who join those below in calling the band back for another encore. Paris has fallen."

The Dutch edition of the single was issued simultaneously in blue and red picture sleeves. The single in the red sleeve, which plays the album version of "Rockville" is more commonly found than that issued in the blue sleeve, which plays the edited version. Both varieties indicate on the cover that the single contains live tracks. The U.K. issues play the album version of the track. The back cover of the Spanish issue differs from the U.S. and U.K. releases of the single in that the tracks are listed much in the same way that the tracks appear on the back of the U.K. "Talk About the Passion" twelve-inch single.

Can't Get There From Here/Bandwagon/Burning Hell

Release date: July 8, 1985

Holland	I.R.S.	A12-6384		**$12-18**
Holland	I.R.S.	A12-6384	(with tour sticker)	**12-18**
U.K.	I.R.S.	IRT 102		**10-15**
U.K.	I.R.S.	IRT 102	(sleeve promotes previously unreleased tracks)	**25-35**

About one month after the release of *Fables of the Reconstruction*, this single was issued in the U.K. and Holland. The heavily imported U.K. edition plays the edited version of the song (3:39), though the label says it plays the LP version, and the sleeve states that the record plays an "extended version" (!). Some copies of the Dutch issue, which is somewhat more scarce than the

U.K. edition, were released with a black sticker on the cover listing European tour dates. An unknown number of copies of the U.K. edition were issued in a slightly different sleeve, which states that the single "Contains previously unreleased tracks 'Bandwagon' and 'Burning Hell.' "

Wendell Gee/Crazy/Driver 8 (live)

Release date: October 1985

Holland	I.R.S.	A12-6587	(b/w "Ages of You"/"Burning Down"/"Driver 8" (live))	**$25-35**
U.K.	I.R.S.	IRT 105		**15-20**

In England, the twelve-inch single of "Wendell Gee" picked up a live cut of "Driver 8" for the B-side, which was recorded at the band's 1984 performance in Seattle. In Holland, the single included two of the tracks that at the time were available on the U.K. double single, "Ages of You" and "Burning Down."

Fall On Me/Rotary 10/Toys in the Attic

Release date: September 1, 1986

U.K.	I.R.S.	IRMT 121		**$10-15**
U.K.	I.R.S.	IRMT 121dj	(promotion only, no PS)	**18-25**

This single, heavily imported to the U.S., features the instrumental "Rotary 10," and R.E.M.'s rendition of Aerosmith's 70's rocker "Toys in the Attic," an outtake from *Lifes Rich Pageant*. White label promotional copies of the single were released in England, without picture sleeves. Interestingly, the labels on the promotional issues do not list "Toys in the Attic."

■ The rare Dutch issue of "Wendell Gee" contains four tracks.

■ The U.K. twelve-inch issue of "Fall On Me"

Superman/White Tornado/Femme Fatale

Release date: March 1987

Holland	I.R.S.	650225-6	(third track is "Perfect Circle")	**$35-50**
U.K.	I.R.S.	IRMT 128		**10-18**
U.K.	I.R.S.	IRMT 128dl	(promotion only, no PS)	**20-25**

For the twelve-inch release of "Superman," the single acquired "Femme Fatale," a *Reckoning* outtake which was also issued as a flexidisc in the U.S. White label promotional copies of the single were issued in England. Curiously, I.R.S. chose to use "Perfect Circle" as the third track on the Dutch issue.

It's the End of the World As We Know It (and I Feel Fine)/This One Goes Out (live)/Maps and Legends (live)
Release date: August 17, 1987

U.K.	I.R.S.	IRMT 105	**$8-12**

Released two weeks before *Document*, this twelve-inch contains two tracks recorded live from the band's May 1987 appearance at McCabe's Guitar Shop in Santa Monica. "This One Goes Out" was an earlier working title for "The One I Love," and as a result of the single's early release, the title of the song differed from the one that eventually appeared on the album.

The One I Love/Last Date/Disturbance at the Heron House (live)
Release date: November 1987

Holland	I.R.S.	651113-6	(b/w "The One I Love" (live)/"Maps and Legends" (live))	**$12-16**
U.K.	I.R.S.	IRMT 146	(released November 1987)	**8-12**
U.K.	I.R.S.	IRMT 173	(b/w "Fall On Me"/"So. Central Rain," released 10/88)	**8-12**
U.K.	I.R.S.	WIRMT 173A	(as above, promotion only, no PS)	**18-25**

This track was first issued as a single from *Document*, and upon the release of *Eponymous*, I.R.S. re-released "The One I Love" as a seven and twelve-inch single, backed by two of R.E.M.'s older singles that appeared on the collection. Both issues were also released as five-inch CD singles. White label promotional copies were released in the U.K. only, without picture sleeves.

■ The U.K. twelve-inch of "It's the End of the World As We Know It (and I Feel Fine)

■ The U.K. promotional issue of "Finest Worksong" in the "media sleeve"

Finest Worksong (Lengthy Club Mix)/Finest Worksong (Other Mix)/Time After Time, Etc. (live)
Release date: April 1988

Holland	I.R.S.	651320-6		**$12-16**
U.K.	I.R.S.	IRMT 161		**8-12**
U.K.	I.R.S.	WIRMT 161ADL	(promotion only)	**32-45**

The "Lengthy Club Mix" of "Finest Worksong" was released as a single in the U.K. and Holland, using slightly different picture sleeves. A special promotional issue of the single was also released in England, which featured a die-cut promotion-only sleeve, or "media sleeve" as it is known.

Finest Worksong (Lengthy Club Mix)/Finest Worksong (Other Mix)/Time After Time, Etc. (live)
Release date: March 1988

Canada	I.R.S.	23850	**$12-18**

This single, nearly identical to the U.S. issue, is the only R.E.M. twelve-inch single thus far released in Canada.

Stand/Memphis Train Blues/Untitled (instrumental remix)
Release date: February 1989

Germany	WB	921 148-0		**$12-20**
U.K.	WB	7577T		**8-12**
U.K.	WB	2833T	(b/w "Pop Song" (acoustic)/"Skin Tight" (live), 8/89)	**10-15**

After an initial go of "Stand" as a single in the U.K. in February 1989, Warner Brothers re-released the single six months later with different B-sides and a different picture sleeve, with the hopes that the relative success of "Orange Crush" would open the door a bit wider for this single. It didn't. Both editions were also available as three-inch CD singles. The original German twelve-inch of "Stand," issued in a hard paperboard sleeve bordered in white, is apparently much more rare than the U.K. releases.

Orange Crush/Ghost Riders/Dark Globe
Release date: June 1989

U.K.	WB	2960T	**$8-12**

This single was very popular among U.S. fans and collectors because at the time of its release, the B-sides were not available in the U.S. "Ghost Riders" was a popular choice during the band's 1987 "Work Tour," and "Dark Globe" has often been performed live *a capella* between songs on the last few tours.

Losing My Religion/Rotary Eleven/After Hours (live)
Release date: March 1991

U.K.	WB	W0015T	**$8-10**

Commercial twelve-inch singles of "Losing My Religion" were available only in the U.K., having been virtually phased out in the U.S. This issue features the identical tracks as the companion CD single, including the live take of the Velvet Underground's "After Hours" from *Tourfilm*.

Shiny Happy People/Forty Second Song/Losing My Religion (live acoustic)
Release date: May 1991

Germany	WB	9362-40078-0	**$8-10**
U.K.	WB	W0027T	**8-10**

This twelve-inch single of "Shiny Happy People" contains the identical tracks as the standard five inch CD single. This was only the second R.E.M. twelve-inch single to be released in Germany, and is distinguishable from the U.K. issue in that it was issued in a hard paperboard sleeve with printing on the spine, rather than in a thin soft sleeve.

Near Wild Heaven/Pop Song '89 (live acoustic)/Half a World Away (live)
Release date: August 5, 1991

Germany	WB	9362-40171-0	**$8-10**
U.K.	WB	W0055T	**8-10**

The three-track single of "Near Wild Heaven," the third single from *Out of Time,* was released on the twelve-inch vinyl format, and was not packaged as a three-track five-inch CD single, unlike the two previous singles from the album. The live version of "Pop Song '89" was recorded at the band's secret show at the Borderline in London in 1991, while the live acoustic version of "Half a World Away" was taken from their radio performance on Rockline in April 1991.

Radio Song/Love is All Around/Shiny Happy People (Music Mix)
Release date: November 4, 1991

Germany	WB	9362-40250-0	**$8-10**
U.K.	WB	W0072T	**8-10**

This twelve-inch single of "Radio Song" was released commercially in the U.K. and Germany, backed with "Love is All Around" as recorded on Rockline, and the "Music Mix" of "Shiny Happy People." The third track was released in the U.S. on the promotional CD and twelve-inch of "Shiny Happy People."

Losing My Religion/Fretless/Losing My Religion (live acoustic)/Rotary Eleven
Release date: March 1992

Germany	WB	9362-40399-2	**$8-10**

"Losing My Religion" was re-released in Germany a full year after its initial issue date, following the nomination of the song for a Grammy as "Song of the Year" in the U.S. A five-inch CD single of "Losing My Religion" was also released, which contains the identical tracks as this issue.

Drive/World Leader Pretend/First We Take Manhattan
Release date: October 1992

Germany	WB	9362-40634-2	**$8-10**

Beginning with *Automatic For the People*, Warner Brothers chose not to release twelve-inch vinyl R.E.M. singles in England, though they remained available in Germany. The twelve-inch of "Drive" was backed with the LP track "World Leader Pretend," and the band's cover of the Leonard Cohen song "First We Take Manhattan."

Man on the Moon (edit)/Turn You Inside-Out/Arms of Love
Release date: December 1992
Germany WB 9362-40698-2 **$8-10**

The second twelve-inch single from *Automatic For the People* was backed with the *Green* LP track "Turn You Inside-Out," and a cover of a Robyn Hitchcock song, "Arms of Love" from his 1993 album *Respect.*

CD SINGLES

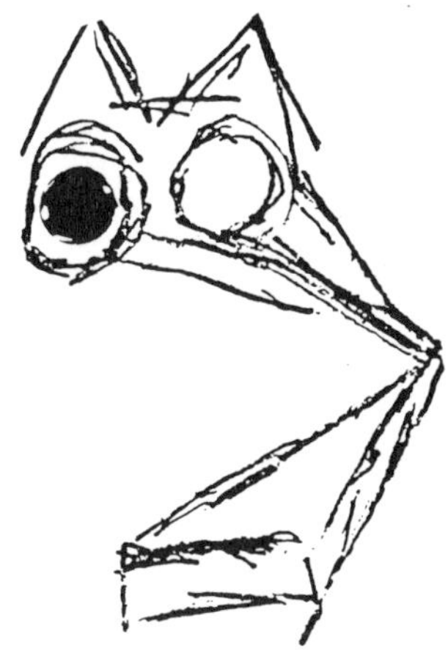

U.S. ISSUES

It's the End of the World As We Know It (and I Feel Fine) (edit)/(album version)
Release date: August 1987

I.R.S. IRSC 53220 (promotion only) **$45-60**

This disc was issued for promotional use in the U.S., and featured the reproduction of the *Rolling Stone* cover from December 3, 1987. The disc plays the 3:29 edit and the LP version of the song. This is easily the most difficult to find of all the U.S. promotional CD singles.

Orange Crush
Release date: December 1988
WB PRO-CD-3306 (promotion only) **$10-15**

Pushing "Orange Crush" as the lead track from *Green*, Warners released this picture disc with color inserts but never released the song as a commercial single in the U.S.

Stand
Release date: January 1989
WB PRO-CD-3353 (promotion only, no PS) **$6-9**

Stand/Memphis Train Blues
Release date: February 1989
WB 2-27688 **$7-12**

The first commercial R.E.M. CD single to be released in the U.S. was this three-inch single, which was the only commercial CD single released in the U.S. by Warner Brothers until the release of "Radio Song" in November 1991.

Turn You Inside-Out
Release date: March 1989
WB PRO-CD-3466 (promotion only, no PS) **$8-12**

Pop Song '89
Release date: May 1989
WB PRO-CD-3357 (promotion only, with back insert) **$6-8**

Get Up/Orange Crush (live)/Turn You Inside-Out (live)
Release date: September 1989
WB PRO-CD-3716 (promotion only, with back insert) **$15-25**

This promotional disc includes two live cuts from the band's 1989 performances in Florida, recorded by Westwood 1. The live tracks also appear on Westwood 1's 3LP "Superstars in Concert" and 2LP "In Concert" radio discs.

Get Up (live)/World Leader Pretend (live)/It's the End of the World As We Know It (and I Feel Fine) (live)/Get Up (video)
Release date: October 1990
WB PRO-CDV-4460 (promotion only) **$20-32**

This nicely packaged promotion-only digi-pack CD plays three live audio tracks and one video track from *Tourfilm*.

Losing My Religion
Release date: February 19, 1991
WB PRO-CD-4707 (promotion only) **$8-15**

The lead single from *Out of Time* was supported by this nicely packaged promotional picture CD, with full inserts.

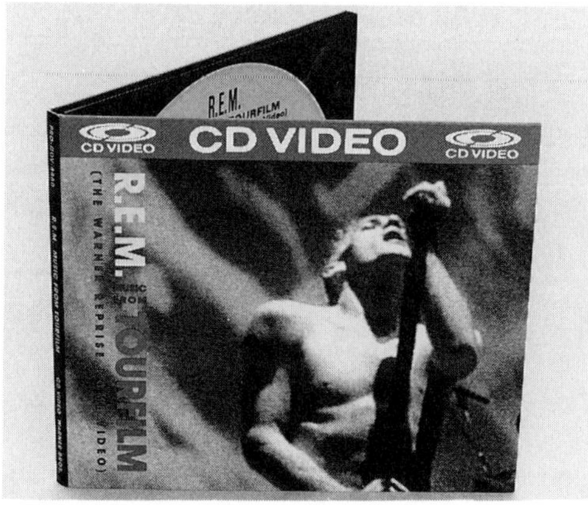

■ The Tourfilm promo CD/video (PRO-CDV-4460)

Texarkana
Release date: May 1991
WB PRO-CD-4826 (promotion only, with back insert) **$8-15**

This promotional picture CD for "Texarkana" was released in the U.S., though the single was never released commercially in any format. The album track enjoyed a brief chart career, peaking at #3 on the Modern Rock chart in mid-June 1991.

Losing My Religion (live acoustic)
Release date: June 1991
WB PRO-CD-4881 (promotion only, with back insert) **$14-18**

This live version of the first single from *Out of Time* was recorded on the syndicated call-in show "Rockline," on April 1, 1991. The live track was issued outside the U.S. on the B-side of the "Shiny Happy People" twelve-inch and CD singles.

Shiny Happy People
Release date: July 1991
WB PRO-CD-4888 (promotion only, with back insert) **$5-9**

"Shiny Happy People" was supported by this promotional five-inch CD single in the U.S., released shortly after the live version of "Losing My Religion."

Shiny Happy People (Music Mix)/Shiny Happy People (Pop Mix)/Shiny Happy People (Hip Mix)
Release date: September 1991
WB PRO-CD-5060 (promotion only) **$15-25**

These remixes of "Shiny Happy People," complete with plenty of scratching and sampling, were also released as a promotional twelve-inch single in the U.S. The "Music Mix" was issued as a B-side on the U.S. "Radio Song" twelve-inch single.

Radio Song
Release date: October 1991
WB PRO-CD-4808 (promotion only, with back insert) **$5-9**

Radio Song (Tower of Luv Bug Mix)/Love is All Around/Belong (live)
Release date: November 1991
WB 9 40229-2 **$5-7**

The remixed version of "Radio Song," along with two live B-sides, was issued in the U.S. as a commercial five-inch CD single, and twelve-inch vinyl single. "Love is All Around" was recorded live on FM on "Rockline" in April 1991, while "Belong" was taken from a performance in Greensboro, North Carolina, in November 1989.

Near Wild Heaven
Release date: March 1992
WB PRO-CD-5058 (promotion only, with back insert) **$5-8**

This promotional CD of "Near Wild Heaven" was scheduled to be shipped to radio the day after the Grammy awards telecast, providing R.E.M. took the Grammy for "Album of the Year" with *Out of Time*. Natalie Cole, not R.E.M., was the big winner at the 1991 Grammys, so the discs were not shipped. Rather than destroy them, Warner Brothers sent 3,500 of the discs to the R.E.M. fan club in April 1992, who mailed them out to members.

Drive/Winged Mammal Theme
Release date: October 1992
WB 9 18729-2 **$5-6**

"Drive," the first single from *Automatic For the People*, was released in the U.S. in three formats, CD, cassette, and seven-inch single. All of the singles play the same B-side, but the CD and cassette singles were released in four different sleeves. Yellow sleeves (with a photo of Michael Stipe on the reverse), blue sleeves (Buck), green sleeves (Berry) and red sleeves (Mills) were all available and all carry the same stock number.

Drive
Release date: October 1992
WB PRO-CD-5700 (promotion only) **$5-8**

This disc was shipped in a cardboard slipcase with a picture sleeve. The reverse depicts each of the four pictures of the band members that graced the backs of the commercial "Drive" singles.

Ignoreland
Release date: December 1992
WB PRO-CD-5844 (promotion only, with back insert) **$5-8**

In addition to the version of this track which appeared on *Automatic For the People* and on this promo CD, the band also recorded another take, which they dubbed the "Bad Horn Version." This unreleased version features the band's engineer on trumpet and Mike Mills on trombone.

Man on the Moon (edit)/(album version)
Release date: January 1993
WB PRO-CD-5894 (promotion only, with back insert) **$5-8**

Man on the Moon/New Orleans Instrumental #2
Release date: January 1993
WB 9 18642-4 **$5-6**

The Sidewinder Sleeps Tonite
Release date: April 1993
WB PRO-CD-5903 (promotion only, with back insert) **$5-8**

The Sidewinder Sleeps Tonite/The Lion Sleeps Tonight
Release date: April 1993
WB 9 18523-2 **$5-6**

U.K. ISSUES

The One I Love/Last Date/Disturbance at the Heron House (live)
Release date: September 1987
I.R.S. DIRM 146 **$15-20**

The first commercial R.E.M. CD single released in the U.K. was this five-inch single of "The One I Love" backed with "Last Date" and a live take of "Disturbance at the Heron House." The back cover misspells "Heron House" as "Henron House." In some cases, the packaging for this disc was also used for U.K. promotional copies of the "It's the End of the World" CD illustrated below, making these discs look very confusing for collectors, because the tracks on the promotional CD ("It's the End of the World"/"Finest Worksong"/"The One I Love") did not match those listed on the cover. As a result, these are sometimes referred to as "mis-pressed" CDs, which they are not. To further confuse matters for collectors, both the stock single of "The One I Love" and promo single of "It's the End of the World" use the same catalog number.

It's the End of the World As We Know It (and I Feel Fine)/Finest Worksong/ The One I Love
Release date: September 1987

I.R.S. DIRM 146 (promotion only) **$30-40**
I.R.S. DIRM 146 (promotional disc in commercial packaging) **22-30**

This three-track promotional five-inch CD single was issued in unique black and white promotional packaging, making it an instant collectible. As stated above, a number of these discs were shipped for promotion using the inserts for the "The One I Love" single.

Finest Worksong (LP version)/Time After Time, Etc. (live)/It's the End of the World As We Know It (and I Feel Fine)
Release date: April 1988

I.R.S. DIRM 161 **$18-25**

A special limited package, this six-inch box with a three-track five-inch CD single was released only in the U.K. The letters R.E.M. on the box are cut out to reveal the disc inside. The CD boxes were numbered, and at least 6,000 were sold. The disc includes the live recording of "Time After Time," which also appeared as a B-side on U.K. seven and twelve-inch singles.

The One I Love/Fall On Me/So. Central Rain
Release date: October 1988
I.R.S. DIRM 173 **$10-12**

One year after "The One I Love" was originally issued, the track was again chosen to be a single, this time from the LP *Eponymous*. A twelve-inch single containing the same three tracks was released along with this CD.

The One I Love/This One Goes Out (live)/Maps and Legends (live)
Release date: October 1991
I.R.S. DIRMT 178 **$10-12**

The release of this "limited edition" CD single (and its companion four-track single) suggested that I.R.S. intended not only to unabashedly duplicate Warner Brothers' marketing scheme for the *Out of Time* CD singles, but that they would also go as far as to nearly duplicate the packaging design for their singles as well. This maneuver was apparently intended to confuse CD buyers as to what exactly was the "new product." I.R.S.'s attempt to copy both Warner Brothers' marketing strategy and product is best summarized by their statement, printed on the CD insert, concerning the live B-sides of the two "The One I Love" singles. The inserts of the

I.R.S. singles state that "Together they will form a unique record of R.E.M. live," whereas in referring to the B-sides of the Warner Brothers limited edition CD singles, the inserts state that "Collectively they will form a unique record of R.E.M. in concert." The two statements are printed in nearly identical type styles and use similar layouts.

The disc insert contains a poorly written ten-page band biography by Ted Mico that is often factually incorrect, and makes no mention of the band's first performance at the church in Athens. The second track on the CD, "This One Goes Out" (live), is identical to the live acoustic version of "The One I Love" that appeared on previous singles.

The One I Love/Driver 8 (live)/Disturbance at the Heron House (live)/Crazy
Release date: October 1991
I.R.S. DIRMX 178 **$10-12**

Released concurrently with the three-track single above was this issue of "The One I Love," backed with two live tracks and the LP track "Crazy" from *Dead Letter Office*. The live version of "Driver 8," recorded in Seattle in 1984, is identical to the version that appears on the U.S. promotional twelve-inch single of "Driver 8" and the U.K. twelve-inch of "Wendell Gee," while the live recording of "Disturbance at the Heron House" was taken from the band's performance at McCabe's Guitar Shop in May 1987. The CD insert contains a four-page discography of the band's commercial U.K. releases.

It's the End of the World As We Know It (and I Feel Fine)/Radio Free Europe/Time After Time, Etc. (live)
Release date: December 2, 1991
I.R.S. DIRMT 180 **$10-12**

The second single from *The Best of R.E.M.* in Europe was "It's the End of the World As We Know It," released as this five-inch CD single, backed with two "rare" tracks. The CD insert contains brief reviews of all of the band's albums, written by Andy Gill of *Q* magazine. Although the second track on the disc contains the I.R.S. version of "Radio Free Europe," discs were printed in error that stated they played the original Hib-Tone version of the song.

It's the End of the World As We Know It (and I Feel Fine)/Radio Free Europe (Hib-Tone version)/Last Date/White Tornado
Release date: July 1992
I.R.S. DIRMX 180 **$10-15**

Though this disc was scheduled to be released alongside the disc above, it didn't made it onto the shelves until seven months later, for as yet unknown reasons. When the disc did finally appear, it surfaced in Germany, and was only available in the U.K. as an import. Less than spectacular sales of the first "End of the World" reissue CD, and legal hassles regarding the release of the single have been cited as possibilities for its being delayed. The single was billed as a "Special edition containing rare and live tracks," though it essentially contained neither. Three of the tracks were available on other albums, and "Last Date" was incorrectly advertised as being a live version.

The One I Love/It's the End of the World As We Know It (and I Feel Fine)/Finest Worksong/Finest Worksong (Lengthy Club Mix)

Release date: March 1992

U.K.	I.R.S. REM-1	**$45-60**

I.R.S. released this promotional disc in order to capitalize on the popularity that R.E.M. enjoyed after *Out of Time* received multiple "Brit" awards in the U.K., the equivalent to the Grammy in the U.S. The disc was designed to promote *The Best of R.E.M.* in the U.K.

GERMAN ISSUES

Stand/Memphis Train Blues/Untitled (instrumental remix)

Release date: January 1989

WEA	W7577CD (921 148-2)	(standard packaging)	**$12-15**
WEA	W7577CDX (921 148-2)	(same disc in leaf shaped holder)	**18-25**

Containing the identical tracks as the British twelve-inch vinyl single, this three-inch CD was issued both in the standard three-inch picture sleeve, and in a special limited edition maple leaf shaped holder for collectors.

Orange Crush/Ghost Riders/Dark Globe

Release date: June 1989

WEA	2960CD (921 219-2)	**$12-15**

This three-inch CD single from *Green* contains the identical three tracks as the "Orange Crush" twelve-inch single released in the U.K.

Stand/Pop Song '89 (acoustic)/Skin Tight (live)

Release date: September 1989

WEA	W2833CD (921 307-2)	(standard packaging)	**$12-15**
WEA	W2833CDX (921 308-2)	(in velcro seal envelope)	**15-18**

Released alongside the "stencil pack" seven-inch single of "Stand," this three-inch disc contained the Westwood 1 live recording of "Skin Tight," a tune originally recorded by The Ohio Players. The black collectors' edition features a cutout window to reveal the disc inside, and seals with velcro.

Losing My Religion/Rotary Eleven/After Hours (live)

Release date: February 25, 1991

WB	W0015CD (9362 40037-2)	**$10-12**

R.E.M. fans in the U.K. were offered this five-inch CD single of "Losing My Religion," and the collector's edition below. No doubt most fans bought both, since their B-sides differed, and since the singles were released prior to *Out of Time*. This disc contains the non-LP track "Rotary Eleven" and a live cover of the Velvet Underground song, "After Hours."

■ The first "Stand" CD single in the leaf envelope

■ The black "collector's edition" of the "Stand" reissue

Losing My Religion/Stand (live)/Turn You Inside-Out (live)/World Leader Pretend (live)
Release date: March 11, 1991

WB	9362 40046-2		**$10-12**
WB	W0015CDX	(for U.K. market)	**10-12**

This "collector's edition" five-inch CD, containing three live tracks from *Tourfilm*, was available for a short time in April 1991 in Europe, and quickly sold out. The color insert for the CD folds out into a 9.5" x 9.5" mini-poster of the band. The disc insert states that these live tracks, along with the live B-side tracks from the forthcoming collector's edition CD singles collectively "will form a unique record of R.E.M. in concert." This, for the most part, would turn out to be quite a disappointment for fans, since Warner Brothers chose to simply use audio tracks from the *Tourfilm* video for many of the live B-sides.

As was the case for all of the collector's edition CD singles from *Out of Time*, the German issues and the editions made in Germany destined for export to the U.K. differ only slightly in appearance. The issues exported from Germany for the U.K. market do not have the words "Made in Germany" printed on the disc, and have a French catalog number printed on the back insert. The discs pressed for the U.K. market (W0015CDX) may climb in value, since the German single was reissued in December 1991 in a CD singles box set.

Shiny Happy People/Forty Second Song/Losing My Religion (live acoustic)
Release date: May 1991

WB	9362 40078-2		**$10-12**
WB	W0027CD	(for U.K. market)	**10-12**

From the *Out of Time* LP, "Shiny Happy People" followed "Losing My Religion" in England and Germany, and this was the standard five-inch CD single, issued in a slimline jewel box. The acoustic version of "Losing My Religion" was recorded on the radio program "Rockline."

Shiny Happy People/I Remember California (live)/Get Up (live)/Pop Song '89 (live)
Release date: May 1991

WB	9362-40079-2		**$10-12**
WB	W0027CDX	(for U.K. market)	**10-12**

This was the second "collector's edition" CD single from *Out of Time*, of which there seem to be considerably more of than the collector's single for "Losing My Religion." The disc was heavily imported into the U.S., and was still available in stores in England weeks after its release, unlike the first single. The live B-sides were taken from the *Tourfilm* video.

Near Wild Heaven/Tom's Diner (live)/Low (live)/Endgame (live)
Release date: August 5, 1991

WB	9362-40178-2		**$10-12**
WB	W0055CDX	(for U.K. market)	**10-12**
WB	9362-40195-2	(October 1991 reissue in slimline jewel box)	**10-12**

The third limited edition CD in Europe featured the single "Near Wild Heaven," plus three live tracks, recorded at a secret gig at the Borderline in London on March 15, 1991, where R.E.M. was booked as "Bingo Hand Job." "Tom's Diner" was originally performed by Suzanne Vega, and can be found on her *Solitude Standing* LP, released in 1987. The song was popularized by DNA in 1990, who added instrumentation and released their rap version of the song.

The four-track "Near Wild Heaven" single was reissued only two months after the initial release in Germany (9362-40178-2), this time packaged in a slimline jewel box rather than in the standard sized box.

Radio Song/You Are the Everything (live)/Orange Crush (live)/Belong (live)
Release date: November 4, 1991

WB	9362-40251-2		**$10-12**
WB	9362-40251-2	(double CD with interview disc)	**20-25**
WB	W0072CDX	(for U.K. market, issued in collector's slipcase)	**12-15**

The final limited edition CD single from *Out of Time* was "Radio Song," backed with three live tracks, once again culled from the *Tourfilm* video. Editions of the single pressed for the U.K. market were issued in a collector's slipcase large enough to hold the four limited edition CD singles, plus an additional disc, presumably the *Out of Time* CD. The German single was also packaged with the U.K. Backtabak *Shiny Chatty People* interview CD (CBAK 4041) and was released in a double CD jewel box in July 1992. The double CD set was advertised as being limited to 500 copies.

Radio Song (Tower of Luv Bug Mix)/Love is All Around/Belong (live)
Release date: December 1991

WB	9362-40229-2	**$10-12**

The "Tower of Luv Bug" mix of "Radio Song" appears on this five-inch CD single, released in a slimline jewel box. The B-sides are identical to those on the commercial U.S. five-inch "Radio Song" CD.

Losing My Religion/Fretless/Losing My Religion (live acoustic)/Rotary Eleven
Release date: March 1992

WB	9362-40399-2	**$10-12**

Shortly after the song "Losing My Religion" was nominated for a Grammy award in the U.S., Warner Brothers put together a special "Song of the Year" edition of the single for release in Germany. The CD release, in a slimline case, includes tracks that had all been previously released.

Drive/World Leader Pretend/First We Take Manhattan
Release date: October 1992

WB	9362-40634-2	**$10-12**
WB	W0136CD	**10-12**

This single was issued alongside the four-track "collector's edition" above. Warner Brothers used the LP version of "World Leader Pretend" from *Green* on the single, a track that surely everyone that bought this single already owned.

Drive/It's a Free World, Baby/Winged Mammal Theme/First We Take Manhattan
Release date: October 1992

WB	9362-40633-2		**$10-12**
WB	W0136CDX	(for U.K. market)	**10-12**

This single was backed by two previously unreleased tracks, as well as "First We Take Manhattan," a song that appeared on the *I'm Your Fan* Leonard Cohen tribute album to which the band contributed. A demo version of "It's a Free World, Baby" had been recorded during the *Out of Time* sessions, but the track did not make the cut on that album or on *Automatic For the People*.

Man on the Moon (edit)/Turn You Inside Out/Arms of Love
Release date: November 1992

WB	9362-40698-2		**$10-12**
WB	W0143CD	(for U.K. market)	**10-12**

For this single, Warner Brothers pulled another track off of the *Green* LP to use as a B-side, this time choosing "Turn You Inside-Out." The tracks on this CD, issued in a slimline case, are identical to those on the twelve-inch single for "Man on the Moon."

Man on the Moon (edit)/Fruity Organ/New Orleans Instrumental #2/Arms of Love
Release date: November 1992

WB	9362-40710-2		**$10-12**
WB	W0143CDX	(for U.K. market)	**10-12**

The second collector's edition five-inch CD single from *Automatic For the People* in Europe contained three non-LP tracks, two instrumentals, and a cover of a Robyn Hitchcock song, "Arms of Love."

The Sidewinder Sleeps Tonite/The Lion Sleeps Tonight/Fretless
Release date: February 1993
WB W0152CD1 (for U.K. market) $10-12

The first of the two CD singles for "The Sidewinder Sleeps Tonite" was backed with two non-LP tracks. "The Lion Sleeps Tonight" was subsequently used as the B-side for U.S. issues of the single.

The Sidewinder Sleeps Tonite/Organ Song/Star Me Kitten (demo)
Release date: February 1993
WB W0152CD2 (for U.K. market) $10-12

Released a few weeks after the above disc, this issue of "The Sidewinder Sleeps Tonite" was backed with two more non-LP tracks, the throwaway instrumental "Organ Song," and an interesting demo version of "Star Me Kitten." The demo is remarkably complete and ends with an amusing, "That's it. Do you like it?" from Michael Stipe.

The Sidewinder Sleeps Tonite/The Lion Sleeps Tonight/Fretless/Organ Song
Release date: March 1993
WB 9362-40782-2 $10-12

A third CD single for "The Sidewinder Sleeps Tonite" was released in Germany sometime after the first two were simultaneously issued. This time the single added three of the non-LP tracks that were used as B-sides on the above two discs. The disc was released in a slimline jewel box.

Everybody Hurts (edit)/New Orleans Instrumental #1 (Long Version)/ Mandolin Strum
Release date: April 1993
WB W0169CD1 (for U.K. market) $10-12

Warner Brothers chose the gentile "Everybody Hurts" as the fourth single from *Automatic For the People* in Europe, electing to use a 4:46 edit of the song rather than the full 5:20 album version. A 3:28 "Long Version" of "New Orleans Instrumental #1" and the non-LP track "Mandolin Strum," an outtake from *Out of Time*, were chosen as B-sides for the first "Everybody Hurts" CD single. "Mandolin Strum" was previously available to collectors on the bootleg CD *Time of Outtakes*.

Everybody Hurts (edit)/Dark Globe/Chance (dub)
Release date: April 1993
WB W0169CD2 (for U.K. market) $10-12

The second collector's edition CD single of "Everybody Hurts" was backed with the non-LP track "Chance," and the band's cover of Syd Barrett's "Dark Globe," recorded during the *Green* sessions. "Dark Globe" was advertised as being "currently unavailable on any other CD," but in fact was released in 1989 on the CD single of "Orange Crush."

DUTCH ISSUES

Finest Worksong (Other Mix)/Finest Worksong (Lengthy Club Mix)/Time After Time, Etc. (live)
Release date: November 1987
I.R.S. ILS 651320 **$15-25**

This three-inch single was issued for the European market in a five-inch case, and came with a free adaptor.

The One I Love/The One I Love (live)/Maps and Legends (live)
Release date: October 1991.
I.R.S. IC (560) 2045372 **$10-12**

With the release of *The Best of R.E.M.* in England and Germany, "The One I Love" was released as a single for the third time in four years. This three-track single, issued in a slimline jewel box, includes B-sides recorded live at McCabe's Guitar Shop in 1987.

It's the End of the World As We Know It (and I Feel Fine)/Radio Free Europe/Time After Time, Etc. (live)
Release date: March 1993
I.R.S. 7 2438 80478 2 **$10-12**

I.R.S. released this five-inch CD single some seventeen months after the above issue of "The One I Love." The three-track single was issued in a slimline jewel box.

FRENCH ISSUES

Half a World Away (acoustic)/Love is All Around (acoustic)/Losing My Religion (acoustic)
Release date: November 1991
WB PRO 2002-2 (promotion only) **$45-75**

Subscribers to the French rock magazine *Les Inrockuptibles* received this three-track CD, which features live acoustic material. The tracks were recorded during an FM radio broadcast from the Rockline studios in Los Angeles in April 1991.

The Sidewinder Sleeps Tonite/The Lion Sleeps Tonight/Fretless
Release date: February 1993
WB 936-40769-9 **$10-12**

This French CD single was issued in a cardboard slipcase.

JAPANESE ISSUES

Stand/Memphis Train Blues
Release date: May 1989
WB 10P3 6078 **$25-35**

The Japanese three-inch single for "Stand" is unique in that the sleeve contains the lyrics for the song on the back, both in English and Japanese. This single is very hard to locate now, though it was easily obtainable in the U.S. when it was first issued.

■ The Japanese CD singles of "Stand" and "Drive"

Drive/Winged Mammal Theme
Release date: November 1992
WB WPDP-6308 **$12-15**

This issue, like that for "Stand," contains lyrics to the song on the back of the sleeve.

Man on the Moon/New Orleans Instrumental #2
Release date: January 25, 1993
WB WPDP-6318 **$12-15**

AUSTRALIAN ISSUES

The Sidewinder Sleeps Tonite/The Lion Sleeps Tonight/Fretless
Release date: February 1993
WB 9362-4077-0-2 **$10-12**

BOXED SETS OF CD SINGLES

R.E.M. Singles Collection
Losing My Religion / Stand (live) / Turn You Inside-Out (live) / World Leader Pretend (live) / Radio Song / You Are the Everything (live) / Orange Crush (live) / Belong (live) / Shiny Happy People / I Remember California (live) / Get Up (live) / Pop Song '89 (live) / Near Wild Heaven / Tom's Diner (live) / Low (live) / Endgame (live)

Release date: December 1991 (Germany); June 1992 (Japan)

Germany	WB	9362-40313-2	**$40-45**
Japan	WB	WPCP-4781-4	**40-50**

The German box set containing all four of the previously released limited edition five-inch CD singles from *Out of Time*, released shortly after the "Radio Song" single, afforded collectors the opportunity to obtain a copy of the elusive "Losing My Religion" single, which had been selling for upwards of three times its original issue price. Six months later, Warner Brothers chose to release a similar 4CD package in Japan, this time in a handsome double jewel box, unlike the German edition, which came in a rather dull cardboard slipcase with no inserts. The Japanese version, subtitled "Pop Game '92," contains a booklet written in Japanese, which tells the history of the band. Also included in the Japanese set is a lyric sheet for all of the tracks, written in English and Japanese. A very rare cassette containing all sixteen tracks from the box was released in Japan for promotion.

CASSETTES

Cassettes are held in very low esteem among those that collect music. The durability of the cassette is generally poor, and their sound quality tends to decay rapidly with repeated playings. In addition, liner notes and lyric inserts (obviously not a problem with R.E.M...) are often omitted in the case of cassettes, in the interest of space. The visual impact of the artwork associated with a band's album is also severely impaired by the small amount of space that a cassette case insert offers.

However, a number of interesting and quite collectible R.E.M. cassettes exist, although they rarely, if ever, are offered up for sale. The most outstanding is clearly the "Cassette Set," which to my knowledge has never been publicly put up for sale. However, advance cassettes and "New Music Seminar" cassettes do appear every so often, and these are an important part of the band's history.

CASSETTE SINGLES

The eighties will be remembered for one thing in particular by record collectors: it's the decade when record companies phased out the seven-inch vinyl single in favor of the cassette. For over forty years the 45 RPM vinyl single, first introduced by RCA in 1949, was the standard format for every artist's releases, but sadly, the tradition seems to have been undermined by the smaller, more mobile and less fragile cassette. The bias of most collectors lies with the vinyl single; nonetheless, cassette singles are still collected.

■ A number of R.E.M. cassette singles have been released, but few collectors seek them out.

The One I Love/Maps and Legends (live)
Release date: August 1987

U.S.	I.R.S.	IRSC 53204		**$5-8**

It's The End Of the World As We Know It/Last Date
Release date: January 1988

U.S.	I.R.S.	IRSC 53220		**$4-7**

Stand/Memphis Train Blues
Release date: January 1989

U.S.	WB	9-27688-4		**$3-4**
U.S.	WB	9-21864-4	(b/w "Pop Song '89"; "Backtrax" oldies issue)	**3-4**

Orange Crush/Ghost Riders
Release date: May 1989

U.K.	WEA	W2960C		**$10-20**

Pop Song '89/Pop Song '89 (acoustic)
Release date: May 1989

U.S.	WB	9-27640-4		**$3-4**
U.S.	WB	9-27640-4	(backwards master)	**15-20**

Get Up/Fun Time
Release date: September 1989

U.S.	WB	9-22791-4		**$3-5**

Losing My Religion/Rotary Eleven
Release date: March 1991 (U.K.: February 1991)

Australia	WB	543919392-4	**$4-6**
France	WB	543919392-4	**4-7**
Holland	WB	300109-4	**4-6**
U.K.	WB	W0015C	**4-6**
U.S.	WB	9-19392-4	**3-4**

Shiny Happy People/Forty Second Song
Release date: July 1991 (U.K.: May 1991)

Australia	WB	543919307-4	**$4-6**
France	WB	543919307-4	**4-7**
Germany	WB	543919307-4	**4-7**
U.K.	WB	W0027C	**4-6**
U.S.	WB	9-19242-4	**3-4**

Near Wild Heaven/Pop Song '89 (live acoustic)
Release date: August 1991

Australia	WB	543919179-4	**$4-6**
France	WB	543919179-4	**4-7**
U.K.	WB	W0055C	**4-6**

The One I Love/Crazy
Release date: September 1991

U.K.	I.R.S.	IRMC 178	**$4-6**

Radio Song/Love is All Around
Release date: November 1991

Australia	WB	543919246-4	**$4-6**
U.K.	WB	W0072C	**4-6**
U.S.	WB	9-19246-4	**3-4**

Radio Song (Tower of Luv Bug Mix)/Love is All Around/ Belong (live)
Release date: December 1991

U.S.	WB	9-40229-4	**$5-7**

It's the End of the World As We Know It/Radio Free Europe
Release date: December 1991

U.K.	I.R.S.	IRMC 180	**$4-6**

Drive/Winged Mammal Theme
Release date: October 1992

Australia	WB	5439-18729-4		
France	WB	9-18708-4	(b/w "World Leader Pretend")	**$4-6**
U.K.	WB	W0136C	(b/w "World Leader Pretend")	**4-6**
U.S.	WB	9-18729-4	(issued in red, yellow, green, and blue picture sleeves)	**3-4**

Man on the Moon/New Orleans Instrumental #2
Release date: January 1993

Australia	WB	5439-18656-4	(b/w "Turn You Inside Out")	**$4-6**
U.K.	WB	W0143C	(b/w "Turn You Inside Out")	**4-6**
U.S.	WB	9-18642-4		**3-4**

The Sidewinder Sleeps Tonite/The Lion Sleeps Tonite
Release date: February 1993

Australia	WB	5439-18634-4	(b/w "Get Up")	**$4-6**
France	WB	5439-18597-4	(b/w "Get Up")	**4-6**
U.K.	WB	W0152C	(b/w "Get Up")	**4-6**
U.S.	WB	9-18523-4		**3-4**

Everybody Hurts/Pop Song '89
U.K. WB W0169C **$4-6**

OTHER COLLECTIBLE CASSETTES

Cassette Set
Sitting Still/Radio Free Europe/White Tornado

U.S. no catalog number **$350-500**

Just before the band was to make the trip up to New York to play The Ritz in June of 1981, they ran off about 400 copies of a three track demo cassette, and bombarded the New York press and club owners with the tape, or "Cassette Set." Recipients of the tape that were brave enough to break the seal warning "Careful- Do Not Open!" found no address or phone number for the band on most copies-- not even their full names. Later, some copies of the demo tape were sent to clubs and radio stations in other cities besides New York, and copies with an address for the band printed on the insert also exist. The tapes contained the two cuts from the Hib-Tone single, plus "White Tornado," and on about 100 copies, Mitch Easter's dub version of "Radio Free Europe." The dubbed version of the track, a severely twisted rendition of the song altered by studio tricks and sound effects, subsequently appeared on a bootleg entitled *Smoking in the Boys Room*, originally released in 1983.

Obviously the tape was in no way typical of a demo that a band would want to send out in order to get press or gigs, and this perhaps is why it was so appealing. "Sitting Still" on the cassette was prefaced by ten seconds of the song done "polka style," and tacked onto the end of the tape, after "White Tornado" was another take of the same track, where the song breaks down following some rather dissonant chords from Peter Buck, who is heard apologizing to the rest of the band for screwing up. In addition, inside the tape boxes were color photocopied pictures of the band, cut into small pieces. Despite the tape's blatant non-commerciality, *New York Rocker* critic Gary Sperrazza helped establish the band as critics' darlings by giving the tape a rave review in his "Crib Death" column. The review was so favorable that it inspired four record companies to write and ask for a copy of the tape. Like any right-thinking young American rock band on the move, R.E.M. threw the letters in the trash and pressed on.

Though no copy of this cassette has been publicly offered for sale in the last eight to ten years, if one were to surface and was offered for sale, it would have to be accompanied by a letter of authenticity or some other means of verifying its authenticity. This is because the cassette insert was made from photocopied white cardstock, and the color photocopied inserts could be easily duplicated. The cassette itself is a plain black plastic cassette, and the labels are simple white stickers with handwritten information by Michael Stipe.

Advance Cassettes

I.R.S.	CS 70502	Chronic Town	(no PS)	**$30-40**
I.R.S.	IRSC 5592	Fables of the Reconstruction		**30-40**
I.R.S.	CS 70054	Dead Letter Office	(no PS)	**15-20**
I.R.S.	IRSC 6262	Eponymous		**15-25**

For some of the R.E.M. albums that I.R.S. released in the U.S., including the *Chronic Town* EP, cassettes of the albums were sent out for promotional purposes, prior to their actual release dates. Both the cassettes themselves and the inserts for these advance releases differ from their commercial counterparts. The *Chronic Town* and *Dead Letter Office* advance cassettes were not issued with inserts. For the later albums on I.R.S., and for the Warner Brothers albums, promotional cassettes have stickers on them indicating that they are not for sale, but are otherwise are identical to the commercial issues.

Of course, all of the band's albums have been released commercially on cassette as well, but these are generally not considered collectible. The only one of real interest is the first edition of the *Murmur* cassette, which on the insert indicates that the cassette includes "There She Goes Again." The track was pulled from the album just prior to its release, but these inserts had already been printed, and were used despite the error.

I.R.S. New Music Seminar cassettes

year	title	R.E.M. track(s)	
1982	Rebellious Jukebox	"1,000,000"	**$25-35**
1983	Hearing Aids	"Talk About the Passion"	**25-30**
1984	Lovelier After Forty	"Pretty Persuasion," "Pale Blue Eyes"	**25-30**
1986	Convention Fever	"Fall On Me," "These Days"	**15-25**
1987	Road Show 1987	"The One I Love"	**15-20**

Perhaps the most interesting cassette compilations featuring R.E.M. tracks are those that were released annually by I.R.S. for promotion. The first of these was the "Rebellious Jukebox" cassette (the name of which was taken from a song by The Fall), which featured "1,000,000" from the *Chronic Town* EP, along with some other interesting releases by other bands from the early days at I.R.S. Records.

■ The New Music Seminar cassettes from I.R.S. contained tracks by R.E.M. as well as other popular I.R.S. artists, including The Go-Go's, The English Beat, and Wall of Voodoo.

Bang Zoom cassette magazine
Release date: 1983
Issue #3 **$15-25**

Issue three of this new music cassette magazine, released in 1983, includes a ten-minute interview with Michael Stipe, and features snippets of "Catapult," "Sitting Still," and "West of the Fields."

R.E.M. Murmur and Reckoning
Release date: 1990
U.K. A&M AMC 24109 **$10-15**

A double length cassette containing both albums.

FULL-LENGTH PROMOTIONAL SAMPLERS ON ALL FORMATS

An AOR Radio Staple

It's the End of the World As We Know It (and I Feel Fine) / The One I Love / Fall On Me / I Believe / Pretty Persuasion / So. Central Rain / Superman / Driver 8 / Can't Get There From Here / Talk About the Passion / Radio Free Europe

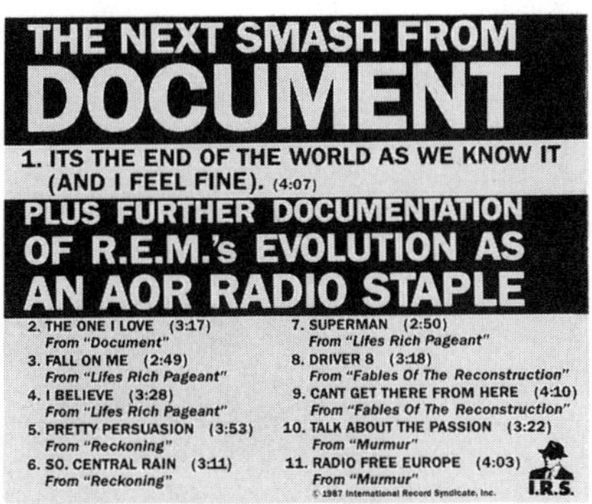
THE NEXT SMASH FROM
DOCUMENT
1. ITS THE END OF THE WORLD AS WE KNOW IT (AND I FEEL FINE). (4:07)
PLUS FURTHER DOCUMENTATION OF R.E.M.'s EVOLUTION AS AN AOR RADIO STAPLE
2. THE ONE I LOVE (3:17) From "Document"
3. FALL ON ME (2:49) From "Lifes Rich Pageant"
4. I BELIEVE (3:28) From "Lifes Rich Pageant"
5. PRETTY PERSUASION (3:53) From "Reckoning"
6. SO. CENTRAL RAIN (3:11) From "Reckoning"
7. SUPERMAN (2:50) From "Lifes Rich Pageant"
8. DRIVER 8 (3:18) From "Fables Of The Reconstruction"
9. CANT GET THERE FROM HERE (4:10) From "Fables Of The Reconstruction"
10. TALK ABOUT THE PASSION (3:22) From "Murmur"
11. RADIO FREE EUROPE (4:03) From "Murmur"
© 1987 International Record Syndicate, Inc.
I.R.S.

■ The back insert from the AOR Radio Staple CD. "AOR" is the abbreviation for "Album-Oriented Rock."

Release date: August 1987

U.S.	I.R.S.	IRSD-seven	(with green and white back insert)	**$75-115**
U.S.	I.R.S.	IRSD-seven	(with black and white back insert)	**75-115**
U.S.	I.R.S.	IRSD-seven	(with "End of the World" front insert)	**100-135**

Released in America in support of *Document*, this compilation featured eleven tracks that spanned the band's career to date. The lead track was "It's the End of the World As We Know It," and the disc featured tracks from all other R.E.M. LPs prior to the release of *Document*, with the exception of *Chronic Town*. Most copies of the disc were packaged with a green and white back insert, however, there are editions with black and white inserts. In addition, the first copies shipped included the *Rolling Stone* cover reproduction that was used for the American promotional CD for "It's the End of the World As We Know It" (IRSC 53220). Though the disc contains nothing but standard LP tracks, it remains a very popular collectible in the U.S. and overseas.

Documenting R.E.M. 1983 to 1987

Finest Worksong / Welcome to the Occupation / Exhuming McCarthy / Disturbance at the Heron House / Strange / It's the End of the World As We Know It (and I Feel Fine) / The One I Love / Fireplace / Lightnin' Hopkins / King of Birds / Oddfellows Local 151 / Radio Free Europe / Pretty Persuasion / So. Central Rain / Life and How To Live It / Can't Get There From Here / Driver 8 / Fall On Me / Superman / Cuyahoga / (All I've Got To Do Is) Dream

Release date: August 1987

Canada	I.R.S.	IRS 14U	**$35-45**

This extremely rare cassette is roughly the Canadian equivalent to the *AOR Radio Staple* CD that was issued in the U.S. to promote *Document*. It is virtually never offered for sale anywhere, probably because so few copies exist. The tape was sent for promotion along with the *Document* press kit in Canada.

Should We Talk About the Weather

Release date: December 1988

U.S.	CD	WB	PRO-CD-3377	**$25-40**
U.S.	LP	WB	PRO-A-3377	**25-40**

This nicely packaged Warner Brothers "Words and Music" release was prepared to promote *Green*, and featured music from the album and interviews with all four members of the band. At least part of all of the *Green* tracks are included on the disc. Portions of the interview material can also be heard on Media America's 1989 "Up Close" CD radio show featuring the band.

■ *Should We Talk About the Weather* was issued on LP and CD in the US to promote *Green*.

■ *Documenting R.E.M.*, a Canadian cassette sampler

R.E.M. Singles Collection

Losing My Religion / Stand (live) / Turn You Inside-Out (live) / World Leader Pretend (live) / Radio Song / You Are the Everything (live) / Orange Crush (live) / Belong (live) / Shiny Happy People / I Remember California (live) / Get Up (live) / Pop Song '89 (live) / Near Wild Heaven / Tom's Diner (live) / Low (live) / Endgame (live)

Release date: March 1992
Japan cassette WB PTS 2039 **$45-75**

Issued in Japan to promote the *Singles Collection* boxed set of CD singles, this rare cassette contains all sixteen tracks found on the four discs. Unlike their German counterparts, the four CD singles in the Japanese boxed set were not released individually prior to the release of the set.

Berry, Buck, Mills, Stipe

Drive / The Sidewinder Sleeps Tonite / Everybody Hurts / Man on the Moon / Find the River / Losing My Religion / Shiny Happy People / Radio Song / Near Wild Heaven / Orange Crush / Stand / Pop Song '89 / Drive

Release date: November, 1992
Japan CD WB PCS-105 **$250-350**

This thirteen track sampler CD was released to promote *Out of Time* in Japan and is evidently very rare, judging by the prices that dealers have gotten for it. Curiously, "Drive" appears twice on the disc.

■ The Japanese CD sampler *Berry, Buck, Mills, Stipe*

The Alternative Radio Sampler

1,000,000 / Talk About the Passion / Pretty Persuasion / Driver 8 / Cuyahoga / It's the End of the World As We Know It (and I Feel Fine) / Gardening at Night (live to two-track)

Release date: November, 1992
U.K. CD I.R.S. CDREM 92 **$75-150**

With the re-release of the I.R.S.-era R.E.M. albums on CD in Holland and Japan in 1992, I.R.S. released this sampler disc, which includes one track from each R.E.M. album originally released on I.R.S. The sampler also includes a version of "Gardening at Night" previously unreleased-- a live to two-track recording of the song made during the *Reckoning* sessions. This version of "Gardening at Night" is not the same one that appeared on the *Dead Letter Office* reissue CD which contained bonus tracks.

R.E.M. SIDE BAND AND SOLO RELEASES

Gonna Have a Good Time Tonight/Narrator (Hindu Love Gods)
Release date: June 16, 1985

■ The Hindu Love Gods sleeve was drawn by Bill Berry.

U.S.	I.R.S.	52867		**$8-15**
U.S.	I.R.S.	52867	(promotional label)	**12-18**
U.S.	I.R.S.	52867	(without picture sleeve)	**7-9**
Canada	I.R.S.	52867		**15-20**

The Hindu Love Gods was a side band that Peter Buck, Mike Mills and Bill Berry created in 1984, with the concept that the Love Gods could have a go at some fun, esoteric cover songs in the small clubs that R.E.M. was too big to play. The original line-up of the then one-single band consisted of Peter Buck, Bill Berry, and Mike Mills along with Warren Zevon and Bryan Cook. Cook, the singer, was a local Athens musician who fronted the band Time Toy, and played in other lesser-known Athens bands, Is Ought Gap and Club Gaga, and can be seen performing in the film *Athens, GA-Inside/Out*. "Gonna Have a Good Time Tonight" was originally recorded by The Easybeats in 1968, and can be heard on their LP *Falling Off the Edge of the World* (United Artists UAS 6667). The B-side of the single, "Narrator," was one of R.E.M.'s earliest compositions. The Love Gods played a few dates around Athens in January 1984, and pressure from a letter writing campaign by R.E.M. fans inspired by the fan club resulted in the single's release. The band played live only a handful of times, the most memorable of which included Zevon belting out "Werewolves of Athens," a slightly skewed rendition of his best known song.

As the press release for the single indicated, there was "No video, no tour, no album." But the relationship with Warren Zevon was a good one, and resulted in the appearances of the three R.E.M. members on Zevon's next album, *Sentimental Hygiene*. Strangely, though, Sandra Lee Phipps' photograph on the back of the "Gonna Have a Good Time Tonight" single was cropped so that Zevon couldn't be seen. White label promotional copies of the single were released, and the single was also released in Canada. The Canadian issue uses the U.S. picture sleeve. In the U.S., I.R.S. shipped out a number of copies of the single without picture sleeves after the sleeves ran out.

My Bible is the Latest TV Guide/Things I'd Like to Say (13111)

Release date: September 1989

U.S.	Dog Gone	DOG 13111	**$8-12**

After about a year of delays, this solo project by Bill Berry was finally released in the fall of 1989 on manager Jefferson Holt's "Dog Gone Records" label. The label and jacket contain no mention of Bill Berry or R.E.M. No word yet as to any hidden meaning behind Bill's pseudonym, "Stashus Mute," but according to Peter Buck, Bill chose the name 13111 for his "band" because when the numbers are written close together, they come close to forming the word "Bill." The B-side is a cover of a tune originally recorded by the New Colony Six in 1968, which was released as a seven-inch single (Mercury 72858), and appeared on the LP *Revelations* (SR-61165).

Hindu Love Gods *Hindu Love Gods*

Release date: October 1990

U.S.	CD/cassette	Giant	2-24406/4-24406	**in print**
U.S.	CD	Giant	9 24406-2 (promotional edition)	**$16-20**
U.S.	cassette	Giant	9 24406-4 (advance promotional edition)	**9-12**
U.S.	press kit			**10-15**
Germany	LP/CD/cassette	Giant	7599-24406-1/2/4	**in print**

U.S. singles

CD	PRO-CD-4414	Raspberry Beret (promotion only)	**$5-9**

U.K. singles

7"	W9502	Raspberry Beret/Wang Dang Doodle	**$5-7**
12"	W9502T	Raspberry Beret/Wang Dang Doodle/Mannish Boy	**8-10**

German singles

7"	5439-19502-7	Raspberry Beret/Wang Dang Doodle	**$5-7**
12"	7599-21798-0	Raspberry Beret/Wang Dang Doodle/Mannish Boy	**8-10**

Most R.E.M. fans probably figured that when the Hindu Love Gods single was released in 1986, it was the beginning and the end of that band's career. To the surprise of many, including perhaps the members of R.E.M., the Love Gods returned in 1990 with a full-length album, released in the U.S., U.K. and Germany. These tracks differed from those that had been released earlier, in that Bryan Cook does not appear on the album, and Warren Zevon handles all of the vocal duties. Indicative of the impromptu nature of the recording session was Michael Stipe's comment in a radio interview, "I would be on that record except I went to dinner and when I came back, the album was finished."

The tracks were originally recorded when R.E.M. was in the studio with Zevon in 1986, backing him on his *Sentimental Hygiene* LP. Their cover of Prince's "Raspberry Beret" was released in the U.S. as a promotional CD single, and in Germany and the U.K. as a seven-inch and twelve-inch single, with the twelve-inch containing the additional track "Mannish Boy." In the U.S., a press kit was released in support of the album as well, as was an advance cassette that differs substantially from the commercial issue. In addition to the above listed singles, "Mannish Boy" was also included on the Reprise CD *Follow Our Tracks vol. V* (PRO-CD-4557). The members of R.E.M. did not appear in the "Raspberry Beret" video, despite the wishes of record company executives.

RADIO SHOWS

Some of the most highly sought-after and highest priced R.E.M. collectibles are the albums and CDs pressed for radio broadcast only. Radio stations subscribe to these programs which are recorded and produced by the companies that distribute them. The largest of these companies in the U.S. is Westwood One (WW1), which has produced a number of R.E.M. shows. The R.E.M. live concert discs are particularly in demand, and prices for the original broadcast discs for R.E.M. shows have escalated rapidly in the past few years.

All of the live R.E.M. radio shows have been heavily bootlegged. At least three different packagings exist for bootlegs of the Seattle Source show, and at least that many exist for the Nottingham show that was recorded in 1984, and the "Superstars in Concert" show from 1989. The original discs sell for over $200 for all of these shows, and that's why the bootlegs are so popular at around $20-30. In addition to the shows listed below, most weekly Top 40 radio shows are pressed as three or four record sets, and for the weeks that R.E.M. had a charting single, these shows will contain the album version of that particular single.

Radio shows are generally worth a bit more when accompanied by their cue sheets, or a copy of them. With the exception of the radio shows that are in the countdown format (Top 40 and the like), radio LPs and CDs that feature one standard studio track from an album are listed in the chapter called "R.E.M. Tracks on Soundtracks and Compilations." All radio shows listed were manufactured in the U.S. unless noted.

Armed Forces Radio
U.S. Army RL 22-7 1LP **$25-35**
One side of this record includes the first three tracks from each side of *Dead Letter Office*, "Crazy," "There She Goes Again," Burning Down," "Windout," "Ages of You," and "Pale Blue Eyes."

BBC Rock Hour/London Wavelength

BBC 603 1LP **$175-250**

Recorded at Rock City, Nottingham, England, November 21, 1984. This is the U.S. version of the BBC Transcription disc, but this show lacks "West of the Fields." The disc contains commercials. Broadcast January 20, 1985.

Tracks: Hyena / Talk About the Passion / (Don't Go Back To) Rockville / Auctioneer / So. Central Rain / Sitting Still / Old Man Kensey / Gardening at Night / 9-9 / Windout / Driver 8 / Pretty Persuasion / Radio Free Europe

Earth News Radio

WW1 Sept. 2, 1985 1LP **$14-18**

Music and interviews, with R.E.M. tracks. This show features two interview tracks with Bill Berry, and one with Peter Buck and Mike Mills (incorrectly identified as Buck). All interview tracks use part of "Can't Get There From Here."

WW1 Dec. 8, 1986 1LP **$14-18**

Includes an interview track with Peter Buck, and uses part of "Superman."

WW1 May 15, 1989 1LP **$14-18**

Includes interview material with Michael Stipe and Bill Berry, and features an excerpt of "It's the End of the World As We Know It (and I Feel Fine)."

Guest DJ

PFM GDJ 84-133 1LP **$75-100**

Peter Buck sits in as Guest DJ for this show. The disc includes the album tracks "So. Central Rain," "Little America," "Windout," and "Radio Free Europe" by R.E.M., and studio cuts from Jason and the Scorchers, The Shangri Las, The Fleshtones, Sly and the Family Stone, Let's Active, Chuck Berry, The Cramps, and Rain Parade. Broadcast October 8, 1984.

■ The "Guest DJ" show with Peter Buck is not as pricey as many of the other full-length R.E.M. radio shows, but is rarely seen for sale.

■ The BBC Transcription disc is one of the top R.E.M. collectibles. It regularly sells for over $500.

In Concert

BBC CN 4516/S 1LP **$425-800**

Recorded at Rock City, Nottingham, England, November 21, 1984. The disc was pressed in the U.K., and contains no commercials. It is widely known as the "BBC transcription disc." Broadcast May 1985.

Tracks: Hyena / Talk About the Passion / West of the Fields / (Don't Go Back To) Rockville / Auctioneer / So. Central Rain / Sitting Still / Old Man Kensey / Gardening at Night / 9-9 / Windout / Driver 8 / Pretty Persuasion / Radio Free Europe

In Concert

WW1 PS-86-24 2LP **$140-225**

One of the two LPs in this set contains excerpts from the band's performance on November 21, 1984 in Nottingham, England. The other disc contains live tracks by The Alarm. Broadcast November 24, 1986.

R.E.M. tracks: West of the Fields / (Don't Go Back To) Rockville / Auctioneer / So. Central Rain / Sitting Still / Driver 8 / 9-9 / Windout / Pretty Persuasion / Radio Free Europe

WW1 90-09 2LP **$125-210**

A re-packaging of the 1989 3LP "Superstars in Concert" show (CO89 143), using the same 20 songs. Broadcast April 30, 1990.

WW1 93-14 2CD **$85-100**

Disc two of this show contains ten of the original fourteen live R.E.M. tracks released on the "BBC Transcription Disc." The first disc contains live material by The Screaming Trees. Broadcast March 29, 1993.

R.E.M. tracks: Talk About the Passion / (Don't Go Back To) Rockville / So. Central Rain / Old Man Kensey / Gardening at Night / 9-9 / Windout / Driver 8 / Pretty Persuasion / Radio Free Europe

In Concert-- The Best of In Concert (Part One)

WW1 92-52 2LP **$25-35**

This "Best Of" show includes three live tracks by R.E.M., all taken from the "Superstars in Concert" package. The R.E.M. tracks are, "Orange Crush," "It's the End of the World As We Know It (and I Feel Fine)," and "Stand." Broadcast December 21, 1992.

Innerview with Jim Ladd

Inner View #33, show 13 1LP **$50-85**

Also released as #37, show 5 and #38, show 10. The disc features interviews with Michael Stipe and includes a number of R.E.M. album tracks. All shows contain the same interview material and cuts, but have different commercials. The tracks are not all played in their entirety. Released in 1985.

Tracks: 1,000,000 / Can't Get There From Here / So. Central Rain / Good Advices / (Don't Go Back To) Rockville / Radio Free Europe / Pretty Persuasion / Second Guessing / Green Grow the Rushes / Driver 8 / Life and How To Live It / Maps and Legends / Talk About the Passion

Isle of Dreams

WW1 9LP **$40-50**

Tracks by various artists, compiled for a Labor Day special. Includes live versions of "Finest Worksong," "Pop Song '89," and "Stand," all culled from the earlier "Superstars in Concert" discs. Broadcast October 1989.

MTV Video Music Awards 1991

Premiere MTV SP 3LP **$25-35**

A promotional radio show for MTV's video music awards for 1991. Includes a segment of "Losing My Religion" on disc 1, and on disc 3, another segment of "Losing My Religion," as well as the full album track. Broadcast August 30, 1991.

Music View

New Program 1P-7865, #50 1LP **$25-30**

R.E.M.'s Peter Buck is the "Feature Interview" for this show. The first segment includes a Buck interview, part of "Gardening at Night," and the full LP track of "Get Up." Later in the show Buck is again interviewed, and part of "Underneath the Bunker" and the LP track "Stand" are heard. Music View shows include a seven-inch single of dailies and promotional spots, and on the disc promoting this show, Buck is interviewed on two separate tracks. Broadcast March 13, 1989.

Joseph Fox 1P-7992, #81 1LP **$15-20**

Show #81. Includes interviews with Pete Buck and Kevn Kinney, and two tracks from Kinney's *MacDougal Blues* LP which Buck produced. Included on the seven-inch single of dailies and promos are two tracks of interview material with Buck and Kinney. Broadcast 1990.

Off the Record with Mary Turner

WW1 OTR 7-30-84 1LP **$16-20**

Includes two brief Pete Buck interviews, and parts of "So. Central Rain" and "Pretty Persuasion." Broadcast July 30, 1984.

WW1 OTR-1-18-88 1LP **$16-20**

Music and interviews, featuring four brief interview segments with Peter Buck. Broadcast January 1988.

WW1 W 89-09 2LP **$45-55**

Music and interviews, broadcast February 1989.

Tracks: These Days / Get Up / Stand / Catapult / Hyena / Orange Crush / I Believe / So. Central Rain / Superman / Fall On Me / The One I Love / Turn You Inside-Out / Finest Worksong / It's the End of the World As We Know It (and I Feel Fine) / Pop Song '89

WW1 91-20 2LP **$40-55**

Music and interviews, broadcast May 13, 1991.

Tracks: Get Up / Orange Crush / Me in Honey / Low / It's the End of the World As We Know It (and I Feel Fine) / Stand / Fall On Me / Radio Song / Pop Song '89 / (Don't Go Back To) Rockville / Belong / Shiny Happy People / The One I Love / Finest Worksong / Losing My Religion

WW1 91-38 2LP **$40-55**

A later issue of the above show, which contains the identical tracks.

WW1 92-47 CD **$40-55**

Music and interviews, broadcast November 16, 1992.

Tracks: Pop Song '89 / Try Not to Breathe / Ignoreland / The One I Love / Drive / Losing My Religion / Nightswimming / Get Up / It's the End of the World As We Know It (and I Feel Fine) / Orange Crush / Man on the Moon / Finest Worksong / Radio Song

On the Edge

WW1 92-48 1CD **$50-70**

Music and interviews with members of the band. Broadcast November 23, 1992.

Tracks: Pop Song '89 / Ignoreland / So. Central Rain / Superman / Drive / The One I Love / Get Up / Losing My Religion / Man on the Moon / Finest Worksong / Orange Crush / Radio Song / Nightswimming

WW1 93-12 1CD **$40-50**

Music and interviews with R.E.M. The disc is basically a repeat of the above show, minus the last four tracks. In place of the last four tracks from the previous R.E.M. *On the Edge* are four tracks by Grant Lee Buffalo. Broadcast March 15, 1993.

R.E.M. tracks: Pop Song '89 / Ignoreland / So. Central Rain / Superman / Drive / The One I Love / Get Up / Losing My Religion / Man on the Moon

On the Radio

WW1 OR 91-20 1LP **$12-15**

Includes brief interviews with Bill Berry and Peter Buck, and the LP versions of "Losing My Religion" and "Stand." Broadcast May 18, 1991.

WW1 OR 91-25 1LP **$12-15**

Includes an interview with Peter Buck, and the LP version of "Losing My Religion." Broadcast June 22, 1991.

WW1 OR 91-28 1LP **$12-15**

Includes interview segments with Bill Berry and Peter Buck, and includes the LP versions of "Losing My Religion" and "Shiny Happy People." Broadcast July 13, 1991.

WW1 OR 91-35 1LP **$12-15**

A countdown companion disc, includes an open-ended interview with Peter Buck. Broadcast August 30, 1991.

Penthouse/Omni Magazine College Rock Special

BBC 1017 1LP **$50-70**

This show centers around Mitch Easter and Let's Active, but also includes the studio takes of "Pilgrimage" and "Carnival of Sorts (Boxcars)" by R.E.M. Broadcast January 29, 1984.

The Rock Chronicles

WW1 85-46 2LP **$35-55**

Music and interview segments with Peter Buck and Mike Mills. Portions of "Driver 8," "Radio Free Europe," "Talk About the Passion," "Catapult" and "So. Central Rain" are heard, plus the LP track "Can't Get There From Here." Broadcast November 1985.

WW1 RC-84-41 2LP **$14-18**

Features a brief interview with Peter Buck, and the studio track of "Fall On Me." Broadcast October 6, 1986.

Rock of the World

MCA ROW 046 1LP **$20-25**

Music and interviews with various artists. This show features Bill Berry interviews, as well as "Superman," "Driver 8," "Fall On Me," and part of "Radio Free Europe." Broadcast November 26, 1986.

MCA 87-06 1LP **$20-25**

This disc includes Bill Berry interviews, plus "I Believe," Radio Free Europe," "Superman," and an excerpt of "Feeling Gravitys Pull." Broadcast February 13, 1987.

MCA 8722 1LP **$20-25**

Includes interviews with Bill Berry and the album cuts "Ages of You," "Fall On Me," "Driver 8," and "Toys in the Attic." Broadcast June 1987.

Rock Over London (AOR version)

R.O.L. ROL 91-22 1CD **$12-20**

This disc contains the live version of "Losing My Religion" as recorded on "Rockline." Broadcast May 27, 1991.

R.O.L. ROL 91-32 1CD **$25-30**

A special "Live Over London" edition, featuring the live version of "Pop Song '89," from *Tourfilm*. Broadcast August 5, 1991.

R.O.L. ROL 91-35 1CD **$12-18**

Includes the live version of "Tom's Diner" recorded in London in March 1991. Broadcast August 30, 1991.

R.O.L. ROL 91-36 1CD **$12-18**

Includes the same track as above. Broadcast September 6, 1991.

R.O.L. 1CD **$12-18**

Includes an R.E.M. track. Broadcast October 14, 1991.

Rock Over London (CHR version)

R.O.L. ROL 91-36 **$12-18**

Includes the live version of "Tom's Diner." Broadcast September 6, 1991.

R.O.L. ROL 91-37 **$12-18**

Includes the live version of "Tom's Diner." Broadcast September 13, 1991.

Rock Stars with Timothy White

WW1 WO 89-C 2LP **$85-120**

Subtitled *The Green Tour of America*, this show contains music and interviews with all four members of R.E.M. This is probably the best of the "music and interview" shows on R.E.M. released, and also contains an exclusive track, the original demo of "Pop Song '89." Broadcast May 1989.

Tracks: Stand / World Leader Pretend / Get Up / Radio Free Europe / (Don't Go Back To) Rockville / Perfect Circle / The One I Love / Fall On Me / Can't Get There From Here / It's the End of the World As We Know It (and I Feel Fine) / Pop Song '89 (original demo) / Orange Crush

Rock Today

MJI RT-71 1LP **$20-25**

Includes an interview with Peter Buck over the intro to "I Believe," as well as the album track "Superman." Broadcast November 10, 1986.

MJI RT-299 2LP **$20-25**

For most of the double LP "Rock Today" shows like this one, only one of the two LPs is the actual radio show, while the other contains open-ended brief interview segments, or actualities. The program disc for this show includes the LP track "Losing My Religion," and an interview segment with Peter Buck, during which part of "Walter's Theme" is heard the background. Buck is also featured on one track on the actuality disc. Broadcast March 25, 1991.

MJI RT-302 2LP **$20-25**

The program disc includes the album version of "Losing My Religion," and contains a scathing review of *Out of Time*, courtesy of Dave Marsh. Broadcast April 15, 1991.

MJI RT-303 2LP **$25-32**

Music and interviews with Michael Stipe. R.E.M. is the "cover story" for this week. In addition to portions of "Belong," "Walter's Theme," "Underneath the Bunker," and "White Tornado," the full LP cuts of "Orange Crush," "Texarkana," "Losing My Religion," and "Radio Song" are heard. The second disc contains five actualities with Michael Stipe. Broadcast April 22, 1991.

MJI RT-304 2LP **$20-25**

The program disc contains "Losing My Religion," and Michael Stipe spins Roger McGuinn's "Someone to Love" in an "Artist's Choice" segment. The actuality disc includes one brief interview with Michael Stipe. Broadcast April 29, 1991.

MJI RT-314 2LP **$25-32**

R.E.M. is the "cover story" for this show. The program disc includes interview segments with Michael Stipe, parts of "Country Feedback," "Walter's Theme," "Underneath the Bunker," and the LP tracks "Texarkana" and The One I Love." The actuality disc includes five interview segments with Stipe. Broadcast July 8, 1991.

MJI RT-319 2LP **$20-25**

The program disc includes a brief interview with Michael Stipe, and the LP track "Shiny Happy People. The actuality disc includes one interview track with Stipe. Broadcast August 12, 1991.

MJI RT-321 2LP **$20-25**

The actuality disc includes one interview and one one-minute "daily" with Michael Stipe. Broadcast August 26, 1991.

MJI RT-342 1LP **$20-25**

R.E.M.'s 1991 Grammy nominations are the lead story on this disc. The show includes a brief interview with Michael Stipe, and plays the album track "Losing My Religion." January 20, 1992.

Rock Trends

MCA 2CD **$22-30**

This top 20 countdown show contains a brief R.E.M. interview. Broadcast August 1989.

Rocklines

Global Satellite Vol 2. 1CD **$15-20**

Contains three short interview segments with Mike Mills from a Rockline radio show. Released 1989.

Rolling Stone's Continuous History of Rock & Roll

ABC vol. II #97 2LP **$35-45**

This show, entitled "The New Americans," profiles R.E.M., and features parts of "Laughing" and "Pilgrimage" as well as the I.R.S. version of "Radio Free Europe." The band is also the subject of one of the show's trivia questions. This radio show was the first to contain R.E.M. tracks or interviews. Broadcast August 14, 1983.

Should We Talk About the Weather
WB PRO-A-3377 2LP and 1CD (PRO-CD-3377) **$25-40**
Though technically not a radio show meant for broadcast, this "Words and Music" promotional release from Warner Brothers is often advertised as a radio show. The program was released in December 1988 to promote *Green*, and features numerous interview segments, but no unusual tracks.
Tracks: Pop Song '89 / Stand / Orange Crush / Get Up / You Are the Everything / The Wrong Child / World Leader Pretend / Turn You Inside-Out / I Remember California

The Source
NBC 84-28 2LP **$700-1,000**
Recorded live at Seattle's Music Hall, June 27, 1984, this double LP was accurately described by one dealer as "The Holy Grail of R.E.M. radio shows." Prices for this show have climbed to astronomical heights in the last few years, because the show is probably the rarest and certainly the most in demand of all the R.E.M. live shows on disc. Broadcast July 20-22, 1984.
Tracks: Moral Kiosk / Driver 8 / Catapult / Hyena / Camera / Pilgrimage / Talk About the Passion / Seven Chinese Brothers / So. Central Rain / Pretty Persuasion / Gardening at Night / 9-9 / Windout / Old Man Kensey / Radio Free Europe / Little America / Sitting Still / Burning Down / Pale Blue Eyes 1,000,000 / So You Want to Be a Rock and Roll Star / Carnival of Sorts (Boxcars) / Skank

■ "The Source" radio discs (NBC 84-28) have sold for as much as $1,000.

The Source Best of New Groups on Tour
NBC 84-38 3LP **$80-125**
A five-sided, various artists radio show. The R.E.M. tracks "Seven Chinese Brothers," "So. Central Rain," and "Pretty Persuasion" from the above July 20, 1984 concert in Seattle make up one entire side.

Stars of the Superstars
WW1 89-33 3LP **$45-65**
A year-end special, which contains "Pop Song '89," "Orange Crush," and "It's the End of the World As We Know It (and I Feel Fine)" from the previously released "Superstars" set. Released December 1989.

Superstars in Concert
WW1 CO89 14 3LP **$175-250**
Recorded in Miami and Orlando, Florida, April 1989. The show was later repackaged in 1990 for the Westwood 1 "In Concert" series. Despite the fact that this show contains the identical tracks as the "In Concert" repackaging, the 3LP version generally sells for more than the 2LP version. Broadcast July 1989.
Tracks: Pop Song '89 / Exhuming McCarthy / Welcome to the Occupation / Disturbance at the Heron House / Turn You Inside-Out / Orange Crush / Feeling Gravitys Pull / Begin the Begin / Pretty Persuasion / I Believe / Swan Swan H / King of Birds / Crazy / Finest Worksong / You Are the Everything / Academy Fight Song / Stand / Perfect Circle / Get Up / It's the End of the World As We Know It (and I Feel Fine)

Up Close

Med. America 89-08 2CD **$195-275**

One hour of music and interviews with R.E.M. The discs are silkscreened with custom graphics. Broadcast March 1989.

Tracks: Turn You Inside-Out / Pop Song '89 / Stand / Radio Free Europe / (Don't Go Back To) Rockville / Perfect Circle / The One I Love / Fall On Me / Can't Get There From Here / Superman / It's the End of the World As We Know It (and I Feel Fine) / The One I Love / Oddfellows Local 151 / Finest Worksong / Exhuming McCarthy / Ages of You / World Leader Pretend / Orange Crush

■ The first R.E.M. "Up Close" radio show, released in 1989

Med. America 91-13 2CD **$90-120**

One hour of R.E.M. music and interviews, with custom graphics printed on the disc. Some copies may not include the live version of "Fall On Me." Broadcast June 1991.

Tracks: Radio Song / Losing My Religion / Near Wild Heaven / Radio Free Europe / So. Central Rain / (Don't Go Back To) Rockville / Driver 8 / Can't Get There From Here / Fall On Me (live from MTV Unplugged) / Superman / It's the End of the World As We Know It (and I Feel Fine) / The One I Love / Oddfellows Local 151 / Finest Worksong / Ages of You / Stand / Turn You Inside-Out / Pop Song '89 / World Leader Pretend / Orange Crush / Shiny Happy People / Texarkana

Med. America 92-24 2CD **$90-120**

One hour of R.E.M. music and interviews, with custom graphics printed on the disc. Broadcast November 16, 1992.

Tracks: Drive / Try Not to Breathe / The Sidewinder Sleeps Tonite / Radio Free Europe / So. Central Rain / (Don't Go Back To) Rockville / Driver 8 / Can't Get There From Here / Superman / Fall On Me The One I Love / It's the End of the World As We Know It (and I Feel Fine) / Finest Worksong / Pop Song '89 / Stand / Orange Crush / Radio Song / Texarkana / Losing My Religion / Shiny Happy People / Nightswimming / Ignoreland

Westwood 1 Rock in Review 1991

WW1 3CD **$25-35**

A triple CD package that contains a few live R.E.M. cuts from previous Westwood 1 recordings.

R.E.M. TRACKS ON SOUNDTRACKS AND COMPILATIONS

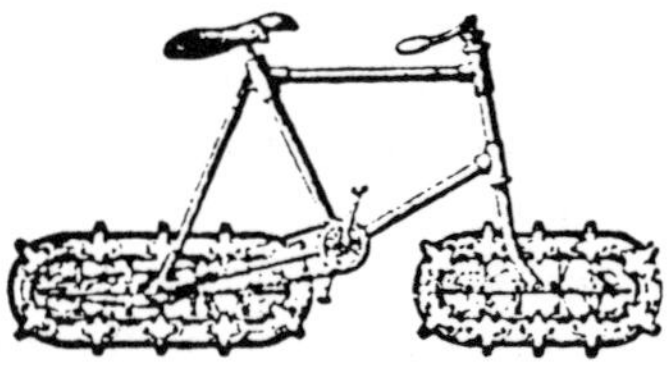

In addition to the items listed below, promotional editions of many compilation and soundtrack LPs with R.E.M. tracks exist, and these are worth slightly more than stock copies to collectors. A few of these promotional issues are valued here, but promotional editions of other items listed exist. In many cases, promotion copies of newer releases issued on CD have the word "promotion" printed in red on the disc, and otherwise do not differ from the stock copies.

Bachelor Party (Motion Picture Soundtrack)
Release date: June 18, 1984

Australia	LP	I.R.S.	ELPS 4444		**$6-9**
U.K.	LP	I.R.S.	IRSA 7051		**6-8**
U.S.	LP	I.R.S.	SP 70047		**4-6**
U.S.	LP	I.R.S.	SP 70047	(with promotional stamp)	**6-8**
U.S.	cassette	I.R.S.	SP 70047		**4-6**

This soundtrack, the first commercially available compilation LP to contain an R.E.M. track, includes "Windout," an outtake from *Reckoning*. The track was later included on *Dead Letter Office*.

Live for Life
Release date: April 21, 1986

Canada	LP	I.R.S.	5371		**$6-9**
U.K.	LP	I.R.S.	MIRF 1013		**6-8**
U.K.	cassette	I.R.S.	MIRFC 1013		**4-7**
U.S.	LP	I.R.S.	5371		**4-6**
U.S.	LP	I.R.S.	5371	(with promotional stamp)	**6-9**
U.S.	cassette	I.R.S.	5371		**4-6**

This album was issued by I.R.S. as a special benefit release for the AMC Cancer Research Center, with all proceeds going to the center. The album includes "Ages of You" by R.E.M., a *Reckoning* outtake, which appeared on *Dead Letter Office*. The record also includes previously unreleased live and studio tracks by Squeeze, The Police, The Bangles, The Go-Go's, and Sting, among others.

Athens, GA-Inside/Out (Motion Picture Soundtrack)

Release date: February 9, 1987

U.K.	LP	Illegal	ILP 017		**$20-25**
U.K.	cassette	Illegal	ILP 017	(advance cassette)	**10-15**
U.S.	LP	I.R.S.	6185		**10-15**
U.S.	cassette	I.R.S.	IRSC-6185		**7-10**

The soundtrack to Tony Gayton's documentary about the Athens music scene circa 1986 included two R.E.M. tracks, an acoustic rendition of "Swan Swan H," and a lighthearted cover of the Everly Brothers' "(All I Have To Do Is) Dream," though it is incorrectly titled (All I've Got To Do Is) Dream" on the LP. The two songs were recorded live in the Lucy Cobb Chapel on Milledge Avenue in Athens. The fact that this album contained R.E.M. tracks was hardly the only reason to buy this record, as it is loaded with great stuff by other combos, in particular two rousing live rockers by the Flat Duo Jets. The hardcore scene is represented by the Bar-B-Q Killers, whose vocalist Laura Carter appears on the album cover. The soundtrack was never issued on CD anywhere, but the two R.E.M. tracks were included on the 1993 European and Japanese CD reissues of *Lifes Rich Pageant*.

Kickin' Back to the Future

Release date: 1987

Japan	CD	CBS/Sony	32DP 843	**$35-55**

This is one of the better compilations that includes R.E.M. tracks, but the disc is virtually never seen for sale. The R.E.M. tracks are "Fall On Me," "Radio Free Europe," and "Ages of You." Also included on the CD are tracks by Concrete Blonde, Wall of Voodoo, Stan Ridgeway, Let's Active, and Timbuk 3.

Made in Heaven (Motion Picture Soundtrack)

Release date: 1988

U.S.	LP	Elektra	60729-1		**$6-8**
U.S.	LP	Elektra	60729-1	(with promotional label)	**7-10**
U.S.	cassette	Elektra	60729-4		**in print**

R.E.M. donated "Romance" to this soundtrack, a song that was originally written in early 1982, and was known to tape traders as "Easy Come, Easy Go." It was during the recording of "Romance" in Atlanta where the band first met and worked with Scott Litt, who would go on to produce *Document*, *Green*, *Out of Time*, and *Automatic For the People*. The track was later made available on the LP *Eponymous*.

Winter Warnerland

Release date: November 1989.

U.S.	2LP	WB	PRO-A-3328	(promotion only)	**$30-35**
U.S.	CD	WB	PRO-CD-3328	(promotion only)	**30-35**
U.S.	cassette	WB	PRO-C-3328	(promotion only)	**15-25**

Warner Brothers released this special collection of music and Christmas greetings for Christmas 1989, with "Deck the Halls" as R.E.M.'s contribution. The double album version of the package contains one red and one green vinyl disc, and the CD version is a picture disc.

Rainbow Warriors

Release date: September 1989

Japan	LP	Geffen	D32Y0312		**$18-22**
Japan	CD	Geffen	D32Y0312		**20-25**
Japan	CD	Geffen	D32Y0312	(promotional edition)	**25-30**
U.K.	LP	BMG/RCA	PL 74065		**12-16**
U.S.	LP	Geffen	GHS 24236-1		**9-12**
U.S.	LP	Geffen	GHS 24236-1	(with promotional stamp)	**10-12**
U.S.	CD/cassette	Geffen	GHS 24236-2/4		**in print**
USSR	LP	Melodia	A60 00439 008		**18-22**

The proceeds from this double album were to go to the establishment of a Greenpeace office in Russia, and sales of the double LP on Melodia were reportedly brisk. The album, which contains tracks by Western bands as diverse as Huey Lewis and The Grateful Dead, was the first of its kind to be released behind the Iron Curtain. The Russian LP contains a 15-page booklet about Greenpeace and the bands that donated the tracks. In Japan, a special promotional double CD issue was released, in a cardboard slipcase with a unique cover. R.E.M. contributed the LP version of "It's the End of the World" to the compilation, and as Michael Stipe put it in a radio interview, "They chose the song-- we didn't. I thought it was kind of an ironic choice. It does mention Brezhnev in it, and I had to submit the lyrics to the government to okay them, and they did okay them so I guess they thought it was okay."

Where the Pyramid Meets the Eye

Release date: November 1990

U.S.	CD/cassette	Sire/WB	2-26422/4-26422		**in print**
U.S.	cassette	Sire/WB	4-26422	(advance promotional cassette)	**$8-12**

When Bill Bentley set out to organize this tribute to 13th Floor Elevators front man Roky Erickson, the first band he asked to contribute to the album was R.E.M. When tours took R.E.M. through Erickson's home town of Austin, Texas, the band members frequently contacted Erickson. Because of these efforts, Bentley knew that R.E.M. were admirers of Erickson, who is widely referred to as the father of psychedelic music. This album features a cover of Erickson's "I Walked With a Zombie" by R.E.M., a song that Erickson originally recorded on the 1980 *Roky Erickson and the Aliens* LP issued in England.

Tom's Album

Release date: September 1991

U.S.	LP/CD/cassette	A&M	75021 5363 1/2/4	**in print**

"Tom's Diner," the popular *a capella* track off of Suzanne Vega's *Solitude Standing* LP, was covered by a number of artists since the album's release in 1987, and Vega herself was responsible for collecting these cover versions together on this album. The contribution from R.E.M. was from their performance as Bingo Hand Job in London, in March 1991.

I'm Your Fan

Release date: November 25, 1991 (U.K. and Germany: September 1991)

Germany	LP/CD/cassette	Columbia/Oscar	COL 469032	**in print**
U.K.	LP/CD/cassette	East West	9031-75598	**in print**
U.S.	CD/cassette	Atlantic	7 82349-2/4	**in print**

R.E.M. contributed the studio track "First We Take Manhattan" for this tribute to Canadian avant-folk singer Leonard Cohen. The album is the brainchild of Christian Fervet, editor of *Les Inrockuptibles*, a French rock magazine. *I'm Your Fan* (the title of which is derived from a Cohen album called *I'm Your Man*) includes seventeen Cohen covers, by The Pixies, James, and Lloyd Cole among others. R.E.M.'s contribution charted briefly in January 1992 on *Billboard*'s Modern Rock chart. U.S. copies of the CD were stickered to indicate that the disc contained an original R.E.M. track.

Until the End of the World (Motion Picture Soundtrack)

Release date: December 10, 1991 (Germany: October 1991)

Germany	LP/CD/cassette	WB	7599-26751	**in print**
U.K.	LP/CD/cassette	WB	7599-26707	**in print**
U.S.	CD/cassette	WB	2 26707/4-26707	**in print**

The soundtrack to the Wim Wendors film *Bis ans Ende der Welt* (translation: "Until the End of the World") contains the R.E.M. track "Fretless," a powerful and moving piece that is easily as compelling as any of the tracks from the *Out of Time* album. R.E.M. had been performing the song under the working title "Benjamin Caroline Love Triangle" for some time prior to the release of the soundtrack on which it would eventually appear. Michael Stipe would go as far as to jokingly introduce the song as "A song by New Order called 'Bizarre Love Triangle' " at the Borderline in London in 1991, playing on the similarity of their working title for the song and the well known New Order song. The studio version of "Fretless" features backing vocals by Kate Pierson of The B-52's. The U.S. and German editions of the soundtrack have entirely different cover designs.

R.E.M. TRACKS ON ADDITIONAL COMPILATIONS:

Promotional Issues and Radio Shows

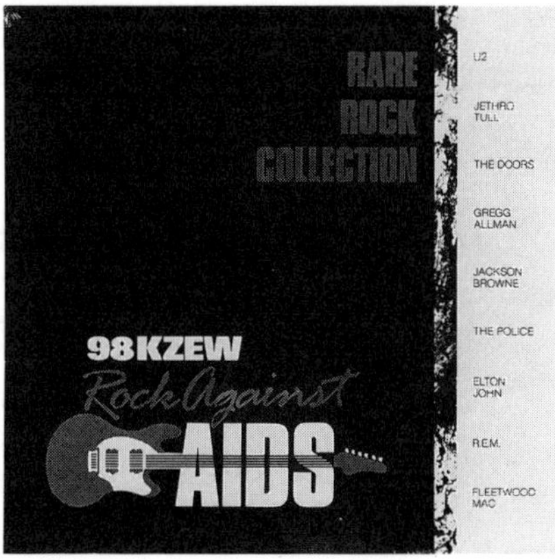

■ *98 KZEW Rock Against Aids* with "Tighten Up"

■ Promo #62 from Brazil includes "Orange Crush."

Radio Free Europe (Hib-Tone version) on C.M.J.'s 10th anniversary set, 1989				
U.S.	5CD	C.M.J.	10-CD 1001	**$50-65**
Radio Free Europe (I.R.S. version) on *Wake Up, It's 1984*				
Holland	cassette	CBS	SAMP MC67	**$12-15**
Radio Free Europe (I.R.S. version) on *Indie City*, 1988				
U.K.	2 LP	NME	Pro 8/036-037 (promotion only)	**$25-50**
U.K.	2 cassette	NME	036-037 (commercial)	**10-20**
So. Central Rain, **Harborcoat**, **Second Guessing** on *Sizzlin' Sounds*, 1984				
Canada	cassette	A&M/IRS	no catalog #	**$15-20**
Can't Get There From Here on *New Rock Collection*, 1985				
Brazil	LP	CBS	950104	**$25-35**
Tighten Up on *98 KZEW Rock Against Aids*, 1987				
U.S.	LP	KZEW	no catalog #	**$20-30**
The One I Love on *CD Tune Up #6*, 1987				
U.S.	CD	Album Net.	6	**$10-12**
The One I Love on *John Landers Hit Music U.S.A.*, December 1987				
U.S.	4LP	USP	12-26-87	**$9-12**
The One I Love on *John Landers Hit Music U.S.A.*, January 1988				
U.S.	4LP	USP	1-31-88	**$9-12**
The One I Love on *John Landers Hit Music U.S.A.*, March 1988				
U.S.	4LP	USP	3-5-88	**$9-12**
The One I Love on *International Record Syndicate, Inc.*, 1989				
Japan	CD	I.R.S.	CDS 20	**$18-25**
The One I Love on *Future Hits*, October 2, 1987				
U.S.	LP	WW1		**$9-12**
It's the End of the World As We Know It on *Rock Trends*, November 16, 1987				
U.S.	2CD	MCA	8746	**$15-20**

Finest Worksong on *Friday Morning Quarterback Album Report #1*, February, 1988
U.S. cassette FMQB 1 **$5-10**

Finest Worksong (Other Mix) on *Album Network CD Tune Up #14*, February 22, 1988
U.S. CD Album Net. 14 **$10-12**

Orange Crush on *Album 88 Alternative CD Sampler #4*, Georgia State University, 1988
U.S. CD Discovery Vol. 4 **$10-15**

Orange Crush on *Warner Brothers New Music Report*, 1988
U.S. CD WB PRO-CD-3339 **$10-15**

Orange Crush on *Future Hits*, January 20, 1989
U.S. LP WW1 **$8-10**

Orange Crush on *Hits: The Bride of Post Modern*, 1989
U.S. CD Hits Mag. HT003 **$12-15**

Orange Crush on *Album Network CD Tune-Up #26*, 1989
U.S. CD Album Net. 26 **$12-15**

Orange Crush on *Promo #62*, 1989
Brazil LP WEA 6WP.0065 **$35-45**

Deck the Halls on *Album Network Christmas CD Tune-Up*, December, 1990
U.S. CD Album Net. A1H00200B **$20-25**

Deck the Halls on *Christmas Rarities on Compact Disc* volume 8, November, 1991
U.S. CD WW1 8 **$22-28**

Stand on *Rock Star Special 1*, 1989
Brazil LP WEA 6WP.1008 **$30-45**

Stand on *Promo Disco Internacional* #33, 1989
Brazil LP WEA 6WP.1033-B **$35-45**

Stand on various artists 12-inch EP "Only For Dee Jays," 1989
Italy LP WEA PROMO 352 (no PS) **$25-35**

Stand on *Rick Dees On the Line*, April 3, 1989
U.S. 2LP DIR RD-OTL 4389, show #892-2 **$8-10**

Stand on *John Landers Hit Music U.S.A.*, March 17, 1989
U.S. 4LP USP 3-17-89 **$9-12**

Stand on *Pioneer Super Stars Super CD*, 1989
U.S. CD WEA WEA/P-SCD-1 **$10-12**

Stand on *Cutting Edge*, 1989
U.S. CD WB OPCD-1592 **$10-12**
U.S. cassette WB OPCS-1592 **5-8**

Pop Song '89 on *Hitmakers Top 40 CD Sampler*, May 5, 1989
U.S. CD Hitmakers 20 **$10-12**

Turn You Inside-Out on *Follow Our Tracks*, 1989
U.S. CD WB PRO-CD-3503 **$10-15**
U.S. LP WB PRO-A-3503 **8-12**

Get Up on *Album Network Rock 40 CD #17*, August 21, 1989
U.S. CD Album Net. 17 **$10-15**

Get Up on *Friday Morning Quarterback* sampler, September 1989
U.S. cassette FMQB no catalog # **$8-10**

Hit Disc promo CD sampler, includes an R.E.M. cut from *Green*, September 22, 1989
U.S. CD HD 807B **$10-15**

Losing My Religion on *Album Network Rock Tune-Up #62*, February 25, 1991
U.S. CD Album Net. 62 **$10-12**

Losing My Religion on *WEA In Store Cassette*, 1991
U.K. cassette WEA #70 **$8-10**

Losing My Religion on *Hitmakers Top 40 CD sampler*, March 8, 1991
U.S. CD Hitmakers 49 **$10-12**

Losing My Religion on *Future Hits*, March 22, 1991
U.S. LP WW1 91-12 **$8-10**

Losing My Religion on *Future Hits*, March 29, 1991
U.S. LP WW1 91-13 **$8-10**

Losing My Religion on *Party America*, May 3, 1991
U.S. LP Cutler 5-3-91 **$7-10**

Losing My Religion on *Party America*, June 7, 1991
U.S. LP Cutler 6-7-91 **$7-10**

Shiny Happy People on *United Kingdom New Releases*, 1991
U.K. CD WB #4 **$10-15**

Shiny Happy People on *Hitdisc*, July 10, 1991
U.S. CD HD 898B **$10-12**

Shiny Happy People on *Party America*, August 23, 1991
U.S. LP Cutler 8-23-91 **$7-10**

Shiny Happy People on *Party America*, August 30, 1991
U.S. LP Cutler 8-30-91 **$7-10**

Shiny Happy People on *Party America*, September 6, 1991
U.S. LP Cutler 9-6-91 **$7-10**

Shiny Happy People on *Party America*, September 13, 1991
U.S. LP Cutler 9-13-91 **$7-10**

Texarkana on *Fluid Formations: Follow Our Tracks volume 6*, May 1991
U.S. CD WB PRO-CD-4634 **$10-15**

First We Take Manhattan on *Rock Over London*, AOR version, October 1991
U.S. CD R.O.L. ROL 91-43 **$10-15**

Radio Song (Tower of Luv Bug Mix) on *Spring Forward, Fall Tracks: Follow Our Trax volume VII*, January 1992
U.S. CD WB PRO-CD-5066 **$10-15**

Half A World Away (live, from Rockline) on *Trademark of Quality*, 1992
U.S. CD WB PRO-CD- **$12-15**

Ghost Reindeer in the Sky on *Rarities on Compact Disc volume 12*, December, 1992
U.S. CD WW1 12 **$16-25**

Losing My Religion (live) on Mountain Stage four-track sampler EP, 1993
U.K. CD **$15-20**

Commercial Issues

Gardening at Night on *Jamming! Presents A New Optimism*, December 1984
U.K. LP Situation 2 SITU 11 **$12-20**

Radio Free Europe (I.R.S. version) on *Just What the Doctor Ordered*, 1985
Greece LP I.R.S. ILP 26807 **$18-25**
Holland LP I.R.S. ILP 26807 **18-25**
Israel LP I.R.S. ILP 26807 **18-25**

So. Central Rain on *Formula 20*, 1984
U.S. 2LP K-TEL NU4300 **$8-10**

Harborcoat on *KROQ Presents the Normal Noise of I.R.S.*, 1984
Japan LP I.R.S. 28AP 2830 **$30-40**
Driver 8 on *American Rock*, 1985
U.S. LP K-TEL TU 1490 **$8-10**

Fall On Me and **(All I Have To Do Is) Dream** on *The Best of I.R.S.*, 1987
Greece LP I.R.S. LSP 980142-1 **$20-25**

Superman on *These People are Nuts*, I.R.S. Records tenth anniversary compilation, 1989

Canada	cassette	I.R.S.	82010	**$6-9**
U.S.	CD	I.R.S.	82010	**12-20**
U.S.	cassette	I.R.S.	82010	**6-8**

The One I Love on *I.R.S. The Singles*, 1990
U.K. LP I.R.S. MIRL 1501 **$10-12**

The One I Love on *L.A. Freeway: The Story of a Journey to L.A.*, October 1991
U.K. LP Dino Ent. DIN-MC25 **$10-12**

The One I Love on *Rock the First* volume 2, February 1992
U.S. CD/cass. Sandstone D233042-2/D233042-4 **in print**

It's the End of the World As We Know It on *Dream a Little Dream* soundtrack, 1989

U.S.	LP	Cypress	14166-0125-1	**$4-7**
U.S.	CD/cass.	Cypress	14166-0125-2/14166-0125-4	**in print**

It's the End of the World As We Know It on *Flashback* soundtrack, 1990

U.S.	LP	WTG	46042-1	**$4-7**
U.S.	CD/cass.	WTG	46042-2/4	**in print**

It's the End of the World As We Know It on *Earthrise-- The Rainforest Album*, 1992
Germany CD E.L.F. EDL 2595-2 **in print**

Orange Crush on *Never Mind the Mainstream...The Best of MTV's 120 Minutes* volume 2, 1991
U.S. CD/cass. Rhino R2 70546/R4 70546 **in print**

Shiny Happy People on *Awesome 2*, October 21, 1991
U.K. CD EMI CDP 7 98249 **in print**

Losing My Religion (live) on *The Best of Mountain Stage volume 2*, December, 1991
U.S. CD/cass. Blue Plate BPM002 CD/BPMC002 **in print**

Losing My Religion on *The Rolling Stone Collection*, March 1993.

U.S.	7 CD	Rolling Stone	**$65-85**
U.S.	7 cassette	Rolling Stone	**40-70**

APPEARANCES AND PRODUCTION BY R.E.M. MEMBERS

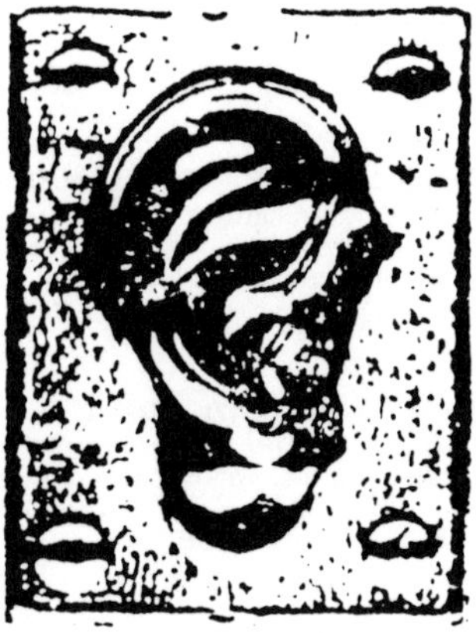

As early as 1983, the members of R.E.M. were lending their talents to their fellow musicians in the studio. Peter Buck is responsible for most of the records being listed in this section, but Michael Stipe and Mike Mills have also produced and performed on a number of albums and singles by other artists. Bill Berry evidently prefers to do otherwise, having only appeared on a handful of other artists records.

Values for some of the items listed in this section are not necessarily due to demand by R.E.M. collectors, but by collectors of the artists on whose albums R.E.M. members performed or produced. For example, fans of Jason and the Scorchers and Michelle Malone are responsible for the values listed for the original *Fervor* and *New Experience* albums. As discussed in the previous section on soundtracks and compilations, gold-stamped promotional copies of many of the LPs in this section exist, and are worth somewhat more than stock copies to collectors.

Jason and the Scorchers *Fervor*

Michael Stipe appears on "Hot Nights in Georgia" and co-wrote "Both Sides of the Line." The EP, originally released in 1983, was re-released on EMI America in 1984 in the U.S. and U.K., and included an extra cut.

U.S.	LP	Praxis	PR 6684	**$25-35**
U.S.	LP	EMI America	SQ-19008	**6-10**
U.K.	LP	EMI	EE24 00801	**10-14**

The Replacements *Let it Be*

Peter Buck appears on "I Will Dare." Released in 1984.

U.S.	LP	Twin Tone	TTR-8441	**$6-9**
U.K.	LP	Zippo Zong	002	**12-15**

singles

12"	Twin Tone	TTR-8440	I Will Dare/20th Century Boy/Hey Good Lookin' (live)	**$12-15**

Spongetones *Torn Apart*
R.E.M. contributes hand claps on "Shock Therapy." Released in 1984.
U.S. LP Ripete 2154 **$4-8**

The Fleshtones *Speed Connection II.*
Peter Buck appears on "Windout," and "When the Night Falls," recorded live at The Gibus Club, Paris, on March 4, 1985. U.K. versions of this album (ILP 26412) include a different version of the song without Peter Buck. Both the U.S. and U.K. LPs were released in 1985. The live version of "Windout" featuring Buck was also included on the Greek LP *The Best of I.R.S.* (LSP 980142-1).
U.S. LP I.R.S 5627 **$5-8**

Dreams So Real "Everywhere Girl"/"Whirl"
Peter Buck produced the single, which was released both in black and white picture sleeves on June 22, 1985. Both tracks were included on a Dreams So Real fan club CD called *Nocturnal Emissions* in November, 1992.
U.S. 7" Coyote TTC 8556 **$10-20**

Full Time Men *Full Time Men*
Peter Buck and Fleshtone Keith Streng perform on and co-produced this three song EP. Mike Mills adds organ on "One More Time." Released in 1985.
U.S. LP Coyote TTC 8652 **$5-10**
U.K. LP What Goes On **8-12**

Kilkenney Cats *Hands Down*
Mike Mills produced the LP. Released in 1986.
U.S. LP Coyote TTC 8670 **$6-10**

The Feelies *The Good Earth*
Peter Buck co-produced the LP with Bill Million and Glen Mercer. Two cuts also appeared on an EP entitled "No One Knows" (TTC 8695, U.K.: Rough Trade RTT 180). Released in 1986.
U.S. LP Coyote TTC 8673 **$6-10**

Dreams So Real *Father's House*
Peter Buck is credited with producing this LP, but as you read in the interview with Buck at the beginning of this book, he had very little to do with its production. Released in 1986.
U.S. LP Coyote TTC 8688 **$12-18**

Woofing Cookies "In the City"/"VB Side (800 miles)"
Peter Buck produced the A-side of the single. Released in 1986.
U.S. 7" Midnight MID 4512 **$4-6**

Hanging Out at Midnight
A Midnight Records compilation LP. Peter Buck produced "Girl Next Door" by Woofing Cookies. Released in 1986.
U.S. LP Midnight MIRLP 127 **$8-12**

Golden Palominos *Visions of Excess*
Michael Stipe is the lead vocalist on "Omaha," "Boy(Go)" and "Clustering Train." Both "Omaha" and "Boy(Go)" appear on a Celluloid anthology entitled *Trilogy* (Cell 80808). *Trilogy* lists the songs as coming from an album entitled *Suitable Grounds For The Blues* using the same record number as *Visions of Excess*. "Boy (Go)" also appeared on a Celluloid promotional cassette (Spin/Celluloid CELC P1). All of the above were released in 1985.
U.S. LP Celluloid CEL 6118 **$4-6**
U.S. cassette Celluloid CEL 6118 **3-5**

U.S. singles

7"	SCEL 56	Omaha/I.D. (Like a Version)	**$6-10**
7"	SCEL 56	Omaha/I.D. (Like a Version) (promotional label, no PS)	**4-7**
7"	SCEL 58	Boy (Go) (edit)/The Animal Speaks	**6-10**
12"	CEL 183	Omaha/For a Few Dollars More	**6-10**
12"	CEL 188	Boy (Go) (edit)/Boy (Go) (LP version)/The Animal Speaks (promotion only)	**8-15**
12"	CEL 187	Kind of True/Clustering Train (Edit)/Clustering Train (LP version) (promotion only)	**8-15**

Community Trolls *Don't Shoot*

Michael Stipe shares lead vocals on "Tainted Obligations," a track that appears only on the U.K. advance promotional cassette for this album. The track was omitted from the commercial release. Released in 1986.

U.K. cassette	Zippo Zong	009	(advance promotional edition)	**$25-50**

The Upbeats *Pop Songs*

Peter Buck plays twelve-string guitar on "Just Another Pop Song." Released in 1986.

U.S. LP	Laser	LLP 102	**$7-12**

Dream Academy *The Dream Academy*

Peter Buck plays twelve-string guitar on "The Party." Released in 1986.

U.S. LP	WB	25265	**$4-6**
U.K. LP	Blanco Y Negro	BYN6	**5-6**

Waxing Poetics *Hermitage*

Mike Mills co-produced with Mitch Easter, and adds piano on "Return." Originally released in 1987, and released sometime later on CD.

U.S. LP	Emergo	EM 9610	**$5-8**
U.S. CD/cassette	Emergo	emd 9610/EMC 9610	**in print**

Warren Zevon *Sentimental Hygiene*

Peter Buck, Mike Mills, and Bill Berry provide backing instrumentals on "Sentimental Hygiene," "Boom Boom Mancini," "The Factory," "Trouble Waiting to Happen," "Detox Mansion," "Bad Kharma," "Even a Dog Can Shake Hands," and "The Heartache." Michael Stipe adds vocals on "Bad Karma." Berry, Buck, and Mills co-wrote "Even a Dog Can Shake Hands" with Zevon. Released in 1987.

U.K. LP	Virgin	V2433	**$7-9**
U.S. LP	Virgin/U.S.	7 90603-1	**5-7**
U.S. CD/cassette	Virgin/U.S.	7 90603-2/4	**in print**

U.S. singles

7"	7-99440	Leave My Monkey Alone/Leave My Monkey Alone (Latin Rascals Dub)	**$2-3**
7"	7-99440	Leave My Monkey Alone/Leave My Monkey Alone (promotional edition)	**2-3**
12"	DMD 1053	Leave My Monkey Alone (extended)/Leave My Monkey Alone (Latin Rascals edit)/Leave My Monkey Alone (Latin Rascals dub) (promotion only)	**3-5**
7"	7-99370	Reconsider Me/The Factory	**2-3**
7"	7-99370	Reconsider Me/The Factory (promotional edition)	**1-2**
12"	PR 2033	Sentimental Hygiene (promotion only)	**3-5**
12"	PR 2062	Detox Mansion/Leave My Monkey Alone (promotion only)	**3-5**

U.K. singles

7"	VS 995	Sentimental Hygiene/The Factory (August, 1987)	**$4-5**
12"	VS 995-12	Sentimental Hygiene/The Factory/Leave My Monkey Alone	**5-7**
CD	VS 995-CD	Sentimental Hygiene/The Factory/Leave My Monkey Alone	**5-8**
7"	VS 1021	Bad Kharma/Boom Boom Mancini (February 1988)	**4-5**
12"	VST 1021	Bad Kharma/Boom Boom Mancini/Leave My Monkey Alone	**5-7**
7"	VS 1055	Reconsider Me/The Factory (February 1988)	**4-5**

12"	VST 1055	Reconsider Me/The Factory/Bad Kharma	**5-7**
7"	VUS 8	Splendid Isolation/Even a Dog Can Shake Hands (January 1990)	**4-6**
12"	VUST 8	Splendid Isolation/Even a Dog Can Shake Hands/Bad Kharma/Gridlock	**5-7**
CD	VUSCD 8	Splendid Isolation/Even a Dog Can Shake Hands/Bad Kharma/Gridlock	**5-8**
7"	VS 976	Leave My Monkey Alone/Nocturne	**4-5**
12"	VS 976-12	Leave My Monkey Alone/Nocturne/Leave My Monkey Alone (Latin Rascals edit)	**5-7**

Our Favorite Band *Saturday Nights... And Sunday Mornings*

Michael Stipe adds vocals on "Dreamin' of Eternity." Released in 1987.

U.S.	LP	Big Time/Praxis	6041-1-B	**$5-8**
U.S.	cassette	Big Time/Praxis	6041-4-B	**5-7**

The Best of I.R.S.

This I.R.S. compilation LP, issued only in Greece, contains the live version of "Windout" as performed by The Fleshtones with Peter Buck. The track originally appeared on the domestic pressing of the Fleshtones LP *Speed Connection II*. Released in 1987.

Greece	I.R.S.	LSP 980142-1	**$6-10**

10,000 Maniacs *In My Tribe*

Michael Stipe adds vocals on "A Campfire Song." The band toured with R.E.M. in 1987, and twelve-inch promotional copies of the single "Don't Talk" have a sticker on the cover that lists the tour dates. Released in 1987.

U.S.	LP	Elektra	60738-1	**$5-7**
U.S.	CD/cassette	Elektra	60738-2/4	**in print**
U.K.	LP	Elektra	EKT41	**in print**

U.K. Singles

7"	EKR 77	Like the Weather/A Campfire Song	**$4-6**
12"	EKR 77T	Like the Weather/A Campfire Song/Poison in the Well (live)/ Verdi Cries (live)	**6-8**

Robyn Hitchcock *Globe of Frogs*

Peter Buck plays twelve-string on "Balloon Man," "Chinese Bones," and "Flesh #1," as well as on the electric version of "A Globe of Frogs." In addition to the singles below, "Balloon Man" appears on *Never Mind the Mainstream... The Best of MTV's 120 Minutes* volume 1 CD and cassette. The demo version of "Flesh #1" was issued as a flexidisc for the U.K. fanzine *Bucketfull of Brains* (flexi 17), released December 1987.

U.S.	LP	A&M	75021-5182-1	**$5-7**
U.S.	CD/cassette	A&M	75021-5182-2/4	**in print**
U.K.	LP	A&M	AMA 5812	**in print**

U.S. singles

7"	AM-3023	Balloon Man/A Globe of Frogs (electric)	**$3-6**
7"	AM-3023	Balloon Man/Balloon Man (promotional edition)	**3-6**
CD	75021 2374 2	Balloon Man/A Globe of Frogs (electric)/The Ghost Ship (5" CD)	**4-7**
CD	CC 31005	Balloon Man/A Globe of Frogs (electric)/The Ghost Ship (3" CD)	**5-7**
12"	SP-17530	Balloon Man/Balloon Man (promotion only)	**5-7**
12"	SP-17530	Balloon Man/A Globe of Frogs (electric)/The Ghost Ship (promotion only, green vinyl)	**10-14**
12"	SP-17549	Flesh #1/Legalized Murder (promotion only, blue vinyl)	**10-14**

The Fleshtones *Fleshtones Present The Big Bang Theory-- Time Bomb!*

This album includes "High on Drugs" by The Full Time Men, a.k.a. Peter Buck and Keith Streng from The Fleshtones. Released in 1987.

France	LP	New Rose	rose 137	**$5-9**
U.S.	LP	Skyclad	(bare)Flesh3	**4-8**

Hugo Largo *Drum*

Michael Stipe co-produced over half of the tracks, added backing vocals on "Eureka" and "Grow Wild" and played some instruments on the EP, which was originally released in 1987. The original release carries a sticker on the cover which reads, "Debut record produced by Michael Stipe and Hugo Largo." The album was remixed and re-released in 1988, this time featuring two additional tracks, including "Harpers," which Stipe co-wrote.

U.S.	LP	Relativity	88561-81671		**$3-5**
U.S.	LP	Opal/WB	1-25768	(reissue)	**3-5**
U.S.	CD/cassette	Opal/WB	2/4-25768	(reissue)	**in print**
U.K.	LP	Land	002	(reissue)	**in print**

Bruce Joyner *Hot GA Nights*

Peter Buck plays guitar on "The World Needs a Little More Love" and "Melrose Avenue." The seven-inch single of "The World Needs a Little More Love" was included in the LP jacket. Released in 1987.

U.S.	LP	New Rose	129	**$4-7**

U.S. singles

7"	NEW 114	The World Needs a Little More Love/In Dreams	**$4-7**

Michelle Malone *New Experience*

Bill Berry plays drums on "Into the Night." Michelle Malone has gone on to a relatively successful career making this album quite valuable. Released in 1988.

U.S.	LP	Aluminum Jane	AJ 01	**$30-40**

The Full Time Men *Your Face My Fist*

Produced by Peter Buck and Keith Streng. Buck plays 6-string on "High on Drugs" and "I Got Wheels." Released in 1988.

U.S.	LP	New Rose	Rose 149	**$3-7**

Charlie Pickett and MC3 *The Wilderness*

Pete Buck produced the LP, and plays guitar on "Death Letter" and "John the Revelator." The CD issue of the album contains five extra tracks, on which Buck does not perform. Released June 6, 1988.

U.S.	LP	Safety Net	Net 15	**$3-6**
U.S.	CD	Safety Net	Tiny Net 15	**in print**
U.K.	LP	Fundamental Music	SAVE 066	**4-6**

The Cynics "What's it Gonna Be"/"Roadrunner" (live)

A seven-inch fan club single pressed on blue vinyl. Pete Buck and Mike Mills appear on the live B-side. Released in 1988.

U.S.	7"	Get Hip	GH-120	**$5-8**

Hetch Hetchy *Make Djibouti*

Michael Stipe produced the LP. Released in 1988.

U.S.	LP	Texas Hotel	151	**$3-6**

Run Westy Run *Hardly Not Even*

Produced by Peter Buck and Grant Hart. Released in 1988.

U.S.	LP	SST	192	**$4-6**

Make the City Grovel in its Dust

A Twilight Records sampler, which includes "What's Left For Today" by Shades of Shame produced by Pete Buck, and "Friends" by Die Monster Die, produced by Michael Stipe. Released in 1988.

U.S.	LP	Twilight	TRO 15	**$9-15**
U.S.	cassette	Twilight	TRO 15	**5-8**

Billy James *Sixes and Sevens*

Mike Mills produced the EP. Released in 1988.

U.S.	LP	Twilight	TRO 16	**$6-8**
U.S.	cassette	Twilight	TRO 16	**4-7**

Drivin' n' Cryin' *Mystery Road*

Peter Buck plays electric dulcimer on the LP, released in 1989. The track "House For Sale" from the album was later issued on the U.K. CD single for "Build a Fire" off the album *Fly Me Courageous*, in 1992.

U.S.	LP/CD/cassette	Island	7 91226-1/2/4	**in print**

Robyn Hitchcock *Queen Elvis*

Pete Buck plays guitar on "Madonna of the Wasps," "Wax Doll," "Swirling," "Freeze" and on the non-LP track "Ruling Class." The promo CD and twelve-inch single of "Madonna of the Wasps" list Hitchcock's 1989 tour dates with R.E.M. Released in 1989.

U.S.	LP	A & M	75021-5241-1	**$5-7**
U.S.	CD	A & M	75021-5241-2	**in print**

U.S. singles

7"	AM-1409	Madonna of the Wasps/Ruling Class (no PS)	**$4-8**
12"	SP 17679	Madonna of the Wasps/One Long Pair of Eyes/More Than This	**5-7**
CD	17718	Madonna of the Wasps/One Long Pair of Eyes/More Than This (promotion only)	**7-10**
CD	17773	Madonna of the Wasps (edit)/(LP version) (promotion only)	**7-10**
12"	SP-17729	One Long Pair of Eyes (edit)/The Ghost In You (live)/ Freeze (Shatter Mix) (promotion only)	**6-9**

Indigo Girls *Indigo Girls*

Michael Stipe adds vocals on "Kid Fears" and Peter Buck, Mike Mills and Bill Berry appear on "Tried To Be True." The sleeve of the U.S. twelve-inch promo of "Kid Fears" bears a sticker listing the duo's tour dates with R.E.M. "Kid Fears" also appears on Epic's *Reverse-1 Live* nine track promo CD (ESK 1670, worth over $35), and on CBS Records "In Your Ear" three-inch CD sampler. Released in 1989.

U.S.	LP	Epic		**$5-7**
U.S.	CD/cassette/minidisc	Epic	EK 45044/FET 45044/EM 45044	**in print**
U.K.	LP	CBS	4634911	**in print**

U.S. singles

12"	EAS 1481	Kid Fears/Closer to Fine/Center Stage/Prince of Darkness (promotion only)	**$10-15**
CD	ESK 1486	Kid Fears/Closer to Fine/Center Stage/Prince of Darkness (promotion only)	**12-16**

Stay Awake

Michael Stipe adds vocals on "Little April Shower," a song from the movie *Mary Poppins*. Released in 1989.

U.S.	CD/cassette	A&M	75021-3918-2/4	**in print**
U.K.	LP	A&M	SP 3918	**in print**

Syd Straw *Surprise*

Michael Stipe adds vocals on "Future 40's (String of Pearls)," a song that he co-wrote with Straw. Released in 1989. U.K. singles were released on September 25, 1989.

U.S.	CD/cassette	Virgin	91266-2/4	**in print**
U.S.	CD	Virgin	no catalog # (promotional edition)	**$10-15**
U.K.	LP/CD/casette	Virgin	VUSLP 6/VUSMC 6/CDVUS 6	**in print**

U.S. singles

CD	PRCD 2788	Future 40's (String of Pearls) (promotion only)	**$5-8**

U.K. singles

7"	VUS6	Future 40's (String of Pearls)/Taken	**$5-7**
12"	VUST6	Future 40's (String of Pearls)/Taken/Learning the Game	**7-9**

Tommy Keene *Based on Happy Times*
Pete Buck adds mandolin on "A Way Out" and guitar on "Our Car Club." Released in 1989.

U.S.	LP	Geffen	GHS 24221	**$3-5**

U.S. singles

12"	PRO-A-3414	Based on Happy Times/Our Car Club (promotion only)	**$3-5**
CD	PRO-CD-3414	Our Car Club (promotion only)	**3-5**

Time Between- A Tribute to The Byrds
Pete Buck plays twelve-string on "Wild Mountain Thyme" with Robyn Hitchcock in their side band Nigel and the Crosses. The CD contains extra tracks, none with Buck. Buck and Hitchcock recorded the Byrds' "Mr. Tambourine Man" at the same session, which has yet to be released. Released in 1989.

U.S.	LP	Imaginary	COMM11	**$6-9**
U.K.	LP/CD	Imaginary	ILL LP 400/ILL CD 400	**7-10**

U.S. singles

7"	no catalog #	Wild Mountain Thyme (one-sided, promotion only)	**$15-25**

Vibrating Egg *Come On In Here If You Want To*
Mike Mills plays bass on selected tracks on this album which features R.E.M. manager Jefferson Holt on vocals. Released in 1989.

U.S.	LP	Dog Gone	DOG 333	**$7-9**

Tater Totz *Mono Stereo*
Michael Stipe produced some tracks, and is credited with hand claps and vibes on "1,2,3, Red Light." Released in 1989.

U.S.	LP/CD/cassette	Giant	GR16027-1/2/4	**in print**

Kevn Kinney *MacDougal Blues*
Pete Buck produced the LP, and plays on most tracks. Mike Mills adds whistling on "Chico & Maria." The title track appears on CMJ's *Certain Damage* CD compilation, volume 25. Released in 1989.

U.S.	LP	Island	91331-1 ("limited vinyl edition")	**$6-9**
U.S.	CD/cassette	Island	91331-2/4	**in print**

The Blue Aeroplanes *Swagger*
Michael Stipe adds backing vocals on "What It Is." Released February 12, 1990.

U.S.	LP	Ensign/Chrysalis	F1 21752	**$4-6**
U.S.	CD/cassette	Ensign/Chrysalis	F2-21856/F4-21856	**in print**
U.K.	LP	Ensign	CHEN 13	**in print**

Run Westy Run *Green Cat Island*
Peter Buck produced the album. Released in 1990.

U.S.	LP/CD/cassette	Twin Tone	TTR 89199-1/2/4	**in print**

Concrete Blonde *Bloodletting*
Pete Buck adds mandolin on "Darkening of the Light." In the U.S., vinyl albums of *Bloodletting* were issued for promotion only and have white labels. Released in 1990.

U.S.	LP	I.R.S.	IRS-82037 (promotion only)	**$6-10**
U.S.	CD/cassette	I.R.S.	X2-13037/X4-13037	**in print**
U.K.	LP/CD/cassette	I.R.S.	064-24 1059 1/2/4	**in print**

Chickasaw Mudd Puppies *White Dirt*
Michael Stipe co-produced the EP with John Keane. A very limited number of burlap-covered promotional copies of the CD were issued in the U.S., as were "test pressing" promo copies of the vinyl album. "McIntosh" also appeared on *Details* magazine's *Music Matters* cassette (MMVOL1), and on Polydor's *In Future* CD (IF2) in 1990. "Raven" appeared on Polygram's *Play* CD sampler (SACD 185). Released April 17, 1990.

U.S.	LP	Polygram	843-217-1	(promotional "test pressing")	**$10-18**
U.S.	CD/cassette	Polygram	843-217-2/4		**in print**
U.S.	CD	Polygram	843-217-2	(promotional edition with burlap cover)	**$15-25**
U.S.	cassette	Polygram	843-217-4	(advance promo edition)	**7-10**
Holland	LP	Polygram	843-217-1		**9-12**

U.S. singles

CD	CDP 233	McIntosh/Lookout (promotion only)	**$6-10**

Nikki Sudden "The Sun is Shining"
Flexidisc given away with *Reflex* magazine, (Flexi #12) volume 2, issue 1. Peter Buck plays guitar. Recorded April 6, 1990, released August 1990.

U.S.	7"	Evatone	106747-1AS	(flexidisc)	**$5-7**

Nigel and the Crosses "The Queen of Eyes"/"Foxy Lady"
Given away with *Bucketfull of Brains* issue #34, August 1990. Pete Buck plays on the A-side, recorded live at The Borderline in London, May, 28, 1989.

U.K.	7"	B.O.B.	BOB.28	**$6-8**

Prisoners of Ecstasy
This U.K. compilation album contains "Such a Little Girl" by Nikki Sudden and Peter Buck, who plays guitar on the track. Released in 1990.

U.K.	LP	Creation	CRELP 082	**$4-7**

Indigo Girls *Nomads*Indians*Saints*
Peter Buck plays electric lap dulcimer on "World Falls." Released September 1990.

U.S.	LP	Epic		**$5-7**
U.S.	CD/cassette	Epic	EK 46820/ET 46820	**in print**
U.K.	LP/CD/cassette	Epic	467308 1/2/4	**in print**

Vic Chestnutt *Little*
Michael Stipe co-produced the LP with John Keane. Released in 1990.

U.S.	LP/CD/cassette	Texas Hotel	20	**in print**

Chickasaw Mudd Puppies *8 Track Stomp*
Michael co-produced the LP with the late blues legend Willie Dixon. Stipe is credited as contributing vocals, keyboards, tambourine, tuba, hand claps and wa wa (!) on seven of the thirteen tracks. The promotional twelve-inch single of "Do You Remember," a track produced by Stipe, includes a three-minute interview with Stipe, Ben Reynolds, and Brant Slay of the Mudd Puppies. Portions of "Cold Blue," "Do You Remember," and "Words and Knives" appeared on the Mercury sampler cassette *Assorted Pies* (SAC 363). In addition, "Do You Remember" appears on The Album Network's *Expando #9* promo CD, released January 21, 1991. The album was released on January 12, 1991.

U.S.	LP	Polygram	843 935-1		**$5-7**
U.S.	cassette	Polygram	843 935-4	(advance promo edition)	**8-10**
U.S.	CD/cassette	Polygram	843 935-2/4		**in print**

U.S. singles

CD	CDP 433	Words and Knives/Cold Blue/Lodi (live)/Nothin' (live) (promotional)	**$6-10**
12"	PRO-912-1	Do You Remember/(interview) (promotion only)	**10-15**

Tame Yourself
Michael Stipe sings "I'll Give You My Skin" with the Indigo Girls on this benefit album for the People for the Ethical Treatment of Animals (PETA). Released February 1991.

U.S.	CD/cassette	R.N.A./Rhino	R2 70772/R4 70772	**in print**
U.S.	cassette	R.N.A./Rhino	R4 70772 (advance promotional edition)	**$5-9**

The Golden Palominos *Thundering Herd: The Best of the Golden Palominos*
This double CD and cassette Celluloid anthology includes "Omaha," the LP version of "Boy (Go)," and "Clustering Train," all featuring Michael Stipe on vocals, and all originally released in 1985 on the *Visions of Excess* LP. The LP version of "Boy (Go)" was also released on *Details* magazine's *Music Matters* compilation CD (DTLS MM-691). Released in 1991.

U.S.	CD/cassette	Oceana	4105-2-Q/4105-4-Q	**in print**

U.S. singles

CD	4183-2QJC	Omaha/Boy (Go)/Something Becomes Nothing (promotion only)	**$5-9**

The Dashboard Saviors "All Before"/"Town"
Both tracks on this seven-inch, pink vinyl single were produced by Peter Buck, and Buck adds twelve-string guitar on the B-side. A limited number of singles were pressed in black vinyl. Released July, 1991.

U.S.	7"	S.O.L.	9114-7	(green vinyl)	**$3-5**
U.S.	7"	S.O.L.	9114-7	(black vinyl)	**5-7**

Robin Hitchcock *Perspex Island*
Peter Buck plays six-string guitar on "Lysander," "So You Think You're in Love," "Child of the Universe," "Earthly Paradise," "Oceanside," "She Doesn't Exist," and twelve-string on "Vegetation and Dimes" and "Ride." Michael Stipe adds backing vocals on "She Doesn't Exist" and on the non-LP track "Dark Green Energy." In addition to the singles listed below, "So You Think You're in Love" also appears on the CD *Album Network Tune Up Rock 70* and on the TDK CD *Mailrock* (SACD 428), along with "Oceanside." Released August 1991.

U.S.	CD/cassette	A&M	75021 5368-2/4	**in print**
U.K.	CD	Go! Discs		**in print**

U.S. singles

12"	75021 7271	So You Think You're in Love/Watch Your Intelligence (promotion)	**$6-9**
CD	75021 7268 2	So You Think You're in Love (promotion only)	**4-7**
CD	75021 7268 2	So You Think You're in Love (promotion only, different cover)	**4-7**
CD	75021 2392 2	So You Think You're in Love/Watch Your Intelligence/ Eight Miles High	**4-7**
CD	75021 7273 2	Ultra Unbelievable Love/Dark Green Energy (promotion only)	**5-8**

U.K. singles

7"	GOD 65	So You Think You're in Love/Watch Your Intelligence	**$5-6**
12"	GODX 65	So You Think You're in Love/Dark Green Energy/ Watch Your Intelligence	**7-9**
CD	GODCD 65	So You Think You're in Love/Dark Green Energy/ Watch Your Intelligence	**7-10**

Billy Bragg *Don't Try This at Home*
Peter Buck plays guitar and mandolin, and Michael Stipe adds vocals on "You Woke Up My Neighborhood," a song co-written by Bragg and Buck. A video was also made for the song, in which Buck and Stipe appear. Buck also adds mandolin on "Everywhere." All tracks from the album were released in a special collectors' edition box of eight 7" singles in the U.K. Released September 18, 1991.

U.S.	CD/cassette	Elektra	9 61121-2/4	**in print**
U.K.	LP/CD/cassette	Go! Discs	828279	**in print**
U.K.	7" box	Go! Discs		**$15-18**

U.S. singles

CD	9 66483-2	You Woke Up My Neighborhood/Ontario Quebec and Me/Bread and Circuses/Heart Like a Wheel/Seven and Seven Is	**$6-8**
CD	PRCD-8462	You Woke Up My Neighborhood (promotion only)	**4-7**

U.K. singles

7"	GOD 60	You Woke Up My Neighborhood/Ontario Quebec and Me	**$4-6**
12"	GODX 60	You Woke Up My Neighborhood/Ontario Quebec and Me/Bread and Circuses/Heart Like a Wheel	**6-9**
12"	GODXDJ 60	You Woke Up My Neighborhood/Ontario Quebec and Me/Bread and Circuses/Heart Like a Wheel (promotion)	**7-10**
CD	GOD CD 60	You Woke Up My Neighborhood/Ontario Quebec and Me/Bread and Circuses/Heart Like a Wheel	**7-9**

The Golden Palominos *Drunk With Passion*

Michael Stipe is lead vocalist on "Alive and Living Now," a track he co-wrote. Released September 1991.

U.K.	CD	Virgin/Venture	CDVE 905	**in print**
U.S.	CD/cassette	Charisma	91745-2/4	**in print**

Spanish singles

7"	Virgin	SP.GOLD 1	Alive and Living Now/same (promo)	**$7-12**

The Daisy Group *The Daisy Group Sings the Hum of Life*

A seven-inch three-track EP produced by Michael Stipe. Released September 1991.

U.S.	7"	Planned Obsolescence	PO2		**$3-5**
U.S.	7"	Planned Obsolescence	PO2	(white and pink marbled vinyl)	**3-5**

Dirt "Rugburn"/"Heavy Petting"

Michael Stipe produced both tracks on this seven-inch single. Released September 1991.

U.S.	7"	Worry Bird	#6	**$3-5**

The Normaltown Flyers *Normaltown Flyers*

Peter Buck adds twelve-string guitar on "I Just Couldn't Stay Away." Released September 1991.

U.S.	CD/cassette	Mercury	848-369-2/4	**in print**

Robbie Robertson *Storyville*

Mike Mills adds backing vocals on "Shake This Town." Released October 1, 1991.

U.S.	CD/cassette	Geffen	GEFD 24303/GEFC 24303	**in print**

Chris Stamey *Fireworks*

Peter Buck adds guitar on "The Brakeman's Consolation." Released October 1991.

U.S.	CD/cassette	Rhino/RNA	R2 70766/R4 70766	**in print**

Nikki Sudden *The Jewel Thief*

Peter Buck co-produced the album with Nikki Sudden. Buck, Bill Berry, and Mike Mills also appear on a number of tracks on the LP, which was released on November 4, 1991. The singles were released in October 1991.

U.K.	LP/CD/cassette	UFO	UFO 4 LP/CD/MC	**in print**

U.K. singles

12"	45003 T	I Belong to You/Alley of the Street/Jigsaw Blues	**$5-8**
CD	45003 CD	I Belong to You/Alley of the Street/Jigsaw Blues	**7-9**

The Troggs *Athens,Andover*
This album was a collaboration between the Troggs and their fans, R.E.M. "Nowhere Road" was co-written by Buck, Berry, Mills, and Peter Holsapple, and was released as the B-side of the first single on February 2, 1992. The album was issued on March 23, 1992.

U.K.	LP/CD/cassette	Castle	ESS LP 180/ESS CD 180/ESS MC 180	**in print**
EEC	LP/CD/cassette	Essential	INT 145.176/INT 845.176/INT 145.176	**in print**

EEC singles

7"	Essential	ESS 2014	Don't You Know/Nowhere Road	**$5-7**
12"	Essential	ESS T 2014	Don't You Know/Nowhere Road	**7-10**
CD	Essential	ESS X 2014	Don't You Know/Nowhere Road	**7-10**
cassette	Essential	ESSM 2014	Don't You Know/Nowhere Road	**3-6**

German singles

12"		INT 125.327	Don't You Know/Nowhere Road	**$7-10**

H.E.A.L., Civilization vs. Technology
Michael Stipe and KRS-1 co-wrote and perform "Civilization vs. Technology" on this album for H.E.A.L., or Humans Educating Against Lies. Also on the compilation is the track, "Tighten Up Your Wig" by Billy Bragg and the Athenians with DJ Woody Dee, with Peter Buck on guitar. Released in February 1992.

U.S. LP/CD/cassette Elektra 9 61141-2 **in print**

The Original Sins *Move*
Peter Buck produced the album, recorded in August 1990 in Athens. The two tracks "Donut Shop Song" and "Drivin' Home" are available on the *Move* LP and cassette only. Released March 1992.

U.S. LP/CD/cassette Psonik Psonik 98 **in print**

The Original Sins *Eat This*
Peter Buck produced the EP, which contains five tracks from the *Move* LP, plus an extra track, "Looking in My Mirror." Released March 1992.

U.S. CD Psonik Psonik 108CD **in print**

The Beats *Up Until Now...*
Peter Buck plays electric guitar on the CD, which was issued in the U.K. Released April 1992.

U.K. CD/cassette Cottage CD COT 102/TC COT 102 **in print**

Drivin' n' Cryin' "Fly Me Courageous" CD single
Peter Buck performs on "With the People" and produced the track "Toy Never Played With." The disc also includes a live version of "Scarred But Smarter" and the studio track "Living By the Book." Released in 1992.

U.K. CD Island CID-523 **in print**

Nenah Cherry *Homebrew*
Michael Stipe sings on "Trout" with Cherry, a song that the two co-wrote. Released November 1992.

U.S.	CD/cassette	Virgin	86516-2/4	**in print**
U.K.	CD/cassette	Circa	25	**in print**

U.S. singles

7"	S7-56975-A	Trout/Buddy X	(white label jukebox release)	**$3-6**

The Dashboard Saviors *Kitty*
Peter Buck produced and performs on the album. Mike Mills adds organ on selected tracks. Released in November 1992.

U.S. CD/cassette Medium Cool **in print**

The Jody Grind *Lefty's Deceiver*
Peter Buck plays mandolin on the track "Third of July." Released in December 1992.
U.S. CD/cassette DB DB155 **in print**

Vic Chestnutt *West of Rome*
Michael Stipe produced the album and adds keyboards on selected tracks. Released in December 1992.
U.S. CD/cassette Texas Hotel 21 **in print**

10,000 Maniacs "Few and Far Between" CD single
Michael Stipe adds vocals on live versions of "Candy Everybody Wants" and "To Sir With Love," as performed by the Maniacs at the 1993 MTV Inaugural Gala. Sales of the single were to benefit Rock the Vote. Released July 8, 1993.
U.S. CD Elektra 66296-2 **in print**

Other projects in the works include Peter Buck's production and/or appearance on records by The Night Porters, Out of the Fire (Bruce Joyner's band), Uncle Tupelo, The Fleshtones, Vigilantes of Love, and on a Gram Parsons tribute album. Buck has also recorded tracks with the Georgia Satellites' Dan Baird under the band name The Nasty Bucks, which have not yet been released. Buck also financed and co-produced an LP by the famed Atlanta band The Fans, the band which inspired him to be in a band of his own. Michael Stipe has also produced yet unreleased tracks for Florida's The Beggar Weeds, The Opal Foxx Quartet, Swell, and Magna Pop. Mike Mills has produced tracks for the Athens band Greenhouse and 3 Walls Down.

R.E.M. SONGS RECORDED BY OTHER BANDS

The Replacements *The Shit Hits the Fans*
A cassette-only release of a live Replacements show in Oklahoma, which includes an R.E.M. cover. Released in 1985.
U.S. cassette Twin Tone **$7-10**

The Butthole Surfers *Butthole Surfers Double Live*
This authorized bootleg includes a cover of "The One I Love," recorded live in Athens. The CD adds ten tracks not on the double LP. Released in 1989.
U.S. LP Latino Bugger Veil LBV 002 **$12-18**
U.S. CD Latino Bugger Veil LBV 002CD **15-22**

Weird Al Yankovick *UHF* (motion picture soundtrack)
Includes "Spam," a parody of "Stand." Released in 1989.
U.S. LP Rock 'n' Roll/CBS SZ 45265 **$5-8**

The Fatima Mansions *Tima Mansio Dumps the Dead*
Included on this ten-track promotional CD, released in 1992, is a rather bizarre version of "Shiny Happy People." The promo CD was issued to promote their album *Viva Dead Ponies*.
U.S. CD Radioactive RAR3P-2109 **$10-12**

Heroina "The One I Love"/"Dancing Barefoot"
The German band Heroina released this twelve-inch single in March 1992.
Germany 12" Strange Ways WAY 17 **$10-12**

Surprise Your Pig– A Tribute to R.E.M.

This tribute album, complete with liner notes by Mitch Easter on the back cover, contains cover versions of 17 different R.E.M. songs by a variety of artists, including Easter and Vic Chestnutt. The LP version contains a yellow vinyl seven-inch single on which three of the tracks are heard. Released in June 1992.

U.S.	LP + 7"	Staplegun	SG001-LP	**$8-12**
U.S.	CD	Staplegun	SG001-CD	**in print**

10,000 Maniacs "Candy Everybody Wants" CD single

This CD, which also includes the non-LP tracks "Everyday is Like Sunday" and "Sally Ann," includes a cover of "(Don't Go Back To) Rockville" by the Maniacs. Released in January 1993.

U.S.	CD	Elektra	2-66342	**in print**

Extrabreit *Hotel Monopol*

"It's the End of the World As We Know It (and I Feel Fine)" is covered on this album by the German band Extrabreit.

Germany	CD	East West	45099 1565 2	**in print**

Flower Pornoes *Mamas Pfirsiche (fur schlechte Zeiten)*

This CD contains the track "Remcover," which is actually a cover of "Losing My Religion" sung in German.

Germany	CD	Moll	Moll 1	**in print**

BOOTLEGS AND INTERVIEW DISCS

Fans of many American rock bands show a passing interest in a band's music, and cast them aside when the next big sound comes over the radio. However, a few select bands, such as The Grateful Dead, Prince, Bruce Springsteen, Led Zeppelin, Frank Zappa, and Bob Dylan, develop a cult following of devout supporters. Many fans of such groups are not satisfied with hearing only the standard studio tracks that are available commercially, and therefore a demand is created for underground recordings.

R.E.M. is currently one of the most popular active bands to bootleg, as proven by the sheer number of illegal discs that have appeared in America, England, Germany and Italy. Unfortunately, many of the bootlegs made from audience recordings are of mediocre to poor quality, making it ridiculous to pay a lot for them. Bootleggers often don't search for high quality material before pressing their records or CDs, and the buyer generally doesn't get to hear the disc before purchasing it, which makes it easier for the bootlegger who is unconcerned with the quality of his releases. The quality of audience-recorded bootlegs will no doubt improve with the availability of small digital recorders, and as is the case for more legitimate releases, the CD has become the preferred format of bootleggers, rather than the LP.

One of the most avid collectors of R.E.M. bootlegs is Peter Buck, who currently owns over forty. Buck and the other band members generally don't disapprove of high quality bootlegs if they are made available at reasonable prices. Warner Brothers probably feels differently about the matter, but the odds are that they are more concerned with stopping the flow of counterfeit cassette tapes of the studio albums than with illegally recorded live albums.

The first R.E.M. bootlegs were *L.I.V.E.*, *Smoking in the Boys Room*, and *Return of the Rickenbacker*, which all appeared in 1983. Since then, almost one hundred bootlegs have surfaced. Though R.E.M. bootlegs are certainly plentiful, many originate from the same source. All of the R.E.M. radio shows have been bootlegged multiple times, though the bootlegs are often advertised incorrectly as having been derived from other sources. For example, the concerts that Westwood 1 recorded in Florida in 1989 and released as the "Superstars in Concert" and "In Concert" radio shows are incorrectly listed on a number of bootleg CDs as being from "Seattle 1989." In addition, the "Source" concert from Seattle in 1984 turned up on the bootleg CD *Boston 1984*. The rule of "buyer beware" certainly applies for the bootleg collector who does not want to waste money buying the same tracks twice.

Not only are bootleggers notoriously sloppy when it comes to providing the buyer with the correct source of the tracks that appear on a particular record or CD, but they are also frequently ignorant of song titles. As a result, many bootlegs contain improperly titled tracks, tracks that are listed but but aren't on the record (and vice versa), and tracks listed out of order. In the list below, song titles have been corrected and properly sequenced. Refer to the *Index To Tracks On Bootlegs* in the back of the book to find individual tracks.

(1) **Acoustic '87**
LP Alpine Records MAC-01 **$20-25**
McCabe's Guitar Shop, Santa Monica, California, May 24, 1987. Includes tracks by Peter Case. A few songs from this performance were recorded on cassette and used as B-sides, but the B-sides were all mastered too fast.
The One I Love / Welcome to the Occupation / Disturbance at the Heron House / Finest Worksong / Maps and Legends / *Tracks by Peter Case:* Walk Don't Run / Baby Please Don't Go / 1,000,000 Miles Away / Trains / *R.E.M. tracks continue:* The One I Love / Spooky / Disturbance at the Heron House / Finest Worksong / Fever / So. Central Rain / Leaving On a Jet Plane

(2) **Acoustic Tour 1991**
CD Real Live RLCD 04 **$20-25**
Eastern Sound Studio 1, Toronto, Canada, May 9, 1991; Cultural Center Auditorium, Charleston, West Virginia, as broadcast on "Mountain Stage," April 28, 1991; KCRW studios, Santa Monica, California, April 3, 1991 as broadcast on "Snap," KCRW FM. Made in Germany.
Toronto: World Leader Pretend / Radio Song / Love is All Around / Losing My Religion / Fretless / *Mountain Stage:* Fall on Me / It's the End of the World As We Know It (and I Feel Fine) / Belong / Dallas / Losing My Religion (alternate) / World Leader Pretend (alternate) / *KCRW, Santa Monica:* Low / Endgame / Swan Swan H / Spooky / Disturbance at the Heron House

(3) **Animal's Attractions**
CD Speedball SPC012 **$22-25**
MTV Studios, New York, New York, April 10, 1991, as broadcast on "MTV Unplugged." Made in Italy.
Half a World Away / Disturbance at the Heron House / Radio Song / Low / Perfect Circle / Fall On Me Belong / Love is All Around / It's the End of the World As We Know It (and I Feel Fine) / Losing My Religion / Pop Song '89

(4) **Applaud**
7" MF03 X3 **$9-12**
MTV Studios, New York, New York, April 10, 1991 (MTV Unplugged) plus other live tracks. Flexidisc from England released in December 1991.
MTV Unplugged: Low / Endgame / *unknown source:* Get Up / Kahoetek / Swan Swan H

(5) **Archival Footage**
LP ARC 10 **$18-24**
Various live and studio demos, 1982-1989.
Four untitled instrumental demos from *Green* / Gardening at Night (live, 9/84) / King of Birds (demo) / Summertime (live, 4/89) / Feeling Gravitys Pull (live, 1985) / Dark Globe (live, 4/89) / 9-9 (live, 9/84) / Carnival of Sorts (Boxcars) (live, 1982)

(6) **Automatically Live**
CD Kiss the Stone KTS 141 **$22-25**
40 Watt Club, Athens, Georgia, November 19, 1992. Made in Italy.
Drive / Monty Got a Raw Deal / Everybody Hurts / Man on the Moon / Losing My Religion / Country Feedback / Begin the Begin / Fall On Me / Me in Honey / Finest Worksong / Drive / Love is All Around / Funtime / Radio Free Europe / *unknown source:* Losing My Religion

(7) Begin the Begin
CD On Stage CD 12033 **$22-25**
Miami Arena, Miami, Florida, April 29, 1989, and Orlando Arena, Orlando, Florida, April 30, 1989. A re-packaging of the Westwood 1 "Superstars in Concert" radio show. The CD omits five songs from the original radio discs. Made in the EEC.
Turn You Inside-Out / Begin the Begin / Disturbance at the Heron House / King of Birds / Finest Worksong / I Believe / Crazy / Swan Swan H / Pop Song '89 / Feeling Gravitys Pull / Welcome to the Occupation / Stand / Exhuming McCarthy / Perfect Circle / Get Up

(8) Blue - The Acoustic Concert
CD Great Live Records GLR 9106 **$22-25**
New York, New York, as broadcast on "MTV Unplugged" in April 1991.
Half a World Away / Disturbance at the Heron House / Radio Song / Low / Perfect Circle / Fall On Me Belong / Love is All Around / It's the End of the World As We Know It (and I Feel Fine) / Losing My Religion / Pop Song '89 (mis-titled as Talk About the Passion)

(9) Blue
2LP Spliff SPLIFF001 **$22-25**
Music Hall, Seattle, Washington, June 27, 1984. Made in England.
Moral Kiosk / Catapult / Hyena / Camera / Pilgrimage / Talk About the Passion / Seven Chinese Brothers / So. Central Rain / Pretty Persuasion / Gardening at Night / 9-9 / Windout / Old Man Kensey / Radio Free Europe / Little America / Burning Down / Pale Blue Eyes / 1,000,000 / So You Want To Be a Rock and Roll Star / Carnival of Sorts / Skank

(10) Bodycount at Tyrone's
LP Brigand Records BRIG 007 **$24-28**
Tyrone's O.C., Athens, Georgia, October 4, 1980. A number of songs are incorrectly titled and sequenced, though the sound quality is fairly good.
Just a Touch / With a Girl Like You / Dangerous Times / There She Goes Again / I Can Only Give You Everything / All the Right Friends / (Don't Go Back To) Rockville / Body Count / Hippy Hippy Shake / Action / Narrator / Hey! Hey! Nadine / Gardening at Night / Scheherazade / Lisa Says / Mystery to Me / Stepping Stone (unknown source) / Permanent Vacation

■ The Tyrone's concert from October 4, 1980 appears here on the vinyl boot *Bodycount at Tyrone's*, as well as on the CD *Twentieth Century Boys volume 2*. At the time it was recorded, the band had only been performing for seven months, making this the earliest show to be bootlegged. The band had yet to write "Radio Free Europe" or "Sitting Still," the two tracks that appeared on their debut single.

(11) Boston 1984
CD Mistral MM9116 **$22-25**
Music Hall, Seattle, Washington, June 27, 1984. Incorrectly identified as a Boston show. Made in Italy.
Moral Kiosk / Catapult / Hyena / Camera / Pilgrimage / Talk About the Passion / Seven Chinese Brothers / So. Central Rain / Pretty Persuasion / Gardening at Night / 9-9 / Windout / Old Man Kensey / Radio Free Europe / Little America / Burning Down / Pale Blue Eyes / 1,000,000 / So You Want To Be a Rock and Roll Star / Carnival of Sorts / Skank

(12) Bucketfull of Worksongs
2CD Rocks 92029/30 **$40-55**
Utrecht, Holland, September 14, 1987, and Werchter Festival, Germany, July, 1985. Made in Luxembourg.

Utrecht: Finest Worksong / These Days / Lightnin' Hopkins / Welcome to the Occupation / Driver 8 Feeling Gravitys Pull / I Believe / The One I Love / Exhuming McCarthy / Wolves, Lower / Fall On Me / Superman / Just a Touch / Oddfellows Local 151 / Strange / Disturbance at the Heron House / Funtime / Time After Time / So. Central Rain / Moral Kiosk / Life and How To Live It / *Werchter Festival:* Feeling Gravitys Pull / Driver 8 / (Don't Go Back To) Rockville / So. Central Rain / Have You Ever Seen the Rain / Can't Get There From Here

(13) **The Byrds Fly South**
LP Sons of Rickenbacker SOR 51188 **$20-25**
Uptown Lounge, Athens, Georgia, May 11, 1988. From a Roger McGuinn concert, with accompaniment by Peter Buck, Bill Berry, and Mike Mills.
Sunshine Love / The Tears / Chestnut Mare / Tiffany Queen 2 / You Ain't Going Nowhere / I'll Feel a Whole Lot Better / Mr. Spaceman / The Bells of Rhymey / Mr. Tambourine Man / Turn, Turn, Turn / Eight Miles High / Knockin' on Heaven's Door

(14) **Can't Get There From Here**
2LP MCP KAXY 002 **$25-35**
Hammersmith Palais Ballroom, London, England, October 28, 1985.
Feeling Gravitys Pull / Harborcoat / Green Grow the Rushes / Maps and Legends / Pilgrimage / Driver 8 / Sitting Still / Good Advices / So. Central Rain / Have You Ever Seen the Rain / Can't Get There From Here / Seven Chinese Brothers / Auctioneer / Old Man Kensey / Pretty Persuasion / Life and How To Live It / Second Guessing / (Don't Go Back To) Rockville / Toys in the Attic / Radar Love / Burning Hell / Talk About the Passion / Little America

(15) **Carnival of Sorts**
CD Great Dane Records GDR CD 9020 **$22-25**
Merlins, Madison, Wisconsin, April 24, 1982. Probably the best sounding bootleg from this period. Made in Italy.
Gardening at Night / 9-9 / Ages of You / Shaking Through / Laughing / Romance / Sitting Still / Pretty Persuasion / That Beat / Catapult / Radio Free Europe / Wolves, Lower / Carnival of Sorts (Boxcars) / White Tornado / West of the Fields / Stumble / Skank / There She Goes Again

(16) **Chestnut**
7" MF01 X1 **$10-15**
Flexidisc from England released in October 1990. Limited to 960 copies.
From Community Trolls cassette, with Michael Stipe on vocals: Tainted Obligations / *Mike Mills and Peter Buck, Atlanta, Ga., live on Rockline 1/14/89:* Ballad of Cat Ballou / *Drive-In Studio, Winston-Salem, N.C., 10/81:* Jazz Lips / *Fan club 1988 single:* Parade of the Wooden Soldiers

(17) **Chronic Murmurings**
2LP Toasted Record Works 1905 **$30-40**
Studio outtakes from five different recording sessions, 1980-1983. The sound quality of this bootleg is somewhat inferior, but the discs contain significant early demo recordings. Probably one of the most popular vinyl bootlegs, but hard to find.
Four-track demos, Tyrone's, Athens, Ga., 1980: Dangerous Times / All The Right Friends / A Different Girl / Narrator / Just a Touch / Baby I / Mystery to Me / Permanent Vacation / *Drive-In Studio, Winston-Salem, N.C., 10/81:* 1,000, 000 / Ages of You / Gardening at Night / Carnival of Sorts (Boxcars) / Stumble / 1,000,000 (different take) / *RCA demos, New York, N.Y., 2/82:* Catapult / Wolves, Lower / Laughing / Easy Come, Easy Go (Romance) / Shaking Through / Carnival of Sorts (Boxcars) / Stumble / *Drive-In Studio, Winston-Salem, N.C., 1/82:* Wolves, Lower (fast version) / *Reckoning outtakes, Reflection Studio, Charlotte, N.C. 12/83:* Windout (sung by Jefferson Holt and Bert Downs) / Just a Touch

(18) **Disturbances**
CD Heartground Records CAR-784 **$20-25**
Aragon Ballroom, Chicago, Illinois, July 7, 1984. Possibly the poorest sounding bootleg ever released.
Letter Never Sent / I Believe / Driver 8 / So. Central Rain / Seven Chinese Brothers / Harborcoat / Hyena / Femme Fatale / Radio Free Europe / Gardening at Night / 9-9 / Windout / Little America / Second Guessing / (Don't Go Back To) Rockville

(19) **Do You Remember (Dead Giveaway Office)**
Stichcraft, Athens, Georgia, September 30, 1983, and other live recordings.
LP C2Y-70054 **$18-25**
Stichcraft, Athens, Ga.: Welcome To The Starlight / Twentieth Century Boy / Pills / Barney Miller theme / Secret Agent Man / Hootenanny / Rave On / I Got You Babe / Moon River / Crazy / *Golden Palominos, The Ritz, New York, N.Y. 1/9/86:* Omaha / *Peppermint Lounge, New York, N.Y. 10/31/83:* DOA / So You Want To Be a Rock and Roll Star / Pale Blue Eyes / I Can't Control Myself / Femme Fatale

(20) **Documentary**
2LP Toasted Record Works TRW 1914 **$30-38**
Bren Events Center, Irvine, California, November 14, 1987.

Finest Worksong / These Days / Welcome to the Occupation / Exhuming McCarthy / Don't Call On Me (Orange Crush) / Feeling Gravitys Pull / King of Birds / I Believe / Maps and Legends / Driver 8 / Superman / Auctioneer (Another Engine) / Oddfellows Local 151 / It's the End of the World As We Know It (and I Feel Fine) / Begin the Begin / Strange / Rollers Show / Cuyahoga / Fall On Me / Harpers / The One I Love / Crazy / Pop Song '89 / Just a Touch / After Hours

(21) **Down South**

LP FTP 0010 **$18-25**

Tyrone's O.C., Athens, Georgia, January 10, 1981; Friday's, Greensboro, North Carolina, March 31, 1981.

Shaking Through / (Don't Go Back To) Rockville / Gardening at Night / Sitting Still / Burning Down / What If We Give It Away? / There She Goes Again / *Friday's:* Chained to the Wall / Ages of You / Laughing / Just a Touch / Radio Free Europe / White Tornado

(22) **The Dream**

CD Red Phantom RPCD 1028 **$22-25**

Pink Pop Festival, Landgraaf, Holland, May 15, 1989; Palartussardi, Milan, Italy, June 15, 1989. Made in Italy.

Landgraaf Holland: Exhuming McCarthy / Turn You Inside-Out / Stand / Orange Crush / Feeling Gravitys Pull / King of Birds / World Leader Pretend / Underneath the Bunker / Pretty Persuasion / Get Up / Auctioneer (Another Engine) / It's the End of the World As We Know It (and I Feel Fine) / Summertime / Swan Swan H / Finest Worksong / *Milan, Italy:* Begin the Begin / Perfect Circle / Dark Globe

■ *The Dream*

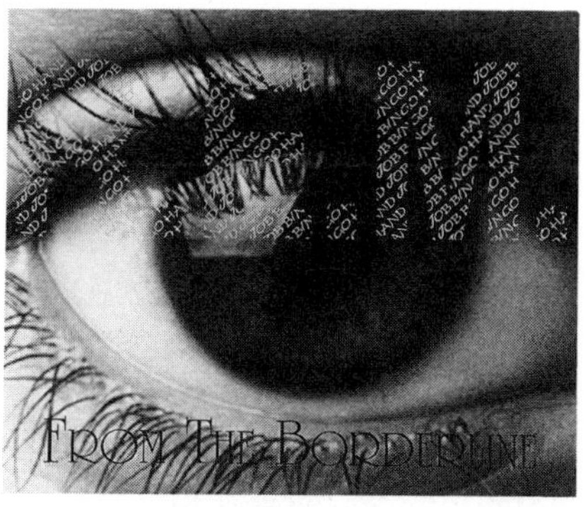

■ The double CD, *From the Borderline*

(23) **The Eighties Do the Sixties: The Beat Goes On**

3LP **$50-75**

Live performances by various artists. Issued in a black box, it includes a twelve page booklet with track listings and photos of the artists. Includes three live R.E.M. tracks, "Rave On," "So You Want To Be a Rock and Roll Star" and "Pale Blue Eyes" from an unknown source.

(24) **Fables of R.E.M.**

7" REM 01 **$18-25**

Rock City, Nottingham, England, November 21, 1984. A bootleg of the BBC Transcription "In Concert" radio disc. Made in England.

Pretty Persuasion / Radio Free Europe / West of the Fields / (Don't Go Back To) Rockville

(25) **The Fan Club Singles Volume One**

7" Small Town Records SMALL2 **$10-18**

This seven-inch single pressed in green vinyl contains the tracks from band's first two fan club singles.

Parade of the Wooden Soldiers / See No Evil / Good King Wenceslas / Academy Fight Song

(26) **The Fan Club Singles Volume Two**

7" Small Town Records SMALL3 **$10-18**

Pressed in pink vinyl, this single contains the tracks from the 1990 and 1991 fan club singles.

Ghost Reindeer in the Sky / Summertime / Baby Baby / Christmas Griping

(27) **Finest Lunchbox**

13LP Toasted Record Works **$195-240**

A 10LP collection of R.E.M. bootleg LPs from Toasted Record Works, including *Chronic Murmurings, Documentary, Mada Mada, Pageantry, Rolling Stone, Working*, and *Nottingham* (in a spray-painted cover using the title *R.E.M.*). The set was issued in a film box with black cloth straps, and included a photocopy book of R.E.M. clippings from magazines and fan club mailouts, a T-shirt, and a postcard. The cover indicates that only 100 were made, and they are numbered.

■ The thirteen-LP *Finest Lunchbox.*

(28) **Finest Worksongs**

LP FWS 889 **$18-24**

John Keane Studios, Athens, Georgia. *Document* and *Green* demos.

Document demos: Finest Worksong / Welcome to the Occupation / Exhuming McCarthy / Disturbance at the Heron House / It's the End of the World As We Know It (and I Feel Fine) / Fireplace / Lightnin' Hopkins / Oddfellows Local 151 / *Green demos:* I Remember California / Get Up / You Are the Everything / Pop Song '89

(29) **From the Borderline**

2CD Red Phantom RPCD 2038/2039 **$45-55**

The Borderline, London, England, March 14, 1991; Shocking Club, Milan, Italy, March 22, 1991. Made in Italy.

The Borderline, London, England: Intro / World Leader Pretend / Half a World Away / Fretless / The One I Love / Hello in There / My Youngest Son Came Home Today (My Eldest Son) / Jackson / Dallas / Disturbance at the Heron House / Belong / Low / Love is All Around / You Are the Everything / Swan Swan H / Radio Song / Perfect Circle / Endgame / Pop Song '89 / Losing My Religion / Fall On Me (part 1) / Fall On Me (part 2) / Tom's Diner / You Ain't Goin' Nowhere / Get Up / Moon River / *Milan, Italy:* Half a World Away / Swan Swan H / Belong / Driver 8 / Low / Fretless / Losing My Religion

(30) **Gravity**

CD Stentor 91.036 **$22-25**

Miami Arena, Miami, Florida, April 29, 1989; Orlando Arena, Orlando, Florida, April 30, 1989. Yet another repackaging of the WW1 "Superstars in Concert" radio show.

Pop Song '89 / Exhuming McCarthy / Welcome to the Occupation / Disturbance at the Heron House / Orange Crush / Turn You Inside-Out / Feeling Gravitys Pull / Begin the Begin / Pretty Persuasion / I Believe / Swan Swan H / King of Birds / Crazy / Finest Worksong / You Are the Everything / Academy Fight Song / Stand / Perfect Circle / Get Up / It's the End of the World As We Know It (and I Feel Fine)

(31) **Green Dreams**

2LP **$22-28**

Miami Arena, Miami, Florida, April 29, 1989; Orlando Arena, Orlando, Florida, April 30, 1989. The WW1 "Superstars in Concert" radio show, plus fan club single B-sides.

Pop Song '89 / Exhuming McCarthy / Welcome to the Occupation / Disturbance at the Heron House / Orange Crush / Turn You Inside-Out / Feeling Gravitys Pull / Begin the Begin / Pretty Persuasion / I Believe / Swan Swan H / King of Birds (mis-titled "Flowers of Guatemala") / Crazy (mis-titled "Shaking Through") / Finest Worksong / You Are the Everything / Academy Fight Song / Stand /

Perfect Circle / Get Up / It's the End of the World As We Know It (and I Feel Fine) / *1988 and 1989 Fan Club single B-sides*: See No Evil / Academy Fight Song

(32) **The Green World Tour**
CD RS Records CD18 **$22-25**
Palasport, Perugia, Italy, June 17, 1989. Made in Italy.
Pop Song '89 / These Days / Exhuming McCarthy / Turn You Inside-Out / Orange Crush / Feeling Gravitys Pull / King of Birds / Shaking Through / World Leader Pretend / Finest Worksong / Underneath the Bunker / Sitting Still / Get Up / Auctioneer (Another Engine) / It's the End of the World As We Know It (and I Feel Fine) / Stand

(33) **Half a World Away Part 1**
CD Mongoose Records MONG CD007A **$22-25**
KCRW studios, Santa Monica, California, April 3, 1991 as broadcast on "Snap," KCRW FM; Warner Brothers promo LP Winter Warnerland; Christmas fan club singles, 1988-90. Made in Germany. The bootleggers who assembled the material for this disc would have been better off omitting the Christmas singles and not deleting the majority of the conversation that took place during the Snap show, which is often hilarious. Skip this bootleg and find a tape of the whole show.
KCRW Studios, Santa Monica: World Leader Pretend / Half a World Away / Fretless / Disturbance at the Heron House / Radio Song / Low / Love is All Around / Academy Fight Song / Tusk / Dallas / Losing My Religion / Mary Tyler Moore theme / Bandwagon / Endgame / Jackson / Swan Swan H / Spooky / Radio Ethiopia / Fall On Me / *Winter Warnerland promo LP:* Deck the Halls / *Christmas fan club singles:* Parade of the Wooden Soldiers / See No Evil / Good King Wenceslas / Academy Fight Song / Ghost Reindeer in the Sky / Summertime

(34) **Half a World Away Part 2**
CD Mongoose Records MONG CD007B **$22-25**
New York, New York, as broadcast on MTV Unplugged on April 24, 1991; Los Angeles, California, as broadcast on Rockline, April 1, 1991; New York, New York, as broadcast on Saturday Night Live, April 13, 1991. Made in Germany.
MTV Unplugged, New York, N.Y.: Half a World Away / Disturbance at the Heron House / Radio Song / Low / Perfect Circle / Fall On Me / Belong / Love is All Around / It's the End of the World As We Know It / Losing My Religion / Pop Song '89 / Endgame / Half a World Away / *Rockline, Los Angeles:* Radio Song / Love is All Around / Losing My Religion / *Saturday Night Live, New York, N.Y.:* Losing My Religion / Shiny Happy People

(35) **Harmonics in Eternity**
LP **$18-25**
KCRW studios, Santa Monica, California, April 3, 1991 as broadcast on KCRW FM. Made in England.
World Leader Pretend / Fretless / Smiling Faces Sometimes / Losing My Religion / Endgame / Jackson / Swan Swan H / Spooky / Fall On Me / Radio Song / I Enjoy Being a Boy

(36) **Here I Am Again**
CD 92-EF-10-101 **$22-25**
John Keane Studios, Athens, Georgia; Bearsville Studios, Woodstock, New York. Studio demos and outtakes from the *Out of Time* sessions. Inferior in quality to *Slightly Out of Time and Time of Outtakes*. Made in Italy.
Losing My Religion / Speed Metal / Shiny Happy People / Me in Honey / Endgame / Belong / Texarkana / It's a Free World Baby (Gave Too Much Away) / Here I Am Again / untitled

(37) **In the Year 2525 - The Cover Versions**
CD Great Live Records GLR 9109 **$22-25**
Various live covers from numerous performances, 1981-1990. Made in Germany.
There She Goes Again / In the Year 2525 / Eight Miles High / Have You Ever Seen the Rain / What's New Pussycat / Radar Love / Gloria / Rave On / Pale Blue Eyes / So You Want To Be a Rock and Roll Star / Moon River / Paint it Black / California Dreamin' / Femme Fatale / Toys in the Attic / See No Evil / Hey Little Girl / The Lion Sleeps Tonight / Behind Closed Doors / Fall On Me / Smokin' in the Boys Room / Sweet Home Alabama

(38) **It's the End of the World**
CD Kiss the Stone KTS 005 **$22-25**
Miami Arena, Miami, Florida, April 29, 1989; Orlando Arena, Orlando, Florida, April 30, 1989. Another re-packaging of the Westwood 1 "Superstars in Concert" radio show. Made in Italy.
Pop Song '89 / Exhuming McCarthy / Welcome to the Occupation / Disturbance at the Heron House / Turn You Inside-Out / Orange Crush / Feeling Gravitys Pull / Swan Swan H / Begin the Begin / Pretty Persuasion / I Believe / King of Birds / Crazy / Finest Worksong / You Are the Everything / Academy Fight Song / Stand / Perfect Circle / Get Up / It's the End of the World As We Know It (and I Feel Fine)

(39) **Latex or Oil Base?**
CD Bullseye Records CD-EYE-11 **$22-25**
Cultural Center Auditorium, Charleston, West Virginia, as broadcast on "Mountain Stage" April 28, 1991; Rockline Studios, Los Angeles, California, April 1, 1991. Made in Australia.
Mountain Stage broadcast: World Leader Pretend / Radio Song / Fall On Me / It's the End of the World As We Know It (and I Feel Fine) / Half a World Away / Belong / Love is All Around / Losing My Religion / *Rockline rehearsal:* Half a World Away / Love is All Around (fragment 1) / Love is All Around (fragment 2) / *Rockline broadcast:* Half a World Away / Radio Song / Love is All Around Losing My Religion / post-show jam

■ The first R.E.M. bootleg was *L.I.V.E.*, also referred to as *Stonehenge*.

■ The *Live in Chicago* picture disc

(40) **L.I.V.E.**
LP Bandido B006 **$40-60**
University of Rochester, New York, April 8, 1983. The first R.E.M. bootleg.
Harlem Nocturn / Moral Kiosk / Catapult / Pilgrimage / Return / Wolves, Lower / Talk About the Passion / Gardening at Night / Radio Free Europe

(41) **Live Collection**
CD Living Legend Records LLRCD 153 **$22-25**
Merlins, Madison, Wisconsin, April 24, 1982; Miami Arena, Miami, Florida, April 29, 1989 and Orlando Arena, Orlando, Florida, April 30, 1989 (from the 1989 Westwood 1 "Superstars in Concert" radio show); MTV Studios, New York, New York, April 10, 1991 as broadcast on "Unplugged." Made in Italy.
Merlins, Madison, Wisc.: Gardening at Night / Radio Free Europe / White Tornado / West of the Fields / There She Goes Again / *Miami Arena and Orlando Arena*: Pop Song '89 / Welcome to the Occupation / Turn You Inside-Out / Orange Crush / Swan Swan H / Begin the Begin / Stand / Perfect Circle / Get Up / It's the End of the World As We Know It (and I Feel Fine) / *MTV Unplugged, New York, N.Y.:* Losing My Religion / Half a World Away / Radio Song / Love is All Around

(42) **Live in Chicago**
LP ME Records 0100 (blue or green picture disc) **$30-35**
LP Juke Box Records London XL2 (black vinyl album) **25-30**
Aragon Ballroom, Chicago, Illinois, July 7, 1984; Rock Influences TV Special, Capital Theater, Passaic, New Jersey, June 9, 1984. Issued as both blue and green picture discs and later on standard black vinyl.
Aragon Ballroom, Chicago: Femme Fatale / Radio Free Europe / Gardening at Night / Sitting Still / 9-9 / Windout / Driver 8 / So. Central Rain / Harbor Coat / Cushy Tush-Behind Closed Doors / Hyena Pretty Persuasion / *Rock Influences TV special:* Pale Blue Eyes / So You Want To Be a Rock and Roll Star (w/Roger McGuinn)

(43) **Love and Squalor**
CD Howdy Records CD 555-07 **$22-25**
Miami Arena, Miami, Florida, April 29, 1989; Orlando Arena, Orlando, Florida, April 30, 1989. A bootleg of the 1989 Westwood 1 "Superstars in Concert" radio show. This disc omits "Turn You Inside-Out" from the original radio LPs. Made in Germany.
Pop Song '89 / Exhuming McCarthy / Welcome to the Occupation / Disturbance at the Heron House / Orange Crush / Feeling Gravitys Pull / Swan Swan H / Begin the Begin / Pretty Persuasion / I Believe / King of Birds (mis-titled "Flowers of Guatemala") / Crazy / Finest Worksong / You Are the

Everything / Academy Fight Song / Stand / Perfect Circle / Get Up / It's the End of the World As We Know It (and I Feel Fine)

(44) Low

CD Templar TCD 28 **$22-25**

Shocking Club, Milan, Italy, March 22, 1991. Two different packagings were used. Made in Italy.

Disturbance at the Heron House / Half a World Away / Swan Swan H / Belong / Driver 8 / Low / Fretless / Love is All Around / Losing My Religion / Fall On Me / Get Up

(45) Mada Mada

2LP Toasted Records 1906 **$30-38**

Larry's Hideaway, Toronto, Canada, July 9, 1983; City Gardens, Trenton, New Jersey, November 16, 1982; Reflection Studios, Charlotte, North Carolina, January 1983.

Larry's Hideaway: Laughing / Pilgrimage / There She Goes Again / Seven Chinese Brothers / Talk About the Passion / Sitting Still / Harborcoat / Catapult / Gardening at Night / 9-9 / Just a Touch / West of the Fields / Radio Free Europe / We Walk / *Murmur outtakes, Reflection Studio, Charlotte, N.C. 1/83:* There She Goes Again / Tighten Up / All the Right Friends / *City Gardens 11/16/82:* Easy Come, Easy Go (Romance) / 1,000,000 / Pretty Persuasion / Ages of You / Pilgrimage / Wolves, Lower

(46) Maps and Legends

CD Mongoose Records MONG CD005 **$22-25**

McCabe's Guitar Shop, Santa Monica, California, May 24, 1987. Features Peter Case and members of 10,000 Maniacs, among other musicians. Made in Germany.

Hello Stranger / The One I Love / Welcome to the Occupation / Disturbance at the Heron House / Finest Worksong / Maps and Legends / *Tracks by Peter Case and others:* Walk, Don't Run / Baby Please Don't Go / 1,000,000 Miles Away / Hello Stranger / A Campfire Song / Stretch Out My Hand *R.E.M. tracks continue:* The One I Love / Spooky / Disturbance at the Heron House / Finest Worksong / Fever / So. Central Rain / Harpers

(47) Mimed

7" MF02 X2 **$10-15**

BBC Studios, London, March 13, 1991, plus live tracks. Flexidisc from England released in August 1990. Issued in white, pink, and purple photocopied sleeves.

BBC Studios: Benjamin Caroline Triangle (Fretless) / Half a World Away / *live tracks:* Wayward Wind / These Days / For the Love of Money

(48) Mumble

LP PSA 101 **$18-24**

John Keane Studios, Athens, Georgia, March 1986 (*Lifes Rich Pageant* demos); Rock City, Nottingham, England, October 24, 1984; Bayfront Center, St. Petersburg, Florida, November 26, 1985; Drive-In Studio, Winston-Salem, North Carolina, April 15, 1981.

Lifes Rich Pageant demos: Underneath the Bunker / PSA / Cuyahoga / *Nottingham, England 11/24/84:* Gardening at Night / 9-9 / Windout / Auctioneer (Another Engine) / West of the Fields / Pretty Persuasion / *Bayfront Center, St. Petersburg, Fla., 11/26/85:* So. Central Rain (acoustic) / Swan Swan H / *unknown source:* White Tornado

(49) New Orleans

2LP OC 89 (marbled vinyl) **$30-35**

2LP OC 89 **25-30**

Lakefront Arena, New Orleans, Louisiana, March 26, 1989.

Welcome to the Occupation / Disturbance at the Heron House / Turn You Inside-Out / Driver 8 / Orange Crush / Cuyahoga / Feeling Gravitys Pull / Time After Time / World Leader Pretend / I Believe / Pretty Persuasion / Get Up / Auctioneer (Another Engine) / It's the End of the World As We Know It (and I Feel Fine) / Stand / Fall On Me / You Are the Everything / Finest Worksong / King of Birds

(50) No. 8, Demos and Outtakes

CD Indian IN02 **$22-25**

Demos and studio outtakes from the *Document*, *Green*, and *Out of Time* sessions. Made in Japan.

Document demos: Exhuming McCarthy / Disturbance at the Heron House / It's the End of the World As We Know It (and I Feel Fine) / Fireplace / Lightnin' Hopkins / *Green demos:* I Remember California / Get Up / You Are the Everything / Orange Crush / *Out of Time demos:* Losing My Religion / Speed Metal / Shiny Happy People / Me in Honey / Endgame / Belong / Texarkana / It's a Free World, Baby

(51) Nottingham

LP TMOQ 71121 **$18-24**

Rock City, Nottingham, England, November 21, 1984. Also included in "Finest Lunchbox" bootleg set. Released on green, clear and red vinyl, as well as mixes of these colors. Covers released were green or red. This was the first bootleg of the BBC Transcription radio disc.

Hyena / Talk About the Passion / (Don't Go Back To) Rockville / Auctioneer (Another Engine) / So. Central Rain / Sitting Still / Old Man Kensey / 9-9 / Windout / Driver 8 / Pretty Persuasion / Radio Free Europe / West of the Fields

(52) **Old Man Kensey**

CD HM4 **$22-25**

Rock City, Nottingham, England, November 21, 1984. Another bootleg of the BBC Transcription radio disc.

Hyena / Talk About the Passion / (Don't Go Back To) Rockville / Auctioneer (Another Engine) / So. Central Rain / Sitting Still / Old Man Kensey / 9-9 / Windout / Driver 8 / Pretty Persuasion / Radio Free Europe / West of the Fields

(53) **Outtakes of Time**

CD R01 **$22-25**

John Keane Studios, Athens, Georgia; Bearsville Studios, Woodstock, New York. Studio demos and outtakes from the *Out of Time* sessions.

Radio Song / Belong / Texarkana / It's a Free World, Baby / Here I Am Again / instrumental / Losing My Religion / instrumental / Shiny Happy People / Me in Honey / Endgame / Half a World Away / untitled / Radio Song / Near Wild Heaven / Fretless / Low / Ghost Reindeer in the Sky / Country Feedback

(54) **Pageantry**

2LP Pharting Pharoah 13154 (original sleeve, with pink vinyl discs) **$32-40**
2LP Pharting Pharoah 13154 (original sleeve, with black vinyl discs) **30-38**
2LP Pharting Pharoah 13154 (reissue) **30-35**

Universal Amphitheater, Los Angeles, California, September 39, 1986.

These Days / Radio Free Europe / Harborcoat / Sitting Still / The One I Love / Shaking Through / Feeling Gravitys Pull / Last Date / Driver 8 / The Flowers Of Guatemala / I Believe / Swan Swan H / Superman / Can't Get There From Here / Pretty Persuasion / Just a Touch / Fall On Me / Cuyahoga / 1,000,000 / Strange / Funtime / Life and How To Live It / Harpers / Begin the Begin / So. Central Rain (acoustic)

(55) **Peace and Love Anyone?**

LP Acme Records ACME 04 **$20-25**

John Keane Studios, Athens, Georgia; Bearsville Studios, Woodstock, New York. Studio demos and outtakes from the *Out of Time* sessions.

Losing My Religion / Speed Metal / Shiny Happy People / Me in Honey / Endgame / Belong Texarkana / It's a Free World Baby / Here I Am Again / untitled

(56) **Perfect Circle**

CD Pluto Records PLR CD 9136 **$22-25**

Miami Arena, Miami, Florida, April 29, 1989; Orlando Arena, Orlando, Florida, April 30, 1989. A bootleg of the 1989 Westwood 1 "Superstars in Concert" radio show. Made in Italy.

Pop Song '89 / Exhuming McCarthy / Welcome to the Occupation / Disturbance at the Heron House / Turn You Inside-Out / Orange Crush / Feeling Gravitys Pull / Swan Swan H / Begin the Begin / Pretty Persuasion / I Believe / King of Birds / Crazy / Finest Worksong / You Are the Everything / Academy Fight Song / Stand / Perfect Circle / Get Up / It's the End of the World As We Know It (and I Feel Fine)

(57) **Philadelphia 1984**

CD Rarities & Few Records GZCD 1010 (original issue) **$22-25**
CD Rarities & Few Records GZCD 1010 (reissue with black inserts) **22-25**
2LP Rarities & Few Records GZLP 2010 BS (reissue with black sleeve) **22-25**

Tower Theater, Philadelphia, Pennsylvania, October 17, 1984. Some collectors feel that this is actually a show from Baton Rouge. Made in Italy.

Radio Free Europe / Hyena / Letter Never Sent / Camera / Gardening at Night / 9-9 / Windout / (Don't Go Back To) Rockville / So. Central Rain / Little America / Second Guessing / Talk About the Passion / Wolves, Lower / Moon River / Ghost Riders in the Sky / There She Goes Again / We Walk

(58) **Pleasant Dreams**

2LP Trademark of Quality, TMOQ 3790 **$30-35**

Music Hall, Seattle, Washington, June 27, 1984. A bootleg of the NBC Source radio discs.

Moral Kiosk / Catapult / Hyena / Camera / Pilgrimage / Talk About the Passion / Seven Chinese Brothers / So. Central Rain / Pretty Persuasion / Gardening at Night / 9-9 / Windout / Old Man Kensey / Radio Free Europe / Little America / Burning Down / Pale Blue Eyes / 1,000,000 / So You Want To Be a Rock and Roll Star / Carnival of Sorts / Skank

(59) Poets of the Wheat
2CD Beech Marten Records BM 149/2 **$45-50**
BBC Studios, London, March 13, 1991; Miami Arena, Miami, Florida, April 29, 1989, and Orlando Arena, Orlando, Florida, April 30, 1989. The tracks recorded in Florida were taken from the Westwood 1 "Superstars in Concert" radio concert discs. These tracks are mis-identified as originating from "Seattle 1989." This 2CD set is particularly annoying because it contains the LP track "Me In Honey" taken directly from *Out of Time*. Made in Italy.
BBC studios: Fretless / *Out of Time LP track:* Me in Honey / *BBC studios:* Half a World Away / Radio Song / Losing My Religion / Love is All Around / *Miami and Orlando, Fla., 1989:* Pop Song '89 / Exhuming McCarthy / Welcome to the Occupation / Disturbance at the Heron House / Turn You Inside-Out / Orange Crush / Feeling Gravitys Pull / Swan Swan H / Begin the Begin / Pretty Persuasion / I Believe / King of Birds / Crazy / Finest Worksong / You Are the Everything / Academy Fight Song / Stand / Perfect Circle / Get Up / It's the End of the World As We Know It (and I Feel Fine)

(60) The Pop Dream
2LP Easy Flyte Records Flight 801 **$35-45**
Various covers from many different performances, 1982-1985. This lengthy collection of cover songs is quite interesting and often amusing, but the quality of the recordings is sometimes poor.
Neverland / Gloria / There She Goes Again / California Dreaming / Toys in the Attic / Paint it Black I Can't Control Myself / Radar Love / So You Want To Be a Rock and Roll Star / I Can Only Give You Everything / Secret Agent Man / See No Evil / Pills / Stepping Stone / Have You Ever Seen the Rain Eight Miles High / Roadrunner / In the Year 2525 / After Hours / God Save the Queen / Twentieth Century Boy / Smoking in the Boy's Room / Sweet Jane / Louie Louie / Pale Blue Eyes / Wild Thing Chicken Train / Be Bop A Lula

■ *The Pop Dream* consists of a collection of live covers from 1982-1985.

■ The double LP *Pretty Pictures*

(61) Pop Songs '89
LP BMPM 8032 **$18-24**
John Keane Studios, Athens, Georgia (*Green* demos); live 1989.
Live tracks: Pop Song '89 / Get Up / You Are the Everything / King of Birds / World Leader Pretend / Orange Crush / Turn You Inside-Out / I Remember California / Rotary 10 / Perfect Circle / *Green demos:* Hairshirt / Untitled

(62) Pretty Pictures
2LP Easy Flyte Records Flyte 130 **$38-45**
Studio outtakes from four different recording sessions, 1980-1983. Like *Chronic Murmurings*, the sound quality on these discs is marginal, but the album contains important demo recordings unavailable elsewhere.
Murmur outtakes, Reflection Studios, Charlotte, N.C. 1/83: That Beat / All the Right Friends / Tighten Up / There She Goes Again / Moon River / *Rhythmic Studios demos, San Francisco, Cal. 11/9/83:* That Beat / Burn it Down (Burning Down) / Burning Hell / The Lion Sleeps Tonight / Skank / Camera / Second Guessing / Just a Touch / Pale Blue Eyes / *RCA demos, New York, N.Y., 2/82:* Catapult / Wolves, Lower / Laughing / Easy (Romance) / Shaking Through / Carnival of Sorts (Boxcars) / Stumble / *Four-track demos, Tyrone's, Athens, Ga., 12/80:* All the Right Friends / A Different Girl / Narrator / Just a Touch / Baby I / Mystery to Me / Permanent Vacation

(63) Radio Free Georgia

2LP Bee Records RM-01 **$25-32**

Stock Pavilion, Madison, Wisconsin, May 10, 1985. Listed as Felt Forum, New York, New York, November 7, 1986. Numerous tracks are improperly titled and ordered.

Feeling Gravitys Pull / Harborcoat / Green Grow the Rushes / Seven Chinese Brothers / Hyena / Good Advices / Talk About the Passion / Driver 8 / Can't Get There From Here / So. Central Rain / Maps and Legends / Auctioneer / Old Man Kensey / Pretty Persuasion / Life and How To Live It / Little America / Second Guessing / (Don't Go Back To) Rockville / Just a Touch / Theme From Two Steps Onward / Gardening at Night / 9-9 / Windout / Pale Blue Eyes / Have You Ever Seen the Rain

(64) Radio Song

CD On Stage OS CD3 **$22-25**

A collection of live recordings. Made in Italy.

Radio Song / Fretless / Me in Honey / Half a World Away / Love is All Around / Swan Swan H / Begin the Begin / Pop Song '89 / Turn You Inside-Out / You Are the Everything / Perfect Circle

(65) Radio Songs

CD CD-101 **$22-25**

NDR Studio 11, Hamburg, Germany, March 5, 1991. A bootleg of a performance taped for radio broadcast where the band performed acoustic versions of songs from *Out of Time*. Includes lengthy amusing segments of the band members talking amongst themselves and to the crew in the sound truck between songs. Apparently, only "Losing My Religion" was broadcast live during this session.

World Leader Pretend / Half a World Away / Belong / Fretless / Radio Song (two false starts) / Radio Song / You Are the Everything / Losing My Religion / Radio Song (false start) / Radio Song (without intro)

(66) Rapid Eye Movement

CD Turtle Records TR8 **$22-25**

Utrecht, Holland, September 14, 1987; Oslo, Norway, October 6, 1985.

Utrecht, Holland: Finest Worksong / These Days / Lightnin' Hopkins / Welcome to the Occupation Driver 8 / Feeling Gravitys Pull / I Believe / The One I Love / Exhuming McCarthy / Wolves, Lower Fall On Me / Superman / Just a Touch / Oddfellows Local 151 / Hyena / *Oslo, Norway:* Letter Never Sent / Driver 8 / Old Man Kensey / Pretty Persuasion / 1,000,000

(67) Rapid Eye Movements, The Georgia Peaches

2LP REM Records L29875 **$25-32**
2LP REM Records L29875 (pink vinyl) **30-40**
2LP REM Records L29875 (reissue) **25-32**

Bayfront Center Theater, St. Petersburg, Florida, November 26, 1985. The same show was re-released using a different cover.

Feeling Gravitys Pull / Harborcoat / Driver 8 / Pilgrimage / Green Grow the Rushes / Maps and Legends / So. Central Rain / Laughing / Seven Chinese Brothers / It's a Restless World / Can't Get There From Here / West of the Fields / Old Man Kensey / Auctioneer (Another Engine) / Pretty Persuasion / Little America / Second Guessing / Shaking Through / So You Want To Be a Rock and Roll Star (w/Roger McGuinn) / Toys in the Attic

(68) Really Exciting Music

LP Easy Flyte Records Flyte 201 **$25-32**

Drive-in Studios, Winston-Salem, North Carolina; Reflection Studios, Charlotte, North Carolina. *Chronic Town*, *Murmur* and *Reckoning* studio outtakes, plus the Hib-Tone cuts. This early bootleg was the first to contain the Hib-Tone tracks.

Chronic Town outtakes, Drive-In Studio, Winston-Salem, N.C. 10/81: 1,000,000 / Ages of You / Carnival of Sorts (Boxcars) / Shut Down (White Tornado) *Drive-In Studio, Winston-Salem, N.C. 4/15/81 (Hib-Tone cuts):* Radio Free Europe / Sitting Still / *Murmur outtake, Reflection Studio, Charlotte, N.C. 1/83:* There She Goes Again (B-side of I.R.S. "Radio Free Europe" single) / *Reckoning outtakes, Reflection Studio, Charlotte, N.C. 12/83:* Windout / Pretty Persuasion / Time After Time / So. Central Rain / Little America

(69) R.E.M. Acoustic 1991

CD Rarities and Few Records RSCD/S 1124 **$10-16**

BBC Studios, London, March 13, 1991. Given away with *Seattle 1989* CD. Made in Italy.

Losing My Religion / Half a World Away / Radio Song / Love is All Around

(70) R.E.M. as Bingo Hand Job

2LP Religious Records PUG-1 **$30-40**

The Borderline, London, England, March 15, 1991. Made in England.

World Leader Pretend / Half a World Away / Fretless / The One I Love / Hello in There / My Eldest Son / Dallas / Disturbance at the Heron House / Belong / Low / Love is All Around / Radio Song /

Pop Song '89 / Losing My Religion / Fall On Me / Tom's Diner / Listening to the Higsons / You Ain't Going Nowhere / Get Up / Moon River

(71) **R.E.M. Live in Chicago**
7" Basil Productions U.S. 84 150 302 **$15-20**
Aragon Ballroom, Chicago, Illinois, July 7, 1984. The A-side of the record is labelled "So. Central Rain" but plays "Harborcoat."
Harborcoat / Pale Blue Eyes

(72) **Reminiscence**
2CD Bullseye CD-EYE-23 **$45-55**
The Forum, Los Angeles, California, March 15, 1989. Made in Australia.
Pop Song '89 / Exhuming McCarthy / Welcome to the Occupation / Turn You Inside-Out / Pilgrimage / Orange Crush / Disturbance at the Heron House / Feeling Gravitys Pull / Time After Time / World Leader Pretend / Begin the Begin / Pretty Persuasion / I Believe / Crazy / Get Up / Auctioneer / It's the End of the World As We Know It (and I Feel Fine) / Stand / Wolves, Lower / Fall On Me / You Are the Everything / Finest Worksong / King of Birds / I Remember California / Strange / Perfect Circle / After Hours

(73) **Return of the Rickenbackers**
LP Kabjdo Records (original issue in picture sleeve) **$30-35**
LP Kabjdo Records (reissue in title sleeve) **25-30**
Paradise Theater, Boston, Massachusetts, July 13, 1983. From a WBCN FM radio broadcast.
Seven Chinese Brothers / Sitting Still / Pretty Persuasion / Harborcoat / West of the Fields / Radio Free Europe / Gloria *(From Tupelo's Tavern, New Orleans, 6/1/82)* / Ages of You / We Walk / 1,000,000 / There She Goes Again / California Dreaming / Carnival of Sorts (Boxcars)

■ *Return of the Rickenbackers*, one of the earlier bootlegs.

■ *Smokin' in the Boys Room*

(74) **Ripe!, The Georgia Peaches**
2LP Parrot REM-7 **$25-32**
Tyrone's O.C., Athens, Georgia, January 10, 1981. Of the bootlegs that contain tracks from the January 10 show at Tyrone's, this one is the most complete.
Rave On / Burning Down / With a Girl Like You / What If We Give It Away? / There She Goes Again / Pretty Persuasion / Body Count / A Different Girl / Action / Narrator / Hey! Hey! Nadine / Baby I / Permanent Vacation / Radio Free Europe / Sitting Still / Dangerous Times / All the Right Friends / Shaking Through / Hey Little Girl / (Don't Go Back To) Rockville / Windout / Gardening at Night / Wait / Scheherazade / Lisa Says / Mystery to Me / White Tornado

(75) **Rock and Roll Stars**
CD Howdy Records, CD 555-19 **$22-25**
Music Hall, Seattle, Washington, June 27, 1984. Made in Germany.
Moral Kiosk / Catapult / Hyena / Camera / Pilgrimage / Talk About the Passion / Seven Chinese Brothers / So. Central Rain / Pretty Persuasion / Gardening at Night / 9-9 / Windout / Old Man Kensey / Radio Free Europe / Little America / Burning Down / Pale Blue Eyes / 1,000,000 / So You Want To Be a Rock and Roll Star / Carnival of Sorts / Skank

(76) **Rolling Stone**

2LP Autodight Records 1345 **$30-35**

Syria Mosque, Pittsburgh, Pennsylvania, October 24, 1986. This bootleg uses the famous Rolling Stone cover photo of R.E.M. from December, 1987 which used the caption, "America's best Rock and Roll band." Unfortunately, the cover is infinitely better in quality than the sound on this release.

These Days / Harborcoat / Sitting Still / The One I Love / West of the Fields / Shaking Through / Feeling Gravitys Pull / White Tornado / The Flowers of Guatemala / Maps and Legends / Driver 8 / I Believe / Seven Chinese Brothers / Superman / Can't Get There From Here / Pretty Persuasion / Auctioneer (Another Engine) / Little America / Fall On Me / Cuyahoga / 1,000,000

(77) **Seattle 1989 (It's the End of the World)**

CD Rarities & Few Records RSCD 1124 **$22-25**

Miami Arena, Miami, Florida, April 29, 1989, and Orlando Arena, Orlando, Florida, April 30, 1989. *R.E.M. Acoustic 1991* CD (RSCD/S 1124) given away with some copies. The tracks were not recorded in Seattle, but were lifted from the Westwood 1 "Superstars in Concert" radio discs. Made in Italy.

Pop Song 89 / Exhuming McCarthy / Welcome to the Occupation / Disturbance at the Heron House / Turn You Inside-Out / Orange Crush / Feeling Gravitys Pull / Swan Swan H / Begin the Begin / Pretty Persuasion / I Believe / King of Birds / Crazy / Finest Worksong / You Are the Everything / Academy Fight Song / Stand / Perfect Circle / Get Up / It's the End of the World As We Know It (and I Feel Fine)

(78) **Slightly Out of Time**

CD 92-R-14-07 **$25-35**

John Keane Studios, Athens, Georgia; Bearsville Studios, Woodstock, New York. Studio demos and outtakes from *Out of Time* recording sessions. This is one of the best quality bootlegs of the *Out of Time* demos, and dealers that handle bootlegs generally ask more for this title than for most of the other common bootleg CDs. Made in Italy.

Radio Song / Belong / Texarkana / Losing My Religion / Speed Metal / Shiny Happy People / Me in Honey / Half a World Away / untitled instrumental / Radio Song / Near Wild Heaven / Fretless / Low / Country Feedback / Ghost Riders (Reindeer) in the Sky / It's a Free World, Baby / Here I Am Again / untitled / Endgame

(79) **Smokin' in the Boys Room**

LP Class Act Records C-116 (original issue in green and white sleeve) **$25-32**
LP Class Act Records C-116 (reissue in yellow and white sleeve) **18-24**

Drive-In Studio, Winston-Salem, North Carolina, April 15, 1981; Agora Ballroom, Hartford, Connecticut, July 20, 1983; Larry's Hideaway, Toronto, Canada, July 1983. Originally issued in 1983 in a paper sleeve with green printing, reissued in paperboard sleeve with yellow printing using a somewhat different layout. This is the only bootleg thus far released with Mitch Easter's "Radio Dub" of the original "Radio Free Europe."

Drive-In Studio, 4/81: White Tornado / Radio Dub (Mitch Easter's remix of Radio Free Europe) / *Agora Ballroom, Hartford:* Smokin' in the Boys Room / *Larry's Hideaway, Toronto, 7/83:* Moral Kiosk / Laughing / There She Goes Again / Talk About the Passion / Sitting Still / Harborcoat / 9-9 / West of the Fields / Pretty Persuasion / Carnival of Sorts (Boxcars)

(80) **So Much Younger Then**

LP FTP-0011 **$18-24**

Tyrone's O.C., Athens, Georgia, January 10, 1981.

Body Count / A Different Girl / Action / Narrator / Hey! Hey! Nadine / Baby I / Permanent Vacation / Wait / Scheherazade / Lisa Says / Mystery to Me / All the Right Friends / Little Girl / Dangerous Times

(81) **Songs For a Green World**

2LP Flashback World Productions Flash L.P. 06.91.0150-33 **$20-25**
CD Flashback World Productions Flash 06.91.0150 **22-25**

Miami Arena, Miami, Florida, April 29, 1989, and Orlando Arena, Orlando, Florida, April 30, 1989. A re-packaging of the Westwood 1 "Superstars in Concert" radio show. The CD version omits "It's the End of the World As We Know It (and I Feel Fine)." Made in Luxembourg.

Pop Song '89 / Exhuming McCarthy / Welcome to the Occupation / Disturbance at the Heron House / Turn You Inside-Out / Orange Crush / Feeling Gravitys Pull / Swan Swan H / Begin the Begin / Pretty Persuasion / I Believe / King of Birds / Crazy / Finest Worksong / You Are the Everything / Academy Fight Song / Stand / Perfect Circle / Get Up / It's the End of the World As We Know It (and I Feel Fine)

(82) **Songs From Little America**

CD Flashback World Productions Flash 09.92.0189 **$22-25**

Music Hall, Seattle, Washington, June 27, 1984.

Moral Kiosk / Catapult / Hyena / Camera / Pilgrimage / Talk About the Passion / Seven Chinese Brothers / So. Central Rain / Pretty Persuasion / Gardening at Night / 9-9 / Windout / Old Man

Kensey / Radio Free Europe / Little America / Burning Down / Pale Blue Eyes / 1,000,000 / So You Want To Be a Rock and Roll Star / Carnival of Sorts / Skank

(83) **The Sound and the Fury**

CD Turtle Records TR-284 **$22-25**

The 9:30 Club, Washington, D.C., March 18, 1983.

Gardening at Night / 9-9 / Catapult / Pilgrimage / Seven Chinese Brothers / Laughing / Wolves, Lower / Romance / Sitting Still / 1,000,000 / West of the Fields / Radio Free Europe / Last Date / Ages of You / We Walk / Carnival of Sorts (Boxcars)

(84) **Stab It and Steer It**

CD Adobe Music CD RAIN 1 **$22-25**

Various live and studio tracks from 1981-1985. Made in England.

Murmur outtakes, Reflection Studios, Charlotte, N.C., 1/83: That Beat / Pretty Persuasion / All the Right Friends / Tighten Up / There She Goes Again / Moon River / *Stock Pavillion, Madison, Wisc., 5/10/85:* Theme From Two Steps Onward / *Brown University, Providence, R.I., 4/27/85:* When I Was Young (I Believe) / *John Keane Studios, Athens, Ga., 3/86:* Bad Day / *Rhythmic Studios, San Francisco, Cal., 11/9/83:* The Lion Sleeps Tonight / Skank / Walter's Theme / Cushy Tush / *Reflection Studios, Charlotte, N.C., 1/83:* Gardening at Night (acoustic) / Mystery to Me / Gardening at Night (acoustic II) / *Community Trolls cassette:* Tainted Obligations

(85) **Standing Room Only**

Swingin' Pig Records **$22-25**

The Muziekcentrum, Utrecht, Holland, September 14, 1987. This was the first R.E.M. bootleg issued on CD.

Finest Worksong / These Days / Lightnin' Hopkins / Welcome to the Occupation / Driver 8 / Feeling Gravitys Pull / I Believe / The One I Love / Exhuming McCarthy / Wolves, Lower / Fall On Me / Superman / Just a Touch / Oddfellows Local 151 / Strange / Disturbance at the Heron House / Funtime / Moral Kiosk / Life and How To Live It

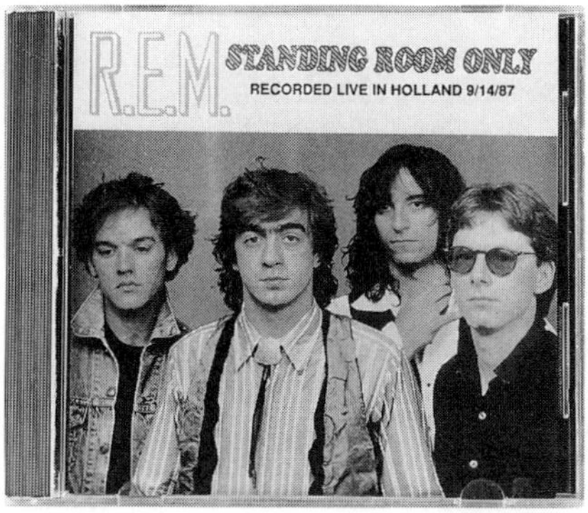

■ *Standing Room Only*, the first R.E.M. bootleg on CD

■ *Tanzplagen*

(86) **Streets of Millionaires**

CD Raid Masters CD 910709 **$22-25**

Larry's Hideaway, Toronto, Canada, July 9, 1983. The inserts indicate incorrectly that the show was recorded in "San Francisco, California, 1983." Inserts with both red and black lettering exist. This bootleg uses the same material (plus the track "1,000,000"), and has the identical cover as the vinyl bootleg, *Mada Mada*. Made in Italy.

Laughing / Pilgrimage / There She Goes Again / Seven Chinese Brothers / Talk About the Passion / Sitting Still / Harborcoat / Catapult / Gardening at Night / 9-9 / Just a Touch / West of the Fields / Radio Free Europe / We Walk / 1,000,000

(87) **Tanzplagen**

CD Strange Ways Records EFA 11056-10 **$18-24**

Studio tracks, plus live at the 40 Watt Club in Athens, Georgia, circa 1981. An early combo featuring Michael Stipe on vocals. Made in Germany.

studio tracks: Treason / Meeting / *live at the 40 Watt:* Living By the Neck / Meeting / Peter Pan

(88) **That Beat in Time**

CD OMK Records OMK CD 001 **$28-34**

Tyrone's O.C., Athens, Georgia, 1980 or 1981. Probably the best sounding bootleg of any of the Tyrone's shows. Contrary to some reports, this is not the oft-bootlegged January 10, 1981 performance. The show probably took place in the winter of 1980 (possibly November 6), because the set includes "Radio Free Europe" but not "Sitting Still."

Hey! Hey! Nadine / Burning Down / Dangerous Times / There She Goes Again / (Don't Go Back To) Rockville / Body Count / Just a Touch / Sitting Still / Permanent Vacation / What If We Give it Away? / Shaking Through / Romance / Laughing / Pretty Persuasion / That Beat / Stumble / Radio Free Europe / Carnival of Sorts (Boxcars) / Skank / Windout / Gardening at Night / White Tornado

■ *That Beat in Time*

(89) **These Days**

CD Why Not WOT 1008 **$22-25**

Hammersmith Palais Ballroom, London, England, October 29, 1985; John Keane Studios, Athens, Georgia, March 1986 (*Lifes Rich Pageant* demos). Made in Italy.

London, 1985: Moral Kiosk / Letter Never Sent / Laughing / Maps and Legends / Driver 8 / Fall On Me / Can't Get There From Here / Seven Chinese Brothers / West of the Fields / Auctioneer (Another Engine) / Old Man Kensey / Gardening At Night / Radio Free Europe / We Walk / Pretty Persuasion / See No Evil / *Lifes Rich Pageant demos:* Theme From Two Steps Onward / These Days / PSA / I Believe

(90) **This Is It**

CD **$22-25**

40 Watt Club, Athens, Georgia, November 19, 1992; MTV Rock & Roll Inaugural Ball, Washington, D.C., January 20, 1993. The two tracks from the inaugural ball feature members of 10,000 Maniacs and U2.

Drive / Monty Got a Raw Deal / Everybody Hurts / Man on the Moon / Losing My Religion / Country Feedback / Begin the Begin / Fall On Me / Me in Honey / Finest Worksong / Drive / Love is All Around / Funtime / Radio Free Europe / *MTV Inaugural Ball:* Candy Everybody Wants / One

(91) **Time of Outtakes**

CD 9201 **$22-25**

John Keane Studios, Athens, Georgia; Bearsville Studios, Woodstock, New York. Demos and outtakes from the *Out of Time* recording sessions. This is probably the best quality boot of the *Out of Time* demos. Made in Germany.

Half a World Away / untitled / Fretless / Mandolin Strum / Texarkana / It's a Free World, Baby / Low / Endgame / Radio Song / Country Feedback / Losing My Religion / Speed Metal / Here I Am Again / Near Wild Heaven / Shiny Happy People / Belong / Radio Song / Me in Honey

(92) **Twentieth Century Boys volume 1**

CD Scorpion REM-92-SC **$25-30**

Stichcraft, Athens, Georgia, September 30, 1983. Made in Italy.

I Got You Babe / Second Guessing / Harborcoat / Pretty Persuasion / Pills / 1,000,000 / Camera / Talk About the Passion / Little America / All the Right Friends / Letter Never Sent / Just a Touch / Secret Agent Man / Hootenanny / Route 66 / Windout / 9-9 / Six Stock Answers / My Roof, Your Roof / Pale Blue Eyes / Tainted Obligations

(93) **Twentieth Century Boys volume 2**

CD Scorpion REM-92-SC **$25-30**

Stichcraft, Athens, Georgia, September 30, 1983; Tyrone's O.C., Athens, Georgia, October 4, 1980. Made in Italy.

Stichcraft: Welcome to the Starlight / Twentieth Century Boy / Seven Chinese Brothers / Crazy / That Beat / (Don't Go Back To) Rockville) / Carnival of Sorts (Boxcars) / *Tyrone's:* Just a Touch / With a Girl Like You / Dangerous Times / There She Goes Again / I Can Only Give You Everything / All the Right Friends / (Don't Go Back To) Rockville / Body Count / Hippy Hippy Shake / Action / Narrator / Hey! Hey! Nadine / Gardening at Night / Scheherazade / Lisa Says / Mystery to Me / Permanent Vacation / ***unknown source:*** Stepping Stone

(94) **Unreleased Live LP**

CD Unbelievable UM 029 **$22-25**

Page Auditorium, Duke University, Durham, North Carolina, September 26, 1984, plus "bonus songs." Rumors circulated for years that I.R.S. was preparing to release a live R.E.M. LP at one time, and the liner notes for this bootleg claim that it is the recording that I.R.S. planned to use. Various sources have indicated that the I.R.S. project got only as far as the making of acetates and test pressings, and that pressure from R.E.M. caused I.R.S. to abandon the live album. Whether or not this is in fact true remains to be proven. A portion of the same concert was released in 1986 on the vinyl bootleg *We Are Having a Heavenly Time*. Made in Germany.

Seven Chinese Brothers / Catapult / Radio Free Europe / 9-9 / Gardening at Night / Windout / Letter Never Sent / Kahoetek / So. Central Rain / (Don't Go Back To) Rockville / 1,000,000 / Hyena / West of the Fields / Old Man Kensey / Second Guessing / *Live Bonus Songs*: Hyena / Letter Never Sent / Driver 8 / Old Man Kensey / Pretty Persuasion / 1,000,000 / Second Guessing

(95) **We Are Having a Heavenly Time**

LP PFM Records Q-9022 **$18-24**

Page Auditorium, Duke University, Durham, North Carolina, September 26, 1984. Purports to be an official fan club issue, but is not.

Seven Chinese Brothers / Catapult / Radio Free Europe / Letter Never Sent / Kahoetek / So. Central Rain / Driver 8 / (Don't Go Back To) Rockville / 1,000,000 / Hyena / Old Man Kensey / Second Guessing

(96) **We Support Greenpeace**

CD Unbelievable UM 034 **$18-24**

40 Watt Club, Athens, Georgia, November 19, 1992. Made in Germany.

Drive / Monty Got a Raw Deal / Everybody Hurts / Man on the Moon / Losing My Religion / Country Feedback / Begin the Begin / Fall On Me / Me in Honey / Finest Worksong / Drive / Love is All Around / Funtime / Radio Free Europe / ***unknown source:*** Losing My Religion

■ R.E.M. with Peter Holsapple on the day of their "Mountain Stage" live radio performance. Parts of the show appear on the bootlegs *Acoustic Tour 1991* and *Latex or Oil Based?*

(97) Welcome to the Hoedown

CD TNT TBU CDA 101 **$22-25**

Stock Pavillion, Madison, Wisconsin, May 10, 1985; Brown University, Providence, Rhode Island, April 27, 1985. Made in Italy.

Harborcoat / Green Grow the Rushes / Seven Chinese Brothers / Hyena / Good Advices / Talk About the Passion / Driver 8 / Can't Get There From Here / So. Central Rain / Maps and Legends / Auctioneer / Life and How To Live It / Little America / Second Guessing / (Don't Go Back To) Rockville / Just a Touch / Theme From Two Steps Onward / Gardening at Night / 9-9 / Windout / Have You Ever Seen the Rain / *Brown University:* I Believe

(98) We're Blinking Just As Fast As We Can

2LP Great Live Concerts GLC3791 **$35-40**

Music Hall, Seattle, Washington, June 27, 1984. This was the first bootleg of the Seattle Source radio show to appear.

Moral Kiosk / Catapult / Hyena / Camera / Pilgrimage / Talk About the Passion / Seven Chinese Brothers / So. Central Rain / Pretty Persuasion / Gardening at Night / 9-9 / Windout / Old Man Kensey / Radio Free Europe / Little America / Burning Down / Pale Blue Eyes / 1,000,000 / So You Want To Be a Rock and Roll Star / Carnival of Sorts / Skank

(99) Working

2LP Autodight 1346 U.S. **$32-40**
2LP Autodight ADR 1346 (reissue with different cover) **20-30**

Universal Amphitheater, Los Angeles, California, November 15, 1987.

Finest Worksong / These Days / Welcome to the Occupation / Pilgrimage / Disturbance at the Heron House / Exhuming McCarthy / Don't Call on Me (Orange Crush) / Feeling Gravitys Pull / King of Birds / I Believe / Sitting Still / Ghost Riders in the Sky / Pretty Persuasion / Superman / Oddfellows Local 151 / It's the End of the World As We Know It (and I Feel Fine) / Begin the Begin / 1,000,000 Wolves, Lower / See No Evil / Pop Hit '89 (Pop Song '89) / Ghost Riders / Cuyahoga / Crazy

The following bootlegs are rumored to exist, but their existence could not be substantiated:

Contents

2LP File Under Grain FUG-1

Auckland, New Zealand, 1989.

titles not available

Green in Concert

LP R.E.M. U.S.A. H2-247

North American tour, 1989.

Be All You Can Be / Pop Song '89 / Get Up / You Are the Everything / Stand / World Leader Pretend / The Wrong Child / Orange Crush / Turn You Inside-Out / Hairshirt / I Remember California / Untitled Army Theme part 2

I Don't Do Autographs

2LP Bbbbbrlech 67

Various Live, 1987, two twelve-inch 45 RPM singles.

Pittsburgh, Pennsylvania: Orange Crush / Stand / Turn You Inside-Out / Pop Song '89 / *unknown source*: Radio Free Europe / Sitting Still / Harborcoat

It Crawled from the South

Peppermint Lounge, New York, New York, October 31, 1983. Cassette tapes of this legendary Halloween show full of one-off cover songs and audience taunting were heavily traded not long after the performance, at which R.E.M. was billed under the moniker "It Crawled From the South." The existence of a vinyl bootleg of this show using the band's stage name from the performance remains extremely suspect, as many long-time collectors have heard that such a record exists, but none have ever been able to verify its existence. The possibility that a vinyl version of *It Crawled From the South* existed was further perpetuated by its inclusion in a 1987 feature on R.E.M. in *Goldmine* magazine. However the author of the piece admitted that he had never actually *seen* a copy.

R=4

2LP Dream Sequence DSR-01/02

Various live, 1985-1989.

It's the End of the World As We Know It (and I Feel Fine) / Driver 8 / Hard Luck Yosemite / Radio Free Europe / Stand / Orange Crush / Pop Song '89 / The One I Love / Fall On Me / Smokin' in the Boys Room / Get Up / Hairshirt / Turn You Inside-Out / Dark Globe / So You Want To Be a Rock and Roll Star / World Leader Pretend / Bandwagon / Finest Worksong / Wendell Gee / Strawberry Fields Forever / Femme Fatale / More This Than That

Rhythmus Et Melos
LP
Music Hall, Seattle, Washington, June 27, 1984
Moral Kiosk / Driver 8 / Catapult / Hyena / Pilgrimage / Old Man Kensey / Radio Free Europe / Little America

They Airbrushed This Box
7" box DSR 03-07
Various acoustic, 1989. Packaged as five seven-inch 45s on green vinyl in a boxed set.
Pop Song 89 / Get Up / Turn You Inside-Out / You Are the Everything / Stand / The Wrong Child / World Leader Pretend / Orange Crush / Hairshirt / I Remember California / Untitled / I Will Follow

INTERVIEW DISCS

R.E.M. Interview picture disc
U.K. LP Baktabak BAK 2057 **in print**
The material from this unauthorized picture disc comes from interviews which took place in November 1984 (with all four band members) and June, 1985 (with Buck and Mills) for Piccadilly radio in England. Released September 1987.

Rapid Mouth Movement
U.K. LP Powwow POW 01 **$15-22**
This 48 minute interview from 1986 was pressed onto green vinyl and sold openly in the U.S., despite the fact that it was unauthorized. Released September 1989.

Shiny Chatty People
U.K. CD Baktabak CBAK 4041 **in print**
This disc includes material previously released on the R.E.M. interview picture disc above, recorded for the BBC, and was released in September 1991. In July 1992, the disc was packaged with the German four track "Radio Song" CD single, and these discs were sold together in a double CD jewel box.

R.E.M. Audio Visual
U.K. CD Bespoke Records BSP.001 **in print**
U.K. LP Bespoke Records BSP.001 **in print**
A compact disc and LP (numbered to 1500) featuring interview material from 1983 (with all four band members), 1987 (with Peter Buck), and 1991 (with Michael Stipe, Peter Buck and Mike Mills), all of which were conducted in the U.K. for the fanzine *Bucketfull of Brains*. The booklet includes the entire text of the interviews on the disc. The disc was also issued in a numbered box set (limited to 1000) entitled *Rapid Ear Movement*, which included the Dutch "nice price" CDs of *Fables of the Reconstruction*, *Dead Letter Office*, *Lifes Rich Pageant*, *Document* and *Eponymous*. Released November 1991.

R.E.M. ON VIDEO

R.E.M. Succumbs

Radio Free Europe / So. Central Rain / Left of Reckoning / Can't Get There From Here / Driver 8 / Life and How To Live It / Feeling Gravitys Pull / Fall On Me

Release date: June 1, 1987

U.K.	A&M Video	089 8373/AM 837	**in print**
U.S.	A&M Video	VC 61710	**in print**
U.S.	A&M Video	LV 38403 (laserdisc)	**in print**

Due to the overwhelming number of requests from fans, R.E.M. and I.R.S. released this collection of videos in 1987. In addition to the standard videos made for the band's singles, the compilation also includes Jim Herbert's twenty-minute film entitled "Left of Reckoning," shot just outside of Gainesville, Georgia, amongst folk artist R. A. Miller's whirligigs. Also included are videos for "Life and How To Live It," and "Feeling Gravitys Pull," neither of which ever ran on music video channels. Jim Herbert had also prepared a video for "Green Grow the Rushes," which didn't make the final cut on the tape. The band had previously filmed a video for "Wolves," which was not included on this collection. Sales of the compilation were extremely strong, and *R.E.M. Succumbs* ended up as the best-selling music video compilation of 1987.

Athens, GA-Inside/Out

Release date: January 1987

U.K.	Polygram 041-650-2	**in print**
U.S.	Polygram 041 650-3	**in print**

Not an R.E.M. item per se, but the band is featured prominently in this documentary about the music scene in Athens, circa 1986. They are seen performing "Swan Swan H" and the Everly Brothers' "(All I Have To Do Is) Dream" live in the Lucy Cobb Chapel in Athens, and Stipe, Buck and Mills are all interviewed.

I.R.S. Records Presents the Best of The Cutting Edge, vol. 1

Release date: 1986

Rhino Video RNVD 2401			**$15-20**

"The Cutting Edge" was a popular fixture on MTV, and parts of R.E.M.'s July 1984 appearance on the show was included on this sixty-minute video cassette, released in 1987. The band is seen performing acoustic renditions of "(Don't Go Back To) Rockville," "Driver 8," "Time After Time," "Wendell Gee," and "Smokin' in the Boy's Room." Also included are interview segments with Michael Stipe, Peter Buck and Mike Mills, and performances and interviews with R.E.M.'s contemporaries, The dB's, The Fleshtones, The Alarm, The Flat Duo Jets, and others.

Pop Screen

The One I Love / It's the It's the End of the World As We Know It (and I Feel Fine) / Finest Worksong / Talk About the Passion / Orange Crush / Stand / Turn You Inside-Out / Pop Song 89 / Get Up

Release date: U.S.: March 6, 1990; U.K.: October 10, 1990.

Japan	Warner Brothers	laserdisc	**$40-55**
U.K.	Warner Reprise Video	7599-38156-3	**in print**
U.S.	Warner Reprise Video	38156-3	**in print**
U.S.	Warner Reprise Video	9 38156-6 (laserdisc)	**in print**

In order to fill the gap between LP releases, Warner Brothers acquired the rights to the later videos that were made while the band was still signed to I.R.S., and together with the videos for *Green*, released this collection. Since some of these videos were rarely played on the major video channels, this cassette was no doubt something that R.E.M. fans were hoping for. Promotional editions of *Pop Screen* were released in the U.S. and U.K.

Tourfilm

Stand / The One I Love / These Days / Turn You Inside-Out / World Leader Pretend / Feeling Gravitys Pull / I Believe / I Remember California / Get Up / It's the End of the World As We Know It (and I Feel Fine) / Pop Song '89 / Fall On Me / You Are the Everything / Begin the Begin / King of Birds / Finest Worksong / Perfect Circle

Release date: September 25, 1990

Japan	Warner Brothers	laserdisc	**$40-55**
U.K.	Warner Music Vision	7599-38184-3	**in print**
U.S.	Warner Reprise Video	38184-3	**in print**
U.S.	Warner Reprise Video	9 38184-6 (laserdisc)	**in print**

This long-awaited live concert video from R.E.M. finally hit the shelves a year after the footage was shot in Macon and Atlanta, Georgia, Hampton, Virginia, and Greensboro, North Carolina. The release marked the first time since the band's founding that live concert footage was released on video which used the actual audio track from the same performance. Some audio tracks and one video track from *Tourfilm* were released as a five-inch promotional CD in October 1990.

Time Piece

Release date: March 4, 1991

U.S.	Warner Brothers	(promotion only)	**$30-45**

This promotional video contains eighteen minutes of "News, views and clues about R.E.M.'s new album, *Out of Time*," plus the video for "Losing My Religion." The interesting and entertaining interview segments are interspersed with off-the-cuff acoustic performances of some of the songs from *Out of Time*, including "Losing My Religion," performed on Peter Buck's porch.

■ The *Timepiece* and *Automatic For the People* promotional videos from Warner Brothers

This Film Is On

Losing My Religion / Shiny Happy People / Near Wild Heaven / Radio Song / Love is All Around / Losing My Religion (acoustic) / Low / Belong / Half a World Away / Country Feedback

Release date: September 1991

Germany	Warner Brothers	7599 38254-3	**in print**
U.K.	Warner Brothers	7599 38254-3	**in print**
U.S.	Warner Brothers	38254-3	**in print**
U.S.	Warner Brothers	9 38254-6 (laserdisc)	**in print**

This Film Is On includes all of the promotional videos prepared from *Out of Time* that you might have seen on music video channels, plus a number of videos that are exclusive to this compilation. The treats for fans are live versions of the Troggs' "Love is All Around" from MTV Unplugged, and "Losing My Religion" from the U.K. TV series "The Late Show." The creative efforts of six different editors appear on the compilation, which results in a collection of videos that maintain a high level of individuality. The title of the collection was lifted from a lyric in the song "Country Feedback."

Automatic For the People video press kit

Release date: October 1992

U.S.	Warner Brothers	(promotion only)	**$25-40**

This promotional video includes interviews with Peter Buck, Mike Mills, and Bill Berry, and shows the band performing "Find the River." Also interviewed is the owner of Weaver D's restaurant in Athens, who shows viewers around his establishment and discusses the restaurant's now famous slogan, "Automatic For the People." Ten-minute and sixteen-minute versions of the video were released, both issued in plastic boxes with album cover artwork on the covers.

Other video appearances

The band has made numerous appearances on TV around the world that fans have been quick enough to record on VCRs. Perhaps the most sought-after appearances are their performances on the David Letterman show in October 1983, and Solid Gold Hits in 1984. Also popular are their performances on England's "The Tube" (the first of which was in November 1983), MTV's "Cutting Edge," Nickelodeon's "Livewire" in 1983, Showtime's "Rock of the 80's," MTV's "Rock Influences," and "Unplugged," and the band's performance on the Arsenio Hall show in October 1989, which never aired in many cities due to an earthquake in San Francisco. Another prized item is the video that was made by Jim Herbert for "Green Grow the Rushes" that was never officially released, but seems to have made its way into the video collections of a few fans. The "Wolves, Lower" video, which was deemed unworthy for inclusion on *R.E.M. Succumbs*, is also actively traded.

Also collectible are the promotional videos sent out by I.R.S. and Warner Brothers for the video singles, and for *R.E.M. Succumbs, Pop Screen, Tourfilm, This Film Is On,* and their 1991 appearance on MTV Unplugged. These are generally packaged in plain plastic cases with the title and running times printed on the outside, and otherwise do not differ from their commercial counterparts. The I.R.S. promotional video for "The One I Love" includes an informative and humorous Michael Stipe interview entitled, "A Conversation with Michael Stipe," in which Jefferson Holt asks Stipe questions about the making and content of the *Document* LP.

In addition to his work with R.E.M., Michael Stipe has made appearances in a number of other commercially available videos. The 10,000 Maniacs' *Time Capsule* collection includes Stipe performing "Hello in There" with Natalie Merchant and Billy Bragg, and the Indigo Girls' *Live at the Uptown Lounge* video features Stipe adding vocals on "Kid Fears." Stipe made his acting debut in a Robert Longo short film entitled *Arena Brains* (1987), now available on video, in which he plays "The Watcher." In addition, the versatile front man can be seen reading a poem in the C-00 film *Lighthearted Nation* (1989). Stipe also made a cameo appearance in the B-52's "Deadbeat Club" video.

With the declining price of the hand-held camcorder, more and more R.E.M. concerts will surely become available to video tape traders. Numerous performances from the *Green* tour, and from earlier tours are in circulation, but they are generally poor in quality.

FAN CLUB ITEMS AND MERCHANDISE

Liz Carter, who ran the R.E.M. fan club from its inception in 1984 to the fall of 1991, described it as "The fan club for people who are not fan club joiners." It is one of the few fan clubs that is truly controlled by the band itself, rather than by a merchandising company. Though the distribution of posters and T-shirts and the like is handled by Nice Man Merchandising in Minnesota, the band oversees all of the designs used and maintains editorial control over the information that is disseminated.

The fan club officially began operation in June 1984 following the release of *Reckoning*, which, together with *Chronic Town* and *Murmur*, inspired hundreds of fans to send letters to the band's address on the album jackets. Those that wrote, many wanting lyrics for the album, received a small card that stated, "Join the club! Be brave-- send $10.00 now to join." The club initially catered to a small family of fans that received regular mailings and offers of eclectic merchandise like the "Gardening at Night" gloves and the Swiss army bags, but by June 1988 its ranks had swelled to 1800 members. Liz Carter was initially hired just to run the club, but as the band became more and more popular, Liz was asked to help with the increasingly more numerous tasks associated with managing the band's affairs. The steady increase in fan club membership coupled with the growing popularity of the band proved to be somewhat of a burden on the club, and mailings become patently less frequent and less informative. The club did, however, begin a popular annual tradition in December 1988 with the release of the first fan club single, "Parade of the Wooden Soldiers." Since that time, members have received a single every December which has a Christmas song on one side, backed with an invariably interesting cover song on the flip. The band had always given fans a special treat of some kind in previous Christmas mailouts, but when the word spread that every year they were sending out records that contained unique tracks, enrollment in the club jumped again. The increased enrollment contributed to the loss of what been an earlier fan club tradition, the mailing of a fully autographed band photo to each member. Today the club's membership stands at about 6,000.

In addition to the items listed here, there are also a number of officially licensed T-shirts that bear the copyright from "R.E.M./Athens, Ltd." The tour shirts, promotional shirts, and special edition T-shirts are generally the only ones that change hands for significant sums of money. Also not listed here are editions of the fan club newsletter entitled "The Latest Word," which debuted in November 1991. The newsletter has much improved the fan club's standing as a source of R.E.M.-related information. If you haven't joined the club yet, send a $10 money order ($12 overseas) to P.O. Box 8032, Athens, GA 30603. Look at all you've missed so far!

■ "The Light is the Way" penlight from 1984. Many who bought these complained because the penlights were disposable and only lasted a few months.

■ The first fan club present for members was the wooden key chain, hand painted and stamped by Liz Carter. The key chain was mailed to members in June 1985 in honor of the fan club's first anniversary.

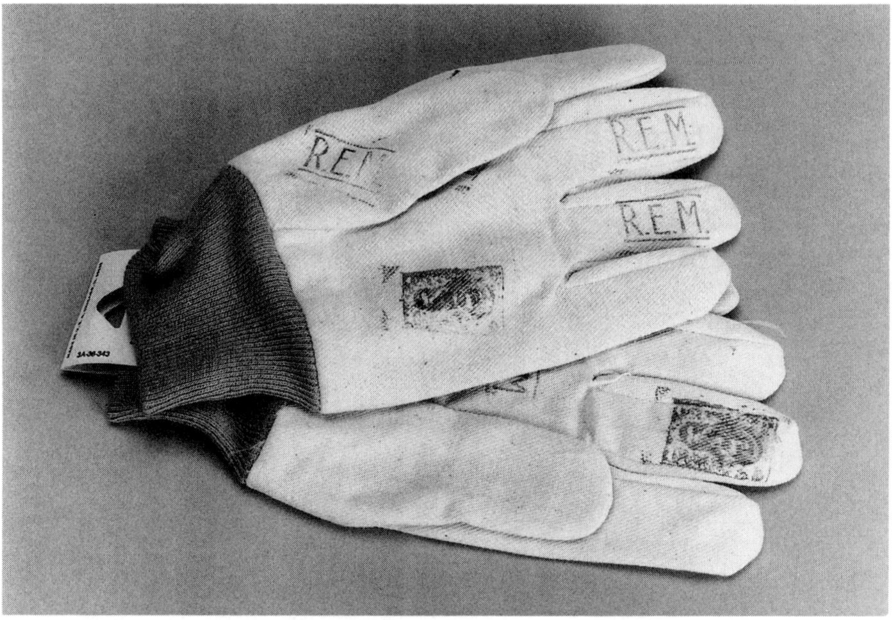

■ With "Gardening at Night" work gloves, R.E.M. fan club members could do their night gardening without getting dirt under their fingernails.

1984

Item	Price
"Join the Club" original announcement postcard (photocopied on cardstock paper)	--
"R.E.M."/"The Light is the Way" blue disposable penlight	**$10-20**
8" x 12" color band photo from Jim Herbert's *Left of Reckoning* film	**12-20**
"Thanks for the Murmuries" postcard showing the band along with Bert Downs and Jefferson Holt	**10-15**
diamond-shaped blue and white "R.E.M." patch	**5-8**

1985

<u>complete Christmas mailout containing:</u>

Item	Price
Christmas card with photograph of a Christmas tree decorated with pictures of the band members and office staff, "There are the Good Old Days."	
Christmas mailout booklet with messages from band members	
Reconstruction tour book	**$60-85**

Item	Price
hand stamped wood block key chain (1.5" cube)	**$35-50**
"Gardening at Night" blue and white cloth hand stamped gardening gloves	**35-50**
Swiss army bag (two different designs)	**30-45**
fan club solicitation card	**25-35**
oval-shaped green and blue "R.E.M." patch with bicycle gear design (not officially released)	**15-20**
Howard Finster "Pilgrims" black bandana (21.5" x 22")	**12-20**
"Driver 8" blue and yellow round cloth patch	**4-5**
"Gravity" blue and white cloth patch showing a man in a parachute	**4-5**
"Fighting Elf" rubber stamp by Good Impressions	**4-8**
"Feeling Gravitys Pull" rubber stamp	**4-8**
"Fighting Elf" 1" button	**2-3**
"Gravity Bicycle" 1" button	**2-3**
"Seven Chinese Brothers" 1" button, shows a drawing of a head	**2-3**
"Scared Guy" 1" button, shows an elf cowering	**2-3**
band photo 1.5" button, blue and gray	**2-3**

■ The fan club solicitation card from 1985. These were found in bags of Wonder Bread and Fritos Corn Chips.

■ These Swiss army bags were offered to members in October 1985 for the bargain price of $13.

1986

<u>complete Christmas mailout containing:</u>
Christmas card depicting red angel holding candelabra
"Merry Crimble"/"Work of folk art No. 1" orange sticker, drawing by Peter Buck (3.75" x 3.75")
"Merry Christmas Everyone" green sticker showing Christmas tree (3.75" x 3.75")
red print of UK "Fall on Me" 45 (IRM 121) with band news on reverse (7" x 7")
"Have a very Berry Christmas" drawing by Bill Berry
"Goal Precision" card with drawings and messages from Michael Stipe **$40-60**

five band postcards in a packet, photos by Ebet Roberts **$6-8**
"Noisy Cat" 1" button, shows a cat drawing by Michael Stipe and "R.E.M." **2-3**
"Seven Continents" 1" button, **2-3**
"Pistol Hot" 1" button **2-3**

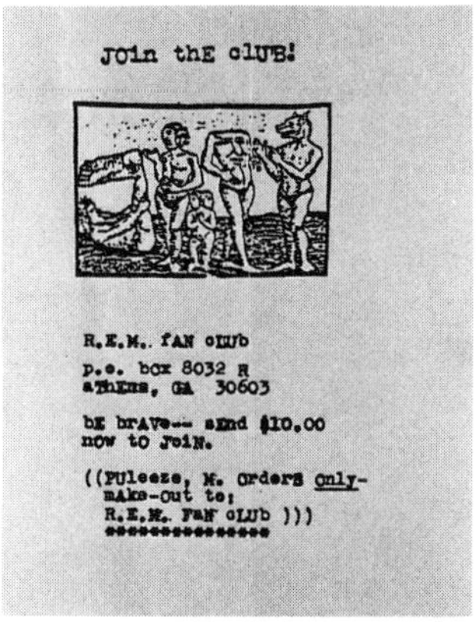

■ The fan club originally announced itself with this postcard.

■ The Howard Finster "Pilgrims" bandana from 1985 originally sold for $5.

1987

Item	Price
complete Christmas mailout containing:	
"You Alone" white round plastic Christmas ornament	
Pete Buck bookmark with Lewis Carroll quotation	
Work Tour embossed black and white guitar pick	
"Important Document Enclosed" sticker	
set of three Polaroids from the "Finest Worksong" video	
"Santa says..." holiday message from Bill Berry	
reprinted set lists	
(no Christmas card was mailed in 1987)	**$60-80**
"Allied" 1.5" button	**$2-3**
"Work Tour" 1" button	**2-3**
Work Tour yellow bicycle cap	**10-20**
one page folded press pamphlet promoting *Document*, with pressed leaf	**7-12**

1988

Item	Price
complete Christmas mailout containing:	
"Parade of the Wooden Soldiers"/ "See No Evil" green vinyl single	
1988 Christmas card booklet with messages and tour dates	
Christmas card in envelope explaining to members that a donation to The Nature Conservancy was made in their name	**$125-185**
"Get Up" 1.5" blue button	**$1-2**
"Green globe" 1.5" black and orange button	**1-2**
"Green World Tour" 2" square button	**2-3**
"R.E.M."/"Direct"/"Peace" set of three 1" buttons	**4-5**
Green World Tour satin laundry tags, set of three different	**5-10**

1989

Item	Price
complete Christmas mailout containing:	
"Good King Wenceslas"/ "Academy Fight Song" single with poster sleeve	
1989 Christmas card printed by Independent Project Press	**$100-125**
Artrock "Green World Tour" postcard	**$3-4**
Green World Tour color 8" x 10" band photo	**7-12**
black and white postcard of the band performing live on the *Green* tour	**2-5**
"50 Ways You Can Save the Earth" book and bookmark	**in print**

■ Most of the annual holiday mailouts since 1985 have included Christmas cards.

1990

<u>complete Christmas mailout containing:</u>
"Ghost Reindeer in the Sky"/"Summertime" single
"The Rainforest Book"
(no Christmas card was mailed in 1990) **$90-110**

1991

<u>complete Christmas mailout containing:</u>
"Baby Baby"/"Christmas Griping" single
"Create" paintbrush
"Fifty Ways to Fight Censorship" book by Dave Marsh
1991 Independent Projects Press wall calendar
1991 Christmas card printed by Independent Project Press **$75-85**

Out of Time black baseball cap **$6-8**
postcards from Mountain Stage concert, photos by James Cohrssen (four different) **5-7**
black and white postcard of the band members with fan club information on reverse **2-4**

1992

<u>complete Christmas mailout containing:</u>
"Where's Captain Kirk"/"Toyland" single
Automatic For the People bar coaster, or
Automatic For the People promotional postcard with stickers
"Find The River" lyric card with stickers
1992 Christmas card printed by Independent Project Press **$75-95**

Automatic For the People bumper sticker **$3-4**
Automatic For the People cloth baseball cap **12-14**
Automatic For the People wool baseball cap **14-16**

PROMOTIONAL MATERIAL

Chronic Town

press kit, with one page biography and one photo	**$40-60**
one-sided display flat (12" x 12")	**8-10**

Murmur

press kit, with one page biography and one photo	**$40-60**
two-sided display flat (12" x 12")	**7-9**
postcard, "There's a kind of Murmur in the air"	**15-25**

Reckoning

press kit	**$35-45**
one-sided display flat (12" x 12")	**4-6**

■ The *Murmur* promotional postcard informed those that received it in 1983 that "There's a kind of murmur in the air."

■ The *Fables of the Reconstruction* cube

■ The *Fables of the Reconstruction* promotional postcard

Fables of the Reconstruction

press kit, with specially printed flyer featuring LP artwork and one photo	**$30-40**
two-sided display flat (12" x 12")	**4-6**
postcard, "LP and cassette out June 10"	**8-10**
cardboard hanging cube display (12" cube)	**25-35**

Lifes Rich Pageant

press kit	**$20-25**
press kit photo with names incorrect (U.K.)	**10-15**
two-sided display flat (12" x 12")	**4-5**
U.K. counter stand-up display using LP cover art (12" x 12")	**12-16**

Dead Letter Office

press kit with one photo	**$20-25**
two-sided display flat (12" x 12")	**3-4**
postcard	**7-9**
plastic letter opener (length = 8.25")	**50-65**

Document

press kit with one photo	**$20-25**
one-page folded press pamphlet with photos by Sandra Lee Phipps	**7-12**
two-sided display flat (12" x 12")	**3-4**
plastic CD bin divider card listing the band's back catalog (6" x 14")	**12-15**
"The One I Love" cardboard window card (8" x 9")	**15-18**
"The One I Love" display card (12" x 12")	**15-18**

■ The *Dead Letter Office* plastic letter opener

■ The "Stand" promotional compass

■ The "Meadow in a Can" promotional can of wildflower seeds

■ A U.K. promotional display for *Green*

Eponymous	
two-sided display flat (12" x 12")	**$3-4**
Green	
press kit, with six page biography and one photo	**$20-25**
two-sided display flat (12" x 12")	**2-3**
postcard, "Two things to do November 8th"	**6-9**
CD bin divider card with album artwork (6" x 15")	**8-10**
"Stand" plastic compass (diameter = 2.5")	**25-35**
Meadow in a Can, custom can of wild flower seeds (height = 4")	**30-40**
round cardboard display, U.K. (diameter = 3')	**40-50**
R.E.M. Succumbs	
large stand-up video box display	**$20-30**
postcard	**5-9**
Pop Screen	
bin divider card (5.5" x 13")	**$7-10**
Tourfilm	
Press kit with two page biography and one photo	**$15-22**
stand-up counter display (two different)	**20-25**
Out of Time	
press kit with seven page biography and two photos	**$20-25**
two-sided display flat (12" x 12")	**2-3**
small counter-top triangular stand-up display with Grammy announcement	**5-9**
folded informational poster detailing marketing plans for the album (15" x 15")	**15-22**
T-shirt iron-on with album logo (6.5" x 9")	**4-9**
yellow album logo sticker (4.5" x 6.5")	**4-7**
"News and Reviews" book of photocopied articles from prominent music magazines	**10-20**
Timepiece video cassette	**30-45**
U.K. promotional items:	
die-cut yellow and black logo board (8" x 11")	**$10-18**
die-cut yellow and black logo board (13" x 19")	**10-18**
two-sided display flat, with press information on reverse (12" x 12")	**15-20**
"Near Wild Heaven" stand-up display (8" x 12")	**12-18**
"Shiny Happy People" stand-up display (8" x 12")	**12-18**
"Radio Song" stand-up display (8" x 12")	**12-18**
embroidered baseball jackets:	
-green body/blue suede sleeves/small logo	**100-200**
-green body/blue suede sleeves/large logo	**100-200**
-black body/black sleeves/large logo	**100-200**
Japanese promotional items:	
sheet of color stickers promoting the Singles Collection CD box (10" x 14")	**$15-25**
the following exist, but are not official promotional items:	
black coffee mug with album logo	**$25-30**
boxed pillow case with album logo (box = 8" square, pillowcase = 19.5" x 38")	**25-30**
"Losing My Religion" black "bible" with blank pages	**10-15**
This Film Is On	
triangular counter stand-up display	**$5-8**
circular sticker, "Includes the award winning video 'Losing My Religion' plus unreleased clips" (5")	**5-7**
The Best of R.E.M.	
"It's the End of the World" U.K. blue counter stand-up display	**$12-20**
Automatic For the People	
press kit	**$18-22**
12" x 12" display flat, two sided (five different)	**2-3**
video press kit	**25-40**
postcard with six stickers	**7-9**
cardboard bar coaster, printed on both sides	**3-6**
small brown bag of peanuts from Weaver D's Restaurant	**10-25**
album cover cardboard display, U.K. (20" x 20")	**10-15**
"Drive" U.K. stand-up display (8" x 11")	**7-12**
"The Sidewinder Sleeps Tonite" U.K. stand-up display (8" x 12")	**7-12**

POSTERS

Promotion is an essential part of making a band or a record a success. One way in which albums are promoted in record stores is by the display of posters made by the record company which advertise the album. These posters are very popular among collectors, as they offer interesting artwork and original band photographs associated with each album, and they are generally hard to find once an album has stopped selling. Official promotional posters have the logo for the record company printed on them, and indicate somewhere in small print that they are "for promotion only, not for sale." The following list of promotional posters does not include gig posters, though these are obviously also collected. In England, a large market for bootlegged R.E.M. posters exists, but these are generally poor in quality, and can usually be differentiated from official posters made by I.R.S. and Warner Brothers because they lack the company logo. In addition to the official R.E.M. promotional posters made by I.R.S. and Warner Brothers, a number of interesting commercial posters also exist, and these are manufactured and distributed by Nice Man Merchandising. The posters made by Nice Man were all sold through the fan club, and have a NM stock number on the bottom.

PROMOTIONAL POSTERS

Hib-Tone single

"Appearing At"/"The single 'Radio Free Europe/Sitting Still' available now" poster used to promote the single, and local appearances (14" x 20")	**$100-130**
"Appearing At" (as above, 9.5" x 14")	**75-100**
promotional poster with press quotes (14" x 20")	**100-130**
"Single Out Now" (11" x 17"; photocopied)	--

Chronic Town

album cover artwork, "$5.98 list" (19.5" x 29")	**$45-75**

Murmur

album cover artwork with inset photos of individual band members (24" x 36")	**$30-45**

■ Two promotional posters for the band's first single on Hib-Tone. Most of these doubled as gig posters.

■ The "Single Out Now" photocopied promotional poster for the Hib-Tone single, and the rare promotional poster for the Tanzplagen cassette, which never materialized. The original Tanzplagen poster, virtually never seen for sale, might cost you over $100.

■ The *Chronic Town* promotional poster sells for around $45 and up in mint condition. A press kit and display flat were also prepared by I.R.S. to promote the EP.

■ Promotional posters for *Murmur* and *Reckoning*. Though the *Murmur* poster has been bootlegged in the U.K., the poor printing quality of the bootlegs make them easily identifiable from originals. The *Reckoning* poster shows the cement sculpture "Seppents in the Wilderness" by Howard Finster. Finster and Michael Stipe collaborated on the artwork for the cover of *Reckoning*.

Reckoning

Howard Finster sculpture and band photo inset "The second album" (23" x 35.5")	**$25-35**
black and white advance promotional poster "Available the week of April 16" (23" x 35")	**30-40**

Fables of the Reconstruction

album cover artwork (24" x 36")	**$15-20**

Lifes Rich Pageant

album cover artwork, "A birdy and a hand for life's rich demand" (24" x 36", vertical)	**$12-15**
album cover artwork, "Featuring the single 'Fall On Me' " (U.K., 24" x 36", vertical)	**14-18**
album cover artwork (24" x 36", horizontal)	**8-10**

Dead Letter Office

album cover artwork (24" x 36")	**$10-12**

Document

album cover artwork (27" x 36")	**$10-12**
two-sided horizontal poster announcing release date (12" x 36")	**14-18**
"Document 1988"; large Mike Mills photo and album catalog pictured (24" x 39")	**10-12**

Eponymous

album cover artwork and album catalog, "(re)-experience the moment" (23" x 35")	**$10-12**

Green

album cover artwork (23" x 35")	**$6-9**
album cover artwork (36" x 55")	**15-18**
Green World Tour 1989, band photographed on the roof of the 40 Watt Club (27" x 39")	**12-15**
album cover artwork with globe and press quotations (U.K., 22" x 31")	**15-20**

Out of Time

photo of band members standing in a field, with album logo inset (23" x 35")	**$7-10**
pre-release poster "coming soon" with album logo (18" x 24")	**7-12**
album logo with checkerboard background (42" x 59")	**10-15**
color shot of band, checkered background (U.K., 23" x 33")	**6-10**
Rolling Stone magazine cover, issue 607, June 27, 1991 (25" x 30")	**10-14**

This Film Is On

band photograph (23" x 35")	**$7-10**

Automatic For the People

album cover artwork (24" x 36")	**$7-10**
album cover artwork, "Coming October 6" (12" x 24")	**7-10**
clear vinyl window poster showing the band walking in Florida (17" x 23")	**15-25**
photo of band walking in Florida, with backwards writing	**10-15**
album cover artwork (U.K.)	**7-10**

OFFICIAL COMMERCIAL POSTERS

1985

April 19, 1985 band photo by Sandra Lee Phipps, stock #8127. The photograph was hand colored by Michael Stipe. (24" x 36")	**$7-10**

1986

Jim Herbert band photo, "Walked, Swam, Hunted, Danced, Sang" (#NM P19, 24" x 36")	**$7-9**

1987

individual band member photos from *Document* period (#NM P37, 24" x 39")	**$6-8**
Mudd Island, Memphis, Tenn., Sept 13, 1986, numbered limited edition concert poster, with photo by Ebet Roberts (22.5" x 30")	**35-45**

1988

band photo by Michael Tighe, "You Are the Everything" (#NM P65, 21" x 30")	**$6-8**
November 1988 photo of the band on a balcony by Bart Everly (#NM P67, 23" x 33")	**6-8**
Green World Tour, made by Artrock, designed by Greg Grimshaw (16.5" x 27.5")	**8-10**
Green World Tour, proof sheet of above, limited to 100 (23" x 31")	**75-100**
Sassy magazine, December 1988 (issue #10) pull-out two-sided poster with band photo by Michael Tighe, and typed ruminations by Michael Stipe (21.5" x 16.5")	**7-10**

1989

"Get Up," issued in U.S. singles box set "Singleactiongreen" (21" x 35") **$8-10**
"Green World Tour"/"Ecology," issued in U.K. "Orange Crush" 7-inch box set (28" x 35") **5-8**
Melody Maker magazine cover, May 27, 1989 (U.K., 25" x 33") **8-12**
poster #76 from the Spanish magazine published by Popular 1, "Con Destino A La Gloria" (54" x 81") **7-10**

1990

Tourfilm poster with video box cover artwork (#NM P99, 23" x 33") **$6-8**
"Read" poster from the American Library Association. The band members are shown holding copies of their favorite books. (22" x 34") **in print**

1991

"NME Classics" U.K. poster of Michael Stipe, photo by Bleddyn Butcher (16" x 23") **$3-6**
band photo by Dennis Keeley (#NM P105, 23" x 33") **$4-7**

1992

band photo by Ronny Johannssen, "Copenhagen" (#NM P123, 23" x 33") **in print**
band photo, all four members walking in Miami (#NM P1686) **in print**

1993

band photo by Anton Corbijn (#NM P2183) **in print**

OTHER R.E.M. RELATED POSTERS

Tanzplagen single "Appearing"/"Cassette available at better record stores now" poster used to promote the two-track cassette (which was never released) and local appearances (14" x 20") **$85-100**

Athens, GA-Inside/Out promotional movie poster (23" x 34.5") **$12-15**

Hindu Love Gods promotional poster with album cover artwork and inset band photo (24" x 36") **$7-10**

MAGAZINES

Since their early days as many a fanzine's favorite, R.E.M. has graced the covers of an untold number of magazines internationally. Probably their most famous cover appearance was *Rolling Stone*'s December 3, 1987, issue that declared R.E.M. "America's Best Rock and Roll Band." *Rolling Stone* had arranged for the cover to be shot weeks before the issue was due to hit the stands, but did not tell the band about the famous caption that ran with it. The caption was a great surprise to the members of R.E.M. and their fans, and certainly made I.R.S. Records employees giddy, but probably angered a number of R.E.M.'s musical contemporaries.

Though most major magazines with R.E.M. covers can be bought for $2-3 at secondhand stores, the more valuable ones tend to be the early local publications and fanzines, and in the U.S., British magazines published before 1987. In addition to the list of magazines below, many magazines have published excellent features on R.E.M. but chose not to put the band on the cover for that particular issue, and thus are not included.

U.S. MAGAZINES WITH R.E.M. COVERS

Aquarian Weekly	July 11, 1984	#531	**$4-6**
Aquarian Weekly	October 21, 1992	#638	**2-4**
Athens Night Life (Athens Observer)	March 7, 1984		**12-20**
Atlanta Journal Weekend	November 21, 1987		**3-5**
Atlanta Journal Weekend	April 1, 1989		**3-5**
BAM	July 13, 1984		**6-9**
BAM	October 3, 1986		**5-8**
BAM	October 9, 1987		**4-8**
BMI Musicworld	Summer 1989		**4-7**
The Bob	September 1986	#27	**6-10**
Bullet	1982	#1	**6-8**
Buzz	February 1988		**3-5**
Classic City Live (Athens Observer)	April 17, 1985		**3-4**
Contrast	Winter 1986	#1	**6-10**
Creem	November 1986		**3-6**
Details	April 1991		**3-5**

Details	February 1993		**2-4**
East Coast Rocker	October 1, 1986	#10	**4-8**
East Coast Rocker	1987	#64	**4-7**
Entertainment Week (Winston-Salem Journal)	December 7, 1985		**4-7**
Flagpole	December 1987	#2	**4-7**
Goldmine	July 31, 1987	vol. 13, #16	**3-5**
Hits	February 6, 1989	vol. 3, #126	**4-6**
The Music Paper	February 1989		**3-5**
The Music Paper	June 1991		**3-5**
The Music Paper	February 1993		**2-3**
Music Pulse	November 25, 1988	vol. 1, #2	**3-5**
Musician	January 1988	#111	**3-6**
Musician	April 1991	#150	**3-5**
Musician	April 1993	#174	**3-4**
Muzik	August 1982	vol. 15	**7-10**
New York Newsday	December 18, 1988		**3-5**
Option	September/October 1990	#34	**3-5**
Pulse	September 1986		**3-6**
Pulse	October 1992		**2-3**
Progressive Media	May 1983		**6-9**
Purple Cow	June 1991	vol. 17, #11	**3-4**
Request	May 1991		**3-5**
Rock & Roll Comics	October 1991	#35	**3-4**
Rockbill	June 1984		**5-9**
Rockbill	September 1986		**4-7**
The Rocket	October 1986		**4-7**
Rolling Stone	December 3, 1987	#514	**3-6**
Rolling Stone	April 20, 1989	#550	**3-6**
Rolling Stone	June 27, 1991	#607	**2-3**
Rolling Stone	March 5, 1992	#625	**2-3**
Spectator	May 30, 1984		**4-8**
Spin	October 1986	vol. 2, #7	**4-6**
Spin	March 1991	vol. 6, #12	**3-5**
The Street	January 1989	vol. 2, #1	**3-4**
Tasty World	September 1985	#6	**8-12**
Trends (Univ. of Ga. Red & Black)	January 25, 1988		**3-5**
West Michigan Music	November 1987	vol.1, #8	**3-5**
Xtra	June 1985		**3-5**

NON-U.S. MAGAZINES WITH R.E.M. COVERS

Bucketfull of Brains (U.K.)		issue 11	**$12-18**
Bucketfull of Brains		issue 37	**6-8**
Bucketfull of Brains		issue 39/40	**6-10**
Buscadero (Italy)	January 1988	#77	**6-9**
Buscadero	November 1988	#86	**6-9**
Hot Press (Ireland)	June 29, 1989	vol. 13, #12	**6-9**
Hot Press	October 21, 1992		**3-5**
Melody Maker (U.K.)	June 15, 1985		**7-10**
Melody Maker	September 6, 1986		**6-8**
Melody Maker	May 27, 1989		**6-8**
Melody Maker R.E.M. supplement	1989		**8-12**
Melody Maker	September 26, 1992		**5-8**
Mucchio (Italy)	June 1991	#161	**6-8**
Musician	January 1989	#123	**3-6**
Muzik Express Sounds (Germany)	January 1992	#1	**5-7**
NME (U.K.)	July 6, 1985		**7-10**
NME	April 2, 1988		**6-8**
NME	August 5, 1989		**6-8**
NME	March 23, 1991		**5-7**
NME	January 2, 1993		**5-7**
Pop Gear 11 (Japan)	November 1992		**5-7**
Popular 1 (Spain)	April 1989		**7-10**
Q (U.K.)	December 1988	#27	**5-7**
Q	April 1991	#55	**5-7**
Q	October 1992	#73	**5-7**
Select	November 1992		**5-7**
Sounds (U.K.)	June 24, 1989		**6-8**
Sounds	March 23, 1991		**5-7**
Vox (U.K.)	April 1991	#7	**5-7**

U.S. MAGAZINES WHERE R.E.M. SHARES THE COVER

Billboard	December 21, 1991		**$3-4**
Classic City Live (Athens Observer)	July 20, 1988		**2-4**
Classic City Live	September 21, 1988		**2-4**
Creem	September 1985		**3-4**
Creem (Best of)	January 1988	vol. 1, #2	**3-5**
Creem (Presents Rock '87)		#4	**3-6**
Discoveries	July 1992	vol. 5, #7	**2-4**
The Georgia Journal	Spring 1990		**3-4**
Guitar	January 1993		**2-3**
Musician	September 1985	#83	**3-4**
Record	June 1984	vol. 3, #8	**4-5**
Rolling Stone	December 14, 1989	#567/568	**2-3**
Rolling Stone	December 12, 1991	#619/620	**2-3**
Rolling Stone	December 10, 1991	#645/646	**2-3**
Southpoint	November 1989		**3-4**
Top	October 1987	#5	**3-4**
Top Presents Nirvana		#3	**3-4**

NON-U.S. MAGAZINES WHERE R.E.M. SHARES THE COVER

Bucketfull of Brains (U.K.)		#23	**$4-7**
Bucketfull of Brains		#34	**4-7**
Hot Press (Ireland)	June 27, 1991	vol. 15, #12	**4-6**
Melody Maker (U.K.)	March 9, 1991		**4-6**
Melody Maker	October 3, 1992		**4-6**
NME (U.K.)	March 30, 1991		**4-6**
Q (U.K.)	January 1992	#64	**4-6**
Q	November 1992	#74	**4-6**
Record Collector (U.K.)	September 1992		**4-6**
Select (U.K.)	February 1991	#8	**4-6**
Select	November 1992		**4-6**
Sounds (U.K.)	March 30, 1991		**4-6**
Vox (U.K.)	November 1992		**4-6**

MAGAZINES WITH R.E.M. MUSIC OR LYRICS

New Sounds	"Radio Free Europe" (lyrics)	January 1984, #1	**$5-8**
Guitar	"Can't Get There From Here" (music and lyrics)	February 1986	**2-3**
Guitar	"The One I Love" (music and lyrics)	January 1993	**2-3**
Guitar	"Man on the Moon" (music and lyrics)	June 1993	**2-3**
Guitar School	"Stand" (music and lyrics)	March 1993	**2-3**
Guitar School	"Losing My Religion" (music and lyrics)	September 1991	**2-3**
Sassy	"Losing My Religion" (lyrics)	April 1991	**3-5**
Song Hits	"Radio Free Europe" (lyrics)	October 1983	**3-5**
Star Hits	"So. Central Rain" (lyrics)	October 1984	**3-5**
NME	"Disturbance at the Heron House" (lyrics)	August 5, 1989	**4-6**

MISCELLANEOUS R.E.M. COLLECTIBLES

AUDIO

"R.E.M." seven-inch EP
Pravda Records PR 4507 **$4-6**
The Chicago band Green named this independent EP *R.E.M.* not long after R.E.M. released their *Green* LP in 1988.

Rock Against Drunk Driving CD **$10-12**
This disc includes two versions of a PSA against drunk driving by Michael Stipe and Peter Buck.

Peach of Immortality *"Jehovah" My Black Ass– R.E.M. is Air Supply* LP
ACR006-B (PRE) **$6-9**
This record made this book only because of its great title. No references are made to R.E.M. on the record, as it consists entirely of utter nonsensical noise.

Polish postcard flexidiscs **$20-35**
About fifteen different R.E.M. tracks have been illegally pressed on "K3 Records" as cardboard flexidiscs with color photos on them. The photos and the artwork on the jacket have nothing whatsoever to do with the band. They were supposedly limited to 50 of each title. Titles include "Radio Free Europe," "Sitting Still," "So. Central Rain," "Femme Fatale," "Can't Get There From Here," "Driver 8," "Fall On Me," "Superman," "Hyena" and "The One I Love."

Other singles on the Hib-Tone label
Since the release of the first R.E.M. single on Hib-Tone in 1981, a few other singles have been released on the label, and these are often sought by R.E.M. collectors.

HT-0002	The Throbs	Just One Dance/Girl Don't Waste Your Tears, 1981	**$3-6**
HT-0003	Harold Kelling	Jezebel/Harlem Nocturne, 1981	**3-6**
HT-8501	The Three Hits	Pressure Dome/Numbers, 1985	**3-6**

CMJ *Certain Damage* CD vol. 23
CD CMJ CD-023/1 **$12-15**
Disc 1 from this two disc set contains a twenty second public service announcement by Michael Stipe and Peter Buck for The National Wildlife Federation. Buck plays an acoustic rendition of "World Leader Pretend" on the PSA, which can be heard nowhere else but on this disc, released in October 1989.

CMJ *Certain Damage* CD vol. 30
CD CMJ CD-030 **$12-15**
This disc, released in September 1990, contains a twenty second public service announcement by Mike Mills for the National Wildlife Federation, with backing guitar work courtesy of Peter Buck.

12 Pack Pretty *Foulmouth* 7" EP
Dr. Strange Records #8 **$3-4**
The South Carolina hardcore band 12 Pack Pretty released this seven-inch EP in 1991, which includes the track "R.E.M. Sucks." Some copies were pressed on yellow vinyl.

DMC EP
U.K. LP DMC records DMC 105-3 **$35-50**
This four-track EP contains a six-minute remixed dance version of "Losing My Religion" shamelessly entitled "Losing My Religion (And Gaining the Rhythm)." It is the product of two English DJ's who license popular songs, remix them, and distribute them as dance mixes. Released in the U.K. in October 1991.

Foreign Bootleg Cassettes of R.E.M. Albums **$6-12**
A vast market exists throughout the world for illegally manufactured cassettes by popular artists. Many such bootleg cassettes originate from Thailand, though bootleg cassettes of standard studio albums are also made and distributed in the U.S. The following R.E.M. bootleg cassettes are known to exist:

Lifes Rich Pageant	Thailand	Michael 642
Document	Thailand	Michael 1006
Document	Indonesia	Billboard BB-10.648
(lacks "Strange" and includes seven tracks from *Lifes Rich Pageant*)		
Eponymous	Thailand	Michael MSC.933
Green	Thailand	Michael 1352
Out of Time	Thailand	1935
The Best of R.E.M.	Thailand	3025
The Best of R.E.M.	Indonesia	Thomsum ENB-1535
Automatic For the People	Thailand	3152

BOOKS AND OTHER PRINTED MATTER

Tour Books

Tour books were issued for the *Fables of the Reconstruction* tour (1985), *Pageantry* tour (1986), *Document* tour (1987), and *Green* tour (1989). The tour book from the 1987 Work Tour is definitely the hardest to find, as the tour was short and not as many books were printed.

Fables of the Reconstruction	**$10-15**
Pageantry	**10-15**
Work Tour	**15-22**
Green World Tour part 1: Japan and Australia	**10-15**
Green World Tour part 2: North America	**10-15**
Green World Tour part 3: Europe, all dates inclusive	**10-15**

■ Tour programs were first printed for the Reconstruction tour in 1985.

Tour Itineraries **$50-75**

The band's spiral-bound tour itineraries are occasionally seen for sale, and surely are extremely rare. Bound itineraries were made as early as 1985.

■ R.E.M. tour itineraries like these are rarely seen for sale. The one on the left covers part of the Reconstruction tour.

Juke Box Strips **$2-4**

In the U.S., juke box title strips have been printed for many of the band's singles, including "Can't Get There From Here," "Fall On Me," "The One I Love," "It's the End of the World," "Stand," "Get Up" and "Losing My Religion."

***Life, How to Live*, by Brivs Mekis** **$25-40**

The story of the inspiration for the song "Life and How To Live It" has been told and retold by Michael Stipe in song intros since early 1985. The song tells of a former Athens resident who owned a house that he divided in half, and lived periodically in one side or the other. The two sides of the house were completely different from one another, and a separate set of clothes, furniture, and other possessions were kept in each side of his house. When he died, and the house was entered some time later, hundreds of copies of a peculiar self-published 418-page book called *Life, How to Live* were found. The book's content is not particularly linear, consisting of the rambling thoughts and opinions from what appears to have been a borderline schizophrenic. The discovery of these bizarre but interesting books stacked high in Mekis' closet inspired Stipe to pen a tribute to this unusual man. At one time R.E.M. considered offering a number of copies of the book for sale to fan club members, but had second thoughts because of the book's content.

Pete Buck and Pete Buck II comic books

Pete Buck **$12-15**
Pete Buck II **8-12**

Comic artist Jack Logan approached Peter Buck after a show that the band played at the Fox Theater in Atlanta in 1986, and asked him if he could do a comic of him. Thinking Logan meant a caricature, Buck agreed, later to be startled to find himself a comic book hero. Both books were published by Mile 9 Comics, Loganville, Georgia.

Document Vol. 2 **$18-25**

This bootleg book was made in Finland and consists of mostly European newspaper and magazine clippings. There evidently was no first volume.

"The One I Love" sheet music

with credit to John Stipe **$10-12**
with credit to Michael Stipe **8-10**

Sheet music was published by Hal Leonard Publishing Corporation in 1987, complete with lyrics, for this popular single. Michael Stipe's first name is listed in the song writing credits as "John" on some copies, and "Michael" on others.

"Losing My Religion" sheet music **in print**

Hal Leonard Publishing Corporation published the sheet music to "Losing My Religion," complete with lyrics, in 1991.

■ The inspiration for the song "Life and How To Live It," and the Pete Buck II comic book by Jack Logan.

A Book of Song Words --
A photocopied lyric book originating from Finland, released in late 1989.

Another Book of Song Words --
As the title suggests, this photocopied book is yet another fan's interpretation of the band's lyrics. This one, released in August 1991, includes the lyrics to B-sides and other non-LP tracks, and does not appear to have been prepared by the same author as the first lyric book.

Remarks: The Story of R.E.M. **in print**
A biography of the band as told by Tony Fletcher. Issued in England in 1989 by Omnibus Press (OP 45442), and in 1990 in the U.S. by Bantam (0553-34920-1). The books have different covers but are otherwise identical. In the U.S., cardboard stand-up displays for the book were issued to book stores.

R.E.M. Bootleg Collectors Guide --
Made available in April 1990, this photocopied guide to R.E.M. bootlegs was compiled by Plastic Pizzeria, 850 Elm Ave., Abescon, New Jersey 08201.

"Mick Steffe" press kit **$10-18**
In the summer of 1990, Michael Stipe toured briefly in Eastern Europe with Natalie Merchant, Billy Bragg, and others, performing songs by R.E.M., Bragg, and 10,000 Maniacs. Bragg and the Maniacs are both on Elektra Records, who sent out this press kit to call attention to the tour. The photo that accompanies the kit shows Stipe standing next to a billboard for the show advertising an appearance by "Mick Steffe" of R.E.M.

Rock the Vote press kit **$10-18**
A press kit was prepared in March 1991 to publicize the band's support of the National Voter Registration Act, better known as the Motor Voter Bill. The band placed "Dear Senator, I support the motor voter bill" postcards on longboxes for U.S. editions of the *Out of Time* CD. The press kit contains a two page description of R.E.M.'s involvement in the campaign, and a photograph of the CD longbox.

Party Out of Bounds **in print**
Subtitled "The B-52's, R.E.M., and the Kids Who Rocked Athens Georgia," this book is Rodger Lyle Brown's accounting of the formation of the new music environment in the late 70's and early 80's in Athens. The book was published by Plume (0-452-26631-9) in July 1991.

Rock 'n' Roll Comics, issue #35 **$3-4**
The October 1991 edition of Rock 'n' Roll comics tells the story of the rise of the band's career. The artwork relies heavily on the photographs in the book *Remarks*. For a copy of the comic, write them at 3841 Fourth Ave. #229, San Diego, CA 92103.

R.E.M. Fanzines --
Over the years, a number of R.E.M. fanzines have come and gone. Two of the earlier ones were "Radio Free Europe," which appeared in October 1985, and "Perfect Circle." Later U.S. fanzines included "The Athens Record," "Dead Letter Office," "Country Feedback," "Pretty Persuasion," and "394 Oconee." Non-U.S. R.E.M. 'zines include "Murmur" from Japan, "Understanding Reconstruction," "Chronic Town," and "Stumble" from England.

A Few Chords and a Cloud of Dust
File Under Water **in print**
These two books, by the editor of the U.K. fanzine *Bucketfull of Brains*, contain R.E.M. discographies and listings of performances.

It Crawled From the South **in print**
An in-depth, and highly analytical treatise on R.E.M., written by Marcus Gray.

OTHER COLLECTIBLES

Backstage Passes and Laminates

cloth backstage passes $5-10
laminated passes 10-18

Custom-made backstage passes for R.E.M. shows were not produced until 1984, when the band was on tour to support *Reckoning*. Since then, quite a few different designs have been used for their tours, and some passes were issued in three or four different colors. Virtually all cloth passes and plastic laminates in the U.S. are made by a company called Otto. Laminates are worth considerably more than cloth passes because they are issued for the band and crew only, and are much more rare. All passes listed below are cloth except as noted.

<u>*Little America Tour, 1984*</u>
Access All Areas, laminate (squished head drawing)
V.I.P.
V.I.P./Guest, "WIQB welcomes R.E.M., Ann Arbor, Mich., October 8, 1984"
V.I.P./Guest, access all areas, after show only

<u>*Reconstruction Tour, 1985*</u>
Guest, Preconstruction, U.S. Colleges 1985, after show only (car being fueled)
Guest, Richmond Mosque, December 5, 1985
Guest, limited access (Fables ear)
Tour laminate (monkey on bicycle)
"Z-92 Celebrates R.E.M., Music Hall, November 5, 1985" (Fables artwork)

<u>*Pageantry Tour, 1986*</u>
After Show, "Mammoth huge colossal understated"
Band, laminate, "What Noisy Cats Are We" (noisy cat drawing)
Crew
Crew, laminate
Guest, "with special guests, Let's Active" (four doodles)

■ A collection of R.E.M. backstage passes and tour laminates.

<u>*Pageantry Tour, 1986*</u>
Guest, "with special guests, The Feelies" (four doodles)
Local Crew, "What Noisy Cats Are We" (noisy cat drawing)
Photo, no backstage access (*Lifes Rich Pageant* artwork)
V.I.P., laminate (man smoking pipe)
V.I.P. (man smoking pipe)

<u>*Work Tour, 1987*</u>
Access All Areas, laminate
After Show Only
Crew
Crew, "It's The End Of The Tour As We Know It, Atlanta's Fox Theater"
It's The End Of The Tour As We Know It, Atlanta's Fox Theater (11/24/87)
It's The End Of The Tour As We Know It, Atlanta's Fox Theater (11/25/87)
It's The End Of The Tour As We Know It, Atlanta's Fox Theater (11/27/87)
It's The End Of The Tour As We Know It, Atlanta's Fox Theater (11/28/87)
Photo/Press
Support Guest, The dB's
Support Guest, 10,000 Maniacs
Tour laminate
V.I.P. (triangular)
V.I.P. (square)

<u>*Green World Tour, 1988/89*</u>
All Areas (earth and power lines)
Guest
Photo, Fall (earth)
Tour laminate

Momos

Momos were small photocopied art books that Michael Stipe made and sold for 25¢ at places like The Koffee Klub in Athens. Three different books are known to exist, all of which were produced at about the time the band formed. The books are essentially composed of Stipe's doodles and of photographs of the people he knew at the time. One interesting photo shows Peter Buck sleeping in what looks to be one of the upstairs bedrooms of the legendary "R.E.M. church." Another shows Alan Vega and Martin Rev from the band Suicide with the caption, "This is Martin. This is Alan. Buy their record." R.E.M. covered "Ghost Rider" by the band eight years later.

■ Michael Stipe's "Momos." The small photocopied books contain interesting artwork, but no references to the band.

■ These small discs were found inserted in Big Gulp cups at 7-11 food stores in 1985.

■ Work Tour mugs were made to commemorate a concert promoted by the legendary Bill Graham in 1987.

7-11 cup insert **$15-25**
This amusing item was issued in 1985 inside the bottom of "Big Gulp" cups at 7-11 convenience stores. And you thought you had seen everything.

Work Tour mug **$40-70**
Given to band members and crew in Los Angeles by promoter Bill Graham in 1987.

Green World Tour water bottle **$25-40**
Given to band members and crew by Bill Graham in 1989.

Green World Tour fanny pack **$25-40**
These were made for the band members and crew for the *Green* tour.

■ The Green World Tour fanny pack

Green World Tour jacket — $450-750

These embroidered red wool jackets with white leather sleeves were made for the band and crew for the *Green* tour. R.E.M. has given at least one of them to be auctioned for charity.

Gold and platinum record awards — $300-800

For fans of any band, gold and platinum record awards given to that particular band by their record company or by the R.I.A.A. are highly coveted. R.E.M. record awards are not frequently seen for sale, but when advertised, they command noticeably higher prices than those for many other bands. *Lifes Rich Pageant* was the first R.E.M. album to be certified gold, and *Document*, *Green*, *Out of Time*, and *Automatic For the People* were certified gold, and later platinum by the R.I.A.A. In general, awards presented to band members are far more valuable than those presented to radio stations, record stores, or music industry personnel.

Michael Stipe playing card — $2-3

Given away with an issue of the magazine *New Musical Express* in the U.K. Just in case you might care, Stipe is on the eight of clubs.

R.E.M. Pro Set Super Stars MusiCards — $1-2

The members of R.E.M. appear on cards numbered 112 and 113 in this series of collector cards, which are often sold alongside baseball cards.

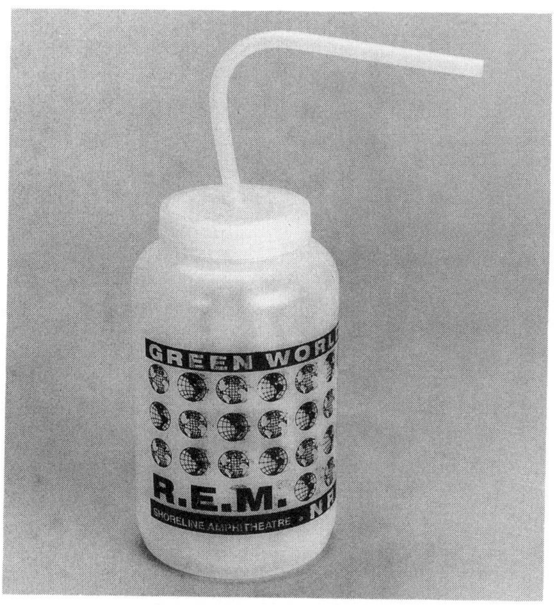

■ Another gift from promoter Bill Graham to the members of R.E.M. and their crew were these Green World Tour water bottles. They were given the night of October 21, 1989 when the band played the Shoreline Amphitheatre in Mountain View, California.

Part 3:

A Compendium of Oddities Collared

PERFORMANCES

Is James Brown really the hardest-working man in show business? The 625 tour dates listed below would indicate that R.E.M. might be in the running for the title. In addition to the dates listed, the band members have all made appearances individually at numerous performances, sitting in with other bands. Peter Buck has toured with Kevn Kinney and Robyn Hitchcock, and regularly hops on stage in Athens when a friend's band is in town. Michael Stipe has performed with The Indigo Girls, 10,000 Maniacs, Chickasaw Mudd Puppies, and The Golden Palominos, and Bill Berry and Mike Mills have made their share of guest appearances as well.

DATE	CITY	VENUE	SUPPORT/HEADLINER
1980			
4-5-80	Athens, Ga.	St. Mary's Episcopal Church	Side Effects/Turtle Bay Band
4-19-80	Athens, Ga.	The Koffee Klub	
5-6-80	Athens, Ga.	Tyrone's O.C.	The Brains
5-12-80	Athens, Ga.	Tyrone's O.C.	The Brains
5-13-80	Athens, Ga.	Tyrone's O.C.	The Swindles
5-15-80	Athens, Ga.	Memorial Hall, U. of Georgia	The Brains
5-21-80	Athens, Ga.	Tyrone's O.C.	
5-31-80	Athens, Ga.	40 Watt Club	The Teevees
6-3-80	Athens, Ga.	Mad Hatter	
6-6-80	Atlanta, Ga.	The Warehouse	Space Heaters/Red Meat & Sprouts
6-30-80	Athens, Ga.	Mad Hatter	
7-7-80	Athens, Ga.	High Shoals	
7-15-80	Atlanta, Ga.	688 Club	
7-18-80	Carrboro, N.C.	The Station	
7-19-80	Carrboro, N.C.	The Station	
7-21-80	Raleigh, N.C.	The Pier	
8-13-80	Athens, Ga.	Tyrone's O.C.	
8-19-80	Atlanta, Ga.	688 Club	Love Tractor
10-4-80	Athens, Ga.	Tyrone's O.C.	
11-6-80	Athens, Ga.	Tyrone's O.C.	Little Tigers
11-20-80	Athens, Ga.	40 Watt Club	
12-6-80	Atlanta, Ga.	Fox Theater	The Police
12/80	*Athens, Ga.*	*First recording session, at Tyrone's. Nine tracks recorded.*	

■ Michael Stipe surveys the audience at Tyrone's, circa 1980. R.E.M. played the club at least 20 times in their early days. After the club burned beyond repair in January 1982, R.E.M. took to other venues in Athens like the I & I Club, and The Mad Hatter.

1981

1-10-81	Athens, Ga.	Tyrone's O.C	
1-30-81	Athens, Ga.	Tyrone's O.C	
1-31-81	Athens, Ga.	Tyrone's O.C	
2-5-81	Augusta, Ga.	New York, New York	
2-8-81	*Smyrna, Ga.*	*R.E.M. make their first studio recording at Bombay Studios. Eight tracks are recorded.*	
2-20-81	Atlanta, Ga.	688 Club	
2-21-81	Atlanta, Ga.	688 Club	
3-13-81	Athens, Ga.	Tyrone's O.C	
3-14-81	Athens, Ga.	Tyrone's O.C	
3-27-81	Nashville, Tenn.	Cantrell's	
3-28-81	Charlotte, N.C.	The Milestone	
3-31-81	Greensboro, N.C.	Friday's	
4-2-81	Augusta, Ga.	New York, New York	
4-3-81	Nashville, Tenn.	Vanderbilt University	
4-4-81	Carrboro, N.C.	The Station	
4-6-81	Raleigh, N.C.	The Pier	
4-10-81	Athens, Ga.	Tyrone's O.C.	
4-11-81	Athens, Ga.	Tyrone's O.C.	
4-15-81	*Winston-Salem, N.C.*	*Drive-in Studio. The tracks that ended up on the Hib-Tone single and Cassette Sets are recorded, along with "White Tornado."*	
4-24-81	Athens, Ga.	B&L Warehouse	XTC
5-25-81	*Winston-Salem, N.C.*	*Drive-In Studio. Radio Free Europe and Sitting Still mixed by R.E.M. and Johnny Hibbert.*	
5-12-81	Athens, Ga.	Tyrone's O.C.	
6-81	Mount Vernon, N.Y.	The Left Bank	Gang of Four
6-16-81	New York, N.Y.	The Ritz	Gang of Four
6-23-81	Atlanta, Ga.	Agora Ballroom	Gang of Four
6-24-81	Athens, Ga.	Tyrone's O.C.	Gang of Four
7-81	*Radio Free Europe/Sitting Still released on Hib-Tone Records*		
7-16-81	New York, N.Y.	The Ritz	

7-24-81	Athens, Ga.	Night Gallery
9-16-81	New York, N.Y.	Pilgrim Theater
9-22-81	Athens, Ga.	Tyrone's O.C.
9-23-81	Athens, Ga.	Tyrone's O.C.
10/2,3,4,7/81	*Winston-Salem, N.C.*	*Drive-in Studio. The Chronic Town tracks are recorded, along with "Ages of You" and "Jazz Lips."*
10-81	New York, N.Y.	The Mudd Club
10-31-81	Athens, Ga.	Tyrone's O.C.
11-5-81	Athens, Ga.	Tyrone's O.C.
11-7-81	Charlotte, N.C.	Viceroy Park

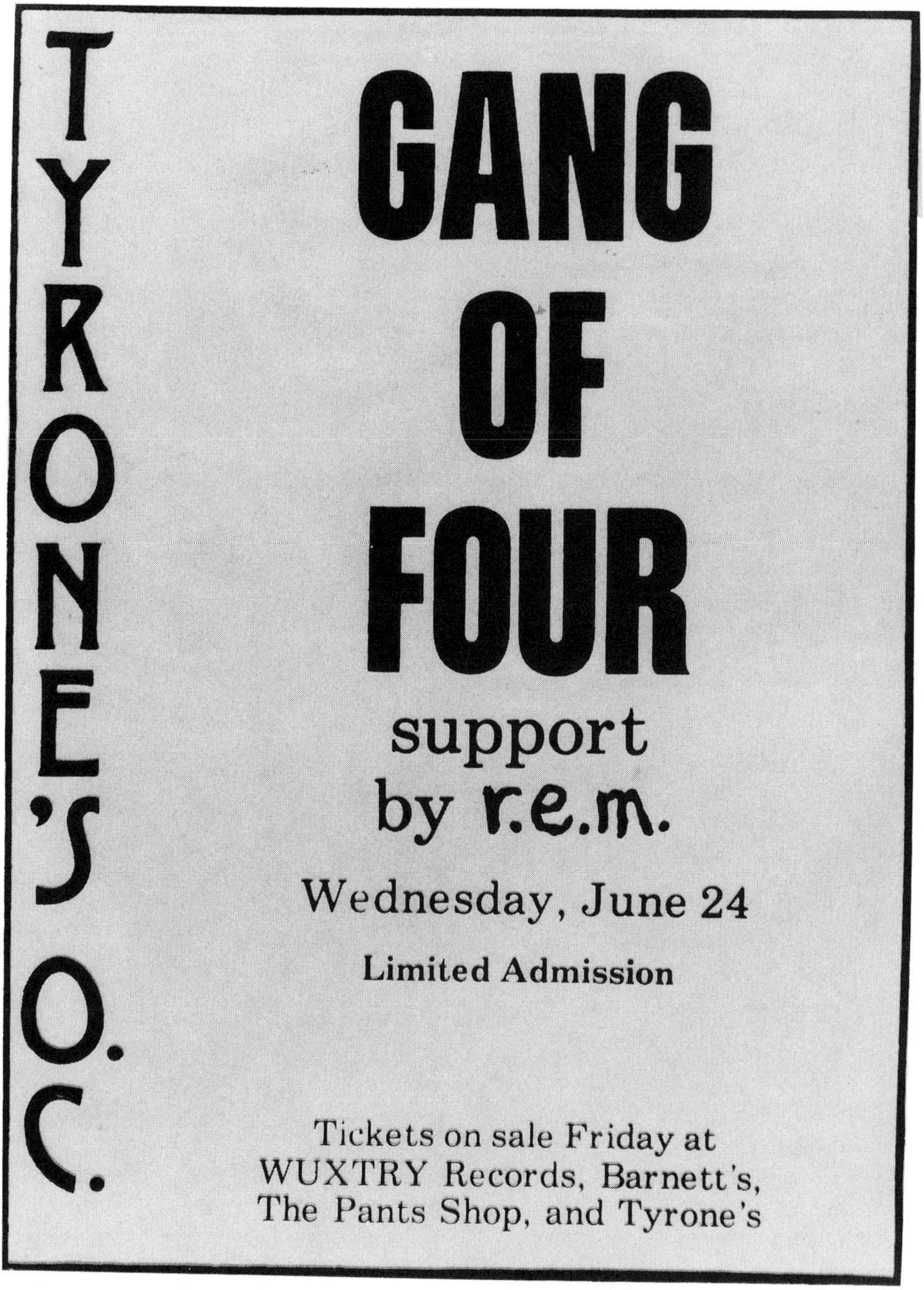

11-17-81	Madison, Wisc.	Merlyn's	
11-26-81	Minneapolis, Minn.	First Avenue Club	
12-5-81	Athens, Ga.	Tyrone's O.C.	
12-13-81	Atlanta, Ga.	Biltmore Hotel	Bow Wow Wow

1982

1-1-82	Hoboken, N.J.	Maxwell's	
1/27,28/82	*Winston-Salem, N.C.*	*Drive-in Studio. R.E.M. records "Wolves, Lower" and re-records "Carnival of Sorts."*	
1-30-82	Hoboken, N.J.	Maxwell's	
2/1,2,8/82	*New York, N.Y.*	*RCA studios. Seven demos are recorded.*	
2-3-82	New York, N.Y.	Danceteria	
2-4-82	New York, N.Y.	Danceteria	
3-10-82	Athens, Ga.	Mad Hatter	
3-12-82	New Orleans, La.	The Beat Exchange	
4-24-82	Madison, Wisc.	Merlyn's	
4-26-82	Minneapolis, Minn.	First Avenue Club	
5-14-82	Atlanta, Ga.	Piedmont Park (Atlanta Arts Festival) (FM broadcast)	
5-31-82	*Winston-Salem, N.C.*	*Drive-in Studio. The band records a slower version of "Wolves, Lower." R.E.M. signs with I.R.S. Records.*	
6-10-82	New Haven, Conn.	Toad's Place	
6-11-82	New Orleans, La.	Tupelo's Tavern	
6-25-82	Athens, Ga.	I & I Club	
7-2-82	Marietta, Ga.	The Strand Cabaret	
7-12-82	Miami, Fla.	The Agora Club	
7-25-82	Athens, Ga.	I & I Club	
8-19-82	Los Angeles, Cal.	The Music Machine	
8-24-82	San Francisco, Cal.	Old Waldorf	
8-24-82	*Chronic Town released*		
9-13-82	Tuscon, Ariz.	Wild Cat House	Gang of Four
9-22-82	Minneapolis, Minn.	First Avenue Club	
9-23-82	Carbondale, Ill.	Southern Illinois University	
9-24-82	Champaign, Ill.	Huff Gym, University of Illinois	
10-6-82	New Haven, Conn.	Toad's Place	Peter Holsapple
10-9-82	Baltimore, Md.	Marble Bar	Peter Holsapple
10-10-82	Raleigh, N.C.	The Pier	
10-19-82	Knoxville, Tenn.	Hobo's	
10-21-82	Athens, Ga.	I & I Club	Blackwater/Peter Holsapple
10-22-82	Athens, Ga.	I & I Club	Blackwater/Peter Holsapple
10-28-82	Hoboken, N.J.	Maxwell's	
10-29-82	Atlanta, Ga.	Agora Ballroom	
10-31-82	Atlanta, Ga.	Georgia Tech	
11-5-82	Baton Rouge, La.	The Bayou	
11-6-82	New Orleans, La.	Tupelo's Tavern	
11-16-82	Trenton, N.J.	City Gardens	
11-19-82	Knoxville, Tenn.	Hobo's	

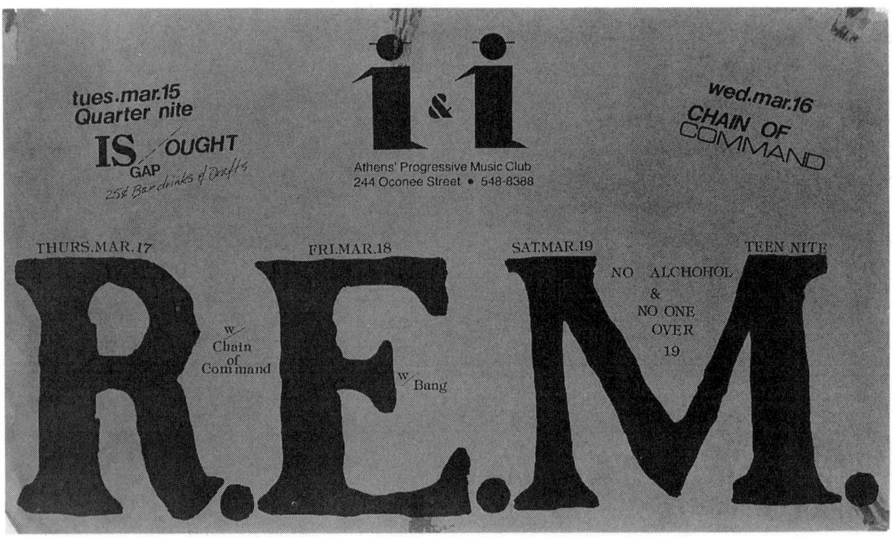

■ R.E.M. sound checking at the University of Georgia Art Department, 1981.

11-21-82	Memphis, Tenn.		
11-22-82	Illinois		
11-23-82	Lawrence, Kan.	Off the Wall Hall	The Micronauts
11-24-82	Uniondale, N.Y.	Nassau Coliseum	The English Beat/Squeeze
11-25-82	New York, N.Y.	Peppermint Lounge	
12-2-82	Greenville, S.C.	UPS Club	
12-7-82	Miami, Fla.	Agora Club	

1983

1-83	*Charlotte, N.C.*	*Reflection Sound Studios. Murmur tracks are recorded, plus Ages of You, Burning Down, Windout, White Tornado, Gardening at Night (acoustic), Just a Touch, Mystery to Me, Voice of Harold, Pale Blue Eyes, Femme Fatale, King of the Road/Walter's Theme and Burning Hell (instrumental).*	
2-12-83	Athens, Ga.	I & I Club	
3-12-83	Washington, D.C.	9:30 Club	
3-17-83	Athens, Ga.	I & I Club	Chain of Command
3-18-83	Athens, Ga.	I & I Club	Bang
3-19-83	Athens, Ga.	I & I Club	
3-26-83	Durham, N.C.	Page Auditorium	The English Beat
3-27-83	Chapel Hill, N.C.	Memorial Hall, UNC	The English Beat
3-31-83	Coral Gables, Fla.	University of Miami	The English Beat
4-13-83	***Murmur released***		
4-13-83	Rochester, N.Y.	Palestra University	The English Beat
4-18-83	Rochester, N.Y.	Palestra University	The English Beat
4-26-83	New York, N.Y.	Spize	The English Beat
4-30-83	New York, N.Y.	The Ritz	
5-3-83	Raleigh, N.C.	The Pier	
5-4-83	Blowing Rock, N.C.	PB Scott's Music Hall	
5-21-83	St. Paul, Minn.	Navy Island	
5-23-83	Madison, Wisc.	Headliners	
5-25-83	Chicago, Ill.	Park West	The dB's
6-1-83	Morrison, Colo.	Red Rocks Amphitheater	
6-12-83	Valencia, Cal.	Magic Mountain	
6-14-83	San Francisco, Cal.	Old Waldorf	
6-20-83	Berkeley, Cal.	Keystone	
6-28-83	Columbia, Md.	Bluenote	
7-8-83	Detroit, Mich.	St. Andrews Hall	
7-9-83	Toronto, Canada	Larry's Hideaway (FM broadcast)	
7-13-83	Boston, Mass.	Paradise Theater (FM broadcast)	
7-15-83	Aberdeen, N.J.	Fountain Casino	
7-17-83	New Haven, Conn.	Toad's Place	The Replacements

7-20-83	Philadelphia, Pa.	Ripley's	
8-18-83	Flushing, N.Y.	Shea Stadium	The Police/Joan Jett
8-20-83	Philadelphia, Pa.	JFK Stadium	The Police
8-21-83	Largo, Md.	Capital Center	The Police
8-26-83	Atlanta, Ga.	Six Flags	The Killer Whales
9-30-83	Athens, Ga.	Stichcraft	
10-3-83	Athens, Ga.	Legion Field	
10-6-83	New York, N.Y.	"Late Night with David Letterman," first live TV appearance	
10-7-83	Washington, D.C.	Ontario Theater	
10-9-83	Piscataway, N.J.	The Good Knight Pub	Let's Active
10-11-83	Poughkeepsie, N.Y.	The Chance	Let's Active
10-12-83	New York, N.Y.		Let's Active
10-13-83	Providence, R.I.		Let's Active
10-14-83	Orono, Me.		Let's Active
10-15-83	Waterville, Me.	Colby College	Let's Active
10-17-83	Syracuse, N.Y.	Drumlins	Let's Active
10-21-83	Flushing, N.Y.	Colton Auditorium, Queens College	Let's Active
10-30-83	New York, N.Y.	"The Cutting Edge" (TV)	
10-31-83	New York, N.Y.	Peppermint Lounge	The Cramps
11-9-83	*San Francisco, Cal.*	*Rhythmic Studios. R.E.M. record 24 demos with producer Elliot Mazer.*	
11-10-83	San Francisco, Cal.	Kabuki Theater	Let's Active
11-11-83	Los Angeles, Cal.	Beverly Theater	Let's Active
11-12-83	San Diego, Cal.	Montezuma Hall, SDSU Campus	Let's Active
11-18-83	Newcastle, England	"The Tube" (TV)	
11-19-83	London, England	Dingwall's	
11-22-83	London, England	Marquee	Jerry Floyd
11-24-83	Paris, France	Les Baines Douches (FM broadcast)	
11-25-83	Roen, France	Exo-7	
11-28-83	St. Petersburg, Fla.		
12-2-83	Greenville, S.C.	UPS Club	
12/8,9,10,12, 13,14,15/83	*Charlotte, N.C.*	*Reflection Sound Studios. Reckoning is recorded, plus Ages of You, Burning Down, Windout (2 takes), White Tornado, Gardening at Night (acoustic, 2 takes), Just a Touch, Mystery to Me, Voice of Harold, Pale Blue Eyes, Femme Fatale, King of the Road/Walter's Theme, Burning Hell (instrumental).*	

1984

1/10,12,13,14, 15,16/84	*Charlotte, N.C.*	*Reflection Sound Studios. Reckoning sessions continue.*	
3-8-84	Athens, Ga.	Mad Hatter	
3-9-84	Athens, Ga.	Mad Hatter	
3-23-84	Cambridge, Mass.	Harvard University	Husker Du
4-6-84	Eindhoven, Holland	The Effener	
4-8-84	Amsterdam, Holland	The Paradiso	
4-10-84	Eindhoven, Holland	The Effener (FM broadcast)	
4-14-84	*Reckoning released*		
4-14-84	Lyon, France	West Side Club	
4-15-84	Clermont-Ferrand, France	town festival	
4-17-84	Roen, France	Exo-7	
4-20-84	Paris, France	El Dorado (FM broadcast)	
4-24-84	Birmingham, England	Tin Can Club	
4-25-84	Manchester, England	The Gallery	
4-26-84	Leeds, England	Warehouse Club	
4-27-84	Glasgow, England	Nightmoves	
4-29-84	Worthing, Sussex, England	Carioca Club	The American Girls
4-30-84	London, England	Marquee Club	
5-1-84	London, England	Marquee Club	
6-9-84	Passaic, N.J.	Capital Theater	
6-14-84	Los Angeles, Cal.	Palace Theater	Dream Syndicate
6-16-84	Fresno, Cal.	Star Palace	Dream Syndicate
6-17-84	Santa Cruz, Cal.	The Catalyst	Dream Syndicate
6-18-84	Santa Barbara, Cal.	Mission Theater	Dream Syndicate
6-19-84	Hollywood, Cal.	Palace Theater "Rock of the 80's" (TV)	
6-20-84	San Diego, Cal.	Del Mar Fairgrounds	Dream Syndicate
6-22-84	San Francisco, Cal.	Warfield Theater	Dream Syndicate
6-23-84	Los Angeles, Cal.	Mountain Air Festival	Huey Lewis/The Cars
6-24-84	Los Angeles, Cal.	Mountain Air Festival	Huey Lewis/The Cars
6-27-84	Seattle, Wash.	The Music Hall (FM broadcast)	Dream Syndicate
6-30-84	Boise, Id.	Mardi Gras	Dream Syndicate
7-3-84	Denver, Colo.	Rainbow Music Hall	Dream Syndicate
7-5-84	Minneapolis, Minn.	Orpheum Theater	Dream Syndicate
7-6-84	Milwaukee, Wisc.	Summerfest Rockstage	Dream Syndicate
7-7-84	Chicago, Ill.	Aragon Ballroom (FM broadcast)	Dream Syndicate
7-8-84	Detroit, Mich.	Royal Oak Theater	Dream Syndicate
7-11-84	Rochester, N.Y.	Minett Hall	Dream Syndicate
7-13-84	Toronto, Canada	Concert Hall	Dream Syndicate
7-15-84	Buffalo, N.Y.	Salty Dog Saloon	Dream Syndicate

7-16-84	Wildwood, N.J.	The Playpen	Dream Syndicate
7-19-84	Boston, Mass.	Orpheum Theater	Dream Syndicate
7-20-84	Hartford, Conn.	Agora	Dream Syndicate
7-21-84	New York, N.Y.	Beacon Theater	Dream Syndicate
7-22-84	New York, N.Y.	Beacon Theater	Dream Syndicate
7-26-84	New York, N.Y.	"Solid Gold Hits" (TV)	Dream Syndicate
7-27-84	Greensboro, N.C.	War Memorial	Dream Syndicate
7-28-84	Atlanta, Ga.	Fox Theater	Dream Syndicate
7-29-84	Los Angeles, Cal.	"The Cutting Edge" (TV)	
9-5-84	Pomona, Cal.	Pomona Valley Aud.	
9-6-84	Los Angeles, Cal.	Greek Theater	
9-8-84	Phoenix, Ariz.	Palace West	
9-11-84	Boulder, Colo.	Macky Auditorium	
9-15-84	Oklahoma City, Okla.	The Bowery	
9-23-84	Charlotte, N.C.	Park Center	
9-25-84	Durham, N.C.	Page Auditorium, Duke University	The dB's
9-26-84	Durham, N.C.	Page Auditorium, Duke University	The dB's
9-28-84	Tampa, Fla.	University of S. Florida	The dB's
9-29-84	Boca Raton, Fla.		The dB's
9-30-84	Gainesville, Fla.		The dB's
10-2-84	New Orleans, La.	McAllister Auditorium	The dB's
10-3-84	Oxford, Miss.		The dB's
10-5-84	Carbondale, Ill.		The dB's
10-6-84	St. Louis, Mo.	Graham Chapel	The dB's
10-7-84	Dekalb, Ill.		The dB's
10-8-84	Ann Arbor, Mich.	Hill Auditorium	The dB's
10-12-84	Scotia, N.Y.		The dB's
10-13-84	Bridgeport, Conn.	University of Bridgeport	The dB's
10-15-84	Amherst, Mass.	Fine Arts Center	The dB's
10-16-84	Providence, R.I.	Veterans Memorial Auditorium	The dB's
10-17-84	Philadelphia, Pa.	Tower Theater	The dB's
11-4-84	Tokyo, Japan	Rehearsal Hall	
11-5-84	Tokyo, Japan	Waseda University	Bokafu Slump
11-8-84	Tokyo, Japan		Bokafu Slump
11-10-84	Tokyo, Japan	Yokahama University	Bokafu Slump
11-11-84	Tokyo, Japan		Bokafu Slump
11-13-84	Oslo, Norway	The Circus (FM broadcast)	
11-15-84	Newcastle, England	Tiffany's	The Lucy Show
11-16-84	Edinburgh, Scotland	Caley Palais	The Lucy Show
11-17-84	Manchester, England	Manchester Polytechnic	The Lucy Show
11-18-84	Liverpool, England	Royal Court Amphitheater	The Lucy Show
11-20-84	London, England	"Old Grey Whistle Test" (TV)	
11-21-84	Nottingham, England	Rock City (FM broadcast)	The Lucy Show
11-23-84	Norwich, England	University of East Anglia	The Lucy Show
11-24-84	Colchester, England	University of Essex	The Lucy Show
11-26-84	Birmingham, England	University	The Lucy Show
11-27-84	Leicester, England	Kiesas	The Lucy Show
11-28-84	Cardiff, Wales	New Ocean Club	The Lucy Show
11-29-84	Dunstable England	Queensway Hall	The Lucy Show
12-2-84	London, England	Lyceum Ballroom	The Lyres
12-4-84	Dublin, Ireland	SFX Centre	
12-6-84	Oslow, Norway	The Circus	
12-31-84	Atlanta, Ga.	Civic Center	Guadalcanal Diary

1985

2-12-85	Athens, Ga.	Uptown Lounge (as "Hornets Attack Victor Mature")	
2-18-85	Atlanta, Ga.	Moonshadow Saloon (L.E.A.F. benefit)	
2-85	*Athens, Ga.*	*John Keane Studios. Sixteen tracks recorded with Joe Boyd.*	
3-85	*London, England*	*Livingstone Studios. Tracks recorded: Fables of the Reconstruction tracks, plus Bandwagon, Burning Hell, Crazy, When I Was Young, Theme From Two Steps Onward*	
4-22-85	Athens, Ga.	Legion Field ("Pre-Construction" Tour begins)	Alex Chilton
4-25-85	Lewisburg, Pa.	Bucknell University	
4-26-85	Binghampton, N.J.	SUNY	
4-27-85	Providence, R.I.	Brown University	
4-28-85	Piscataway, N.J.	Rutgers University	
4-30-85	Madison, N.J.	Drew University	
5-3-85	Cambridge, Mass.	New Athletic Center, M.I.T.	The Neats
5-4-85	Williamstown, Mass.	Lansing Arena	
5-5-85	Buffalo, N.Y.	University, Alumni Arena	
5-8-85	Evanston, Ill.	McGaw Arena, Northwestern U.	
5-9-85	Iowa City, Ia.		
5-10-85	Madison, Wisc.	Stock Pavillion	
5-12-85	Richmond, Va.		
5-27-85	Raleigh, N.C.	Meridith College Amphitheater	
5-30-85	Madison, N.J.	Drew University	
6-10-85	*Fables of the Reconstruction released*		
6-22-85	England	Milton Keynes Bowl	U2

6-24-85	Manchester, England	International Ballroom	
6-25-85	Edinburgh, Scotland	Coasters	
6-26-85	Newcastle, England	Tiffany's Ballroom	
6-27-85	Coventry, England	Workroom, Warwick University	
6-29-85	Dublin, Ireland	Slane Castle	
7-6-85	Belgium	Torhout/Werchter Festival	
7-7-85	Belgium	Torhout/Werchter Festival	
7-11-85	Portland, Ore.	("Reconstruction I" begins)	
7-12-85	Seattle, Wash.	Paramount Theater	True West
7-13-85	Vancouver, B.C., Canada	Commodore Ballroom	
7-15-85	Edmonton, Alberta, Canada	S.U.B. Theater	
7-16-85	Calgary, Alberta, Canada	McEwan Hall	
7-19-85	Fresno, Cal.	Warner Theater	Robyn Hitchcock
7-20-85	Berkeley, Cal.	Greek Theater	Robyn Hitchcock
7-22-85	Santa Rosa, Cal.	Sonoma County Fairgrounds	Robyn Hitchcock
7-23-85	Santa Cruz, Cal.	Civic Auditorium	Robyn Hitchcock
7-24-85	Santa Barbara, Cal.	Arlington Theater	Robyn Hitchcock
7-26-85	San Diego, Cal.	Open Air Theater	Robyn Hitchcock
7-27-85	Hollywood, Cal.	Greek Theater (w/Warren Zevon)	Robyn Hitchcock
7-28-85	Irvine, Cal.	Irvine Meadows	Robyn Hitchcock
7-29-85	Phoenix, Ariz.	Palace West	
7-31-85	San Antonio, Tex.	Majestic Theater	
8-1-85	Austin, Tex.	Austin Coliseum	
8-2-85	Houston, Tex.	Cullen Auditorium	
8-3-85	Dallas, Tex.	Bronco Bowl	
8-5-85	Minneapolis, Minn.	Roy Wilkins Auditorium	
8-6-85	St. Paul, Minn.	Civic Center Forum	
8-7-85	Chicago, Ill.	U.I.C. Pavillion	
8-9-85	Kalamazoo, Mich.	State Theater	
8-10-85	Detroit, Mich.	Fox Theater	
8-12-85	Cleveland, Oh.	Music Hall	The Three O'Clock
8-13-85	Pittsburgh, Pa.	Syria Mosque	The Three O'Clock
8-15-85	Rochester, N.Y.	Auditorium Theater	The Three O'Clock
8-16-85	Toronto, Canada	Toronto Concert Hall	The Three O'Clock
8-17-85	Ottowa, Ontario	Barrymore's	The Three O'Clock
8-18-85	Montreal, Quebec	Le Vieux Port Dome	The Three O'Clock
8-20-85	Portland, Me.	Cumberland County Civic Center	The Three O'Clock
8-21-85	Boston, Mass.	Walter Brown Arena	The Three O'Clock
8-23-85	Pawtucket, R.I.	Leroy Theater	The Three O'Clock
8-24-85	Hartford, Conn.	Agora	The Three O'Clock
8-25-85	Albany, N.Y.	J.B. Scott's Theater	The Three O'Clock
8-26-85	Baltimore, Md.	Lyric Theater	The Three O'Clock
8-28-85	Philadelphia, Pa.	Tower Theater	The Three O'Clock
8-29-85	Washington, D.C.	DAR Constitution Hall	The Three O'Clock
8-30-85	Pasiac, N.J.	Capital Theater	The Three O'Clock
8-31-85	New York, N.Y.	Radio City Music Hall	The Three O'Clock
10-1-85	Amsterdam, Holland	Paradiso ("Reconstruction II" begins) (FM broadcast)	
10-2-85	Zeche Bochum, Germany	Rockpalast (FM broadcast)	
10-3-85	Rotterdam, Holland	Arena	
10-5-85	Gent, Belgium	Vooruit	
10-6-85	Frankfurt, Germany	Batschfopp	
10-7-85	Munich, Germany	Alabamahalle (TV)	
10-9-85	Berlin, Germany	Metropol	
10-10-85	Hamburg, Germany	Markethalle	
10-11-85	Koln, Germany	Luxor	
10-13-85	Saarbrucken, Germany	Uni Aula	
10-14-85	Paris, France	Eldorado	
10-15-85	Lyon, France	Salle Maleire	
10-16-85	Geneva, Switzerland	Salle du Faubourg	
10-18-85	Mannheim, Germany	Feuerwache	
10-20-85	Manchester, England	Ritz Ballroom	The Faith Brothers
10-21-85	Nottingham, England	Rock City	The Faith Brothers
10-22-85	Sheffield, England	Octagon Centre, University of Sheffield	The Faith Brothers
10-23-85	Glasgow, Scotland	Barrowlands Ballroom	The Faith Brothers
10-25-85	Newcastle, England	"The Tube" (TV)	The Faith Brothers
10-26-85	Liverpool, England	Royal Court	The Faith Brothers
10-27-85	Birmingham, England	Powerhouse	The Faith Brothers
10-28-85	London, England	Hammersmith Palais	Misdemeanor/The Faith Brothers
10-29-85	London, England	Hammersmith Palais	The Jazz Butcher/The Faith Brothers
11-2-85	Boulder, Colo.	C.U. Events Center ("Reconstruction III" begins)	10,000 Maniacs
11-3-85	Laramie, Wyo.	U. Of Wyo., A & S Auditorium	10,000 Maniacs
11-5-85	Omaha, Neb.	Music Hall	10,000 Maniacs
11-6-85	Kansas City, Mo.	Memorial Hall	10,000 Maniacs
11-7-85	Champaign, Ill.	Assembly, Aud.	10,000 Maniacs
11-8-85	Bloomington, Ind.	UI Auditorium	10,000 Maniacs
11-9-85	New York, N.Y.	Beacon Theater, CMJ Awards	10,000 Maniacs
11-11-85	Lexington, Ky.	U.K. Memorial Coliseum	10,000 Maniacs
11-12-85	Nashville, Tenn.	Vanderbilt U. Gym	10,000 Maniacs
11-13-85	Memphis, Tenn.	Orpheum Theater	10,000 Maniacs
11-15-85	Ames, Ia.	U. of Iowa, CY Stephens Auditorium	10,000 Maniacs

11-16-85	Champaign, Ill.	U. of Illinois, Folinger Auditorium	10,000 Maniacs
11-17-85	St. Louis, Mo.	Kiel Opera House	10,000 Maniacs
11-19-85	New Orleans, La.	Saenger Theater	10,000 Maniacs
11-21-85	Tuscaloosa, Ala.	U. of Alabama, Focter Auditorium	10,000 Maniacs
11-22-85	Tallahassee, Fla.	Leon County Civic Center	The Minutemen
11-23-85	Jacksonville, Fla.	U. of Florida	The Minutemen
11-24-85	Miami, Fla.	Knight Centre	The Minutemen
11-26-85	St. Petersburg, Fla.	Bayfront Center (w/Roger McGuinn)	The Minutemen
11-27-85	Savannah, Ga.	Civic Center	The Minutemen
11-29-85	Atlanta, Ga.	Fox Theater	The Minutemen
11-30-85	Atlanta, Ga.	Fox Theater	The Minutemen
12-2-85	Raleigh, N.C.	Civic Center	The Minutemen
12-3-85	Columbia, S.C.	Township	The Minutemen
12-4-85	Norfolk, Va.	Chrysler Auditorium	The Minutemen
12-5-85	Richmond, Va.	The Mosque	The Minutemen
12-6-85	Lexington, Va.	Washington and Lee University	The Minutemen
12-8-85	Winston-Salem, N.C.	Reynolds Auditorium	The Minutemen
12-9-85	Radford, Va.	Radford University	The Minutemen
12-10-85	Columbus, Oh.	Veterans Memorial Auditorium	The Minutemen
12-11-85	Indianapolis, Ind.	Clowes Auditorium	The Minutemen
12-13-85	Charlotte, N.C.	Park Center	The Minutemen
12-14-85	Augusta, Ga.		The Minutemen

1986

1-20-86	Athens, Ga.	40 Watt Club (D. Boon benefit)	
3-8-86	Athens, Ga.	Mike Mills and Bill Berry in "The Corn Cob Webs"	
4/5-86	*Bloomington, Ind.*	*Belmont Mall Studios. Tracks recorded: Lifes Rich Pageant tracks, plus Toys in the Attic, Rotary 10*	
7-28-86	*Lifes Rich Pageant released*		
9-5-86	Birmingham, Ala.	Oak Mountain Theater	Fetchin' Bones
9-6-86	Bloomington, Ind.	Indiana University Auditorium	Fetchin' Bones
9-7-86	Cincinnati, Oh.	Taft Theater	Fetchin' Bones
9-8-86	Louisville, Ky.	Memorial Auditorium	Fetchin' Bones
9-10-86	Nashville, Tenn.	Grand Ole Opry	Fetchin' Bones
9-11-86	Jackson, Miss.	Municipal Auditorium	Fetchin' Bones
9-12-86	New Orleans, La.	Saenger Theater	Fetchin' Bones
9-13-86	Memphis, Tenn.	Mudd Island Amphitheater	Fetchin' Bones
9-15-86	Little Rock, Ark.	Robinson Auditorium	Fetchin' Bones
9-17-86	Oklahoma City, Okla.	Civic Center	Fetchin' Bones
9-18-86	Austin, Tex.	Coliseum	Fetchin' Bones
9-19-86	Houston, Tex.	Southern Star Amphitheater	Fetchin' Bones
9-20-86	Dallas, Tex.	Dallas Fair Park Bandshell	Fetchin' Bones
9-22-86	Las Cruces, N.M.	Pan American Center	10,000 Maniacs
9-23-86	Mesa, Ariz.	Mesa Amphitheater	Guadalcanal Diary
9-24-86	Costa Mesa, Cal.	Pacific Amphitheater	10,000 Maniacs
9-26-86	Berkeley, Cal.	Greek Theater	10,000 Maniacs
9-27-86	Santa Barbara, Cal.	Arlington Theater	10,000 Maniacs
9-28-86	San Diego, Cal.	U.C.S.D. Gym	10,000 Maniacs
9-30-86	Universal City, Cal.	Universal Amphitheater	10,000 Maniacs
10-1-86	Oakland, Cal.	Coliseum Arena	10,000 Maniacs
10-2-86	Eugene, Ore.	Holt Center	10,000 Maniacs
10-3-86	Portland, Ore.	Civic Auditorium	10,000 Maniacs
10-4-86	Seattle, Wash.	Paramount Theater	10,000 Maniacs
10-5-86	Vancouver, B.C.	U.B.C. Gym	10,000 Maniacs
10-7-86	Salt Lake City, Ut.	Fairgrounds Coliseum	10,000 Maniacs
10-9-86	Boulder, Colo.	C.U. Events Center	Camper Van Beethoven
10-10-86	Lincoln, Neb.	Pershing Auditorium	Camper Van Beethoven
10-11-86	Kansas City, Kan.	Memorial Auditorium	Camper Van Beethoven
10-12-86	St. Louis, Mo.	Kiel Opera House	Camper Van Beethoven
10-14-86	Minneapolis, Minn.	Roy Wilkins Auditorium	Camper Van Beethoven
10-15-86	Iowa City, Ia.	Hancher Auditorium	Camper Van Beethoven
10-17-86	Milwaukee, Wisc.	Oriental Theater	Camper Van Beethoven
10-18-86	Grand Rapids, Mich.	Grand Center	Camper Van Beethoven
10-19-86	Chicago, Ill.	U.I.C. Circle Pavillion, U. of Illinois	Camper Van Beethoven
10-21-86	Dekalb, Ill.	Chick Evans Fieldhouse, North. IL U.	Camper Van Beethoven
10-22-86	Detroit, Mich.	Fox Theater	Camper Van Beethoven
10-23-86	Cleveland, Oh.	Public Hall	Camper Van Beethoven
10-24-86	Pittsburgh, Pa.	Syria Mosque	Camper Van Beethoven
10-26-86	Buffalo, N.Y.	Shea's Theater	Camper Van Beethoven
10-27-86	Toronto, Canada	Massey Hall	Camper Van Beethoven
10-28-86	Montreal, Quebec		Camper Van Beethoven
10-30-86	Durham, N.H.	University of N.H. Fieldhouse	Camper Van Beethoven
10-31-86	Burlington, Vt.	Patrick Gym	Camper Van Beethoven
11-1-86	Boston, Mass.	Wang Centre	The Feelies
11-2-86	Boston, Mass.	Wang Centre	The Feelies
11-4-86	Portland, Me.	C.C.C.C.	The Feelies
11-6-86	New York, N.Y.	Felt Forum	The Feelies
11-7-86	New York, N.Y.	Felt Forum	The Feelies

■ The band's first performance in 1986 was a benefit at the 40 Watt Club for D. Boon of The Minutemen, who died in a car accident shortly after supporting R.E.M. during the Reconstruction tour.

11-8-86	New Haven, Conn.	Coliseum	The Feelies
11-9-86	Philadelphia, Pa.	Spectrum Showcase	The Feelies
11-12-86	Washington, D.C.	Smith Center	Let's Active
11-14-86	Williamsburg, Va.	William and Mary Hall	Let's Active
11-15-86	Durham, N.C.	Cameron Indoor Stadium	Let's Active
11-16-86	Wilmington, N.C.	Trask Auditorium	Let's Active
11-17-86	Columbia, S.C.	Township	Let's Active
11-19-86	Statesboro, Ga.	Georgia Southern College	Let's Active
11-20-86	Jacksonville, Fla.	Civic Auditorium	Let's Active
11-21-86	St. Petersburg, Fla.	Bayfront Center (w/Roger McGuinn)	Let's Active
11-22-86	Miami, Fla.	James L. Knight Center	Let's Active
11-24-86	Atlanta, Ga.	Fox Theater	Let's Active
11-25-86	Atlanta, Ga.	Fox Theater	Let's Active
11-26-86	Atlanta, Ga.	Fox Theater	Let's Active

1987

1-23-87	*Lifes Rich Pageant certified gold*		
3-25-87	Athens, Ga.	Uptown Lounge	Charlie Pickett
4-27-87	*Dead Letter Office released*		
4/5-87	*Nashville, Tenn.*	*Sound Emporium. Document is recorded.*	
5-24-87	Santa Monica, Cal.	McCabe's Guitar Shop	
8-19-87	Athens, Ga.	40 Watt Club	
8-31-87	*Document released*		
9-3-87	Athens, Ga.	40 Watt Club	
9-12-87	London, England	Hammersmith Odeon	10,000 Maniacs
9-14-87	Utrecht, Holland	Muziekcentrum (FM broadcast)	10,000 Maniacs
9-16-87	Paris, France	La Cigalle	10,000 Maniacs
9-18-87	Dusseldorf, Germany	Tor 3	10,000 Maniacs
10-1-87	Knoxville, Tenn.	Stokley Athletic Center	10,000 Maniacs
10-2-87	Clemson, S.C.	Little John Coliseum, Clemson U.	10,000 Maniacs
10-3-87	Durham, N.C.	Cameron Indoor Stadium, Duke U.	10,000 Maniacs
10-4-87	Durham, N.C.	Cameron Indoor Stadium, Duke U.	10,000 Maniacs
10-6-87	New York, N.Y.	Radio City Music Hall	10,000 Maniacs
10-7-87	New York, N.Y.	Radio City Music Hall	10,000 Maniacs
10-9-87	Williamsburg, Va.	William and Mary College	10,000 Maniacs
10-10-87	Fairfax, Va.	Patriot Center	10,000 Maniacs
10-11-87	State College, Pa.	Penn State University	10,000 Maniacs

10-12-87	Charlottesville, Va.	University Hall, U. of Virginia	10,000 Maniacs
10-14-87	Charleston, W.Va.	Charleston Auditorium	10,000 Maniacs
10-16-87	Philadelphia, Pa.	Spectrum Theater	10,000 Maniacs
10-17-87	New Haven, Conn.	Coliseum	10,000 Maniacs
10-18-87	Worcester, Mass.	Centrum	10,000 Maniacs
10-19-87	Providence, R.I.	Performing Arts Center	10,000 Maniacs
10-21-87	Rochester, N.Y.	War Memorial	10,000 Maniacs
10-22-87	Piscataway, N.J.	Louis Brown Athletic Center	10,000 Maniacs
10-23-87	Pittsburgh, Pa.	Civic Arena	10,000 Maniacs
10-24-87	Columbus, Oh.	Memorial Coliseum	10,000 Maniacs
10-26-87	East Lansing, Mich.	Michigan State University	10,000 Maniacs
10-27-87	West Lafayette, Ind.	Elliot Hall, Purdue University	10,000 Maniacs
10-29-87	Ann Arbor, Mich.	Chrysler Arena	10,000 Maniacs
10-30-87	Oxford, Oh.	Millet Hall	10,000 Maniacs
10-31-87	Davenport, Ia.	Palmer College	10,000 Maniacs
11-2-87	St. Paul, Minn.	Civic Center	10,000 Maniacs
11-2-87	*Document certified gold*		
11-3-87	Madison, Wisc.	Dane County Coliseum	The dB's
11-4-87	Chicago, Ill.	U.I.C. Circle Pavillion	The dB's
11-5-87	Chicago, Ill.	U.I.C. Circle Pavillion	The dB's
11-7-87	Champaign, Ill.	Assembly Auditorium, University of Illinois	The dB's
11-8-87	Kansas City, Mo.	Soldiers Memorial Hall	The dB's
11-9-87	Lincoln, Neb.	Pershing Auditorium	The dB's
11-10-87	St. Louis, Mo.	Fox Theater	The dB's
11-13-87	Oakland, Cal.	Henry Kaiser Center	The dB's
11-14-87	Irvine, Cal.	Bren Events Center	The dB's
11-15-87	Universal City, Cal.	Universal Amphitheater	The dB's
11-16-87	Tempe, Ariz.	Gammage Auditorium	The dB's
11-18-87	Dallas, Tex.	Moody Coliseum, So. Methodist U.	The dB's
11-19-87	College Station, Tex.	Rollie White Coliseum	The dB's
11-20-87	Houston, Tex.	Sam Houston College	The dB's
11-22-87	Oxford, Miss.	U. of Mississippi	The dB's
11-23-87	Auburn, Ala.	Auburn University	The dB's
11-24-87	Atlanta, Ga.	Fox Theater	The dB's
11-25-87	Atlanta, Ga.	Fox Theater	The dB's
11-27-87	Atlanta, Ga.	Fox Theater	The dB's
11-28-87	Atlanta, Ga.	Fox Theater	The dB's

1988

1-25-88	*Document certified platinum*		
4-20-88	*R.E.M. signs with Warner Brothers Records*		
5-11-88	Athens, Ga.	Uptown Lounge (Berry, Buck and Mills backing Roger McGuinn)	
5-20-88	Athens, Ga.	The Grit	
5 to 7-88	*Memphis, Tenn.*	*Ardent Studios. Tracks recorded: Green tracks, plus Memphis Train Blues, Pop Song '89 (acoustic), See No Evil, Parade of the Wooden Soldiers, and other untitled songs.*	
7-8-88	Athens, Ga.	40 Watt Club	The Primates
9-25-88	Athens, Ga.	Athens Music Festival (Michael Stipe w/ Indigo Girls)	
10-3-88	*Eponymous released*		
11-8-88	*Green released*		

1989

1-9-89	Atlanta, Ga.	Buck and Mills perform on Rockline (FM broadcast)	
1-10-89	*Green certified gold*		
1-26-89	Tokyo, Japan	MZA Stadium (Green World Tour part I begins)	
1-27-89	Tokyo, Japan	MZA Stadium	
2-2-89	Christchurch, New Zealand	Town Hall	The Bats
2-3-89	Wellington, New Zealand	Town Hall	
2-4-89	Auckland, New Zealand	Logan Campbell Centre	
2-8-89	Perth, Australia	Concert Hall	
2-9-89	Perth, Australia	Concert Hall	
2-11-89	Adelaide, Australia	The Barton Theater	
2-12-89	Melbourne, Australia	Festival Hall	
2-14-89	*Green certified platinum*		
2-15-89	Brisbane, Australia	Festival Hall	
2-17-89	Sydney, Australia	Hordern Pavillion	
3-1-89	Louisville, Ky.	City Gardens (Gren World Tour part II)	Robyn Hitchcock
3-2-89	Carbondale, Ill.	S.I.U. Arena	Robyn Hitchcock
3-3-89	St. Louis, Mo.	Arena	Robyn Hitchcock
3-4-89	Kansas City, Mo.	Kemper Arena	Robyn Hitchcock
3-6-89	Chicago, Ill.	Rosemont Horizon	Robyn Hitchcock
3-7-89	Iowa City, Ia.	Hawkeye Arena	Robyn Hitchcock
3-8-89	Minneapolis, Minn.	Met Center	Robyn Hitchcock
3-10-89	Omaha, Neb.	Civic Coliseum	Robyn Hitchcock

3-13-89	Sacramento, Cal.	Arco Arena	Robyn Hitchcock
3-14-89	Oakland, Cal.	Coliseum	Robyn Hitchcock
3-15-89	Los Angeles, Cal.	Forum	Robyn Hitchcock
3-16-89	San Diego, Cal.	Sports Arena	Robyn Hitchcock
3-18-89	Phoenix, Ariz.	Arizona State University	Robyn Hitchcock
3-20-89	San Antonio, Tex.	Municipal Auditorium	Robyn Hitchcock
3-21-89	Austin, Tex.	Frank Erwin Center	Robyn Hitchcock
3-22-89	Dallas, Tex.	Reunion Arena	Robyn Hitchcock
3-23-89	Houston, Tex.	Summit	Robyn Hitchcock
3-25-89	Shreveport, La.	Hersh Memorial Auditorium	Indigo Girls
3-27-89	New Orleans, La.	Lakefront Arena	Indigo Girls
3-28-89	Birmingham, Ala.	Jefferson County Civic Auditorium	Indigo Girls
3-30-89	Memphis, Tenn.	Midsouth Coliseum	Indigo Girls
3-31-89	Murphreesboro, Tenn.	Murphy Center	Indigo Girls
4-1-89	Atlanta, Ga.	The Omni	Indigo Girls
4-2-89	Atlanta, Ga.	The Omni	Indigo Girls
4-4-89	Cincinnati, Oh.	Riverfront Coliseum	Indigo Girls
4-5-89	Detroit, Mich.	Cobo Hall	Indigo Girls
4-6-89	Cleveland, Oh.	Richfield Coliseum	Indigo Girls
4-7-89	Morgantown, W.Va.	The Coliseum	Indigo Girls
4-9-89	Worcester, Mass.	The Centrum	Indigo Girls
4-10-89	New York, N.Y.	Madison Square Garden	Indigo Girls
4-11-89	Syracuse, N.Y.	War Memorial	Indigo Girls
4-12-89	Toronto, Ontario	Maple Leaf Gardens	Indigo Girls
4-14-89	Montreal, Quebec	Forum	Indigo Girls
4-15-89	Portland, Me.	Civic Center	Drivin n' Cryin'
4-16-89	Boston, Mass.	Boston Garden	Drivin n' Cryin'
4-18-89	Landover, Md.	Capital Center	Drivin n' Cryin'
4-20-89	Philadelphia, Pa.	Spectrum	Drivin n' Cryin'
4-21-89	Richmond, Va.	Coliseum	Drivin n' Cryin'
4-22-89	Chapel Hill, N.C.	Dean Smith Center	Drivin n' Cryin'
4-23-89	Charlotte, N.C.	Coliseum	Drivin n' Cryin'
4-25-89	Columbia, S.C.	Carolina Coliseum	Drivin n' Cryin'
4-26-89	Savannah, Ga.	Civic Center	Drivin n' Cryin'
4-28-89	Tampa, Fla.	Sundome	Drivin n' Cryin'
4-29-89	Miami, Fla.	Miami Arena	Drivin n' Cryin'
4-30-89	Orlando, Fla.	Orlando Arena	Drivin n' Cryin'
5-2-89	Tallahassee, Fla.	Leon County Civic Center	Drivin n' Cryin'
5-3-89	Huntsville, Ala.	Von Braun Arena	Drivin n' Cryin'
5-9-89	Dusseldorf, Germany	Philipshalle (Green World Tour part III)	The Go Betweens
5-10-89	Munich, Germany	Circus Krone	The Go Betweens
5-12-89	Bielfeld, Germany	PC 89	The Go Betweens
5-14-89	Hamburg, Germany	Grosse Freiheit	The Go Betweens
5-15-89	Landgraaf, Holland	Pink Pop Festival	
5-17-89	Leicester, England	De Montfort Hall	Blue Aeroplanes
5-18-89	Newport , England	Newport Centre	Blue Aeroplanes
5-19-89	Portsmouth, England	Guild Hall	Blue Aeroplanes
5-21-89	Liverpool, England	Royal Court Theatre	Blue Aeroplanes
5-22-89	Nottingham, England	Royal Centre	Blue Aeroplanes
5-23-89	Edinburgh, Scotland	Playhouse Theatre	The Go Betweens
5-24-89	Glasgow, Scotland	Barrowlands Ballroom	Blue Aeroplanes
5-26-89	Newcastle, England	City Hall	Blue Aeroplanes
5-27-89	Manchester, England	Apollo Theatre	Blue Aeroplanes
5-28-89	London, England	Hammersmith Odeon Theatre	Blue Aeroplanes
5-29-89	London, England	Hammersmith Odeon Theatre	Blue Aeroplanes
5-30-89	London, England	Hammersmith Odeon Theatre	Blue Aeroplanes
5-31-89	Birmingham, England	Birmingham International Arena	Blue Aeroplanes
6-4-89	Seinajoki, Finland	Provinssi-Rock Festival	
6-6-89	Stockholm, Sweden	Gotha Lejoh	
6-7-89	Oslo, Norway	Rockerfeller Music Hall	
6-8-89	Oslo, Norway	Rockerfeller Music Hall	
6-9-89	Copenhagen, Denmark	Saga Rockteater	
6-11-89	Berlin, Germany	Metropol	The Go Betweens
6-13-89	Zurich, Switzerland	Volkshaus	The Go Betweens
6-15-89	Milan, Italy	Palatrussardi	The Go Betweens
6-16-89	Bologna, Italy	Palasport	The Go Betweens
6-17-89	Perugia, Italy	Rockin Umbria Festival	The Go Betweens
6-20-89	Paris, France	Le Grand Rex	The Go Betweens
6-22-89	London, England	Wembley Arena	Throwing Muses
6-24-89	Dublin, Ireland	R.D.S. Simmons Court	The Go Betweens
6-28-89	Frankfurt, Germany	Kongresshalle	The Go Betweens
7-1-89	Belgium	Rock Torhout Festival	
7-2-89	Belgium	Rock Werchter Festival	
9-8-89	Indianapolis, Ind.	Market Square (Gren World Tour part IV)	Throwing Muses
9-9-89	Clarkeston, Mo.	Pine Knob	Throwing Muses
9-10-89	Pittsburgh, Pa.	Civic Arena	Throwing Muses
9-12-89	Buffalo, N.Y.	Memorial Auditorium	Throwing Muses
9-13-89	Hartford, Conn.	Civic Center	Throwing Muses
9-15-89	Boston, Mass.	Great Woods	Throwing Muses
9-16-89	Boston, Mass.	Great Woods	Throwing Muses

9-17-89	Philadelphia, Pa.	Mann Music Center	Throwing Muses
9-19-89	East Rutherford, N.J.	Meadowlands	Throwing Muses
9-20-89	Hempstead, N.Y.	Nassau Coliseum	Throwing Muses
9-22-89	Columbia, Md.	Merriwether Post Pavillion	Throwing Muses
9-23-89	Columbia, Md.	Merriwether Post Pavillion	Throwing Muses
9-26-89	Dayton, Oh.	Ohio Center	Throwing Muses
9-27-89	Champaign, Ill.	U. of Illinois Assembly Hall	NRBQ
9-29-89	South Bend, Ind.	Joyce Center, University of Notre Dame	NRBQ
9-30-89	East Troy, Wisc.	Alpine Valley	NRBQ
10-1-89	Ames, Ia.	Hilton Coliseum	NRBQ
10-3-89	Lincoln, Neb.	Nebraska Devaney	NRBQ
10-5-89	Denver, Colo.	McNichols	NRBQ
10-7-89	Salt Lake City, Ut.	Salt Palace	NRBQ
10-9-89	Boise, Id.	University Center	NRBQ
10-10-89	Pullman, Wash.	Beasley Center	NRBQ
10-11-89	Seattle, Wash.	Seattle Center	NRBQ
10-13-89	Portland, Ore.	Portland Memorial	NRBQ
10-14-89	Vancouver, B.C.	Pacific Coliseum	NRBQ
10-16-89	Anchorage, Alas.	Sullivan Arena	NRBQ
10-17-89	Los Angeles, Cal.	"The Arsenio Hall Show" (TV)	
10-20-89	Concord, Cal.	Pavillion	NRBQ
10-21-89	Mountain View, Cal.	Shoreline Amphitheater	NRBQ
10-22-89	Costa Mesa, Cal.	Pacific Amphitheater	NRBQ
10-24-89	Phoenix, Ariz.	Compton Terrace	Pylon
10-25-89	Tuscon, Ariz.	Community Center Arena	Pylon
10-26-89	Las Cruces, N.M.	Pan Am Center	Pylon
10-28-89	Oklahoma City, Okla.	Myriad	Pylon
10-29-89	Little Rock, Ark.	Barton Coliseum	Pylon
10-30-89	Baton Rouge, La.	Louisiana State University	Pylon
11-1-89	Tallahassee, Fla.	Leon County Civic Center Arena	Pylon
11-3-89	Chattanooga, Tenn.	University of Tennessee	Pylon
11-4-89	Knoxville, Tenn.	Thompson-Boling Assembly	Pylon
11-5-89	Lexington, Ky.	Rupp Arena	Pylon
11-7-89	Roanoke, Va.	Civic Center	Pylon
11-8-89	Hampton, Va.	VA Coliseum	Pylon
11-10-89	Greensboro, N.C.	Coliseum	Pylon
11-11-89	Macon, Ga.	Coliseum	Pylon
11-13-89	Atlanta, Ga.	Fox Theater (C.P.G./L.E.A.F. Benefit)	Pylon

■ In March 1991, the band performed for a nationwide "Mountain Stage" radio audience and for the privileged few present at the Cultural Center Auditorium in West Virginia. Peter Holsapple, Robyn Hitchcock and Billy Bragg also performed.

1990

1 to 7-90	*Athens, Ga/Woodstock, N.Y.*	*John Keane Studios and Bearsville Studios. Tracks recorded: Out of Time tracks plus Rotary Eleven, Forty Second Song, Radio Song (acoustic), Fretless, Night Swim, It's a Free World Baby, Speed Metal, Kerouac No. 4, Love is All Around, First We Take Manhattan, I Walked With a Zombie, Mandolin Strum, Ghost Reindeer in the Sky, Summertime*	
4-5-90	Athens, Ga.	40 Watt Club (R.E.M.'s 10th anniversary)	Beast Penis/Jarvik 8
7-31-90	Athens, Ga.	40 Watt Club (Berry, Buck, and Mills)	
12-19-90	Athens, Ga.	40 Watt Club (Buck, Mills, and Stipe)	

1991

3-5-91	Hamburg, Germany	NDR Studio (FM broadcast)	
3-7-91	Dallas, Tex.	KDGE Studios (FM broadcast)	
3-10-91	Denberg, Holland	Bulletsound Studios (FM broadcast)	
3-12-91	Amsterdam, Holland	2 Meter Vara Studios (FM broadcast)	
3-12-91	*Out of Time released*		
3-13-91	London, England	BBC studios (Radio 1 FM broadcast)	
3-14-91	London, England	"The Late Show" (TV)	
3-14-91	London, England	The Borderline	Chickasaw Mudd Puppies
3-15-91	London, England	The Borderline	Chickasaw Mudd Puppies
3-22-91	Milan, Italy	Shocking Club	
4-1-91	Los Angeles, Cal.	Rockline studios (FM broadcast)	
4-3-91	Santa Monica, Cal.	KCRW studios (FM broadcast)	
4-10-91	New York, N.Y.	MTV studios, "MTV Unplugged" (TV)	
4-13-91	New York, N.Y.	"Saturday Night Live" (TV)	
4-25-91	Chicago, Ill.	WXRT Studios (FM broadcast)	
4-28-91	Charleston, W.Va.	Cultural Center Auditorium (FM "Mountain Stage" broadcast)	
5-9-91	Toronto, Canada	Eastern Sound Studio 1 (FM broadcast)	
5-18-91	*Out of Time hits #1 on the Billboard chart*		
5-29-91	Athens, Ga.	40 Watt Club (Buck, Mills, and Stipe)	
6-15-91	Athens, Ga.	40 Watt Club	Vic Chestnutt
11-27-91	Atlanta, Ga	MTV's 10th anniversary (TV)	

1992

1-31-92	Athens, Ga.	40 Watt Club	5-8/Michelle Malone
10-6-92	*Automatic For the People released*		
11-19-92	Athens, Ga.	40 Watt Club (Greenpeace benefit)	

1993

1-20-93	Washington, D.C.	MTV Rock & Roll Inaugural Ball (Michael Stipe and Mike Mills performed with members of U2 and 10,000 Maniacs)	

U.S. AND U.K. BILLBOARD CHARTING HISTORY

Albums:	U.S. Top Pop Albums		U.K. Chart	
Chronic Town	*did not chart*		*did not chart*	
Murmur	**#36**	August 13, 1983	*did not chart*	
Reckoning	**#27**	June 30, 1984	**#91**	April 28, 1984
Fables of the Reconstruction	**#28**	August 10, 1985	**#35**	July 29, 1985
Lifes Rich Pageant	**#21**	October 11, 1986	**#43**	September 6, 1986
Dead Letter Office	**#52**	June 13, 1987	**#60**	May 16, 1987
Document	**#10**	November 17, 1987	**#28**	September 26, 1987
Eponymous	**#44**	November 19, 1988	*did not chart*	
Green	**#12**	March 4, 1989	**#27**	November 19, 1988
Out of Time	**#1**	May 18, 1991	**#1**	March 23, 1991
The Best of R.E.M.	*not issued in the U.S.*		**#7**	October 19, 1991
Automatic For the People	**#2**	October 24, 1992	**#1**	October 17, 1992

U.S. Singles:	Hot 100		Album Rock		Modern Rock	
Radio Free Europe	**#78**	8/13/83				
So. Central Rain	**#85**	7/14/84				
(Don't Go Back To) Rockville	*did not chart*					
Can't Get There From Here	*did not chart*					
Driver 8	*did not chart*					
Fall On Me	**#94**	10/11/86	**#5**	9/6/86		
Superman	*did not chart*		**#17**	11/22/86		
The One I Love	**#9**	12/5/87	**#2**	10/10/87		
It's the End of the World	**#69**	2/20/88	**#16**	1/9/88		
Finest Worksong	*did not chart*		**#28**	2/26/88		
Orange Crush	*did not chart*		**#1**	11/26/88	**#1**	11/26/88
Stand	**#6**	4/22/89	**#1**	2/11/89	**#1**	2/4/89
Pop Song 89	**#86**	6/24/89	**#14**	6/17/89	**#24**	6/17/89
Turn You Inside-Out	*did not chart*		**#7**	4/22/89	**#10**	4/15/89
Get Up	*did not chart*		*did not chart*		*did not chart*	
Losing My Religion	**#4**	6/22/91	**#1**	4/13/91	**#1**	3/16/91
Texarkana	*did not chart*		**#7**	6/15/91	**#3**	6/22/91
Shiny Happy People	**#10**	9/28/91	**#9**	8/24/91	**#5**	7/6/91
Radio Song	*did not chart*		**#43**	10/19/91	*did not chart*	

First We Take Manhattan	*did not chart*		*did not chart*		**#11**	1/25/92
Drive	**#28**	12/26/92	**#2**	11/7/92	**#1**	10/19/92
Ignoreland	*did not chart*		**#4**	1/23/93	**#1**	10/17/92
Man on the Moon	**#30**	3/27/93	**#5**	2/20/93	**#2**	1/30/93
The Sidewinder Sleeps Tonite	*did not chart*		**#28**	5/29/93	**#24**	5/15/93

U.K. Singles

The One I Love	**#51**	November 28, 1987	(previous singles did not chart)
Finest Worksong	**#50**	April 30, 1988	
Stand	**#51**	February 4, 1989	
Orange Crush	**#28**	June 3, 1989	
Stand (reissue)	**#48**	August 12, 1989	
Losing My Religion	**#19**	March 16, 1991	
Shiny Happy People	**#6**	June 15, 1991	
Near Wild Heaven	**#17**	August 24, 1991	
The One I Love (reissue)	**#16**	October 19, 1991	
Radio Song	**#28**	November 16, 1991	
It's the End of the World	**#39**	December 21, 1991	
Drive	**#6**	October 10, 1992	
Man on the Moon	**#19**	December 5, 1992	
The Sidewinder Sleeps Tonite	**#17**	March 6, 1993	
Everybody Hurts	**#7**	May 22, 1993	

CATALOG

ALBUMS AND EPs

Chronic Town		**LP**	**CD**	**Cassette**	**release date**
Canada	I.R.S.	SP 70502	--	CS 70502	1984
Greece	Illegal	ILP 26097	--		1984
Holland	I.R.S.	ILP 26097	--		1984
Japan	CBS/Sony	20AP 2958	--		1984
U.S.	I.R.S.	SP 70502	--	cs70502	8/24/82
Murmur					
Australia	I.R.S./Epic	ELPS 4380		EPC 4380	1983
Australia	I.R.S.	SP 70014	025433 2		1991
Canada	I.R.S.	SP 70604	--	CS 70604	1983
Greece	I.R.S.	ILS 4653781			1983
Holland	Illegal	ILP 25433			1983
Holland	I.R.S.	ILP 465378 1	ILP 465378 2		1990
Holland	I.R.S.	--	713158 2	--	8/92
Japan	CBS/Sony	25 AP 2659	CD-70014		1983
Japan	CBS/Sony		CSCS 6080		1990
Japan	I.R.S./EMI	--	TOCP-7266	--	1992
South Africa	CBS	ASF 2886			1990
U.K.	I.R.S.	SP 70604	CD 70014	CS 70604	8/83
U.K.	I.R.S.		CDMID 129		1990
U.S.	I.R.S.	SP 70604	-	CS 70604	4/13/83
U.S.	I.R.S.	SP 70014	CD 70014	CS 70014	9/1/83
Reckoning					
Australia	I.R.S./Epic	ELPS 4439	--	EPC 4439	4/84
Canada	I.R.S.	SP 70044	VPCD 70044	CS-70044	4/84
Greece	Illegal	ILP 25915			4/84
Holland	I.R.S.	ILP 25915			4/84
Holland	I.R.S.	ILP 465379 1	ILP 465379 2		1990
Holland	I.R.S.	--	713159 2	--	8/92
Israel	I.R.S.	CBS 25915			4/84
Japan	CBS/Sony	28 AP 2847	--		4/84
Japan	CBS/Sony	--	VICP-5129	--	1987
Japan	CBS/Sony		CSCS 6081		1990
Japan	I.R.S./EMI	--	TOCP-7267		1992
New Zealand	Illegal	ELPS 4439			4/84
Spain	Illegal	ILP 25915			4/84
U.K.	I.R.S.	IRSA 7045	CD 70044	IRSC 7045	4/84
U.S.	I.R.S.	SP 70044	CD 70044	CS-70044	4/14/84

Fables of the Reconstruction		**LP**	**CD**	**Cassette**	**release date**
Argentina					6/85
Australia	I.R.S./Epic	ELPS 4105		EPC 4105	6/85
Brazil	I.R.S./Epic	144.877			6/85
Canada	I.R.S.	5592	MC 5592	IRSC-5592	6/85
Greece	Illegal	ILP 26525			6/85
Holland	I.R.S.	ILP 26525	CDILP 26525		6/85
Holland	I.R.S.	ILP 465380 1	ILP 465380 2		1990
Holland	I.R.S.	--	713160 2	--	8/92
Israel	I.R.S.	CBS 26525			6/85
Japan	I.R.S./Sony	28 AP 3058	CDILP 26525		6/85
Japan	I.R.S.		CSCS 6082		1990
Japan	I.R.S./EMI	--	TOCP-7268	--	1992
New Zealand	Illegal	ELPS 4495			6/85
Philippines	Epic	QEL 25105			6/85
Portugal	I.R.S.	ILP 26525			6/85
Spain	I.R.S.	ILP 26525			6/85
U.K.	I.R.S.	MIRF 1003	DMIRF 1003	MIRFC 1003	6/85
U.K.	I.R.S.		DMIRL 1503	MIRLC 1503	1986
U.S.	I.R.S.	5592	IRSD-5592	IRSC-5592	6/10/85

Lifes Rich Pageant					
Australia	I.R.S./Epic	ELPS 4550		EPC 4550	7/86
Brazil	Epic	144.905			7/86
Canada	I.R.S.	5783	IRSND-5783	IRSC 5783	7/86
Greece	I.R.S.	ILP 57064			7/86
Holland	I.R.S.	ILP 57064	CDILP 57064		7/86
Holland	I.R.S.	ILP 465381 1	465381 2		1990
Holland	I.R.S.	--	713201 2	--	2/93
Japan	I.R.S.	28 AP 3240	CDILP 57064		7/86
Japan	I.R.S.		CSCS 6083		1990
U.K.	I.R.S.	MIRG 1014	DMIRG 1014	MIRGC 1014	7/86
U.K.	I.R.S.		MIRC 1507		1990
U.S.	I.R.S.	5783	IRSD-5783	IRSC 5783	7/28/86

***Dead Letter Office* (all CDs include *Chronic Town*)**					
Australia	I.R.S./Epic	450961	--	450961-4	4/87
Brazil	Epic	235.502			4/87
Canada	I.R.S.	70054	CD 70054	CS 70054	4/87
Greece	I.R.S.	ILP 450961			4/87
Holland	I.R.S.	ILP 450961	ILP 450961.2		4/87
Holland	I.R.S.	ILP 465382 1	ILP 465382 2		1990
Holland	I.R.S.	--	713199 2	--	2/93
Japan	CBS/Sony		32DP 799		4/87
Japan	I.R.S.		CSCS 6084		1990
U.K.	I.R.S.	SP 70054	CDA 70054	CS 70054	4/87
U.S.	I.R.S.	SP 70054	CD 70054	CS 70054	4/27/87

Document					
Australia	I.R.S./Epic	460105			10/87
Canada	I.R.S.	42059	MC 42059	IRSC 42050	10/87
Holland	I.R.S.	ILP 460105 1	ILP 460105.2		10/87
Holland	I.R.S.	ILP 465383 1	ILP 465383 2		1990
Holland	I.R.S.	--	713200 2	--	2/93
Japan	I.R.S.	28 AP 3382	32 DP 842		10/87
Japan	CBS/Sony		CSCS 6085		1990
South Africa	CBS	ASF3174			10/87
U.K.	I.R.S.	MIRG 1025	DMIRG 1025	MIRGC 1025	10/87
U.K.	I.R.S.		DMIRC 1508		1990
U.S.	I.R.S.	42059	IRSD-42059	IRSC 42050	8/31/87

Eponymous					
Australia	I.R.S./Lib.	LIB 5165	CDLIB 5165		10/88
Canada	I.R.S.	6262	IRSD 6262	IRSC 6262	10/88
Greece	I.R.S.	463 147			10/88
Holland	I.R.S.	463 147 1	463147 2		10/88
Holland	I.R.S.	ILP 466338 1	ILP 466338 2		1990
Japan	I.R.S.	UDP 1426	VDP-1426		10/88
U.K.	I.R.S.	6262	DMIRG 1038	MIRGC 1038	10/88
U.S.	I.R.S.	6262	IRSD-6262	IRSC 6262	10/3/88

Green		LP	CD	Cassette	release date
Argentina	WEA	80127			11/88
Australia	WB	25795.1	25795.2	25795.4	11/88
Brazil	WB	670.8035			11/88
Canada	WEA	92-57951	CD 25795	9 25795-4	11/88
Germany	WB	925 795-1	925 795-2	925795-4	11/88
Greece	WB	2-25795	925 795		11/88
Israel	WB	BAN 925733-1			11/88
Japan	WB	25P2-2389	25P2-2389		11/88
Mexico	WEA	LXWB 6813			11/88
Spain	WB	925 795			11/88
U.K.	WEA	WX234	WX-234CD	WX 234C	11/88
U.S.	WB	9 25795-1	9 25795-2	9 25795-4	11/8/88
Out of Time					
Australia	WB	7599 264961	7599 264962	7599 264964	3/91
Canada	WEA	92-64961	CD 26496	9 26496-4	3/91
Czechoslovakia	Popron	50 139-2			3/91
Germany	WB	7599-26496-1	7599-26496-2	7599-26496-4	3/91
Greece	WB	7599-26496-1			3/91
Hungary	WB				3/91
Israel	WB	9-26496-1	9 26496-2	9 26496-4	3/91
Japan	WB		WPCP 4195		3/91
Russia	BRS	no number			1992
South Africa	WB				3/91
U.K.	WB	WX 404	WX 404CD	WX 404C	3/91
U.S.	WB	9 26496-1	9 26496-2	9 26496-4	3/12/91
U.S. (DCC)	WB	9 26496-5	--	--	1992
Yugoslavia	Jugoton			303277-7	1991
The Best of R.E.M.					
U.K.	I.R.S.	MIRH-1	DMIRH 1	MIRHC 1	9/30/91
Holland	I.R.S.	(068) 7131281	(568) 7131282	(268) 7131284	9/30/91
Japan	I.R.S./EMI	--	TOCP-7265	--	9/30/91
Automatic For the People					
Australia	WB	--	9362-45055-2	9362-45055-4	10/6/92
Croatia	WEA	LP-71203931-3		MC-7S303931-2	1992
Germany	WB	9362-45055-1	9362-45055-2	9362-45055-4	10/6/92
Japan	WB		WPCP-4970		10/6/92
U.K.	WB	WX 488	WX 488CD	WX 488C	10/6/92
U.S.	WB	9 45055-1	9 45055-2	9 45055-4	10/6/92
U.S. (ltd. edition)	WB	--	9 45122-2	--	10/6/92
U.S. (in longbox)	WB	--	9 45138-2	--	10/6/92
U.S. (minidisc)	WB	9 45055-8	--	--	10/6/92

Boxed Sets Of Albums

Holland	I.R.S.	465885	Collection (*Fables of the Reconstruction*, *Lifes Rich Pageant*, *Dead Letter Office*, *Document*, and *Eponymous* CDs)	8/90
Holland	I.R.S.	131762	R.E.M. (*Murmur*, *Reckoning* and *Fables of the Reconstruction* remastered CDs with bonus tracks)	11/92

7-INCH SINGLES

7-inch singles, Australia

Illegal	ES 875		Radio Free Europe (edit)/There She Goes Again	1983
Illegal	ES 875		Radio Free Europe (edit)/There She Goes Again (white label, promotion only)	1983
Illegal	ES 971		So. Central Rain/King of the Road	1984
Illegal	ES 971		So. Central Rain/King of the Road (white label, promotion only)	1984
Epic	ES 1082		Can't Get There From Here/Driver 8 (promotion only)	1985
I.R.S.	ES 1170		Fall On Me/Rotary 10	1986
I.R.S.	650225 7		Superman/White Tornado	1986
I.R.S.	6511137	PS	The One I Love/Maps and Legends (live)	1987
I.R.S.	6513487		It's the End of the World As We Know It (and I Feel Fine) (edit)/Last Date	1987
WB	7-27652	PS	Orange Crush/Memphis Train Blues	1989
WB	7-27577	PS	Stand/Memphis Train Blues	1989
WB			Pop Song '89/	1989
WB	543919392-7	PS	Losing My Religion/Rotary Eleven	1991

7-inch singles, Canada

I.R.S.	IR9927		So. Central Rain/King of the Road	1984
I.R.S.	52642	PS	Can't Get There From Here (edit)/Bandwagon	1985
I.R.S.	52642	PS	Can't Get There From Here (edit)/Bandwagon (promotion only)	1985
I.R.S.	IRSP 857		Wendell Gee/Just Friends/Without You (tracks 2 and 3 by Beat Rodeo; promo)	1985
I.R.S.	52883	PS	Fall On Me/Rotary 10	1986
I.R.S.	52971	PS	Superman/White Tornado	1986
I.R.S.	52971	PS	Superman/White Tornado (promotion only)	1986
I.R.S.	53171	PS	The One I Love/Maps and Legends (live)	1987
I.R.S.	53171		The One I Love/The One I Love (promotion only)	1987
I.R.S.	53220	PS	It's the End of the World As We Know It (and I Feel Fine) (edit)/Last Date	1987
I.R.S.	53220		It's the End of the World (edit)/Last Date (promotion only)	1987
WB	PRO-76887		Stand/Stand (promotion only)	1989
WB	76887		Stand/Memphis Train Blues	1989
WB	PRO-76407		Pop Song '89/Pop Song '89 (promotion only)	1989
WB	76407		Pop Song '89/Pop Song '89 (acoustic)	1989
WB	27917		Get Up/Funtime	1989

7-inch singles, Ecuador

WEA	45-80156	Stand/Memphis Train Blues	1989
WEA	45-80155	Get Up/Funtime	1989
WEA	45-80163	Losing My Religion/Texarkana	1991
WEA	45-80165	Shiny Happy People/Forty Second Song	1991

7-inch singles, France

WB	5439-19392	PS	Losing My Religion/Rotary Eleven	3/91
WB	5439-19307	PS	Shiny Happy People/Forty Second Song	5/91
WB	5439-19179	PS	Near Wild Heaven/Pop Song '89 (live acoustic)	3/92
WB	5439-18708	PS	Drive/World Leader Pretend	10/92

7-inch singles, Germany

WEA	927652-7	PS	Orange Crush/Memphis Train Blues	1989
WEA	PRO 523	PS	Orange Crush/Orange Crush (promotion only)	1989
WEA	PRO 541	PS	Pop Song '89/Orange Crush (promotion only)	1989
WEA	927577-7	PS	Stand/Memphis Train Blues	1989
WB	PRO 607	PS	Near Wild Heaven/Losing My Religion (promotion only)	4/91
WB	PRO 610		World Leader Pretend (live, edit)/Turn You Inside-Out (live) issued with limited edition of Out of Time LP	3/91
WB	5439-19392	PS	Losing My Religion/Rotary Eleven	3/91
WB	5439-19307	PS	Shiny Happy People/Forty Second Song	5/91
WB	5439-19179	PS	Near Wild Heaven/Pop Song '89 (live)	8/5/91
I.R.S.	2045377	PS	The One I Love/Maps and Legends (live)	9/8/91
WB	5439-19246	PS	Radio Song/Love is All Around	11/4/91
WB	5439-18963	PS	Losing My Religion/Losing My Religion (acoustic)	3/92
WB	5439-18708	PS	Drive/World Leader Pretend	10/92
WB	5439-18656	PS	Man on the Moon (edit)/Turn You Inside-Out	12/92
WB	5439-18597	PS	The Sidewinder Sleeps Tonite/Get Up	2/93
WB	5439-18513	PS	Everybody Hurts (edit)/Pop Song '89	4/93

7-inch singles, Holland

Illegal	A3567	PS	Radio Free Europe (edit)/There She Goes Again	1983
I.R.S.	A4255	PS	So. Central Rain/King of the Road	1984
I.R.S.	A4734	PS	(Don't Go Back To) Rockville/Wolves	1984
I.R.S.	A6384	PS	Can't Get There From Here (edit)/Bandwagon	1985
I.R.S.	A6587	PS	Wendell Gee/Crazy	1985
I.R.S.	A7302	PS	Fall On Me/Rotary 10	1986
I.R.S.	6502257	PS	Superman/White Tornado	1986
I.R.S.	6511137	PS	The One I Love/Maps and Legends (some copies in German promotional sleeve)	1987
I.R.S.	6513207	PS	Finest Worksong/Time After Time, etc. (live)	1987

7-inch singles, Italy

WB	Promo 412	Losing My Religion/Call it Poison (B-side by Escape Club; juke box edition)	4/20/91

7-inch singles, Japan

I.R.S.	XDSP 93083	PS	Superman/The Future's So Bright (B-side by Timbuk 3; promotion only)	1986
I.R.S.	04SP1072	PS	The One I Love (one-sided)	1987

7-inch singles, Philippines

WB	WB-77-661	Stand/Stand (promotion only)	1989

7-inch singles, South Africa

CBS	SSC 6067	The One I Love/Maps and Legends (live)	1987

7-inch singles, Spain

Illegal	ILSA4734	PS	(Don't Go Back To) Rockville/Wolves	1984
Illegal	ILSA4734	PS	(Don't Go Back To) Rockville (one-sided, promotion only)	1984
Illegal	ILSA6384	PS	Can't Get There From Here (edit)/Bandwagon	1985
Epic	M20618	PS	Can't Get There From Here (LP version) (one-sided, promotion only)	1985
Illegal	ARI 2066	PS	It's the End of the World (edit) (one-sided, promotion only)	1987
WEA	1008	PS	Orange Crush/Orange Crush (promotion only)	1989
WEA	1033	PS	Stand/Stand (promotion only)	1989
WEA	1078	PS	Turn You Inside-Out/Turn You Inside-Out (promotion only)	1989
WEA	1378	PS	Shiny Happy People/Shiny Happy People (promotion only)	1991
WEA	1425	PS	Losing My Religion (live acoustic)/Losing My Religion (live acoustic) (promo)	1991
I.R.S.	4024097	PS	It's the End of the World/It's the End of the World (promotion only)	12/91

7-inch singles, U.K.

I.R.S.	PFP 1017	PS	Radio Free Europe (edit)/There She Goes Again	8/83
I.R.S.	PFP 1017	PS	Radio Free Europe (edit)/There She Goes Again (promotion only)	8/83
I.R.S.	PFP 1026		Talk About the Passion/Talk About the Passion (promotion only)	11/83
I.R.S.	105	PS	So. Central Rain/King of the Road	3/84
I.R.S.	105	PS	So. Central Rain/King of the Road (promotion only)	3/84
I.R.S.	107	PS	(Don't Go Back To) Rockville (LP version)/Wolves	6/84
I.R.S.	107(DJ)	PS	(Don't Go Back To) Rockville (edit/LP versions)	6/84
B.O.B.	5/LYN15742		Tighten Up (given away w/Bucketfull of Brains magazine)	3/85
I.R.S.	IRM 102	PS	Can't Get There From Here (edit)/Bandwagon	7/85
I.R.S.	IRMD 105	PS	Wendell Gee/Crazy/Ages of You/Burning Down (double single)	10/7/85
I.R.S.	IRM 105	PS	Wendell Gee/Crazy	9/30/85
I.R.S.	IRM 121	PS	Fall On Me/Rotary 10	7/86
I.R.S.	IRM 128	PS	Superman/White Tornado	11/86
I.R.S.	IRM 145	PS	It's the End of the World As We Know It (edit)/This One Goes Out (live)	8/17/87
I.R.S.	IRM 146	PS	The One I Love/Last Date	11/87
I.R.S.	IRM 161	PS	Finest Worksong/Time After Time, etc. (live)	4/18/88
I.R.S.	IRM 173	PS	The One I Love/Fall On Me	10/88
WEA	W7577	PS	Stand/Memphis Train Blues	1/23/89
WEA	W7577X	PS	Stand/Memphis Train Blues (recycled paper sleeve)	1/23/89
WEA	W2960	PS	Orange Crush/Ghost Riders	5/89
WEA	W2960X	PS	Orange Crush/Ghost Riders (recycled paper sleeve)	5/89
WEA	W2960B	PS	Orange Crush/Ghost Riders (in boxed set with Ecology poster)	5/89
WEA	W2833	PS	Stand/Pop Song '89 (acoustic version, recycled paper sleeve)	8/89
WEA	W2833W	PS	Stand/Pop Song '89 (acoustic version, recycled paper sleeve, stencil pack)	8/89
WB	W0015	PS	Losing My Religion/Rotary Eleven	2/25/91
WB	W0027	PS	Shiny Happy People/Forty Second Song	5/91
WB	W0055	PS	Near Wild Heaven/Pop Song '89 (live)	8/5/91
I.R.S.	IRM 178	PS	The One I Love/Crazy	9/9/91
WB	W0072	PS	Radio Song/Love is All Around	11/4/91
I.R.S.	IRM 180	PS	It's the End of the World As We Know It (and I Feel Fine)/Radio Free Europe	12/2/91
B.O.B.	B.O.B.32	PS	Academy Fight Song (live)/B-side by The Coal Porters	3/92
WB	W0136	PS	Drive/World Leader Pretend	9/92
WB	W0143	PS	Man on the Moon (edit)/Turn You Inside-Out	11/92
WB	W0152	PS	The Sidewinder Sleeps Tonite/Get Up	2/93
WB	W0169	PS	Everybody Hurts (edit)/Pop Song '89	3/93

7-inch singles, U.S.

Hib-Tone	HT-0001	PS	Radio Free Europe/Sitting Still (first pressing)	7/81
Hib-Tone	HT-0001	PS	Radio Free Europe/Sitting Still (second pressing)	7/81
Tr.Press	Flexi 12		Wolves, Lower/Russian Roulette (B-side by Lords of the New Church)	12/82
I.R.S.	IR9916	PS	Radio Free Europe (LP version)/There She Goes Again	4/13/83
I.R.S.	IR9916		Radio Free Europe (edit)/Radio Free Europe (edit) (promotion only)	4/13/83
I.R.S.	IR9927	PS	So. Central Rain/King of the Road	4/14/84
I.R.S.	IR9927		So. Central Rain/So. Central Rain (promotion only)	4/14/84
I.R.S.	IR9931	PS	(Don't Go Back To) Rockville (edit)/Catapult (live)	8/84
I.R.S.	IR9931		(Don't Go Back To) Rockville (edit)/(Don't Go Back To) Rockville (edit) (promo)	8/84
I.R.S.	52642	PS	Can't Get There From Here (edit)/Bandwagon	6/10/85
I.R.S.	52642	PS	Can't Get There From Here (edit)/Can't Get There From Here (edit) (promotion)	6/10/85
I.R.S.	52678	PS	Driver 8/Crazy	9/3/85
I.R.S.	52678	PS	Driver 8/Driver 8 (promotion only)	9/3/85
The Bob	REAL 005	PS	Femme Fatale (some copies on red plastic)	6/86
I.R.S.	52883	PS	Fall On Me/Rotary 10	8/18/86
I.R.S.	52883	PS	Fall On Me/Fall On Me (promotion only)	8/18/86
I.R.S.	52971	PS	Superman/White Tornado	11/3/86
I.R.S.	52971	PS	Superman/Superman (promotion only)	11/3/86
I.R.S.	52971	PS	Superman/White Tornado (promotion only)	11/3/86
I.R.S.	53171	PS	The One I Love/Maps and Legends (live)	8/24/87
I.R.S.	53171	PS	The One I Love/Maps and Legends (live) (promotion only)	8/24/87
I.R.S.	53171	PS	The One I Love/The One I Love (promotion only)	8/24/87
I.R.S.	53220	PS	It's the End of the World As We Know It (and I Feel Fine) (edit)/Last Date	1/88
I.R.S.	53220	PS	It's the End of the World (edit)/It's the End of the World (edit) (promotion only)	1/88
fan club	U-23518M	PS	Parade of the Wooden Soldiers/See No Evil	12/88
WB	7-27688	PS	Stand/Memphis Train Blues	1/89
WB	7-27688		Stand/Stand (promotion only)	1/89

WB	7-27640	PS	Pop Song '89/Pop Song '89 (acoustic version)	5/89
WB	7-27640		Pop Song '89/Pop Song '89 (promotion only)	5/89
WB	7-22791	PS	Get Up/Funtime	9/89
WB	7-22791		Get Up/Get Up (promotion only)	9/89
Evatone	105900-1S		Dark Globe (6" flexidisc given away with Sassy magazine)	11/89
fan club	122589	PS	Good King Wenceslas/Academy Fight Song	12/89
WB	7-21864		Stand/Pop Song '89 (Back to Back Hits issue)	9/90
fan club	122590	PS	Ghost Reindeer in the Sky/Summertime	12/90
WB	7-19392		Losing My Religion/Rotary Eleven	5/91
WB	7-19242		Shiny Happy People/Forty Second Song	9/91
WB	7-19246		Radio Song/Love is All Around	10/91
fan club	122591	PS	Baby Baby/Christmas Griping	12/91
WB	7-18729		Drive/Winged Mammal Theme	10/92
fan club	REM-92	PS	Where's Captain Kirk/Toyland	12/92
WB	7-18642		Man on the Moon/New Orleans Instrumental #2	2/93

Boxed Sets Of 7-inch Singles

U.S.	WB	7-22780	Singleactiongreen (Get Up, Stand, Pop Song '89, Orange Crush (U.K.) + poster)	11/89

12-INCH SINGLES

12-inch singles, Canada

I.R.S.	23850	PS	Finest Worksong (Lengthy Club Mix)/(Other Mix)/Time After Time, etc. (live)	1988

12-inch singles, Germany

WB	921 148-0	PS	Stand/Memphis Train Blues/Untitled (instrumental remix)	5/91
WB	9362-40078-0	PS	Shiny Happy People/Forty Second Song/Losing My Religion (acoustic)	5/91
WB	9362-40171-0	PS	Near Wild Heaven/Pop Song '89 (live)/Half a World Away (live)	8/5/91
WB	9362-40250-0	PS	Radio Song/Love is All Around/Shiny Happy People (Music Mix)	11/4/91
WB	9362-40399-0	PS	Losing My Religion/Fretless/Losing My Religion (acoustic)/Rotary Eleven	3/92
WB	9362-40634-0	PS	Drive/World Leader Pretend/First We Take Manhattan	10/92
WB	9362-40698-0	PS	Man on the Moon/Turn You Inside-Out/Arms of Love	12/92

12-inch singles, Holland

I.R.S.	A12-4255	PS	So. Central Rain/Voice of Harold/Pale Blue Eyes	1984
I.R.S.	A12-4734	PS	(Don't Go Back To) Rockville/Wolves/9-9 (live)/Gardening at Night (live)	1984
I.R.S.	A12-4734	PS	(Don't Go Back To) Rockville (edit)/Wolves/9-9 (live)/Gardening at Night (live)	1984
I.R.S.	A12-6384	PS	Can't Get There From Here (edit)/Bandwagon/Burning Hell	1985
I.R.S.	A12-6587	PS	Wendell Gee/Driver 8 (live)/Ages of You/Burning Down	1985
I.R.S.	650225-6	PS	Superman/White Tornado/Perfect Circle	1986
I.R.S.	651113-6	PS	The One I Love/The One I Love (live)/Maps and Legends (live)	1987
I.R.S.	651320-6	PS	Finest Worksong (Lengthy Club Mix)/(Other Mix)/Time After Time, etc. (live)	1987

12-inch singles, Spain

I.R.S.	ILSA 12.4734	PS	(Don't Go Back To) Rockville/Wolves/9-9 (live)/Gardening at Night (live)	1984

12-inch singles, U.K.

I.R.S.	PFSX 1026	PS	Talk About the Passion/Shaking Through/Carnival of Sorts/1,000,000	11/11/83
I.R.S.	IRSX 105	PS	So. Central Rain/Voice of Harold/Pale Blue Eyes	3/26/84
I.R.S.	IRSX 107	PS	(Don't Go Back To) Rockville/Wolves/9-9 (live)/Gardening at Night (live)	6/18/84
I.R.S.	IRT 102	PS	Can't Get There From Here/Bandwagon/Burning Hell	7/8/85
I.R.S.	IRT 105	PS	Wendell Gee/Crazy/Driver 8 (live)	10/85
I.R.S.	IRMT 121	PS	Fall On Me/Rotary 10/Toys in the Attic	9/1/86
I.R.S.	IRMT 121dj		Fall On Me/Rotary 10/Toys in the Attic (promotion only)	9/1/86
I.R.S.	IRMT 128	PS	Superman/White Tornado/Femme Fatale	3/87
I.R.S.	IRMT 128dl		Superman/White Tornado/Femme Fatale (promotion only)	3/87
I.R.S.	IRMT 145	PS	It's the End of the World/This One Goes Out (live)/Maps and Legends (live)	8/17/87
I.R.S.	IRMT 146	PS	The One I Love/Last Date/Disturbance at the Heron House	11/87
I.R.S.	IRMT 161	PS	Finest Worksong (Lengthy Club Mix)/(Other Mix)/Time After Time, etc. (live)	4/88
I.R.S.	WIRMT 161ADL	PS	Finest Worksong (Lengthy Club Mix)/(Other Mix)/Time After Time, etc. (live) (promotion only, in "media sleeve")	4/88
I.R.S.	IRMT 173	PS	The One I Love/Fall On Me/So. Central Rain	10/88
I.R.S.	WIRMT 173A		The One I Love/Fall On Me/So. Central Rain (promotion only)	10/88
WEA	W7577T	PS	Stand/Memphis Train Blues/Untitled (instrumental remix)	1/89
WEA	W2960T	PS	Orange Crush/Ghost Riders/Dark Globe	5/89
WEA	W2833T	PS	Stand/Pop Song '89 (acoustic)/Skin Tight (live)	8/89
WB	W0015T	PS	Losing My Religion/Rotary Eleven/After Hours (live)	3/91
WB	W0027T	PS	Shiny Happy People/Forty Second Song/Losing My Religion (acoustic)	5/91
WB	W0055T	PS	Near Wild Heaven/Pop Song '89 (live)/Half a World Away (live)	8/5/91
WB	W0072T	PS	Radio Song/Love is All Around/Shiny Happy People (Music Mix)	11/4/91
WB	W0184TP	PS	Nightswimming/World Leader Pretend (live)/Belong (live)/Low (live)	7/93

12-inch singles, U.S.

I.R.S.	SP 70968		Talk About the Passion/Catapult/Sitting Still (promotion only)	1983
I.R.S.	SP 70979		Pretty Persuasion/(Don't Go Back To) Rockville (edit; promotion only)	1984
I.R.S.	SP 70982	PS	(Don't Go Back To) Rockville (edit)/Catapult (live) (promotion only)	8/84
I.R.S.	L33-17004	PS	Can't Get There From Here (edit)/Driver 8/Life and How To Live It (promotion)	6/10/85
I.R.S.	L33-17034	PS	Driver 8/Driver 8 (live) (promotion only)	8/8/85
I.R.S.	L33-17060	PS	Life and How To Live It/Bandwagon/Crazy (promotion only)	10/21/85
I.R.S.	L33-17159	PS	Fall On Me/Fall On Me (promotion only)	7/21/86
I.R.S.	L33-17200	PS	Superman/Superman (promotion only)	10/20/86
I.R.S.	L33-17199	PS	I Believe/Toys in the Attic (promotion only)	1/5/87
I.R.S.	SP 70146		Ages of You/Ages of You (promotion only)	4/7/87
I.R.S.	L33-17384	PS	The One I Love/The One I Love (promotion only)	9/87
I.R.S.	23792	PS	The One I Love/The One I Love (live)/Maps And Legends (live)	9/7/87
I.R.S.	L33-17430	PS	It's the End of the World/Disturbance at the Heron House (live) (promotion only)	12/87
I.R.S.	L33-17510	PS	Finest Worksong/Finest Worksong (media version) (promotion only)	2/88
I.R.S.	23850	PS	Finest Worksong (Lengthy Club Mix)/(Other Mix)/Time After Time, etc. (live)	3/88
WB	PRO-A-3306	PS	Orange Crush/Orange Crush (promotion only, orange vinyl)	11/88
WB	PRO-5060		Shiny Happy People (Music Mix)/(Pop Mix)/(Hip Mix) (promotion only)	9/91
WB	9 40229-0	PS	Radio Song (Tower of Luv Bug Mix)/Love is All Around (live)/Belong (live)	11/26/91
WB	PRO-A-5263	PS	Radio Song (Tower of Luv Bug Mix)/(Monster Mix) (promotion only)	2/92
WB	PRO-A-5942	PS	Drive (Primary Remix)/Drive (Secondary Remix) (promotion only)	12/92

CD SINGLES

CD singles, Australia

WEA	9362-4077-0-2	PS	The Sidewinder Sleeps Tonite/The Lion Sleeps Tonight/Fretless	1993

CD singles, France

WB	PRO 2002-2	PS	Half a World Away/Love is All Around/Losing My Religion (all acoustic, promo)	11/91
WEA	936-40769-9	PS	The Sidewinder Sleeps Tonite/The Lion Sleeps Tonight/Fretless	1993

CD singles, Germany

WEA	W7577CD	PS	Stand/Memphis Train Blues/Untitled (remix) (three-inch single)	1/89
WEA	W7577CDX	PS	Stand/Memphis Train Blues/Untitled (remix) (in leaf shaped envelope, 3" single)	1/89
WEA	W2960CD	PS	Orange Crush/Ghost Riders/Dark Globe (three-inch single)	5/89
WEA	W2833CD	PS	Stand/Pop Song '89 (acoustic)/Skin Tight (live) (three-inch single)	8/89
WEA	W2833CDX	PS	Stand/Pop Song '89 (acoustic)/Skin Tight (live) (ltd. edition three-inch single)	8/89
WB	W0015CD	PS	Losing My Religion/Rotary Eleven/After Hours (live)	3/91
WB	W0015CDX	PS	Losing My Religion/Stand (live)/Turn You Inside-Out (live)/World Leader Pretend (live)	3/91
WB	9362-40046-2	PS	Losing My Religion/Stand (live)/Turn You Inside-Out (live)/World Leader Pretend (live)	3/91
WB	W0027CD	PS	Shiny Happy People/Forty Second Song/Losing My Religion (acoustic)	5/91
WB	9362-40078-2	PS	Shiny Happy People/Forty Second Song/Losing My Religion (acoustic)	5/91
WB	W0027CDX	PS	Shiny Happy People/I Remember California (live)/Get Up (live)/ Pop Song '89 (live)	5/91
WB	9362-40079-2	PS	Shiny Happy People/I Remember California (live)/Get Up (live)/ Pop Song '89 (live)	5/91
WB	W0055CDX	PS	Near Wild Heaven/Tom's Diner (live)/Low (live)/Endgame (live)	8/5/91
WB	9362-40178-2	PS	Near Wild Heaven/Tom's Diner (live)/Low (live)/Endgame (live)	8/5/91
WB	W0072CDX	PS	Radio Song/You Are the Everything (live)/Orange Crush (live)/Belong (live)	11/4/91
WB	9362-40251-2	PS	Radio Song/You Are the Everything (live)/Orange Crush (live)/Belong (live)	11/4/91
WB	9362-40229-2	PS	Radio Song (Tower of Luv Bug Mix)/Love is All Around/Belong (live)	12/91
WB	9362-40399-2	PS	Losing My Religion/Fretless/Losing My Religion (acoustic)/Rotary Eleven	3/92
WB	W0136CD	PS	Drive/World Leader Pretend/First We Take Manhattan	10/92
WB	9362-40634-2	PS	Drive/World Leader Pretend/First We Take Manhattan	10/92
WB	W0136CDX	PS	Drive/It's a Free World, Baby/Winged Mammal Theme/First We Take Manhattan	10/92
WB	9362-40633-2	PS	Drive/It's a Free World, Baby/Winged Mammal Theme/First We Take Manhattan	10/92
WB	W0143CD	PS	Man on the Moon/Turn You Inside-Out/Arms of Love	11/92
WB	9362-40698-2	PS	Man on the Moon/Turn You Inside-Out/Arms of Love	11/92
WB	W0143CDX	PS	Man on the Moon/Fruity Organ/Arms of Love/New Orleans Instrumental #2	11/92
WB	9362-40710-2	PS	Man on the Moon/Fruity Organ/Arms of Love/New Orleans Instrumental #2	11/92
WB	W0152CD1	PS	The Sidewinder Sleeps Tonite/The Lion Sleeps Tonight/Fretless	2/93
WB	W0152CD2	PS	The Sidewinder Sleeps Tonite/Organ Song/Star Me Kitten (demo)	2/93
WB	9362-40782-2	PS	The Sidewinder Sleeps Tonite/The Lion Sleeps Tonight/Fretless/Organ Song	3/93
WB	W0169CD1	PS	Everybody Hurts (edit)/New Orleans Instrumental #1 (Long Vers.)/Mandolin Strum	4/93
WB	W0169CD2	PS	Everybody Hurts (edit)/Chance (dub)/Dark Globe	4/93
WB	W0184CD	PS	Nightswimming/World Leader Pretend (live)/Belong (live)/Low (live)	7/93

CD box sets, Germany

WB	9362-40313-2	PS	R.E.M. Singles Collection (four limited edition CD singles from Out of Time LP)	12/91

CD singles, Holland

I.R.S.	ILS 651320	PS	Finest Worksong (Other Mix)/(Club Mix)/Time After Time, etc. (live), (3" single)	4/87
I.R.S.	2045372	PS	The One I Love/Maps and Legends (live)/The One I Love (live)	9/8/91
I.R.S.	7 2438 80478 2	PS	It's the End of the World/Radio Free Europe/Time After Time, etc. (live)	3/93

CD singles, Japan

WB	10P3 6078	PS	Stand/Memphis Train Blues (three-inch single)	5/89
WB	WPDP-6308	PS	Drive/Winged Mammal Theme (three-inch single)	11/92
WB	WPDP-6318	PS	Man on the Moon/New Orleans Instrumental #2 (three-inch single)	1/25/93

CD box sets, Japan

WB	WPCP-4781-4	PS	R.E.M. Singles Collection ("Pop Game '92"; four singles from *Out of Time*)	6/92

CD singles, U.K.

I.R.S.	DIRM 146	PS	The One I Love/Last Date/Disturbance at the Heron House	9/87
I.R.S.	DIRM 146	PS	It's the End of the World/Finest Worksong/The One I Love (promotion only)	9/87
I.R.S.	DIRM 161	PS	Finest Worksong/Time After Time, etc. (live)/It's the End of the World (limited edition in die-cut box)	4/88
I.R.S.	DIRM 173	PS	The One I Love/Fall On Me/So. Central Rain	10/88
I.R.S.	DIRMT 178	PS	The One I Love/This One Goes Out (live)/Maps and Legends (live)	10/91
I.R.S.	DIRMX 178	PS	The One I Love/Driver 8 (live)/Disturbance at the Heron House (live)/Crazy	10/91
I.R.S.	DIRMT 180	PS	It's the End of the World/Radio Free Europe/Time After Time, etc. (live)	12/2/91
I.R.S.	REM-1	PS	The One I Love/It's the End of the World/Finest Worksong/Finest Worksong (Lengthy Club Mix) (promotion only)	3/92
I.R.S.	DIRMX 180	PS	It's the End of the World/Last Date/White Tornado/Radio Free Europe (Hib-Tone)	7/92

CD singles, U.S.

I.R.S.	CD45-17476	PS	It's the End of the World (edit)/(album version) (promotion only)	8/87
WB	PRO-CD-3306	PS	Orange Crush (promotion only)	12/88
WB	PRO-CD-3353		Stand (promotion only)	1/89
WB	2-27688	PS	Stand/Memphis Train Blues (3" single)	2/89
WB	PRO-CD-3466		Turn You Inside-Out (promotion only)	3/89
WB	PRO-CD-3357		Pop Song '89 (promotion only)	5/89
WB	PRO-CD-3716		Get Up/Orange Crush (live)/Turn You Inside-Out (live) (promotion only)	9/89
WB	PRO-CDV-4460	PS	Get Up (live)/World Leader Pretend (live)/It's the End of the World (live)/ Get Up (video) (promotion only)	10/90
WB	PRO-CD-4707	PS	Losing My Religion (promotion only)	2/19/91
WB	PRO-CD-4826		Texarkana (promotion only)	5/91
WB	PRO-CD-4881		Losing My Religion (live) (promotion only)	6/91
WB	PRO-CD-4888		Shiny Happy People (promotion only)	7/91
WB	PRO-CD-5060		Shiny Happy People (Music Mix)/(Pop Mix)/(Hip Mix) (promotion only)	9/91
WB	PRO-CD-4808		Radio Song (promotion only)	10/91
WB	9 40229-2	PS	Radio Song (Tower of Luv Bug Mix)/Love is All Around (live)/Belong (live)	11/91
WB	PRO-CD-5058		Near Wild Heaven (promotion only)	3/92
WB	9 18729-2	PS	Drive/Winged Mammal Theme (issued in four different picture sleeves)	10/92
WB	PRO-CD-5700		Drive (promotion only)	10/92
WB	PRO-CD-5844		Ignoreland (promotion only)	12/92
WB	PRO-CD-5894		Man on the Moon (edit)/(album version) (promotion only)	1/93
WB	9 18642-2	PS	Man on the Moon/New Orleans Instrumental #2	1/93
WB	PRO-CD-5903		The Sidewinder Sleeps Tonite (promotion only)	4/93
WB	9 18523-2	PS	The Sidewinder Sleeps Tonite/The Lion Sleeps Tonight	4/93

Full-length promotional samplers

I.R.S.	CD	IRSD-seven		An AOR Radio Staple	8/87
I.R.S.	cassette	IRS 14U	PS	Documenting R.E.M. 1983-1987 (Canada)	1987
WB	CD/LP	PRO-A/CD-3377	PS	Should We Talk About the Weather	12/88
WB	cassette	PTS 2039	PS	Singles Collection (Japan)	3/92
WB	CD	PCS-105	PS	Berry, Buck, Mills, Stipe (Japan)	11/92
I.R.S.	CD	CDREM 92	PS	The Alternative Radio Sampler (U.K.)	11/92

CASSETTES

Cassette singles, Australia

WB	543919392-4	PS	Losing My Religion/Rotary Eleven	3/91
WB	543919307-4	PS	Shiny Happy People/Forty Second Song	7/91
WB	543919179-4	PS	Near Wild Heaven/Pop Song '89	8/91
WB	543919246-4	PS	Radio Song/Love is All Around	11/91
WB	543918729-4	PS	Drive/World Leader Pretend	10/92
WB	543918656-4	PS	Man on the Moon/New Orleans Instrumental #2	1/93
WB	543918634-4	PS	The Sidewinder Sleeps Tonite/Get Up	2/93

Cassette singles, France

WB	543919392-4	PS	Losing My Religion/Rotary Eleven	3/91
WB	543919307-4	PS	Shiny Happy People/Forty Second Song	7/91
WB	543919179-4	PS	Near Wild Heaven/Pop Song '89	8/91
WB	543918597-4	PS	The Sidewinder Sleeps Tonite/Get Up	2/93

Cassette singles, Germany

WB	543919392-4	PS	Shiny Happy People/Forty Second Song	3/91

Cassette singles, Holland

WB	300109-4	PS	Losing My Religion/Rotary Eleven	3/91

Cassette singles, U.K.

WEA	W2960C	PS	Orange Crush/Ghost Riders	1989
WB	W0015C	PS	Losing My Religion/Rotary Eleven	2/91
WB	W0027C	PS	Shiny Happy People/Forty Second Song	5/91
WB	W0055C	PS	Near Wild Heaven/Pop Song '89	8/5/91
I.R.S.	IRMC 178	PS	The One I Love/Crazy	9/8/91
WB	W0072C	PS	Radio Song/Love is All Around	11/4/91
I.R.S.	IRMC 180	PS	It's the End of the World As We Know It (and I Feel Fine)/Radio Free Europe	12/2/91
WB	W0136	PS	Drive/World Leader Pretend	9/92
WB	W0143	PS	Man on the Moon (edit)/Turn You Inside-Out	11/92
WB	W0152	PS	The Sidewinder Sleeps Tonite/Get Up	2/93
WB	W0169	PS	Everybody Hurts (edit)/Pop Song '89	3/93

Cassette singles, U.S.

I.R.S.	IRSC 53204	PS	The One I Love/Maps and Legends (live)	8/87
I.R.S.	IRSC 53220	PS	It's the End of the World As We Know It (and I Feel Fine)/Last Date	1/88
WB	9-27688-4	PS	Stand/Memphis Train Blues	1/89
WB	9-27640-4	PS	Pop Song '89/Pop Song '89 (acoustic)	5/89
WB	9-22791-4	PS	Get Up/Funtime	9/89
WB	9-21864-4	PS	Stand/Pop Song '89 (Backtrax issue)	5/90
WB	9-19392-4	PS	Losing My Religion/Rotary Eleven	3/91
WB	9-19242-4	PS	Shiny Happy People/Forty Second Song	7/91
WB	9-19246-4	PS	Radio Song/Love is All Around	11/91
WB	9-40229-4	PS	Radio Song (Tower of Luv Bug Mix)/Love is All Around/Belong (live)	12/91
WB	9 18729-4	PS	Drive/Winged Mammal Theme (issued in four different picture sleeves)	10/92
WB	9 18642-4	PS	Man on the Moon/New Orleans Instrumental #2	1/93
WB	9 18523-4	PS	The Sidewinder Sleeps Tonite/The Lion Sleeps Tonight	4/93

Other collectible cassettes

--	--	PS	R.E.M. Cassette Set (Sitting Still/Radio Free Europe/White Tornado)	1981
A&M	AMC 24109	PS	R.E.M. Murmur and Reckoning (U.K.)	1990

R.E.M. side band and solo releases

I.R.S.	52867	Gonna Have a Good Time Tonight/Narrator (Hindu Love Gods)	6/16/85
I.R.S.	52867	Gonna Have a Good Time Tonight/Narrator (promotion only)	6/16/85
I.R.S.	52867	Gonna Have a Good Time Tonight/Narrator (Canada)	1985
Dog Gone	DOG 13111	Thirteen One Eleven (Bill Berry solo)	9/89
Giant	9 24406	Hindu Love Gods LP/CD/cassette (U.S.)	10/90
Giant		Hindu Love Gods LP/CD/cassette (U.K.)	10/90
Giant	7599-24406	Hindu Love Gods LP/CD/cassette (Germany)	10/90
Giant	W9502	Raspberry Beret/Wang Dang Doodle (U.K. 7-inch, Hindu Love Gods)	11/90
Giant	5439-19502	Raspberry Beret/Wang Dang Doodle (German 7-inch single)	11/90
Giant	W9502T	Raspberry Beret/Wang Dang Doodle/Mannish Boy (U.K. 12-inch single)	11/90
Giant	7599-21798	Raspberry Beret/Wang Dang Doodle/Mannish Boy (German 12-inch single)	11/90

Videos

A&M Vid.	VC 61710	R.E.M. Succumbs	6/1/87
Polygram	041 650-3	Athens, GA-Inside/Out	1/87
W/Reprise	38156-3	Pop Screen	3/6/90
W/Reprise	38184-3	Tourfilm	9/25/90
WB	--	Timepiece (promotion only)	3/91
WB	38254-3	This Film Is On	9/91
WB	--	Automatic For the People video press kit (promotion only)	10/92

Laserdiscs

A&M Vid.	LV 38403	R.E.M. Succumbs	1990
Warner	9 38156-6	Pop Screen (also issued in Japan)	1990
Warner	9 38184-6	Tourfilm (Japan: WPLP-9046)	1990
Warner	9 38254-6	This Film Is On (Japan: WPLP-9066)	9/91

WHERE TO FIND R.E.M. ITEMS

As you probably surmised from some of the prices in this book, the more valued R.E.M. collectibles are getting increasingly difficult to find at any price. The following mail order businesses and shops regularly have R.E.M. items in stock, and in general, have the most reasonable prices, though some of the dealers are more pricier than others. In general, prices for R.E.M. collectibles are higher in the U.K. than in the U.S.

U.S. sources

Athens Records
c/o Eclipse Publishing
P.O. Box 398
Bala Cynwyd, PA 19004

B & B Music Express
1341-E George Washington Way
Richland, WA 99352
(509)-943-0449

CVC Collectables
12228 Venice Blvd. #219
Los Angeles, CA 90066
(213)-313-0102
FAX: (213)-397-3695

The Disc Junkie
One Summit Place
Suite 204
Branford, CT 06405
(203)-483-8317

Intergalactic Garage
P.O. Box 3047
Shepherdstown, WV 25443
(304)-876-6818

Metro Music
P.O. Box 10004
Silver Spring, MD 20904-0004

Mod Lang
P.O. Box 10111
Berkeley, CA 94709-0111
(415)-526-8777

Music Machine
10367 Reistertown Rd.
Owings Mills, MD 21117
(301)-356-4693

The Old Hippie
P.O. Box 5
Ottowa, KS 66067
(913)-242-2879

Todd Ploharski
335 Ankonian
Alpharetta, GA 30201
(404)-475-2204

Rockaway Too
2395 Glendale Blvd.
Los Angeles, CA 90039
(213)-664-3232

Vinyl Ink Records
955 Bonifant St.
Silver Spring, MD 20910
(301)-588-4695

Vinyl Vendors
1800 S. Robertson Blvd. #279
Los Angeles, CA 90035
(213)-935-6553

Jack Wolack's Rare Necessities
P.O. Box 88
North Syracuse, NY 13212
(315)-452-1355

Yesterday and Today Records
1327-J Rockville Pike
Rockville, MD 20852
(301)-279-7007

Yodelin' Pig CD & Collectables
109 Melrose Ave.
Catonsville, MD 21228
(410)-788-5463

U.K. sources

Adrians Records
36 High Street
Wickford
Essex SS12 9AZ
England
phone: 0268-733318/19
FAX: 0268-764507

Beanos
27 Surrey St.
Croydon, Surrey CRO 1RR
England
phone: 081-680 1202

Bob Clayton
12 Clement Court
Maidstone
Kent ME 16 0EW
England
(R.E.M. list available)

Quickstep Mail Order
36 High Street
Northwood
Middlesex HA6 1BN
England
phone: 09274-28832

Minus Zero Records
2 Blenheim Crescent
London W11
England
phone: 071-229-5424
(R.E.M. list available)

Swordfish Mail Order
P.O. Box 1882
Great Barr
Birmingham B42 1ED
England
phone: 021-358-7041

Greg Vandyke
1 Delgany Villas
Derriford
Plymouth
Devon PL6 8AG
England
phone: 0752-773531

Vinyl Experience
20 Hanway St.
London W1
England
phone: 071-636-1281

Vinyl Solution
231 Portobello Road
London W11
England
229-8010

INDEX TO NON-LP TRACKS

INDEX TO TRACKS ON BOOTLEGS

Numbers refer to bootleg numbers, not page numbers in this, and the following sections.

Index To Live R.E.M. Songs On Bootlegs

Index To Studio Demos On Bootlegs

Index To Live Cover Versions On Bootlegs

NOTES

NOTES

NOTES

NOTES

NOTES

NOTES